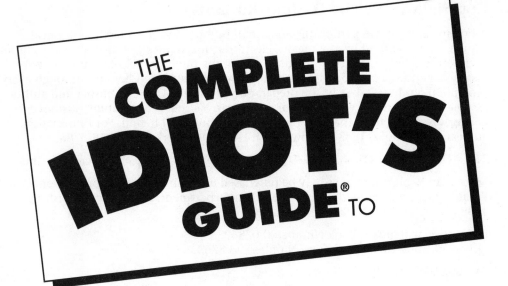
THE COMPLETE IDIOT'S GUIDE® TO

Dating,
Second Edition

by Dr. Judy Kuriansky

alpha books

A Division of Macmillan General Reference
A Simon & Schuster Macmillan Company
1633 Broadway, New York, NY 10019-6785

Macmillan Publishing books may be purchased for business or sales promotional use. For information please write: Special Markets Department, Macmillan Publishing USA, 1633 Broadway, New York, NY 10019-6785.

International Standard Book Number: 0-02862739-3
Library of Congress Catalog Card Number: 98-89623

01 00 99   8 7 6 5 4 3 2 1

Interpretation of the printing code: The rightmost number of the first series of numbers is the year of the book's printing; the rightmost number of the second series of numbers is the number of the book's printing. For example, a printing code of 99-1 shows that the first printing occurred in 1999.

Printed in the United States of America

Alpha Development Team

Publisher
Kathy Nebenhaus

Editorial Director
Gary M. Krebs

Managing Editor
Bob Shuman

Marketing Brand Manager
Felice Primeau

Editor
Jessica Faust

Development Editors
Phil Kitchel
Amy Zavatto

Production Team

Development Editor
Nancy Mikhail
Betsy Thorpe

Production Editor
Stephanie Mohler

Copy Editor
Krista Hansing

Cover Designer
Mike Freeland

Photo Editor
Richard H. Fox

Cartoonist
Jody P. Schaeffer

Designer
Scott Cook and Amy Adams of DesignLab

Indexer
Mary Gammons

Layout/Proofreading
Angela Calvert
Mary Hunt
Julie Trippetti

Contents at a Glance

Contents

Introduction

This book is intended for anyone who is looking for love—whatever your age, background, dating history, or sexual intentions.

In the search for love, many people display their deepest fears—that they are unlovable, or that there is something wrong with them. I offer this book to reassure you, to give you hope that your quest will be successful! Your dreams can come true—but first you must be clear about what you are really looking for. And most of all, you must feel good about yourself.

This book is a guide to dating—from meeting and starting a relationship to making a commitment. It contains facts, corrections of myths, tips, and plenty of simple as well as sophisticated how-to's and exercises that you can immediately put to use. It also includes valid psychological principles, which will help you understand your own personal dynamics on a deeper level. The more you know about what makes you tick, the better prepared you will be when approaching potential loves.

Many people in the dating game are in the dark about human behavior. Men and women alike ask me, "Why did she say that?" "What does he mean by that?" "How can she do this to me?" When you understand what motivates and immobilizes people, as I help you to do in this book, you'll feel more empowered and in control. In addition, as you increase your self-esteem through self-knowledge, you'll improve your chances of dating success.

How to Use This Book

Treat this book as a good friend who supports you at any time and in many situations, who calms you down and peps you up.

- ➤ Keep it by your bedside to read before you go to bed.
- ➤ Discuss it with your friends.
- ➤ Refer to it before a date.
- ➤ Read sections and do the quizzes *with* a date.

Use it as a great conversation opener, or a means of learning about one another in a non-threatening way. Blame the book for making you ask some tough questions like: "What are we each looking for?" "Are you into commitment?" "When is the right time for us to have sex?"

In the front of the book is a reference card with some dating pointers. Tear it out and keep it in your pocket. Refer to it when you want a boost and a reminder that I'm always there with you in spirit. I'll always remember the first acting class I ever took, where the coach told us, "Take your biggest fan with you on an audition," (meaning, imagine them in the audience). So, imagine me cheering you on as you set out on a date!

To help you get the most out of this book, you'll see the following information boxes scattered throughout:

Dating Data

These boxes offer research and statistics relating to human behavior and relationships.

Smooth Talk'n

Make a good impression! These boxes give you everything from flirting advice to plain 'ole dating know-how so you can capture and keep your new-found love interest.

Home Alone

These boxes help you steer clear of potential dating pitfalls so you're not stuck in front of your television set on a Friday night!

Throughout the book, you will encounter the three A's: *acceptance*, *appreciation*, and *adjustment*. The three A's are guideposts; when you're feeling confused about a person, or are having trouble remembering what you're after, the three A's can help restore your focus. You'll find them helpful in all kinds of situations—whether you're ready to make a commitment or trying to resolve an argument.

Mastering dating and mating is a metaphor for mastering your life. Here are some metaphors about dating that can also be helpful to you:

➤ *Love is art.* You start out with an empty canvas, a tabula rasa, then you layer on the shapes and colors. The details are all of your choosing. What picture are you painting of your love life? Who's in it? What are you doing?

➤ *Life is a play.* As Shakespeare said, "All the world's a stage and we are but players on it, who strut and fret their hour upon the stage." Realize that you create your own play of your love life. You select the leading lady or man, and you cast them in your story line. You have a script in your mind, even if you're not aware of it. What have you been putting on your love screen—a romantic drama where man and woman fall deeply in love and live happily ever after, or an action adventure where they encounter violence, enemies, and end up alone?

➤ *Dating is about selling.* Forget the cynicism; the truth is that, in dating, you're selling yourself to others. So follow certain tried-and-true rules of selling. Go after your prospects. Make cold calls (without formal introductions). Don't be discouraged by a "no," but see each as an opportunity to get to a "yes." If you can't get to "yes," go quickly on to the next "no," since that will bring you closer to a "yes" merely by the rule of odds (at least nine "no's" may be necessary before one "yes").

➤ *Dating is like a deal.* Put aside how unromantic this sounds. The truth is that you each bring something to the table when you meet. As you evaluate your assets, think about what you think you need, and think about what a date has that you would consider of value in the merger.

➤ *Dating is an adventure.* When you are feeling "lost" in the dating world, desperate to find love, frustrated with rejections, reframe your situation to feeling awe over the twists and turns in the road on your journey to love.

Being Single Today

These days, one out of every three people in the United States is single. This means there are about 50 million singles age 20 to 55 across America. That's a lot of people to reassure you that you are not alone, and that there are a lot of choices out there for you!

The U.S. Bureau of the Census shows that there are increasing numbers of singles these days, and that the estimated age of those getting married for the first time is higher than in recent years (26.5 for males and 24.4 for females in 1992, compared to 22.6 for males and 20.2 for females in 1955). The proportion of men and women in their twenties and thirties who have never married has grown substantially since 1970. Among women age 20 to 24, two-thirds had never been married in the 1990s, compared to just over one-third in 1970. About one-third of women in their late twenties and early thirties, and about 20 percent of women age 35 to 39, were unmarried. These proportions tripled and doubled over the past 20 years. Similarly, 80 percent of men age 20 to 24 and nearly half of men age 25 to 29 had never been married, and about one-third of men in their thirties were unmarried in the 1990s—this number tripling over the past two decades.

Though strong in numbers, singles unfortunately are not equally strong in attitude. Facing the perennial question "Why haven't you found anyone?" many wonder, "What's wrong with me?" I am painfully reminded that my mother's generation dreaded being the "old maid," and even in my college days, you had to graduate with an engagement ring and an "MRS." Degree or you were looked upon askance. Times have changed; in the past 20 years, more and more people spend their twenties and thirties focusing on career goals rather than commitment goals. But they still need their self-esteem to catch up with their choices. And society's attitudes and laws need to offer support to validate these choices.

My Philosophy of Life

I hope you come away from this book trusting that you can have what you need in life. This message came across to me powerfully during a recent trip to India's Taj Mahal, where our guide ended up taking me to a carpet store. Initially, I had no desire to buy Indian carpets, but the owner spread them out, inviting me to appreciate the art. I ended up buying several rugs to the tune of several thousand dollars, and asked him, "How did you get me to buy these when I had no intention of bringing carpets back to America, much less spending so much money?" What he said rings in my ears, in his Indian accent: "Whatever is yours will come to you." It seemed a wise message for life and love: The love that is yours will come to you.

Of course, not all is fate. You are in control by your thoughts and actions. Remember one of my favorite phrases: Whatever you believe and conceive you can achieve. And then you must take steps to realize your dreams.

The fundamental message in *The Complete Idiot's Guide to Dating*, Second Edition is that the key to success is to be happy with yourself. Happiness is not just the fulfillment of needs; it's how you choose to think and feel every second. So make each second count by thinking good thoughts and feeling good about yourself!

While other guides may tell you to play games in dating (to hold out, or maintain mystery), I do not believe in game-playing. Real love comes from being appreciated for who you are—not who you pretend to be. And finally, because I am on my own course to be completely authentic and more spiritual in life, I encourage you to consider dating as simply meeting kindred souls, teaching and supporting each other in life's journey. Useful in this is the Sufi principle: Show up, pay attention, tell the truth, and don't be attached. Trusting and valuing yourself, with few demands or expectations on others, will bring you a purer love.

Acknowledgments

This book continues to be the result of sharing from thousands of amazing, wonderful callers to my call-in advice radio show, "LovePhones;" letters from newspaper columns I write; guests and audience members from innumerable talk shows I have appeared on; men and women in lectures and seminars I have led; and precious friends. Blessings to all those who have revealed such an open heart, and to everyone I acknowledged in the first edition of *The Complete Idiot's Guide to Dating*, from family and friends to professional colleagues, editors, and agents who helped set the foundation for this evolution. Thanks to all those at Macmillan Publishing for their help on the making of this edition, and in particular: publisher Kathy Nebenhaus, senior editor Nancy Mikhail, managing editor Bob Shuman, production editor Stephanie Mohler, editor Betsy Thorpe, illustrator Jody P. Schaeffer, publicity director Margaret Durante, publicist Gardi Ipena Wilkes, and marketing manager Felice Primeau. Deep appreciation for the ongoing support of *Newsday* editor Barbara Schuler, *Penthouse* editor Peter Bloch and senior editor Lavada Blanton Nahon, and my teams at "LovePhones." What a gift to come from the original magical mix of Steve Kingston, Jagger, and Sam Milkman, to the current dream team headed by the inimitable magician Jay Clark and made up of the nightly joyous gathering in the studio of producer Scott "Badger" Hodges, engineer Brother, and interns Emily, Lee, and Chantal—offered inspiration by Bruce Goldberg and Sean Compton, and now backed by the whole team at WinStar and Global. Special soulfelt gratitude, too, to the angels in my life—mother Sylvia; father Abe in spirit; brother Robert; sister Barbara; soulmate Edward; soul sisters

Voltage, Edie Hand, Rhea Ross, Susan Cingari, Jill Marti, and Lucille Luongo; soul Brothers Alex Lessin and Brian Courtney; cherished friends Allan Rose, Maxine Figatner, Stanley London, Teri Whitcraft, and Fred Barron; healers Deborah Young, Reverend Pamela Wangler, Dawnea Adams, Carole Maracle and Dr. Robert Frey; The Woman Within program; Louise Koeghan and everyone at E! Entertainment; the socially responsible Ron Higgins at Dimensional Marketing; my fellow "goddesses" Laurie Sue Brockney, Joan Heartfield, Caroline Muir, Jaiia Earthschild, and Marci Javril; tantric master Charles Muir; "Warrior" poet Matt Feinberg; and second family Sandy and Jay Pollack—for their ever-present love and devotion—and to Alissa Pollack, who is a most trusted, cherished, and beloved gem and inspiration throughout this project, and my life.

Trademarks

All terms mentioned in this book that are known to be or are suspected of being trademarks or service marks have been appropriately capitalized. Alpha Books and Macmillan General Reference cannot attest to the accuracy of this information. Use of a term in this book should not be regarded as affecting the validity of any trademark or service mark.

Part 1
The Hunt—The Real Rules

It's a jungle out there. So many men, so many women, so many possibilities. Yet, dating has never been so exciting. But, between the hundreds of different types of dates you can go on and the zillions of ways you can meet people (even on the Internet), it's enough to make your head spin.

With so many routes to take, not to mention so much conflicting guidance (should you feign not being shy, prepare opening lines, hold back interest), you can easily feel like leaving the jungle altogether and instead, run to a deserted island. Don't give up! In this section, we will take a look at how dating has changed over the past few years, determine what kind of prey you should be hunting, where he may be hiding, and how to keep her from escaping.

Keep in mind that dating is fun! The word doesn't necessarily have to give you butter-flies, sweaty palms, and heart palpitations. Instead, when you think of the word D-A-T-I-N-G, I want you to think of it as away for you to meet people, learn about yourself, and, if all goes well, experience love. Most importantly, it's time to be yourself. To help you with your search, here are some opening tips to keep in mind:

➤ *Let people know you're available*

➤ *Know—but be flexible about—your "love criteria"*

➤ *Don't be afraid of rejection*

➤ *Go to places and see things that you enjoy*

➤ *Boost your self-esteem and mates will flock to you*

➤ *Remember that you have the power to get what you want*

➤ *Always have hope—you can meet someone special anytime and anywhere*

➤ *Meet as many people as you can*

➤ *Be ready and open for love*

So, get your compass and gear out—and take your armor off—it's time to snag some prey . . .

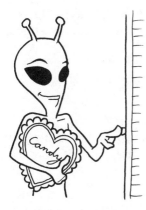

Chapter 1

Dating Today, in the New Millennium, and Beyond

In This Chapter

➤ How dating has changed in recent years

➤ What's useful and dangerous about *The Rules*

➤ Realistic rules

➤ What's ahead in the new millenium

In the two years since the first edition of *The Complete Idiot's Guide to Dating* was published, some major world events have affected relationships. These have been significant enough for me to notice a shift in the way people behave and the way they seek—and express—love. It is important to review these major events and trends, in order to refine the best approach for your search and strategy for love.

For sure, as we enter the new millennium, it's a good opportunity to realize changes you need to make to adapt to a new century. This doesn't just mean updating your computer, but *yourself*. Let's consider it the real "New Age."

In addition, the yet two more years of my conducting call-in advice on the radio, answering letters through various columns and articles, and doing various television shows on dating (particularly several specials for E! Entertainment Television on "What Women Want" and "What Men Want"), have proven that some always popular problems still persist in the world of dating. The most common questions still seem to be "Where do I go to meet someone?" and "What do I say?" But also, some questions have moved up the Top 10, like whether Internet and long-distance relationships can work. And there's good news: I've also witnessed a greater desire for openness as time has marched on, as well as more yearning for intimacy in men, as well as women.

And over this time, I have become even more convinced of the validity of the two basic principles about dating that I've developed during my many years as a therapist and advisor. These principles have been even more justified in light of the events I will share with you in this chapter that have changed the course of dating. Keep these principles in mind always, as you read this book, and as you go through your dating experiences:

1. Your ultimate goal—and the goal of this book—is not about dating, per se. It's about getting to know someone, getting to know yourself, and enjoying yourselves individually and together. Yes, this results in a date, but that word has become too loaded, so take the pressure off yourself from that word, by not worrying about "dating" or "getting a date."

2. Dating is not about playing games. It's about being yourself. Put aside the fear of being foolish. If you're shy, be shy. If someone is going to love you, they'll love you as you are, not as something (cool or suave) you're trying to be.

How the '90s Changed the Dating Scene

From the increase in financial independence to the panic of being prepared for the year 2000 to the Sexgate Scandal, here's a review of some events of the 1990s that have changed dating habits—and that continue to affect how men and women behave.

Love Online

With the advent of the computer age, meeting online has become the new means of finding someone to love. Read Chapter 5 for all the ins and outs and etiquette of computer dating.

Working Hard for the Money . . .

The media gets blamed for many problems in society, but in this case print, radio, and TV are being helpful, creating an awareness and interest in financial matters. Just turn on the TV or look at a rack of magazines to see the many sources of information about money.

Who doesn't want to win the lottery? But, luck and fantasy aside, in this age, men and women—especially those in their 20s and 30s— have become more finance-savvy than ever before. Not only do both sexes understand the importance of being financially responsible, but more people also are investing their money in mutual funds, 401(k)s, and the stock market, in the hopes of becoming as financially independent—and rich—as possible.

A significant trend affecting dating involves women setting aside the Cinderella fantasy that someday their prince will come, and instead facing reality, learning that they have to take responsibility for their own future, including their financial security.

More women are working and gaining exposure to financial matters. Girls are being raised differently: They're no longer expecting to be taken care of by a man, but they're taking responsibility for their own financial security—partly because their parents (and their mothers) had to do this themselves. As a result, financial issues involving dating and mating (who pays, who earns more) have changed substantially. On the potentially negative side, couples are more sensitive to who has money (how much and how much *more*) and who pays for what. On the positive side, both people are expected to take responsibility for making—and potentially sharing—money. As another bonus, women who earn their own money can choose partners without making a man's portfolio their primary criteria.

Dating Data

In this communication age of beepers, fax, e-mail, the Internet, and cell phones, technology offers more ways to start a relationship, more opportunities to develop a relationship, and more possibilities to make a long-distance relationship last!

Sexual Matters

Some shocking statistics of the late 1990s have shown an increase in some sexually transmitted diseases—to the point of near-epidemic proportions in some cases. You've heard a lot about herpes and HIV, but, for example, by the end of the century, the American Social Health Association warns that gonorrhea will spread dramatically, and media articles also report a new threat of Hepatitis C.

Before I totally scare you, let me add that some heartening trends are also influencing the dating scene. For one thing, I have noticed an increased awareness in my radio audience of more obscure STDs. For instance, a woman caller said she was worried about catching chlymydia, an STD that is dangerous but not commonly known. More men and women today are paying attention to their health and considering more carefully what they're doing before jumping into bed with someone.

Increase in Abstinence

Besides being more careful about a particular partner, surveys also reveal that more men and women—especially young people—are thinking twice about being sexually active. I hear from more older virgins who are less worried that there is something wrong with them. A 1997 survey by the Centers for Disease Control (CDC) found that more than half of America's high-schoolers are saying no to sex. Of more than 16,000 students surveyed nationwide, 52 percent said they had never had sexual intercourse. This represented a decrease from the 57 percent who admitted to sex in 1988.

Condom Use

Further encouraging news comes from surveys showing an increased use of condoms. In a CDC survey, 57 percent of students in 1997 said they used condoms the last time they had sex, compared to 46 percent in 1991. Another survey of more than 10,000 people showed that more women are taking responsibility for using condoms.

The credit for the increased use of condoms has been given to individuals themselves for being responsible for their own health, to friends for spreading their knowledge and experiences to each other, to educators for their dedication to develop helpful programs, and to parents for communicating more openly with their children.

Love Drugs

The ever-lasting search for an aphrodisiac hit new highs in 1998 with the long-awaited FDA approval of the drug Viagra, which promised men potent erections. The drug's proven effectiveness in reversing impotence for men with physical as well as psychological problems became the top story in newspapers and on network TV. Within days of its announcement, millions of sales registered, and the stock of the manufacturer, Pfizer, soared. Soon, men who didn't have erection problems, but who simply wanted to be "studs," were getting prescriptions. And, inevitably women started trying Viagra to increase their sexual pleasure as well. Also inevitably, studies got underway to test similar medications for women.

The love drug brought hope that men could achieve sexual satisfaction despite any physical problems or psychological blocks (inhibitions, fears, guilt). But also, it brought upset—with news of men leaving their wives (after discovering their newfound potency), and even dying (from complications with heart problems). The bottom line: Beware of shortcuts to good sex! No drug can replace a solid relationship, self-confidence, and good communication.

The Sexgate Scandal

Having an affair, lying, falling in love with the wrong person—all issues in dating that singles struggle with and that were never before so publicly highlighted as in our time—in the Sexgate scandal. Probably the biggest news story of the decade was the Bill Clinton–Monica Lewinsky scandal that emerged from sexual charges against the most powerful man in our country and the world—our President. The affair, called Sexgate and Zippergate, grew out of a sexual harassment suit brought against the President by a former government employee, Paula Jones. Although that case was dismissed, revelations emerged that the President had had an affair with a former White House intern. Nine months after the President denied the charges publicly, shaking his finger in a televised statement, he recanted his denial and admitted the affair. The intern's testimony to a grand jury called by independent counsel Ken Starr (in the infamous Starr Report), opened the President up to charges of perjury and obstruction of justice.

The nation—and the world—read about the sex acts the White House intern reported happened between her and the President. These included oral sex performed on him (in the hallway of the White House and while he was on the phone with staff and politicians), his groping her breasts and vagina, and his inserting a cigar in her vagina and then in his mouth. Politicians and other commentators called the acts "disgusting, gross, and pornographic"—hardly true, in my estimation, since such oral sex acts are a favorite male fantasy and the other sex acts described are tame in comparison to what people do, or want to do. Despite the arguments, rumors, lies, and accusations of a political witch hunt, many issues of relationships and sex came to light during the proceedings. These include lying (the President denied the affair to his wife, the country, and his political friends), the morality of extramarital affairs, the "normality" of certain sex acts, betrayal (Lewinsky's former friend Linda Tripp released secretly taped conversations between Lewinsky and herself), and forgiveness (or the lack thereof).

In addition, the characters of the three major players became mirrors for "Everyman" and "Everywoman" to examine themselves in their own roles in relationships today and explore the labels applied to those who venture beyond the limits of propriety.

As part of the fallout, the President was even accused of having a sex addiction (a problem estimated in 1 out of 15 Americans), focusing our attention on how much is too much of a sex drive. Furthermore, though supported by the Women's Coalition, he was also accused of being a misogynist (woman-hater) by some, including Speaker of the House Newt Gingrich, a Miss America, and Monica's Rabbi. His wife, Hillary, was also criticized for her role: Was she a victim or a co-dependent enabler? And Monica was called a modern-day, Generation X example of the '80s classic love addict—a desperate, needy, overweight young woman and child of divorce who seduced older, married and powerful men to satisfy her own needs for attention, love, and power.

The tragedy of this scandal, though, served as a lesson for men and women: Because we live in a day and age where scandal and exploitation abound, we must choose our partners wisely. (That's where this guide to dating comes in: We'll cover ways to do just that, starting with the next chapter.)

Conscious Dating

What does this mean? This is my new term that takes off on a wonderful concept that my friends, tantra masters Charles and Caroline Muir, use called "conscious loving," whereby couples put thoughtfulness, attention, and nurturing into their relationship (and lovemaking) as they would to a career, family, or cause. You can certainly tell from the word itself that being "conscious" requires being aware of who you are, and also appreciating who you are. This is of course consistent with my major point in this book—that in finding love (dating) you need to be yourself and love yourself, and love will find you.

To help in this process, think of practicing meditation to reduce stress, but more importantly to get in touch with your inner spirit to find out and express who you are without fear. Also consider taking yoga classes, to both quiet your mind and stretch your body, allowing for limberness of movement, but moreover for ease of the breathing that is essential for confidence and openness to intimacy and love.

Conscious dating involves truly getting into one another's soul. From the exercises that the Muirs teach brilliantly, here are some suggestions. (It's interesting that these exercises can delay having sex in dating, because they help you connect on a deep spiritual level.)

➤ **Conscious touching.** You can "run energy" between you by resting hands upon each other on nonsexual parts without moving. Face each other and place your right hand on the space over your heart and the left hand on the center of the back, imagining energy flowing through your right hand into your love and back into you through your left hand (like a game of catch). Or you can imagine kissing each other with your hands.

➤ **Eye gazing.** The eyes are indeed the window to the soul. Face each other and look into each other's eyes, without speaking. Let your eyes communicate what you feel.

➤ **Massaging.** Explore and please each other physically without any intention to arouse sexually. Take turns for a discrete amount of time, to prevent worry. Give in to receiving, and practice totally focused giving. Experiment with different touches (long strokes, tapping, squeezing, pinching), different directions (lengthwise, circles, zigzags), and seven levels of pressure (from light to firm).

Smooth Talk'n

Use my favorite words to refer to your date: See the Goddess in her and the God in him. Sweep her off her feet by asking her, "What can I do to please my Goddess?"

Other activities you can do together consciously: singing or chanting, playing musical instruments, building something, fixing something in your home, making a flower arrangement, doing puzzles, reading a book aloud, or composing poetry.

Following the principle of conscious dating, you would never experience the desperation of losing love that so many singles go through and that leads to that dramatic fear of rejection. Why? Because you would always keep in mind that you never lose love, that no one takes love away from you, because love is always inside you. It is you who created it. And you can keep love inside you even if a lover takes himself away.

Dating Data

The Muirs' tantra workshops that teach conscious loving apply to singles as well as couples. Groups specifically for men are a new offering. Contact the Source School of Tantra at (808) 572-8364.

An Increase in Spirituality

As we approach the new millennium, men and women of all religions are becoming more conscious of spirituality and of improving their overall lives. As a therapist, I have been on a similar journey in my personal and professional growth, exploring the needs of the soul in seeking love and fulfilling its destiny. Men and women no longer want to simply find a date that they can have fun with; instead, they're looking to find someone who touches—and connects with—their soul.

You can test your "soul connection" by thinking back about those people you date (or have dated) to whom you seem inextricably attracted. These undoubtedly have some soul connection to you, indicating that you can learn something valuable from each other. My friend, San Diego spiritual counselor Deborah Young, explains that these dates may be part of your "soul family."

Appreciation for Intuition

Reason certainly helps in dating because it assists you with picking the right person, making compromises, and dealing rationally with rejection without falling apart emotionally. But the New Age brings a new appreciation for intuition, that sixth sense inside that tells you what is right without any rational thought. More men and women today are trusting and relying on their instincts when it comes to dating. If something just doesn't feel right, they are acting on that sixth sense. That means either giving the relationship some breathing room or ending it—especially if their needs are not being met.

Remember the terror in dating in the '90s that always arose with that dreaded phrase "I need more space"? In this New Age, instead of being blindsided by such rejection, men and women are getting smarter—sensing when a lover needs more space, and giving it before being asked. She will know which men want her to encourage them to get closer and which ones will not budge. He will know when she really needs to "find herself" and will detach without blaming himself.

In dating in our New Age, you will be good at sensing when you need to back off from a relationship and give it time to breathe and grow slowly—and when it's time to get out if your needs are not being met. Put simply, pay attention to your intuition: It's probably right.

Past Lives

One of my favorite new awarenesses is that we may all indeed have lived past lives. You might not believe this, but I have seen how people attracted to each other can seem to "sense" that they have known each other before.

Here's one powerful example of this. In one intimate moment of kissing her new boyfriend, Angie started whispering in his ear about how she felt like a Guineviere from medieval times, a princess locked in a tower who had to be rescued by him. Astounded, her boyfriend told her how as a child he had listened to the music of the play *Camelot* over and over, imagining that he was Lancelot. Coincidence, you might say, but the shared fantasy of the two characters from another time certainly brought them closer together.

The Rules: What's Right and Wrong About Them

The Rules, a book by two women survivors of the dating wars, became a bestseller in the late '90s. Women seemed both relieved and desperate to follow the steps outlined to ensure they would get their man. Groups sprung up, with women encouraging each other to continue following the book's advice to snag a mate with coy games and clever tactics. Even the authors didn't deny that it was a throw-back to the early days of dating.

But over time, *The Rules* experienced a backlash: The book came to be called an "un-popular" bestseller, and its tenets fell out of favor. Women who bought into its advice came to feel that they were being told to behave in a way that was not authentic for them, forcing them to put on a tougher exterior and deny their truer sensitive selves.

Pretty soon media producers began booking the authors not to promote the book, but to confront critics. I was one of those chosen for that role and was invited on shows like *Geraldo* and on CNN. At first I hesitated because I appreciated the *basic* message in the book: that a woman should not be desperate, but should love herself; expect to be treated well; and not settle for anything less than being respected, adored, and pursued. But I finally agreed, because my *approach* to the same goal was exactly the opposite to theirs: Instead of playing games to trap your man, just be yourself from beginning to end.

Specific Objections to *The Rules*

The most troublesome message in *The Rules* is one that insists that a woman must "play hard to get." Certainly, a woman should be strong and independent—not needy or desperate. And, yes, there is a sense of mystery to a woman, and that mystique captures a man's attention. But who do you capture when you play hard to get but an elusive, non-committal man? How long can such a man's attention be kept (even though one author swears she transformed one of this type of man into a devoted husband)? Additionally, doesn't this hard-to-get game show that he doesn't care for the real you (at least what you *want* to be loved for)? And how long can the façade last?

Here's another dilemma: What about all the nice guys who really are ready for commitment and want honesty? A great cry of protest arose on my own radio show—and other shows—from the nice guys who felt *The Rules* overlooked them, giving women tricks to trap the elusive players who really didn't appreciate women or treat them well.

To test *The Rules*, Geraldo sent out his charming female co-host to meet a car salesman. On the show, the salesman talked about how he wanted her to accept his offer for a first date with enthusiasm, not following *The Rules* authors' advice that she pretend not to be interested, to spark his pursuit. "I want her to be herself, and show me she's interested," he said emphatically. The audience cheered. This fit so much feedback I get from men who are shy about dating, and feel relieved when women show their interest and *don't* play hard to get.

Another objection I have to *The Rules* is that it forces men and women to take on stereotypic roles where the woman is still being cast as the desperate, longing one, and the man as in control, with the rules attempting to switch that balance, so the woman takes more control. While admittedly attempting an honorable goal to empower women, *The Rules* threatened to disempower women by insisting that they put on an act, and to disempower men, reducing them to their traditional role as pursuer. This contrasts with a more flowing, natural evolution of a healthy love relationship, which involves not a battle over who's on top, but two people simply responding to each other.

Here are some specific rules discussed in that book that women should be particularly cautious about following, as they prevent you from expressing yourself.

Remember, I suggest you DO NOT do the following:

Home Alone

Many modern men enjoy being pursued and want a woman to make advances.

➤ Play hard to get.

➤ Don't talk to a man first.

➤ Don't call a man or return his calls.

➤ Pretend you're busy when a man calls, and end the call first.

➤ Don't accept a date on Saturday if a man calls after Wednesday.

➤ Drop his hand before he drops yours.

➤ Don't ask a man out first.

➤ Don't go Dutch (where both parties equally split the cost of a date).

➤ Don't open up first or easily.

➤ Don't leave things at his apartment.

A New Millennium Concept of Dating

Over the years of responding to my radio show callers' basic dating questions, as well as my lecturing about *The Complete Idiot's Guide to Dating* at bookstore signings and workshops around the country, I found myself saying over and over not to get stuck on the word "dating." This can create too much pressure and anxiety, negating the positive effects. Instead, think more about the concept of what a date is: It's a means of getting together with someone with whom you would like to share an enjoyable experience. Don't think of dating as "dating."

Sure, it's a simple principle, but it makes so much sense! The word "dating" alone creates pressure, as an anxiety-producing reminder from high school days of asking someone out and risking rejection. Hence, a more constructive way is to reframe the word, thinking not of a date, but of getting together to do something that is enjoyable for both of you. That concept better accomplishes your goal of bonding by sharing an experience that brings you closer.

Through my years of experience, I have learned what dating is—and what it is not:

➤ Dating is not a game. There are no winners or losers. Dating is a learning experience that should allow both people to grow.

➤ Dating is not about "looking for love." The truth is, dating should not be a desperate search for the perfect mate who will make you feel loved. Instead, you need to find love inside you and let that radiate outward. That's why you often find love when NOT specifically looking, since those are the times you are most naturally yourself.

➤ Dating is not about complaining about who you're with (whining that he doesn't bring flowers or fuming that she never calls back fast enough). Instead, it's about who you choose to be with. There is a world of people out there. Whatever is going on in the relationship reflects what you need to learn. Dating is about your choice of who enters your space and your thoughts. Imagine yourself as a gate, with lots of people walking by, but only those you invite being allowed in.

Review these changes in the old versus the new rules:

PASSÉ RULE: The man has to love a woman more than she loves him. This seems justified when you think that men are more distractible and have traditionally been more unfaithful than women.

IN THE NEW MILLENNIUM: Both people need to love each other equally.

PASSÉ RULE: You need someone to date to validate.

IN THE NEW MILLENNIUM: You are fine on your own; a date merely annotates.

PASSÉ RULE: Play games.

IN THE NEW MILLENNIUM: Be yourself.

PASSÉ RULE: Play hard to get.

IN THE NEW MILLENNIUM: Show interest when you feel it.

PASSÉ RULE: Pretend you're not interested.

IN THE NEW MILLENNIUM: Show you're interested.

PASSÉ RULE: Withhold about yourself to keep the mystery.

IN THE NEW MILLENNIUM: Reveal yourself to be intriguing.

Energetics

Watch—you'll hear the word "energetics" more and more. It's the new word of the new millennium, emerging in the language of sophisticated and holistic relationship counselors and guides. I often hear fellow colleagues ask, "What are the energetics between the two of them?" or comment, "They have positive energetics."

The word technically evolved from magnetic therapy, which involves placing magnets on body parts to balance energy within the body. Think of a magnet surrounded by metal pieces. The pieces automatically gravitate toward the magnet, attaching themselves to it. Pull away the magnet, and watch the iron pieces move toward it, attempting to get closer, and to attach. Relationships can operate in much the same way, where one person draws the other inextricably and uncontrollably into the relationship.

Home Alone

You might feel drawn to him like a moth to flame if you have deeper, unresolved issues (called "Karma") with that person, or within yourself.

These are signs that you are experiencing positive energetics:

➤ You smile when you see your partner.

➤ You feel comfortable in his/her presence.

➤ Your body internally feels at peace when you are together.

➤ You want to get closer to him/her.

➤ You feel like you "know" your partner.

➤ Your movements seem to be synchronized and flow without effort.

➤ You feel a "pull" toward each other, as if magnetized.

Signs of poor energetics include the opposite of the above:

➤ You feel like you're not on the same wavelength.

➤ You feel bad vibes between you.

➤ You feel uncomfortable in each other's presence.

➤ You find that you're always frowning.

➤ His/her actions make you want to move away.

Trends to Watch for in the New Millennium

In light of all the changes previously mentioned, some trends will emerge in the coming years of dating.

➤ **The speed of love:** Relationships will undoubtedly get more intense as life moves faster and will produce pressures to form relationships more quickly—pressures that sometimes would best be resisted for love to be allowed time to grow, but which can also lead to a strong bond.

➤ **New male-female complications:** As women become increasingly independent, they also expect more from men. In addition, men are increasingly threatened by women's increase in independence. Both sexes must continue to reject stereo-typic male and female roles and continue progress already made whereby men become more in touch with their sensitive side, and women with their power and assertiveness.

➤ **The importance of love:** Think about what the movie *2001: A Space Odyssey* meant to you. What were the images conjured up in your mind about what life would be like? No doubt you see space-like clothing, industrial buildings, mono-rail transportation, and unusual flying spaceships for cars. What do the relation-ships look like when you imagine the people encountering each other? The picture in your mind likely is not two people cozily hunkering down in a soft plush red couch, but rather a bare bench and stiff bodies. Images stick in your mind and research even shows that what we imagine affects how we behave, as if living out a pre-determined story.

But this is hardly what you want in the coming millennium. Isn't that cozy, warm interaction more what you want in your life? Now, think about what the phrase "New Age" connoted. Likely you think of the pictures invoked by the hippie term of the '70s, with people walking around in tie-dye clothes, smiling, and trying out non-traditional health remedies and lifestyles. Isn't that warmer vison more conducive to what you want? That New Age of the '70s emerged during the "flower child" and "free love" period in our history. While we have to be more responsible these days (to resist the casual sex of that era), we *can* welcome back that innocent concept of "love."

In the '90s, we undoubtedly witnessed society growing more consumed with materialism. However, I predict that once again we will begin to see an emphasis on the things that really matter: love, trust, and happiness. When I have asked my radio audience, "Would you marry for love or money?" the majority of the answers from both men and women have been "love." That's not to say money isn't of major importance, but at least they are saying that "love" matters more. Even more heartening, when I gave my audience the classic choice provoked by the movie *Indecent Proposal*—where the married woman played by Demi Moore had to decide whether to accept $1 million in exchange for a sexual evening with the rich bachelor played by Robert Redford—more men and women said they would rather turn down the money than risk upsetting their love relationship.

Each one of you has responsibility to set the trends for the new millenium in how you think and behave. Contribute to a better age by considering these:

➤ Respecting what feels right for you

➤ Getting rid of fear—or feeling it and acting anyway

➤ Relying on your intuition as well as logic

➤ Re-evaluating and starting afresh in patterns; giving up what doesn't work and having courage to step into the unknown

➤ Constructing a new view of sex that requires love

New Ways to Stay in Touch in the New Age

This is the communication age, with there being more ways to get in touch, and keep in touch. That means there are more ways to start a relationship and more opportunities to develop a relationship. It also means there are fewer excuses as to why you can't be in touch, no matter where you are.

What ways are you in touch (besides the traditional telephone)?

➤ Long-distance services. Keep track of the connecting lines that are constantly offering cheaper prices for long-distance calling. Many are now at 5 cents a minute. Some require a monthly fee ($4.95), so be sure to read the fine print or ask for any hidden costs.

➤ Car phones.

➤ Cell phones. The deals on these are endless, so here too, you have to do your research. Ask friends who use them frequently for referrals. Find out when you do most of your talking so you can sign up for an economical plan with free minutes when you need them.

➤ Beepers, with or without features like voice messages.

➤ Fax. There are even fax machines on airport telephone lines now.

Smooth Talk'n

When you fall for someone, you can create special codes (on your beeper, for example) to get in touch, but be sure this won't wreak havoc if you happen to break up.

➤ E-mail.

➤ Overnight mail services. These include the local post office and special services like Federal Express, Airborne, and DHL. These run about $15 for a letter and more for packages. Compare prices, as the U.S. postal service seems to be the least expensive. Many will pick up at your home or office for an extra charge than if you go to a drop-off center. You can send things overnight or less expensively if they are delivered in two days.

➤ Airfares. If you're in a long-distance relationship, you can still arrange for visits by saving up your money. Airfares fluctuate, so you have to stay abreast of changes and keep checking with them directly, with your local newspaper, and with a good travel agent for deals. Also, keep on the alert for TV and radio ads about new, smaller airlines that fly specialty routes for low fares (but they may have limited seats at those fares).

Special Issues Depending on Your Background

All the issues in this book apply to everybody. But, of course, there are always special issues faced by singles depending on age, cultural upbringing, religious teachings, and even socio-economic background. In order to trace the effects of these on your current approach to dating, and male-female relationships, ask your parents to help you trace the influences on you during your childhood. What did they teach you? What traditions did they follow themselves that they wanted you to carry on? For example, parents from a Middle Eastern or Fundamentalist background may have been against your "dating" at all, or with anyone who wasn't from a similar sect. Mothers who have been abused might give messages to their daughters about men being abusive and untrustworthy. Decide what positive influence you would like your background to have on your dating now, and concentrate and build on those. For example, if you were adored by your father, choose men who equally adore you.

Special Issues for Teens

You've probably heard the phrase once or twice, or said it yourself: "The future is our young people." All the more reason to need—and offer to them—help in dating. After all, young people face all the dilemmas explained in this book, as do adults. But when we are young, we seem to face added anxieties—about growing up, self-consciousness about appearance, insecurities in self-esteem, and challenges in developing friendships. As life becomes more complicated in the new millennium, these anxieties will only increase, demanding that much more support from friends, parents, and advisors about all the ins and outs of falling in love, asking someone out, and dealing with rejection.

Teens have asked me whether they can "fall in love" at their age. Of course they can, but lasting love takes time to grow and obviously prove itself to be lasting! Innumerable teens call me about when to have sex, with girls needing to resist agreeing to pressure in order not to lose their boyfriend. An unfortunate number of teens call me about what I call "double betrayals," an exceptionally painful experience, where you find out about your best friend hitting on your girlfriend or having sex with your girlfriend (my advise: consider a break-up with both). One of the most common questions teens have is one expressed by Jared, who asked me, "I really like this girl, but she's my best friend and I don't want to lose her friendship. What should I do?" (I answer this question in Chapter 21.)

Another common dilemma for teens is like Max's, "I'm still in high school and my girlfriend went off to college this year and I'm worried that she is dating other guys." The truth is that going away to school often spells the end of committed relationships, as both male and female coeds get tempted to party and have innumerable opportunities for meeting others—making it wise not to have grand expectations that a love will last. But, of course, your relationship *can* survive, if you both want it to.

What do you do in that situation? Max's girlfriend was feeding his anxiety by telling him about some guy that she met on the way to English class and another guy she talked to in the cafeteria. She may have been trying to allay his fears that she is really dating them, but she is also unnecessarily raising his fears by mentioning them at all. It is better for her to avoid talking about other guys, and if it bothers Max, he should ask her not to say those things, and to give him the reassurance that he needs. They also need to plan as many contacts as possible between them, including phone calls, sending packages, and planning visits, and even a romantic vacation where they can be alone.

From Me to You . . .

It has been heartening for me to see over these past years since *The Complete Idiot's Guide to Dating* first edition how much appreciation there has been for this book, men and women alike have told me, "I read your book cover to cover," "I used your advice and found a wonderful woman," or "I keep your book by my bedside." I am grateful because I put my heart and soul into these pages, and have reflected the hearts and souls of many who have called me or written to me over the years. I have reviewed each section to include the most up-to-date information so you can have the most fulfilled love life! I invite you to learn, grow, and enjoy.

> ### The Least You Need to Know
>
> ➤ Changes in people's habits and philosophies, as well as current events, require you to re-think your dating strategies.
>
> ➤ Be aware of some of the frustrations, challenges, and opportunities that the computer age puts on dating.
>
> ➤ Always remember that being yourself is the best guiding principle.

Chapter 2

The Prey

In This Chapter

➤ The meaning of attraction

➤ Making a love deal

➤ Your chances of finding a partner

➤ Do nice guys really finish last?

➤ Test your compatibility

"It ain't gonna be no pickle man!"—Amy Irving's character in Crossing Delancey

Of course you want to fall in love, but, like many singles, you despair of finding that "right" one. You may have some idea of your perfect man or woman—he should be good-looking, rich, and powerful; she should be beautiful, sexy, and smart.

One single guy I know explains, "In real estate you look for three things: location, location, location. But in the dating market, a lot of women look for three things: cash, cash, cash." In a culture where the free love of the 1970s has emerged into high commercialism, love has been reduced to the "BBD"—the "Bigger Better Deal." But when it comes down to it, the "right" person might seem quite plain at first, but turn out to be exactly what you need and be the best lover you ever had. For Amy Irving's character in the movie *Crossing Delancey*, the pickle man she first dismissed turned out to be just the Mr. Right she needed. Similarly for Meg Ryan's character in *When Harry Met Sally*, the best friend she complained to about all her other dates ended up capturing her heart.

The Mystery of Attraction

In many ways, attraction is a mystery, but there are some guideposts to help you understand the process. First off, I'd like to introduce you to my concept of "The Mirror Law of Attraction." According to this principle, we attract, and are attracted to, those people who have something we desire or wish to defy. For example, people who have commitment problems (but deny it) frequently attract unavailable types who wear their noncommittal status like a badge. Another example: People who are insecure about their appearance become obsessed with finding the most attractive dates (to compensate for their own looks).

Another one of my concepts that I'd like to introduce to you is what I call "love antennae." We are all equipped with "love antennae" that tune us into certain types of people. It's like we are each a radio station or satellite dish sending out and receiving signals. But beware, your love antennae may be improperly programmed, leading you to make choices that end up making you unhappy.

Your love antennae get tuned by your particular "love criteria"—things you think you must have in a partner. But on closer examination, searching for someone with those qualities may not work for you, and you may have to change your criteria to find a relationship that lasts. Michelle, a radio DJ from Duluth, dated a string of "losers" until I explained the concept of love antennae to her. She realized what she was broadcasting and said, "I see—I have to change my signal!"

The frequency of your love antennae is affected by what's called an "eligibility score," in which we assess our "market" worth, and that of potential mates. To understand how we assess our worth, try this exercise. Think of the qualities you think you have (looks, intelligence, sense of humor, etc.). Assess each quality from 0 (= zero) to 10 (= hero) by putting a check in the appropriate column. Now do the same for your ideal mate.

My Qualities	0	1	2	3	4	5	6	7	8	9	10
_____	—	—	—	—	—	—	—	—	—	—	—
_____	—	—	—	—	—	—	—	—	—	—	—
_____	—	—	—	—	—	—	—	—	—	—	—
_____	—	—	—	—	—	—	—	—	—	—	—

Qualities in Someone I Look for	0	1	2	3	4	5	6	7	8	9	10
_____	—	—	—	—	—	—	—	—	—	—	—
_____	—	—	—	—	—	—	—	—	—	—	—
_____	—	—	—	—	—	—	—	—	—	—	—
_____	—	—	—	—	—	—	—	—	—	—	—

If you rate yourself a "9" in looks but a "4" in intelligence, see if you also look for someone who ranks a similar high score in attractiveness but a "9" in smarts—so your scores even out. If you feel you have a quality "covered" (with a high score), you may find yourself going after someone who offers something that you don't quite have (a high score in a different quality). No scoring is "right" or "wrong," but just helps you get an idea of your dating choices.

What Is Chemistry? (and Does It Exist?)

You spot her across a crowded room and you just know she's the one. His eyes meet yours, and you melt into each other. It's the dream of a lifetime. You feel that chemistry, the thrill coursing through your body. Your heart pounds, and you feel that the two of you are meant to be together. Books, songs, and movies are replete with these scenarios. The stories fuel our hope about that exquisite high, and we despair when it doesn't happen to us.

But just what is "chemistry"? Love, attraction, or lust—call it what you will—does trigger physiological reactions. In a heightened state of arousal, our bodies release a number of hormones and chemicals. One of these, adrenaline, triggers the "fight-or-flight response" that explains symptoms such as sweaty palms, palpitations, and weak knees—similar to anxiety symptoms triggered by a final exam or the near-miss of a traffic accident. Other chemicals flood into your system, including oxytocin (the "cuddle chemical"), phenylethylamine (the "natural high chemical"), and endorphins (the "pleasure chemicals").

Dating Data

Research indicates that the brain plays a large role in our experience of love. A study of youngsters who underwent surgery for the removal of pituitary tumors found that these individuals were later able to form friendships, but had more trouble than other people falling in love. The pituitary gland releases hormones essential to "mating" behavior. Scientists think that during surgery, crucial pathways can be blocked, preventing the hormones from reaching their proper receptor sites in the brain.

The feeling of being magnetically attracted to someone may also have to do with the bioelectric fields that surround our bodies. Remember I described this in Chapter 1 as "energetics," where you feel that electricity between you.

A cycle between the physiological and psychological aspects of attraction is created: When we are aroused, our bodies release chemicals, which in turn stimulate the smooth muscles and sensitize the nerve endings. This makes us even more sensitive to pleasure and more emotionally responsive. As you interpret your body signals to mean you are "in love," your enthusiasm escalates.

Making Your Love Deal

Remember I said earlier that you can think of picking a mate like the art of the deal. There are qualities you definitely want in a mate ("deal points"), conditions that you won't accept or live with under any circumstances ("deal-breakers"), and points you are willing to negotiate.

List the qualities you want in a mate. Check back with the list you made in the previous exercise. While I've only made room for five, list more if you wish.

1. _____
2. _____
3. _____
4. _____
5. _____

Now go back over your list and circle the qualities that are non-negotiable—the real deal-breakers. Put a question mark next to the ones that are negotiable—things you are willing to compromise on, or could learn to live with or without. Next, put an "x" next to the points that continually cause you trouble in relationships—these may be things you should consider dropping from your list or giving up on when looking for a mate.

Dating Data

Research indicates that 8 out of 10 men still consider looks their primary "deal point." In comparison, women rank personality characteristics tops, such as sensitivity and caring. Research shows that physical attractiveness does affect how people react. In one study, people at the controls of a vibrating chair that created pleasurable sensations gave more vibrations to the people they rated as more attractive looking.

Love Scripts

Chemistry and deal points are just part of the reason we choose the people we do. We also use a "love script." This is like a blueprint that tells a story about how we'd like our love lives to go. Think of it as a movie of your love life, where you are casting a partner for the leading role. Our love scripts come from several sources, including our emotional needs, experiences, beliefs, and desires.

Our love scripts often lead us to people who offer us some measure of emotional protection. The most common example is women who date unavailable men like their father in order to get the love they always wanted but never got. But here's a poignant, more extreme example. Geoffrey told me that he had "a special thing" for women who weighed over 200 pounds. "If they're not that fat," he said, "I won't date them." Terribly insecure about his own underdeveloped body, Geoffrey convinced himself that such full-figured women would never reject him, so he felt safe. To find out why you are attracted to a particular trait, ask yourself: What meaning does this have for me? How does being with a person like that make me feel (safe, protected, important, powerful)?

Love scripts are affected by our early childhood experiences. It's sometimes obvious, like when you keep picking women to date who look like the girl in grade school you had a crush on but who never noticed you. Sometimes it's helpful to dig deeper. For example, when I examined Geoffrey's background to find the sources of his attraction to large women, I discovered he had had a frail mother who never hugged him. This helped explain his distaste for slim-framed women, whom he expected would be as cold. A very overweight aunt came to visit infrequently, and her arms around him were his only fond memory of nurturing—making him pleasantly predisposed to other women with a similar body type.

Conditions That Enhance Attraction

In one study, men who had exercised vigorously found a pretty woman even more appealing than those who had exercised for only a short period of time. In another study, men coming off a narrow, swaying footbridge, 230 feet above the rocks, asked a female research assistant out on a date more often than men walking across a low concrete span. The explanation: Arousal (as from the pounding heart and pumping blood associated with fear) can be interpreted as excitement, making the men more susceptible to attraction.

Experiencing grief or loss stimulates a desire to reaffirm life, bringing people together in the face of tragedy. Sometimes these relationships flower beautifully. For example, Susie lost her fiancé to cancer, but at a memorial service, she met Kurt. Although an unlikely pair (she was a banking executive in New York, and he was a pilot living on a farm in Idaho), they bonded with memories of their cherished friend. Despite their apparent lifestyle differences, they discovered emotional similarities and, in sharing their pain, found a new love that was deep and lasting to this day (her ongoing updates of their love are inspiring).

Home Alone

While Kurt and Susie's relationship (described on the previous page) worked out, there is a danger in forming bonds based on temporary need. After Lance broke his arm playing football, he ended up in physical therapy three times a week. Finding solace in the sweet physical therapist who carefully bandaged his arm and exercised his fingers, Lance felt he was falling in love. But once on the mend, Lance called his nurse less and less often, until he finally felt no desire to see her at all. When his need diminished, the attraction faded.

Many people have had the experience of falling for a co-worker or fellow cast member in a play, only to have the relationship fall apart at the end of the project. Mutual endeavors are very erotic, but don't guarantee lasting love. If you fall for someone during an intense project at work, or while you are both performing in a community play, don't be surprised if the relationship fizzles after the common bond dissipates.

Opposites Attract

You know the old saying, "Opposites attract," and we have all seen this adage in action. But over time, differences that were once appreciated can become sources of irritation. Renée called my radio show, "LovePhones," to say that her boyfriend loves country music and honky-tonk bars. At first she was captivated by this because she's more the alternative music, pierced belly-button type. But the novelty of their differences was beginning to wear thin. If Renée and her boyfriend want to keep the relationship going, they both have to learn to accommodate their differences.

To this end, I suggest that couples keep in mind the three A's necessary for a lasting relationship: acceptance, appreciation, and adjustment. New York mayor Rudy Guiliani and his wife, TV reporter and actress Donna Hanover, are a good example of how opposites can attract and require the three A's. When they met, she loved country music, he loved opera; he was into football, and she loved baseball. Joking about these differences helped them appreciate each other all the more when they first fell in love.

Common Dating Myths

When you become depressed about dating, it might be because your mind is telling you discouraging thoughts. Many of these are blatantly untrue! Here are some common misconceptions, and the truth about them.

MYTH: There is no one for you. All the good ones are taken.

REALITY: Negative thoughts create negative outcomes; positive thoughts allow positive realities. Remember, the world is full of possibilities. There is a cover for every pot. Even the gloomy forecast years ago that single women over 35 had as much a chance of finding a man as being attacked by a terrorist was subsequently proved misleading. Instead of worrying about your chances, look upon dating as a series of separate events: All that matters is what happens to you. In the movie *Dumb and Dumber*, Jim Carrey falls hard for Lauren Holly and asks God what his chances are. "One in a million" is the answer. Carrey then cheers, "I have a chance!" Even if it's true that you have a one in 7,397,685 chance of winning a multimillion-dollar lottery, someone has to win it—and it could be you!

You always have a chance. Be encouraged by Nilly's example. He called my radio show and admitted, "I'm not attractive and I fell for this gorgeous girl. I thought she'd never look at me once, much less twice, but surprisingly I won her heart. We started out as friends and we got to talking. She told me she had been abused when she was younger, and that I made her laugh. Now she says she never felt as comfortable with anyone in her life."

If you do need statistics, be heartened by these, shown in the following chart. The U.S. Bureau of the Census reports show there are more single men for women than you might think (especially for those under 40 years of age).

Ratio of Unmarried Men Per 100 Unmarried Women by Age: 1992

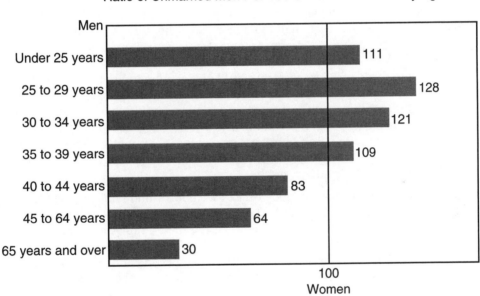

Source: U.S. Bureau of the Census, March 1993

MYTH: There is only one person right for you.

REALITY: There are many fish in the sea. There is no "one and only" Mr. or Ms. Right, and no "perfect" person—only real people, with real imperfections. It's totally true that finding love means being open to many possibilities and making compromises.

Rather than looking for "the one," be open to "dating around." Make the most of every date, not in terms of success or failure, or expectations or desperation, but look at it as an adventure, a way of enjoying and learning about yourself and others. Beat any

Smooth Talk'n

Chronic pessimists may have only themselves to blame! I've found in years of counseling singles that women and men who insist they can't find anyone are often afraid, unwilling, or not ready to commit themselves. Overcome this problem, adjust your too-rigid criteria, or tune your love antennae to whir for the right kind of date.

man (or woman) shortage odds: Instead of insisting on a certain height, salary, or status, be open to possibilities of who might be good for you.

For example, consider white-collar/blue-collar unions. Princess Stephanie of Monaco had two children by her bodyguard before she married him, and Elizabeth Taylor married carpenter Larry Fortensky (even though both marriages ended up in divorce). Roseanne divorced her producer-husband Tom Arnold to marry her chauffeur-bodyguard. More secure women today consider repairmen, chauffeurs, and bodyguards, not fearing "marrying down," but welcoming the man's love and support.

Also consider May–December and December–May (age gap) relationships. Research shows the ideal relationship was once considered to be the man being three-and-a-half years older than the woman (anthropologically, younger, more fertile females were desirable to propagate the species). But today's trend of older women with younger men (made popular by celebrities like Cher, who in her forties dated twenty-something lovers) can be a successful coupling. The younger man has grown up respecting independent, mature women and is more comfortable with equality than many older men. Lots of guys, including my "LovePhones" co-host Chris Jagger, admit proudly to losing their virginity to the "Mrs. Robinson" (from the movie *The Graduate*, in which Dustin Hoffman had an affair with a woman old enough to be his mother), revering the sexually confident "teacher."

Differences in culture, race, and religion can seem insurmountable. C.J. is black and attracted to a Pakistani Muslim girl. Abe's girlfriend is Lutheran, but he's Jewish. Parents and friends may warn and object, causing these couples to argue. Instead of succumbing to others' criticisms, get past your own and society's prejudices. Be prepared for life changes, understand each other's background and perspective, and agree on important lifestyle decisions. Appreciate the reasons for your attraction: for him as a person or what you provide for each other (protection, nurturance, support). Hopefully your relationship is built on a true connection, and not on rebellion, obstinacy, or defiance.

I maintain that any difference can be overcome if you truly appreciate each other and work out major lifestyle decisions (about kids, careers, family visits). If others' objections get to you too much, realize that they are triggering your *own* hesitations. Examine these doubts within yourself. Are you worried that your attraction is an escape, or a challenge, or proof of your independence? Declare a moratorium on the worries and spend time strengthening your relationship so it can withstand objections.

Myth: It's impossible to find someone to love.

Reality: Love can come in unexpected places and times, and in unexpected partners. For example, Jeannette was morose in her search. She told all her friends to be on the lookout, went to all the "right" parties, and joined all kinds of clubs, but seemingly to no avail. Finally, while visiting her sister in another state, she went to a museum exhibit. As she stood in front of a painting, a man with a small child asked her what she thought of the work. As she wandered to the next painting, and then the next, he seemed to follow her. Finally, he asked her to join him for lunch. They've been painting the town together ever since.

MYTH: Finding the right person is simply a matter of "fate"—being in the right place at the right time.

REALITY: As Jeanette's story shows, fate and timing are important, but you have to be open, receptive, and ready! You may not be able to ensure that any one activity or place will manifest love (in fact, you should not have any expectations), but when you are open to possibilities, feeling good about yourself, and going about your life with joy, more people are bound to be drawn to you.

MYTH: All the "good ones" are taken. There are no good men or women left.

REALITY: Even if many "good ones" are taken, it only takes one. You may even know that good person now and just need to open your eyes.

So Who Is Ms./Mr. Right?

A few years ago I wrote a book, *How To Love A Nice Guy*, because I found that people were constantly drawn to lovers who were wrong for them. Unfortunately, things haven't changed enough in the five years since then, and men and women still need to be wary of dream lovers and need to learn to appreciate the "nice" guy or gal. He might be a cook or a carpenter instead of a CEO, or she may look like a Plain Jane compared to Michelle Pfeiffer, but that person might be exactly who you need for a lifetime of lasting love.

Fortunately, as women become more emotionally, financially, and sexually secure and independent, they increasingly choose men who treat them well instead of those who are thrilling, "hot," or who fill some inadequacy in their lives. My own research shows that the top three qualities women want in a man are sensitivity (expressed as understanding, kindness, caring), intelligence, and a sense of humor (while men still go for looks). These are far more substantive than looking for someone who is a challenge. Undesirable qualities in men include arrogance, dishonesty, and selfishness. Both sexes say a sense of humor is a winner.

Nice Guys Don't Have to Finish Last

The lament of the nice guy is a common one that I hear a lot on my radio show. Vincent echoes the troubled refrain of many guys: "Why is it that girls stay with guys who treat them poorly but nice guys get stepped on?" Vincent is right—many women *are* attracted to "bad guys." As Christie says, "I like exciting guys. I know they're jerks and I'd like to like another guy I know who's sweet, but I can't help it. The rats just turn me on." Some women, like some men, find themselves in this trap of being torn between two loves—one nice and one "exciting." What's really going on is that they are addicted to a challenge, and need to prove they are desirable. They can only escape this trap when they feel secure within themselves and find their own life exciting.

Like Vincent, Billy is similarly befuddled: "I spared no expense romancing this girl for two weeks, opening doors for her, taking her horseback-riding, buying her gifts. But she said I was too nice and left me for some guy who acts tough and treats her rough. What's wrong with me?"

What's wrong with Billy is that he opened his bank account and his heart too fast. Showering someone with gifts does not ensure her approval. But before he jumps to conclusions that being nice isn't worth it, Billy has to examine what else he might be doing wrong, such as choosing a woman who is unavailable and unattainable, who only wants a challenge in a man, and who may have such low self-esteem that she can't let herself be loved. His love antennae need re-tuning.

Following my "Mirror Law of Attraction," if you're always attracted to unavailable, unattainable dates, look at why you need to have partners who don't appreciate you. It might be to prove that you're okay (because of low self-esteem; if so, value yourself as you are), or because you need to prove that all people are hard to please (look at your history and see why you resent men or women), or because you are really afraid of commitment (so you pick partners who would never want to settle down either).

"Nice" used to be the kiss of death, implying doormat, nerd, or wimp. But the new nice (male or female) can be good-looking and exciting. The one thing the nice guy or gal may lack is mystery or elusiveness—in its place is sensitivity, caring, sincerity, and reliability. Which qualities would you rather have over the long term? Nice people are there for you in an emergency, give even more than they take, and listen when you need to talk. They're your best friend, the ones you call to complain about all the others who treat you poorly. Like Harry in the movie *When Harry Met Sally*, or the pickle salesman in *Crossing Delancey*, they love you for you. They may not show up like fireworks, but they'll warm your heart by the fire. And they'll probably remember your birthday. One guy I met on a talk show in Boston, Craig Sutton, started a club for nice guys, with dances and T-shirts that read, "This is what a nice guy looks like."

I'm often asked, "Where do I go to meet someone nice?" The nice guy or gal often shows up as somebody's good friend. So look right under your nose. Ask friends, relatives, and co-workers to introduce you to their best friends. The nice guy may be the one who lets you out of the elevator first in your office building or the one who offers you a seat on the bus. The nice gal's the one with the smiling face you bump into many mornings at your favorite coffee shop. Once you've determined that "nice" is the one quality you won't compromise on, your "love antennae" will be attuned to that type of person, and he or she will show up in your life.

The Good Friend Test

I always marvel at how people accept things from lovers that they would never accept from a friend. As Zenia says, "My boyfriend cheats on me, he lies, he always forgets to call me . . . but I still love him."

Before you set out to find your ideal date, think about what friendship means to you. After all, you want your lover to be your friend, don't you? List the things that are important in a friend (steadfastness, honesty, reliability), and then consider whether your current or past lovers have these qualities. If anything, you can be a little more lenient with friends, but should compromise less when it comes to a love partner—where you have more to invest and more to gain or lose.

Expecting Change

Part of love is supporting each other to become your best. But if you choose partners with the expectation of changing them, you're courting serious disappointment. Tara learned this the hard way. As she explained, "I've been seeing Ben for six years. He's really smart, but he's lazy. He's been working on his dissertation for years and just can't finish it. I keep encouraging him because I know he's talented, but now I feel like I'm just pushing him. Lately he's said that he's not interested in a career—that he'd rather do something simple. I'm afraid he'll never make anything of himself."

While it is wonderful to be a partner's cheerleader and inspiration, if you both have decidedly different goals, it might be time to either accept your mate or cut your losses. Eventually, Tara decided she could never be happy being a constant nag, nor could she be happy with someone who wasn't as ambitious as she was, so she and Ben parted ways.

Compatibility Test

Let's close this chapter with a simple compatibility test that helps you gauge if a relationship is going to work. If you're not seeing someone right now, remember to turn back to this test when you start dating. Compatibility is essential if a relationship is going to work. Ask yourself these questions:

➤ **Do the two of you have similar values?** Research shows that shared values are crucial in keeping a relationship together.

➤ **Can you resolve your differences?** Every couple has arguments, but can you resolve them, respecting one another's opinions and needs? If you argue more often than you agree, you're in trouble.

➤ **Do you have similar needs for closeness or separateness?** If one person wants to be inseparable while the other feels suffocated with too much togetherness, you're in trouble.

➤ **Do you have similar sex drives?** Sex doesn't have to be on top of the list for every couple (and keep in mind sex drives can ebb and flow), but in most happy relationships, partners have similar feelings about sex.

Dating Data

A good test of what you're looking for is the "romantic resumé" in the book *Network Your Way to Endless Romance: Secrets to Help You Meet the Mate of Your Dreams* by Bob Burg and Laurie Sue Brockway.

➤ **Do you have similar lifestyles and goals?** Some differences can be worked out (he's an early riser while she comes alive late at night), but others can tear couples apart (she wants children and he doesn't).

A "no" answer to any one of these questions could spell trouble. Since each one of these can determine whether your relationship is happy and lasting, concentrate on how you may differ and make efforts to apply the three A's: acceptance, appreciation, and adjustment.

The Three-Month Observation Period

Of course I believe in love—or rather lust—at first sight. But before jumping to conclusions about any relationship, make sure you observe your partner over time. Follow my "three-month observation period" guideline—this is the minimum amount of time necessary to truly assess someone's character (trustworthiness, security, reliability, kindness). Falling too fast leads to trouble, so take things slow. You don't want to cast someone into your love script without really knowing that person.

The Least You Need to Know

➤ Attraction seems to be a mystery, but can actually be explained (by your experience, physical reactions, and the situation).

➤ We often seek in others what we wish for in ourselves.

➤ It is possible to open yourself up to fall in love with a different "type" of love partner.

➤ Ultimately, the best partner is someone who is secure and who really cares about you. Pick the woman idolizer instead of the womanizer.

➤ Remember, you always have a chance.

➤ Treat dating as an adventure.

Chapter 3

The Trenches—Getting Down and Dirty to Clean Up in Love

In This Chapter

➤ The best hunting grounds

➤ Improving your chances of meeting someone

➤ Where the single men and women are

"Where do I go to meet someone?" This is the MOST common question that single men and women of all ages have asked me over the years. If there is one lesson about this that you learn from this book, let it be the following: Don't worry about where you go, just be open! You don't always have to do something special or go out of your way to meet your future mate. In fact, you can meet her this morning while waiting for the train, at lunchtime while standing in line for your grilled chicken sandwich, or even this evening while riding the elevator. The point is to enjoy your life. Wherever you are, send out vibes that you're happy, open, and available!

Rule 1: Get Going!

When the energy is right, people will come into your energy field without any huge effort. It happened to Janey. Desolate and depressed, she turned down many invites so she could stay home and feel sorry for herself. Then one day an electrician came to rewire her apartment—and now he is igniting her passion as well.

Research shows meetings are conducive in places close to home where people feel comfortable and safe to talk to strangers. You become attractive when you are going about your normal activities because you are unself-conscious and just being yourself—which is, after all, what everyone really wants to be loved for! So, shop at the supermarket, go to the cleaners, and visit the health club—and stay open and keep your love antennae tuned.

Smooth Talk'n

More singles today are finding themselves new and alone in town because of job transfers or breakups after following lovers to different cities. To help make new friends, talk to neighbors; attend local events; and check out local newspapers, tourist magazines, and pamphlets that cover what's going on around town.

Rule 2: Be Proactive

Although it's not necessary to travel far and wide to find a mate, you can improve your chances of meeting someone by being proactive in your search. There are three strategies to this plan:

1. Do something you enjoy. This maneuver has a number of benefits. First of all, when you are actively engaged in something that interests you, you automatically become excited and emanate sex appeal. Secondly, you'll meet people who have similar interests to yours—one of the best foundations for a relationship. Meeting through a common interest provides both an instant bond and ice-breaker for that dreaded first conversation.

To help you accomplish this, do this exercise. Write down three interests you have and where you would go to pursue them:

Interest Inventory

Interest	Where to Go
1.	
2.	
3.	

Use the following table to help you with this exercise.

If Your Interest Is:	You Might Meet People Here:
Spiritual exploration	Holistic health expos, encounter group meetings, weekend getaways, trips to holy places
Sports	Health clubs, tennis lessons, pool halls, teams at local schools, Y's, sports bars
Dancing	Parties, dancing lessons, clubs, weddings
Art	Classes, museum exhibits and courses, art supply shops
Music	Classes, concerts, record stores
Health	Health clubs, retreats, health food stores

2. Choose places to go and things to do based on your personality style. For example, if you are a quiet person who loves to spend time reading or listening to

music, go to a bookstore—preferably one of the superstores where you can discuss your favorite novel or CD over a cappuccino. Or attend lectures where authors speak—during a break, you can talk to people who like the book or author.

If you're more adventurous, go where the action is—amusement parks, sporting events, and concerts. Places like these give you the freedom to release your inhibitions. Excitement tends to get you "pumped up," causing your heartbeat to race and your blood pressure to rise—all of which make you and others more turned on and more likely to fall in love.

3. Go to places where the type of mate you're looking for might be. Vinny wanted to know where he could meet a classy girl. The key to finding your ideal person is to pretend that you are that person. Vinny needed to consider, if he were a classy girl, where would he go? Maybe to a health club, a fancy restaurant, or an art history class. If you're looking for a wealthy person, you might try a golf course, stock exchange, charity ball, or chic vacation spot. If you're looking for a sports nut, go to a football game or sports bar.

Smooth Talk'n

The best time to meet working people is early in the morning, at lunchtime, after work, and over weekends. The best time to meet freelancers is during midday hours.

Always be ready—you can meet that special someone at the most unexpected times and places. Dawn went on a fishing trip with her friend even though she hates to fish, and met James, an avid fisherman, who hooked her line and sinker!

Make up an activities calendar of places to go and things to do for the week, for fun and singles scouting.

Activities Calendar

	Mon.	Tues.	Wed.	Thurs.	Fri.	Sat.	Sun.
9 a.m.							
Noon							
7 p.m.							
10 p.m.							

Do Your Homework!

Remember what it was like to do a term paper? At first, your mind was probably blank. But as soon as you began to research the topic, ideas popped into your head and your creative juices started flowing. Trying to meet someone is like writing a term paper. At first you may be void of clues of where you can meet him, but once you do a little research of your own and brainstorm with friends, you will come up with fresh ideas. For now, use the following sources to get you started in your research:

➤ Yellow pages for clubs and groups

➤ Local or neighborhood newspapers—special sections on activities and events

➤ Magazines for special interests

➤ National newspapers for travel ideas

➤ Friends and other singles

➤ Newspaper gossip columns that cover upcoming events

➤ Chamber of Commerce listings and pamphlets

➤ "Around town" books and pamphlets found in hotel rooms and lobbies that describe where to go and things to do

➤ Mailing lists—various clubs and party promoters use mailing lists to produce new events. Often there are sign-up sheets at clubs that will circulate them to other related establishments.

Dating Networks

Think of trying to find a partner like trying to find a job. Besides doing the obvious, like going through the want ads or visiting employment agencies (or going to bars, clubs, or singles parties), you also have to do the not-so-obvious—and that's network. I'm sure you know people who got their jobs through a friend or contact they met at some business function, or a chance meeting.

Now ask yourself how many couples do you know who met through a friend or co-worker, or at the gym? The point is that many means can work, so in order for you to find your prey, you have to be willing to search every hunting ground—whether that be a class, concert, or restaurant. And during your search, you'll meet other people—networks—who can introduce you to more people and maybe your Ms./Mr. Right!

The Little Black Book

Once you develop your network, you have to keep track of it. Remember the infamous "little black books"—those "hands-off" address/ratings books that men used to keep of women? Well, as you begin your hunt, you need your own "track record" of who you meet. Think of your black book less as a record of dates, and more as a working list of possibilities. In sales, it's called a prospecting list, but I call it a "dating networking list." Include people you haven't yet met but who you would like to date (your "wish list"), as well as people you can call on for other possibilities (for example, as an escort for an upcoming event).

A Little Help from Friends

According to numerous surveys, friends are the number-one source for finding a mate. The more dangerous life becomes, the safer people feel being introduced to someone by friends. Friends can offer a ready-made character reference, as well as a ready ear for feedback about the relationship.

"Do I have a girl for you!" Who hasn't cringed at the thought of Aunt Abby setting you up, or your mother wanting you to meet the son of one of her friends. However, don't cut off any possibilities— open your heart, mind, and spirit to all possibilities. Frank's "Aunt Abby" was right on target, and he ended up marrying her referral.

Smooth Talk'n

Blind dates don't have to be a total mystery—or surprise—if you talk a lot on the phone beforehand, and get a good description from the referral and the date himself.

Distant Co-Workers

Although love affairs at the office are often too close for comfort, look beyond immediate co-workers and partners. For example, you may find potential mates in other departments or working other shifts.

Also consider attending industry-related workshops and seminars. Conventions are a hotbed for contacts. With everything from social hours to exhibition halls, they offer lots of opportunities to mingle. Billy met Patty Sue at the jalapeño-eating contest at their district advertising convention. And when Candace stopped by Cal's booth at the annual gift show, he offered her free samples—and dinner. Plan your schedule to stay that extra day for the golf tournament, party, or tour.

Classroom Connections

Who hasn't fallen in love with someone they met in class, in a club, or in the cafeteria? School provides a fertile meeting and mating ground for all ages. Where else can you take an interesting class in history or photography, and at the same time meet like-minded people? Use local newspapers, school newspapers, and special-interest publications to find out what kinds of courses are being offered. You might also find listings and free publications at bookstores, music stores, newspaper stands, convenience stores, health food stores, doctors' offices, school lobbies, popular nightspots, and libraries.

Smooth Talk'n

When you do finally take a class, don't immediately take a seat. Instead, stand by the door or wander around until you spot someone you want to sit next to.

Religious and Community Groups

What's a safer and a more common-ground place to meet than in a religious institution? Most churches and synagogues have special singles' clubs that sponsor evening events and trips where you can meet other singles trying to find that special someone, while strengthening your ties to religion. You don't always have to be a paying member to attend. Stop in and pick up a listing of lectures, discussion groups, dances, holiday services, and parties. Also, volunteer to be a speaker at events so that you are the center of attention—drawing others to you without any effort.

Because connecting on familiar home territory can be comfortable and less awkward, also consider joining a community group. Here you can meet someone as you lobby for mutually-important issues or plan block parties.

Cafes, Restaurants, and Shops

Because food is already a symbol of love, eating can easily set the stage for romance. Additions such as fireplaces and piano bars in restaurants, and coffee bars in bookstores, have made finding opportunities to chit-chat much easier. Theme restaurants for sports, movies (such as Planet Hollywood), and music (such as the Hard Rock Cafe) feature all sorts of memorabilia that can be used as ice-breakers.

One of the latest craze in the cafe scene is the "cyber-cafe." These are restaurants and coffee shops set up with computer stations, so you can log on while you hang out. These experience a surge in popularity whenever some major news event happens, and people all log on to the same site for similar information, making it really easy to talk to one another. This happened during the release of the Starr Report on the Sexgate scandal between the President and Monica Lewinsky, when the report was released first on the Internet. Hungry for information, and unable to get it so instantly anywhere else, people flocked to cyber-cafes. There's probably no topic that feels safer, and lends itself to more discussion in this new age, than computers. So what better spot to meet someone than in a place filled with them? Ask questions about the latest programs—and then about each other.

Dating Data

Coffee shops are becoming a really "in" place to go and even to hang out, thanks to some big coffee companies' marketing campaigns. Discuss what flavor is "hot," then sit down together and test it—and each other.

Believe it or not, supermarkets are also great spots to meet someone. They offer a safe environment and easy opportunities to strike up conversation: "Do you think this cantaloupe is fresh?" or "I recommend this brand of spaghetti sauce because . . ." You can also observe a person's eating habits by taking quick glances at his shopping cart or food basket. Good single shopping hours are between 6 p.m. and closing, particularly in the frozen-food aisle!

Picking up people in specialty shops is a tried-and-true trick. Men should go to the women's wear floors in department stores and ask for help in choosing a gift for mom or sis, and women should browse in the men's wear department (because single guys have to buy their own clothes). Different stores cater to different ages and types, so your prey comes presorted. Women should also hang out at electronic and hardware stores, and new or used car lots. Try this new type of window-shopping.

Laundromats

With the addition of coffee stands, video games, and other diversions, Laundromats have given singles opportunities to socialize while they suds their duds. You can be creative and discuss detergents or help someone fold their sheets. You also have an opportunity to examine someone's lifestyle through her wash load ("Is he washing mostly dress shirts?" "Did she throw in lots of workout clothes?").

Parties

Meeting people at parties is easier for more confident and adventurous souls, but even shy people can grow from the challenge of throwing themselves into party-type situations. There are many types of parties: small friendly gatherings, special-event parties (such as birthdays, art openings, and weddings), singles parties, and formal events. Some singles parties have ice-breaker techniques; for example, write on a card what your main interest is and find someone in the room who has the same interest.

Here are some strategies to adopt when at a party:

➤ Place yourself in a strategic position so you're easily seen, or "cruise" the room to get comfortable with your environment (a good way to reduce anxiety before a speech, for example, is to survey the room beforehand). Also, strike up a conversation by asking a DJ or bartender for help in finding a pay phone or restroom. Adopt an inviting "look."

➤ Have a positive attitude. Don't feel embarrassed or ashamed to be there ("I'm a loser")

Smooth Talk'n

It's easier to approach someone who's alone rather than in a pack. In roping a steer, a cowboy isn't supposed to throw his lasso into the herd, but coax one selected animal aside. When Patty goes skiing with her girlfriends, she always gets on the singles line for the ski lift so she can pair up with another single for the ride up the mountain.

or think of past failures ("I was always a wallflower in high school"). Instead, think positive thoughts ("I'm attractive" and "I'm having a good time"). At the very least, distract yourself from negative thoughts by observing the color of the room or how the food is displayed.

➤ Amuse yourself. Survey the crowd for someone who interests you. Be aware of the superficiality of such attractions, but enjoy playing mental games by yourself, fixing on someone and imagining what that person is like. Become aware of what makes your love antennae whir and what makes it wilt (such as hair length, style of clothes, and certain postures).

Self-Improvement Workshops, Retreats, and Expos

Last year, I returned to the granddaddy of all "new-age" retreats—Esalen—on the Big Sur. Esalen became famous in the l960s for self-awareness seminars (and hot tubs) where you could "let it all hang out." As soon as I stepped foot on the grounds again, I felt myself opening up, relaxing, breathing easier, and smiling to everyone who walked by. "How nice it would be," I thought, "if I could bring those feelings back home with me to the rat race and shark waters of New York City!"

Besides getting in touch with yourself, being in an atmosphere where people expect to spiritually grow and meet others facilitates confidence, communication, and openness. Because everybody comes to a self-improvement workshop with the intention of being open, half your work is done, and half your fear is erased. Women will be especially glad to meet the more sensitive men who are drawn to these experiences. Courses usually last for a day, a weekend, or even longer. They also usually consist of group mealtimes, and classes with built-in exercises designed for interaction and group activities, which are instant structured ways to get to know other people.

Seminars on money management, financial planning, time management, and general management skills are also great places to meet men and women climbing up their career ladders. These seminars are usually held at hotels or other rented meeting rooms. Many are run by professional organizations that can charge several hundred dollars, but some are offered by networking clubs for $20 or so. You can even find a few free seminars that serve as introductions to a company's service. Refer to listings in newspapers and newsletters and in Appendix B of this book. Also, call brokerage firms and financial companies and ask if they're offering any such seminars.

You can also find someone with similar interests at expos that are advertised in publications and booklets distributed free of charge in various stores and street vending boxes. Popular health expos include the New Life Expo and the Whole Life Expo held in cities around the country several times a year. They feature lectures and exhibit booths on everything from clothes and jewelry to "magnet mattresses" (to balance your energy) and powdered health potions. You can get a Reiki massage, remove ear wax with candles, and find your soulmate.

Health Clubs and Health Stores

In the past decade, health clubs have become the hotspot for singles to meet. Pumping up your muscles also pumps up your self-esteem. Making conversation is easy, with built-in ice-breakers about workout routines, help on using machines, and nutrition. You can even offer to "spot" someone who's weight training. Many clubs offer classes in everything from karate to ballroom dancing, and trips for sports and socializing.

Health enthusiasts hungry for love can also frequent health-food stores and check out customers while buying soybean milk. Men should take health-food cooking classes, which are usually loaded with women. Refer to health newsletters to find out where health enthusiasts hang out.

Political Campaigns and Volunteer Organizations

Politics make not-so-strange bedfellows, because strong competition can spark an attraction between two opponents. (Remember the marriage of Republican television commentator Mary Matlin and Democratic party leader James Carville?) On the other hand, when two people team up against a common enemy, they grow to protect and value each other—making political volunteering a good hunting ground. Be prepared, though. Don't walk in blindly; instead, make sure you know the issues of the candidate you are working for. Being informed and committed offers you an even better chance to get into an impassioned conversation with someone.

Volunteering as a way to meet people is rewarding because you are contributing to the world in a worthwhile way. Remember that unselfishness is a top quality valued in the mating world, by both men and women. By volunteering, you are likely to meet others who are also giving and have similar values as you.

Pick a cause that you feel strongly about and that has some meaning in your life. For example, if your sister has multiple sclerosis, work for an M.S. charity. If you love animals, volunteer at the local zoo. If you enjoy reading, raise money for the local library or literacy foundation (they have major celebrity fundraisers with the likes of gossip columnist Liz Smith and TV newswoman Barbara Walters). Jill found the man of her dreams by working at a bachelor auction. Ivy and Dino hooked up working at a table collecting contributions and giving out information on Lifebeat (the music industry's fight against AIDS) at rock concerts. Will and Gina bonded over planning a Greenpeace demonstration. The possibilities for good Samaritans are endless.

Smooth Talk'n

A good way for single parents to meet other single parents is to go to children's school and after-school activities (dances, sports, classes, and rehearsals), and single-parent clubs, meetings, or events (listed in local newspapers and singles newsletters). While their kids were watching the puppet show at the Renaissance Fair, Al and Francine started talking about the puppet shows they used to put on when they were kids, and found a common interest in drama—and each other.

Concerts, Museums, and Cultural Events

Jackie was marveling over Janis Joplin's 1969 painted Porsche in the Rock-and-Roll Hall of Fame. "Can you believe it really only cost $3,500 back then? I'd sure love to own one now," she said, half to the display case, and half to the guy next to her—who ended up offering her a ride home in his Porsche.

Jeannette and Larry both lingered over a Degas painting and ended up going through the rest of the art exhibit together. There are an infinite number of museums, art galleries, and dance and theater groups that you can get involved with by taking classes or attending special showings or performances. Barbara met Kent while she was playing the lead in a community play he directed. She's a magazine editor and he's a doctor; they probably would not have met had they not both decided to pursue their amateur theatrical interests.

If you've ever been to Woodstock, a rock concert, or even a karaoke or piano bar, you know how music can bring people together. Feeling at one with a large group of people can create an open spirit, facilitating communication between strangers. Music causes chemicals to flow in the body that physiologically creates a feeling of relaxation or excitation, making you more open to falling in love. You won't have to worry about what to say when it's so easy to talk about the song and what it sounds like—or to dance and let your bodies do the talking!

Conventions

Conventions are a great way to meet people, because they usually draw huge crowds. Check with the local Chamber of Commerce, the concierge at local hotels that often host such events, and the large convention and concert halls in your area for their schedules. Sometimes admission is not restricted, and you can just pay to get in. For example, the Nassau Coliseum holds a magic convention that is open to the public.

Busy Spots: From Malls to Your Building Lobby

Research has shown that people form relationships more quickly in crowded places. So go where lots of people are—for example, to shopping malls. Most feature food courts, scattered benches, entertainment, and even art galleries, all of which can facilitate your hunt.

People also feel more comfortable close to home. If you live in an apartment building, try to hang out in your lobby, in the laundry room, or around your mailbox (repeated encounters also breed familiarity). Also keep your eye on local papers for lists of festivals, arts and crafts shows, and street fairs in your neighborhood. Even public parks have become great places for people to meet while they jog, play Frisbee, or walk their dogs.

Sporting Events

If you're an active participant—whether in softball or scuba diving—get out there! Sports, especially team sports, easily bring people together who share a common interest. Most clubs team you up with others, so you don't have to worry about making your own contacts.

If you're more of an observer, go to sporting events (football, baseball, basketball, even rodeos). Talk to people sitting around you. Don't spend halftime in your seat, but wander in the memorabilia shop, or wait on the food line and strike up a conversation about the game with someone. Attend tournaments (like golf and tennis) where you can wander around instead of staying put in your seat. Stand next to an interesting stranger and talk about a player's great line drive or an incredibly fast serve.

Instead of watching games at home, go to sports bars that have giant-screen TVs, electronic sports games, and lots of food and drinks. You'll have a chance to mingle with other fans while watching your favorite sport.

Support Groups

Although they're divorced now, Elizabeth Taylor once fell in love with unlikely match Larry Fortensky at a rehab center. The bonding makes sense; when you've seen each other at your worst, there's nowhere to go but up. Sharing your deepest, darkest feelings and fears with someone establishes a strong connection and is key to intimacy. There are support groups to deal with everything from pet loss and shyness to alcoholism, love addiction, and codependency. Refer to your local hospital or telephone directory for local 12-step self-help programs that offer regular meetings (e.g. Sex and Love Addicts Anonymous, Alcoholics Anonymous, or Alanon).

Dating Data

Many organizations hold social events for gays and lesbians. Check local and specialty newspapers that are distributed free in many stores and on college campuses. Also, check the phone directory for clubs and organizations listed under "Gay" and "Lesbian."

Openings and Fundraisers

There are innumerable public events in every town, from free openings of museums, community centers, and health organizations to invitation-only galas and expensive fundraisers. Make sure you make it to the cocktail party where the real mingling takes place, or you'll be limited to just meeting the people at your table. Call the organizer beforehand to arrange to be seated at a table with interesting people.

Smooth Talk'n

Single parents can attend any one of these activities. You can go alone, or bring your children along (kids can be company and great conversation pieces), as long as you make it obvious that you're single.

Marathons are popular big events these days—from Walk-a-Thons to Dance-a-Thons. You'll find many singles who've come to raise money for their various charities. Because you don't have to be an expert in any of these activities, you'll meet all kinds of people with shared spirits, "do-gooder" attitudes, and interests in being active.

Dating Data

Surveys of towns across America have found that cold Northwestern states—such as Alaska and Washington—have impressively high percentages of single men to women.

Travel

If you've got the time, the money, and the interest, traveling to some exotic spot—for a weekend getaway or a longer journey—can be the perfect setting for possible romance. Just as places that are close to home facilitate comfort for meeting strangers, the escape from daily life and excitement in a new adventure can allow just the right freedom (from stress or old patterns) and sex appeal for romance. The thrill alone of chance meetings in romantic settings can create sparks.

Most people feel safer having a companion or friend along on a trip, but going alone can afford just the open space for you to befriend others on your trip, talk to strangers, or spend time with someone you might meet.

Some people feel more comfortable going on a singles' trip arranged by an organization. Other more adventurous souls might take off by themselves. I'll never forget the year I had an unexpected week off from work. Because no one could take the same time off with me, I simply called United Airlines and told them to book me a ticket to the farthest place they could fly me. I ended up in Australia where I made lots of new friends—whom I still have and probably would never have met had I not gone alone.

When planning trips, pick destinations that are known for drawing singles or that have things to do for singles (such as clubs and shows). Do some research on airlines and travel organizations that book vacations, tours, camps, cruises, and trips for singles to resorts, sports outings, and exotic destinations. Consider all-inclusive packages such as those offered by Club Med, where you don't have to worry about what to do and where to eat, since the set-up provides instant playmates and meal companions.

Also know the type of vacation you want: Do you want to loll around the beach all day, or be active and go horseback riding or scuba diving? There are all kinds of organized outdoor singles trips that feature special interests, such as hiking, biking, rafting, safaris, archeology, and more.

Consider spiritual trips to sacred destinations where you are ensured that even if you don't meet your soulmate, you can get more in touch with your own inner soul. Outward Bound–type trips have become popular in the past decade; while embarking on a journey for survival, you discover yourself as well as bond with others. Who isn't familiar with the fun and camaraderie of camp as a child? Look into adult camps, such as Club Getaway, where you can recapture those experiences.

Buying a share in a summerhouse is a popular way to cut costs for a vacation and to increase your social contacts. Everyone chips in for food, so dinners can be parties, and there are always new people dropping by to visit friends.

Dating Data

Pittsburgh and Seattle have been rated as the most livable cities, while Rochester, N.Y.; East Lansing, Mich.; and Nashville, Tenn. scored as the most kind. Although New York and Los Angeles have been rated as the rudest cities, big urban cities generally offer a wider variety of people to meet.

Amusement Parks

When fun and fear mix, they create arousal and open the doors to falling in love. Based on this theory, and my research at Universal Studios Florida, I've developed what's called "Theme Park Therapy." It's easy to meet someone special or spice up your love life at an amusement park, theme park, state fair, or the like, because of the magical mixture of the four F's:

➤ **Feelings** (allowing yourself free expression)

➤ **Fear** (getting "scared" on rides, while knowing you're safe)

➤ **Fantasy** (suspending reality in imaginative settings and rides)

➤ **Fun** (experiencing uninhibited glee reminiscent of childhood)

Smooth Talk'n

From Albuquerque's Hot Air Balloon Festival to Milwaukee's Harley Davidson Festival, many cities have county fairs, festivals, and street fairs. Use these events to meet locals as well as tourists. The easy browsing pace and friendly atmosphere are conducive to casual chats with interesting-looking strangers at booths and in bleachers watching events.

In addition, chemicals flow in the body as you get excited on a theme park ride. Besides the physiological high, there are psychological benefits, such as returning to the joy of childhood. These benefits put you in a positive and open mental state to fall in love.

Going to a theme park is also a good way for single parents to meet someone and at the same time entertain their kids. Or you can take a date and allow your child to get to know the new person in your life in a fun and nonthreatening way.

Life is full of interesting and fun things to do and places to go. As you explore all of these possibilities, you're bound to meet new friends, and some relationships may blossom into love. At the very least, you'll be enjoying your first love and number-one date—yourself!

Video Arcades

Though a craze of the '80s and '90s, video arcades are still around, especially as the video age continues. These entertainment centers are getting more elaborate, with games of virtual reality, where you strap yourself in or step onto a tarp, and get a sense of playing golf, skiing, or racing, as if it is really happening. The benefits of places like these are similar to amusement parks.

Comedy Clubs

Since I mentioned to you that humor is the most attractive quality in both men and women these days, a great place to meet people is in comedy clubs. While also a great place for a date, comedy clubs are often frequented by groups of single friends going together for a fun night out. The very experience of laughing itself brings out the best in you, reduces your discomfort about approaching someone, and helps you be yourself (your real dating selling point).

Piers, Boardwalks, and Marketplaces

Many cities have centralized sections of town where restaurants, museums, specialty shops, and other places are centralized. Some examples include the Flats in Cleveland, where you can go from clubs to concerts and Pike's market in Seattle, where you can shop for fresh fish and watch vendors making potpourri. On any given day on the Santa Monica Pier in Los Angeles there might be a dance or music festival. Window shopping, club hopping, and people-meeting in the French Quarter in New Orleans is alive all night. Almost every city has some such entertaining section. Check the city guides.

Public Plazas or Atriums

Far simpler than piers or marketplaces, public plazas are still a potential meeting ground. Many are tucked in the middle of city streets, between tall buildings, where you can eat your lunch by a man-made waterfall or patch of garden. Some are even adding attractions, like wall climbing. The casual and safe atmosphere can lend itself to talking to strangers. Besides, you will likely see the same person return, giving you a chance to watch someone over time before you make your approach.

Smooth Talk'n

Look for any place in your city that is along a waterway. There are bound to be people hanging out, skating, walking their dog, roller-blading, and lots of attractions and distractions.

Making "Outdated" Places "In" Again

Let's face it. The dating scene is constantly evolving. You may remember when it was hip to go to discos, ice skating rinks, and carnivals to meet fellow singles. Now, you probably wouldn't be caught dead at these and other places. However, you probably felt the same way about hip huggers, bell-bottoms, and platform shoes. But we all know that the retro look is "in" again. Well this same turn-around-of events also applies to the dating scene.

Smooth Talk'n

Driving ranges, shooting ranges, putting greens, batting cages, and any place that people go to learn an activity are great places to meet others. Through expert secrets and other tips you can learn from each other, and you have tons of ice-breakers to pick from!

Bar Hopping

What's "out" about bar hopping is the idea of picking someone up for casual sex. But bars are still a fun place to go and socialize. Even without drinking, you can listen to music, play games, or watch your favorite sport. Visit a "theme" bar that features anything from uniforms and trophies to celebrity clothing—which provides material for starting up a conversation (versus picking up someone with idle chatter). For example, at the Fashion Café in New York City (owned by three high fashion models), you can remark how she would look great in a particular outfit being displayed. Or at a sports bar you can ask which team jersey is his favorite.

45

Clubbing

A spin-off of the typical bar is a club. These are usually open to the public, although some may require a membership fee. One example involves a recent craze—cigars. Cigar clubs are offering a very enjoyable, elegant atmosphere—even if you don't smoke (excuse me, anti-smokers).

Large, comfortable couches and a generally friendly attitude of those who come to such clubs make it conducive to meeting new people.

Singles Dances

One of the hottest places to go in the '70s was discos, when *Saturday Night Fever* was hot and happening. In recent years, retro dance music, as well as dance clubs, has experienced a resurgence. While none of the dance clubs reach the fervor and intensity of New York's famed Studio 54 (where celebrities like Halston, Bianca Jagger, and Andy Warhol appeared regularly), almost every city features dance clubs with reflecting disco balls and pounding music. The fun atmosphere and general high in the room is a great place for meeting someone.

Dating Data

Another type of club that is really in these days is the swing club—not mate-swapping but jitterbugging! Be careful suggesting this to someone, though. I must admit when I first heard of swing clubs I thought someone was suggesting sex—not the dance!

Another type of dance that is becoming "in" again is the sock hop, where people literally dance in their socks. In fact, one of my radio callers, a 25-year-old guy, met a girl at once of these dances.

Ballroom dancing and the Tango are also types of dance that are great ways to meet other singles. In fact, if you don't have a date on Saturday night, go to one of these events because you are expected to circulate and socialize with the other dancers. We all know how scary it feels to approach a stranger and ask him or her to dance. However, since you are expected to go up to someone and ask for a dance and then find other partners, you are less likely to be turned down. Also, you may discover that after an enjoyable dance, a person you initially felt was not your "type" becomes suddenly quite attractive. To find these types of dances, keep on eye on flyers at libraries and coffee shops and your local newspaper listings.

Shop 'Til You Drop

I'll never forget how longtime *Cosmo* editor Helen Gurley Brown advised over 20 years ago that a girl can talk to a guy who catches her eye while browsing through ties. All she would have to do was simply say that she needs to buy a tie for her brother and ask the object of her desire which tie he would prefer. Or to turn the tables around, a man could saunter over to a counter of scarves and ask a lady which she would recommend he get for his mother.

This old idea still works, so give it a try, but not just with clothing. Try other merchandise, from electronic gadgets to plants to in-line skates. You have all the material you need to strike up a conversation with a stranger—in fact, probably with someone who shares your same interests.

The trend of the new age is superstores, where everything from electronics to toys to clothing to food is collected under one roof, allowing you more choices of items that you are comfortable and interested in talking to someone about.

Unexpected Places

Anywhere can be a place to meet someone. You can be on a bus, waiting in a line, buying something, stopped at a stoplight. All it takes is being open, and having the guts to make a move, or to respond to someone else's approach, to show your interest.

Smooth Talk'n

Don't be afraid to go places alone. If you like, bring along a conversation tool like a magazine or your favorite book.

Smooth Talk'n

With women as well as men interested in cars and computers these days, and those purchases being complicated, they are ripe for taking the opportunity to ask other attractive shoppers about their recommendations. Who knows—he could go out on that test drive with you. Or you could end up exchanging e-mail addresses.

Your flight's delayed and you're stuck at the airport for two hours. You're about to settle a case in small claims court. You notice an unusual building down the street. At first sight, these events and situations don't seem like a means to finding a date. Well, look again . . .

Airports

Everyone is more mobile in this new age, between making business trips and pleasure excursions. Consider airports like the grocery store. With check-in lines, vendors, and coffee stands, there are endless opportunities to meet someone and strike up a conversation. Of course, let's not forget, that guy sitting next to you on your flight could be a fascinating catch.

Smooth Talk'n

When you don't look or feel your best, you're not likely to be open to seduction. Because you can meet anyone anywhere, it's always a good idea to be as well put together as possible. As a hairdresser once said to me, "Every day is show time."

Smooth Talk'n

There are endless ice-breakers to start a conversation—from bad airline food to headlines in the local newspaper. Think how easy it is to ask "Where are you traveling to?" and transition into what work you do. Ask if she lives to travel, or where he would most like to go.

Home Alone

The one potential draw-back to meeting potential dates while traveling is that they most likely live in a distant place. Be prepared for a long-distance relationship!

Every flight that isn't to a "hub" city has a connection that can entail waiting time of up to an hour. With airline delays the way they are, you can be waiting for many hours! One woman, Jackie, whose plane was canceled, requiring a six-hour wait for the next flight, used that time to sit in a chair at the gate next to a man with a large cowboy hat whom she thought looked cute. It was easy to start a conversation about where they were both coming from and how to use the delay time. Before you know it, they took off in a cab and went to the beach together, spent a romantic two hours under a tree, and the next year in a hot and heavy long-distance romance, heating up the phone lines, and making several visits to one another.

Hotels

Hotel lobbies are also a potentially great place to meet people. Yes, travelers may be tired and preoccupied, but they also could be lonely and receptive to you extending a warm welcome. Many hotel bars and restaurants are extremely popular even among locals.

Tourist Attractions

Rarely when you live in a city do you think of actually seeing the sights in your own backyard. But consider checking out the sightseeing opportunities and listings in the back of your local city magazine, or the tourist flyers from hotel lobbies and your own city cultural center. Select certain tours that you would find interesting. Despite the fact that you can expect more couples and families to be on these tours, as well as tourists from out of town (risking long-distance relationships), the tours might just turn up a like-minded local. In any case, the experience can help acquaint you with sights that you may have never discovered on your own (like museums and entertainment centers), where you can return and that could lead to meeting people closer to home.

Clubs and Hobbies

Remember how there were tons of extra curricular activities in high school and college that you could participate in? I remember belonging to the ski club, journalism club, and drama club. These activities were great places to bond with friends with similar interests. These same opportunities exist outside of school. For instance you could join a wine club, a tennis club, or a golf club. There are even clubs that are quite formal, as in the case of Kiwanis Clubs, or the Friars Club (which I belong to) where you have to meet certain requirements and/or be invited to join.

The purpose of joining a club is to belong to an association that offers you services and a network of people with common interests. Clubs are usually mainly eating clubs, with dining facilities. But many offer a wide range of other activities for their members, from golf and tennis outings to theater performances—some of which are geared to singles. Think of ones you might already be eligible for—by virtue of your school, job, or even armed services. Call your college alumnae office about their club in your city or ask your human resources director at work for references to any clubs that you might be eligible for. National associations for professional groups (from sanitation workers to psychologists) have societies that their constituency can join, for benefits, as well as trip offerings. Once you have joined, make sure you take full advantage of the social activities offered (for example, my own school's club—the Smith Club—has events specifically geared toward singles, including cocktail parties, singles dances and events, and even a matchmaking service to meet alums from other schools). Then read the newsletter, which usually advertises even more applicable events and services.

Smooth Talk'n

You don't always have to travel far. Be a tourist for a day and take a tour of your local city. Stacy met John on a Rock-and-Roll bus tour of New York City, while Pam fell for Larry on a behind-the-scenes tour of Madison Square Garden.

Smooth Talk'n

One of the best classes to enroll in these days is computer training. What could be easier to break the ice than a discussion about which model machine to buy, modems, Internet service providers, and the myriad of sites to find your way through? The conversation is ripe for advice and sharing, and developing a potential "connection."

Dating Data

When you "target" potential customers, you zero in on their specific interest. In dating this would mean you would follow up my favorite suggestion about going to courses you (and potential partners) have a mutual interest in, or places where the type of person you would like to meet is likely to be (for example, go to a boating regatta for an upscale outdoorsy man, or volunteer to work with underprivileged children to meet a caring, devoted woman).

Courts

Let's face it: The law is "in." You cannot turn on TV without *Judge Judy*, *People's Court*, *Law and Order*, or some other courtroom drama popping up on the screen. There's even a whole cable channel, Court TV. Chances are, you will find yourself in court for one reason or another—it may be just to renew your license or perform jury duty. Whatever your reason for being in court, you can rest assured that your visit will involve long lines, leaving you frustrated and restless. Why not take this opportunity to talk to those around you who are probably feeling exactly the same way?

The Least You Need to Know

➤ You can meet that special someone simply during the course of your daily life.

➤ To increase your chances of finding someone to love, get involved in an activity you enjoy doing.

➤ Think of where your ideal person might be, and then go there.

➤ Go where lots of men (sports events, loading docks) or women (dance lessons, self-improvement classes) are.

➤ Keep a "dating networking list" of contacts and possibilities.

➤ Be open to all possibilities.

Chapter 4

"Catalog" Shopping

In This Chapter

➤ Services that make a match

➤ The best policy: honesty and creativity, too

➤ Checking out a service

Aah, you may think there is no one out there for you, but the truth is there are so many options, so little time. The dating scene is definitely a world of its own with so many people to meet—in every shape, size, and style. So where do you start? If there were only a magical way you could "order" your soulmate, have the "package" sent to you overnight . . . and be able to return it if it doesn't "fit."

In ancient days, marriages were arranged to ensure fiefdoms and obtain dowries. Over time, matchmaking became somewhat nobler and less opportunistic, with good-natured relative and friends pitching in to bring two people together. In more recent years, matchmaking became big business, with dating services charging big bucks for the promise of love. Of course the newest way to meet people in this new era has become the Internet. There are innumerable sites and opportunities to meet people on the Internet that I will address in Chapter 5.

In this chapter I talk about various services that'll help you do your own "catalog shopping." Each has benefits, drawbacks, and limitations. I encourage you to give these a try, but don't be overly optimistic. Also, check Appendix B for more suggestions and details about these services.

Whatever means you use to hunt for that special someone, think of dating as a lesson in sales and marketing. That means keep looking for new leads. Like a good salesperson, you need exposure (play sports, sign up for classes, etc.). You can "target potential new customers" (meaning a specific guy to date) or you can send out a "mass mailing" (meaning joining a dating service) to cast a wide net to a larger audience.

Dating Data

When sending out "mass mailings," keep in mind that a 1–2 percent response rate is considered acceptable. Therefore, don't get discouraged if you receive only a handful of responses to a personal ad—especially when only a smaller percentage is worth a follow-up anyway.

Oldies but Goodies

Personal ads, video dating, and plain old matchmaking have been around for several years. They may seem "passé" or old, but they are still worthwhile. In fact, since they've been around for a while, some of these services have expanded into different territories, like onto the Internet (see Chapter 5 for more details on cyberdating). Such services have also become more socially acceptable. As a result, a wider group of people are participating, giving you a better chance of meeting someone "right" for you. So go ahead and try them out. As long as you are exercising your usual precautions, you don't have much to lose. In fact, the costs of many of these services, especially personal ads and cyberconnecting can be so reasonable that you're bound to find one suited to your budget.

Smooth Talk'n

Keep in mind that repeated efforts are usually necessary in order to get your message out (like in advertising or public relations). Don't be discouraged if your first attempts do not lead to big success.

Personal Ads

One of the least expensive matchmaking services, personal ads are carried in a tremendous number of publications, ranging from local newspapers and singles newsletters to national magazines. Before placing an ad, think carefully about the type of person you are trying to reach. Study the contents of the publication and assess the readership so that you get responses from the type of person you are looking for. For example, someone advertising in *Screw* magazine would probably not have the same intentions as someone placing an ad in *New York Magazine*.

Remember, when you submit a personal ad, you are an advertiser selling yourself. As such, you want to "break out of the clutter" (one of my favorite phrases), meaning stand out from the crowd. You also want to attract the desired "customer" to your "product"—you. Remember, the goal is not the quantity of responses, but the quality.

In writing your ad, be honest, creative, and descriptive about what you offer and what you want. Make sure your personality shines through. For example, a funny person might say, "Why can't Miss Piggy count to 70? For the answer, call me." Or a spontaneous person might say, "Want to fly off to Bali tomorrow?" Or a romantic might say, "Come sit by my fire and share dreams . . ."

I'm always encouraged by success stories. My cousin placed an ad in which she described her love of cats, the poet Baudelaire, and sonatas by Bach. Her passionate descriptions drew her now-husband to her ad and the altar. Another friend met his wife through the personals by describing himself this way: "36-year-old dancing psychiatrist likes ballet and sports, prefers nonsmoker 25–35. Hopes for lasting relationship and family."

Dating Data

A good tip: Answering a personal ad that required paying money is likely to net a higher quality date than one that was free.

If you have trouble describing yourself, ask a friend to help. Also, have a friend help you go over responses to your ad to get an objective perspective.

Personals do have a downside. It takes time to get responses, and you can count on some people being less than truthful in their advertising.

Answering Ads

In answering an ad, the same rules apply: Be honest, creative, and descriptive. Use the guidelines for good communication and listening described in Chapter 15. Besides telling about yourself, respond to the specific points the person wrote about, with comments or questions (just as you would in a good conversation).

Smooth Talk'n

Most personal ads have voice mail as an added feature. A lot of people prefer speaking to a recorded response because it is more immediate. Besides, a pleasant voice is revealing. If you decide to try it, write out your voice-mail message before you record it. Be creative. Instead of saying "Call me" and leaving your number, respond as if you were giving your own personal ad. Remember, as in advertising, you have to stand out from the crowd, so add intriguing details (talk about interests, your dreams, your ambitions, your desires).

Do a background check. Investigate this stranger, just as you would a job prospect. Get as much information as you can. Call him at work. Ask if you can call friends she talks about during your conversations.

Ask for a photo—not just to see if the person is your type, but to try to get a "sense" of the person. "Read" it: Is his posture open or closed (arms crossed, hands hidden)? Is she stern or smiling? What's the setting: a stark background or warm surroundings? Kathie sends a picture of herself hugging her puppy, and not surprisingly she wants a guy to snuggle with. Paul is standing by his Harley; you can imagine he has a wild streak.

Be cautious about getting together. Be sure that you have several phone calls before you meet for a date. During the calls, interview the person, asking direct questions. Meet during the day, in a public place, preferably with a friend.

If the date doesn't work out, or if there is no spark, don't waste time dragging it out. You can simply say, "It was nice meeting you, but I guess it wasn't a match made in heaven."

Video Dating

The more senses you can use to get an impression of a stranger, the easier it is to determine whether you are simpatico. Seeing a person and watching how he moves and talks gives you much more information than a written personal ad. It also saves time and energy in helping you make a decision faster. But you won't save money—video ads are more expensive than personal ads.

Video dating involves joining a private club, filling out a computerized personal profile, and making a videotape. Your profile, photo, and tape become part of the club's library, available to other members. You, in turn, can look at the library offerings, and if you see someone on video you would like to meet, submit a meeting request. If the person is interested, she can screen your video. If both are in agreement, phone numbers can then be swapped.

Video dating boomed in the 1980s, but like all other means, is being overshadowed somewhat by the latest flurry over computer dating services.

Dating Lines

Telephone party lines were popular in the early 1990s, when ads for these services flooded late-night cable TV. The premise is simple: By dialing a certain number, you gain access to a public phone line with other callers who want to talk or make dates. These lines tend to cater to young people. While these numbers may seem inexpensive, they can be costly—you are charged per minute, and when you are chatting on the phone it's very easy to lose track of time. Be wary of using these!

Cyberdating

It's the latest craze in the dating game, the next generation of personals and dating services. All you need is a computer and a modem (so you can access the Internet), then you enter different chat rooms, write messages, and send them via e-mail. More about this is discussed in the next chapter.

Professional Matchmakers

Like Yentl of *Fiddler on the Roof* fame (a perfect example of a "yenta" who loves to fix people up), matchmaking has a long tradition, especially among certain ethnic groups. Many matchmakers are fixtures in a given community, and spend considerable time really getting to know the singles. Their matches are based more on intuition and experience rather than on answers to a prescribed set of questions.

Many people like the personal touch that matchmakers provide. And some matchmaking services are as difficult to get into as some of our nation's finest schools. For example, one matchmaker puts a whole team of professionals on your case, including a handwriting analyst, private investigator, psychologist (for a battery of tests), and an image consultant (for fashion and make-up advice, as well as for advice on weight reduction and plastic surgery). Costs can range from the reasonable hundreds ($250) to the stratospheric thousands ($5,000).

Dating Services

These services run the gamut, with some offering parties, socials, and other singles events, and others sticking to simple introductions based on answers to a questionnaire and photographs. Some specialize in fixing up successful professionals, others say they cater to the sports-minded, and others are for specific religious groups. Call several to get information and recommendations. Ask for success rates and feedback from customers. Don't feel obligated or pressured. Read all the fine print about what you get for your money, including how many dates you're entitled to and over what period of time. Be sure you're provided with a member-services coordinator as your contact person, and call often with questions or to ask for advice.

Home Alone

To avoid rip-off or fly-by-night dating services, investigate what you're buying. Check prices (some limits are set by law) for membership and matches. Ask how long they've been in service, who owns the business, and the number of clients. Stick with busy, reputable businesses.

Dining Clubs

Some restaurants and clubs sponsor events, such as wine-tastings or movie screenings, designed to bring singles together. These events can provide a comfortable meeting atmosphere, reducing pressures and expectations. A well-known franchise that I've written about over the years is the "Single Gourmet." Now franchised in various countries around the world, the "Single Gourmet" offers dinners as well as day, week-end, or week-long trips. Most of the members have an interest in food and wine.

Dating Data

Hats off to the innovative Japanese for coming up with this unique dating service: on-site matchmaking at major corporations! These "matrimonial" companies act as commercial nakodo (go-betweens) for omiai (marriage interviews), introducing prospective brides and bridegrooms. Some boast about a 50 percent success rate. Granted, the need is there: Japanese workers spend most of their waking hours on the job. By contrast, American companies tend to actively discourage office romances.

The Least You Need to Know

➤ There are endless options for finding a date, from the low-tech to the high-tech.

➤ Whatever your method of contact, always be honest about yourself.

➤ Keep your expectations in check and be on the lookout for stories that sound too good or too wild to be true.

➤ Put potential dates and services through strict, extensive questioning.

➤ Exercise caution when getting together with strangers.

Chapter 5

Ineedadatebad.com

In This Chapter

➤ Chat rooms, bulletin boards, and home pages for finding a cyberdate

➤ Cyberdating pros and cons

➤ Turning a cyber-interest into a real-life date

➤ Flirting online—do's and don'ts

Gone are the days when Grandma insisted, "Have I got a girl for you," and friends insisted on fixing you up. The computer age has produced the next generation of personals and dating services: modem mating. Finding love online is now possible through e-mail, chat rooms, and online dating services. You now have access to do-it-yourself, instant intimacy with complete strangers—all with a switch of a button.

Cyberdating is definitely a cheaper and more convenient alternative to meeting people. It saves you the cost of using a real-life dating service, it takes less time to find people to "chat" with, and it provides instant gratification. In addition, it's a great service to those who are too shy to strike up a conversation face-to-face with a stranger; it allows more exposure for those who live in small, isolated towns; and it's perfect for those who can't easily get out due to physical limitations, illnesses, or other conditions. Geography and demographics suddenly melt away with taps on the keyboard. And, let's face it, we all know that time stands still out in cyberspace when you have the ability to connect 24–7 (meaning *all* the time) in the comfort of your home—despite lousy weather, having "nothing to wear," or having a plain old bad hair day!

With the increased popularity of using computers to find dates, I have gotten a lot of questions about this method of looking for, or finding, love. I'll address the answers to these questions, and more, in this chapter. Many of the questions and answers are similar to those that apply to printed "personals." Some of the most common ones are listed here:

➤ "Can you find true love on the Web?"

➤ "I've been chatting with a great person online for some time now. We want to meet, but I'm afraid that it won't work out. Should we take a chance and ruin a good online relationship?"

➤ "Can you really trust what someone is like from talking to them in a chat room?"

This chapter offers you the answers to these questions and gives you the inside scoop on finding and capturing your love interest on the Web.

Dating Data

Cyberdating can be credited for producing more passionate male lovers. How? Men are learning to express themselves (the very complaint women have always had), and though they feel more comfortable doing so computer-to-computer rather than in person, at least they're "talking."

In addition, communicating through the Internet forces men to focus on something other than a woman's looks (that is, until downloading photos and visual images become a much more common feature). This gives women not in the Julia Roberts–Cindy Crawford categories (which is nearly 100 percent of us) a far better fighting chance! Cyber-hooking-up accomplishes what I have often joked about—that men who are obsessed with a lover's looks should try going out with a bag over their head—so they can see potential mates with their hearts instead of with their eyes! Of course, this cerebral lovemaking works in men's favor, too, giving the poetic but unsightly Cyrano de Bergerac a fair chance to win the lady of his dreams over a more handsome—but perhaps less articulate—Prince Charming.

Connecting online can also be a useful training ground for practicing the flirting skills necessary in dating (outlined in Chapter 9). You can make mistakes without severe consequences since you never have to "see" the person again. No one even needs to know about these strikeouts. That gives you more courage to try things out, and to get closer to your goals.

Dating Data

For women who have ever complained there aren't enough men to go around, the electronic age has solved that problem. The popularity of electronics and gadgets among men means that computer dating holds great odds for females. The typical ratio of male to female users ranks well over five to one. Some services report 75 percent male users.

Keyword: Date Me!

With so many thousands of Web sites, it can be hard to know exactly where to go in cyberspace to meet someone. The task can seem as daunting as it is in real life. That's why certain services have evolved—just as in the "real world"—to make connecting easier for you.

Dating Data

With the popularity and increased affordability of laptops, you can have constant access to dating opportunities wherever you go. That means you never have to lose touch or worry about not being around for a crucial "call."

Chat Rooms

Online chat rooms are probably the easiest places to meet someone via computer. Chat rooms exist for almost every hobby, television show, and news headline. Some target specific age groups, geographical locations, nationalities, and just about any type of dating criteria people have. You can locate the chat room that interests you through specific Web servers, such as American Online, Yahoo, or Excite. Or, because these appear on many sites all over the Internet, you can simply spend some time surfing the Net exploring sites.

The ideal part about finding a chat room that appeals to you is that you'll meet other people who share your similar interests. From the initial chat room and discussion group, you can even enter a private room for a chat if you find someone who interests you. This fulfills my basic principle in dating: Much like going to a club you like, you can use a chat room to meet people with like interests and take advantage of an easy way to connect.

Smooth Talk'n

Certain sites require particular software or technological know-how. Don't be discouraged if you're not Internet-savvy. Ask a friend, your local computer store, or your service provider for help.

Bulletin Boards

Just as with chat rooms, hundreds of bulletin board services advertise new Web sites, upcoming Web events, and chat rooms. Thousands of people all over the country browse these sites. Use them to contact people, find out about new chat rooms, and make more personal connections. From these, you can contact people to make more personal connections, perhaps inviting them into a chat room.

Home Pages

Major companies set up Internet sites to advertise their products, services, and overall philosophies. These sites can cost thousands of dollars to set up and run. However, these days, any person can set up their own personal home page without spending an exorbitant amount of money. You can use your own home page to post your photo, list your favorite hobbies, and even post your favorite jokes. For singles, a home page can provide others a window to your life and a means of discovering someone they'd like to know more about.

Free Online Dating Registries

Just as in magazines and newspapers, you can answer personals at various sites on the Web. One of the easiest to use is www.webpersonals.com. Usually, you can use the same guidelines used in printed ads for writing and answering personals.

Dating Data

Some traditional dating services have gone "electronic" and now have sites on the Internet. You can find these by inputting their name in a search engine.

Online Communities

Have you ever been a member of a fraternity or sorority? You can think of online communities like such a group. For example, http://www.theglobe.com is a homogeneous group of people with the same interests and goals. Basically, you get to interact and exchange information with the security of knowing that the members have been pre-screened and that those who don't share the same philosophies are "screened out."

E-mail

The simplest form of communicating with a love interest is through e-mail, much like writing a letter to someone or making a phone call. All you need, of course, is an e-mail address. Obviously, it's more difficult to e-mail strangers, but this is a perfect way to send a quick note to someone you just met. Think of how easy it would be to send a short e-mail to ask how that person's day is going or to even ask someone out for dinner—it's certainly easier and more casual than making that dreaded phone call! Of course, it also means you have to keep track of people's e-mail addresses now, in addition to their address and phone number and fax number!

Home Alone

When giving out your e-mail address, use the same discretion as you would with your telephone number. One option is to set up different e-mail addresses for close friends, potential dates, and people you've met in chat rooms you want to keep at more distance. Think of it as having an unlisted and listed phone number.

Can You Find Love on the Web?

The possibility of finding true love on the Internet is one of the most popular new questions I'm asked as online dating heats up.

The answer to whether you can find love from cyberconnecting is a resounding "yes." The results have as much potential as in the case of personals and video dating. Of course there are no promises, no guarantees. But, the more exposure you get to different people, the more circles you form and the greater your likelihood of meeting someone that interests you.

I'm sure you've heard of successful Web matches. Take, for instance, the story of Carla, a 32-year-old divorced mother of two from Long Island, who took part in a poetry chat room. She met a man from New Mexico who not only shared her same interest in Elizabeth Barrett Browning's works, but who was also newly divorced with a son. Soon they began to "chat" about their children and the mutual problems of being a single parent. Months later, she moved to his town with her children, and they are still living happily together.

Another success story involves "Scottso," once my radio show engineer. A single guy who worked nights and lived far from the studio, Scott barely had time to go out to meet people. Being a computer geek, though, he would often surf the Net and check out people's home pages. In one of his random searches, he came upon a young woman's home page, with photos of her with her two young boys. As he read her statements about how she loves her children, his heart went aflutter. He sent her an e-mail, she responded, and they exchanged computer messages and later phone calls. Months later, he flew to her hometown in Rochester to meet her, and they fell in love. Sometime thereafter, tragedy struck, as she developed breast cancer and needed treatment. Yet Scott was by her side, and they are, to this day, planning their wedding.

Upsides to Cyberdating

On the upside, cyberdating can help you vastly expand your universe of contacts. Remember, this is an approach to selling, throwing out a wide net and searching for leads in less-than-traditional places.

Other advantages to communicating on the Internet are listed here:

➤ It's readily possible, immediate, and convenient.

➤ It's less costly than a date and can cost less than even phone calls.

➤ Because you type your messages, you get insight into how articulate and expressive your love interest is (it's wise to pay attention to those English composition classes in school!).

➤ You start out relating to someone whose physical characteristics are a mystery—that can make the connection based on more substantial qualities.

Imagine going into a large room, having innumerable choices, feeling free to approach anyone without fear, and then being able to move on to the next if necessary.

Cyberdating is a wonderful arena for building your confidence to date in person. By hiding behind the anonymity of words, you can be freer to express who you really are as a person. Without the burden of having to physically interact, you can gain skills that help you over the next hurdle: the actual face-to-face meeting. The thousands of people chatting online give you a wide selection with whom to test your moves. And if you are unhappy with one interaction, there are thousands more to peruse.

A unique feature of cyberdating is that you have total control. After all, you do not have to respond to anyone. You are the ultimate judge of what, where, and with whom you connect.

Dating Data

Computer contact can also help foster the friendship that is the basis for a long-lasting love by allowing the time and safety for a relationship to grow.

Other advantages to cyber-connecting are listed here:

➤ Immediacy. You can be in the middle of working on your computer and easily switch over to send an e-mail to someone. Others can also instantly contact you, so you don't have to wait for a phone call back.

➤ Cost-effectiveness. Communicating through the computer is cheaper than making phone calls, as your computer can connect you to people around the world for no more money than you pay for your monthly connecting service. The actual "date" is cheaper as well. Dinner and a movie can cost $50, while logging on together for a chat is far less expensive over the long run.

➤ Accessibility. Wherever there is a telephone line, you can be hooked up on your computer.

➤ Convenience. You don't have to answer or communicate back and forth on the spot, but can choose to send an e-mail whenever you're in the right mood.

➤ Unlike phone conversations but like letters, you can save people's messages, by creating a special file.

Dating Data

For those on the go, look for computer access lines in airports and other public places. If you don't see one readily available, ask an information booth or a store owner. Look for banks of telephones, as these are now being outfitted for fax and computer hook-ups. (NOTE: Be sure your computer is outfitted for the desired applications.) Also, don't forget the business centers of hotels. Even if you are not a guest, you can use their services.

Downsides to Cyberdating

For all the convenience of online romances, there's also a downside to cyberspace dating. These include cautions, dangers, and compromises that are similar to those for other dating services (described in the previous chapter). And because of the Internet's widespread reach—it's accessible to all kinds of people, including characters with less-than-pure motives, there are even more dangers.

Take heed of the following cautions:

Home Alone

Newblies (new Internet users) have to be especially careful. Just like in the dating game, certain "players" are waiting to take advantage of computer "virgins."

Home Alone

Some married people take advantage of the Internet to have affairs online, misleading singles into relationships. These can lead to disappointment for the single person, and also in divorce for the married person whose spouse finds out about the cyber-affair.

➤ Dishonesty of others. The biggest danger of the Internet involves one of its biggest advantages: You can be anything or anybody you want. As result, you must be extremely wary of liars and con artists. Don't immediately believe everything you read. Remember, it's very easy to deceive someone online or be someone or something other than yourself. If you're really interested in someone you meet on the Web, take the next step and meet over the phone, see a photo, and so forth.

➤ Your own dishonesty. As with other personals, you can also hide behind the anonymity of words, making up stories about who you really are or what you really look like. But it is best to be honest about yourself, especially if you really want to meet someone in person. If you get to that point, you'll have a lot of explaining to do if you haven't been completely above board.

➤ Escaping real relationships. Cyberlove junkies can escape real-life, person-to-person relationships without even realizing it. Online minutes easily become online hours, without the everyday dating problems. In-person love and sex can be replaced by eroticism from a distance. Don't get off on netsex, but get an offline life and a lover you can see and feel!

Online Dating Etiquette: Dos and Don'ts

Just as there is etiquette in dating (see Chapter 9 on flirting), there are also guidelines if you want to be a graceful and gentlemanly user of the Internet to meet people—and if you want cyberlove to cross over into real-life. Just as you would never talk with your mouth full, you should follow some codes of etiquette when communicating, hooking up, and "dating" via the Internet:

➤ DO be honest about yourself. Should you ever get to the stage of meeting your love interest in person, it could be a rude awakening for him if you fabricated a few key things about yourself (as in, you're not a 105-pound blonde . . .).

➤ DON'T reveal everything there is to know about yourself, as in dating in real-life. Leave something to the imagination (and also wait until you really know the person).

➤ DO be respectful of the other person's privacy, without demanding too much.

➤ DO refrain from profanity.

Home Alone

Don't jump too quickly into "talking" about sex, just as in a real-life encounter. Also avoid any impulse to be lewd or to say sexually abusive things. Watch out for people who use the Internet to purge their angry feelings from past rejections or hurts from relationships.

Other do's and don'ts of cyberdating to keep in mind include the following:

➤ DON'T reveal too much about yourself until you know the person better, as you would if you met in person.

➤ DON'T use your real name, phone number, or other information that could identify you until you know the person for several months or completely feel that this is a person you can trust. If you do make phone contact, use a phone at work rather than your home number, or even call from a local phone booth (as super-cautious as this sounds, it is a real protection).

➤ DO be wary of "lurkers" (unless you're in a private chat room). These are people who read along during a discussion without contributing.

➤ DO be wary of life stories that are too fantastic, glamorous, or dramatic. These people are likely lying.

➤ DO carefully pick your e-mail address and username. Using a gender-specific name that can help others choose you has certain advantages, but tricksters and prowlers often look for women (or youngsters) who come across as vulnerable or desperate. (For example, steer clear of names such as "kitten girl" or "lovelonging;" you don't want to be a target for cyber-abusers.) Also, certain names can put off others. For instance, referring to yourself as "Loverboy" can imply that you're a player or a womanizer. You can always try out different names and see what happens.

➤ DO find out what information is available about you online. Log onto your e-mail address at one of the finger services on the Net. Your finger (also called a "plan file") can contain all the information you used when you signed up with

Home Alone

Cyber-dumps (rejections) happen either by the other person ceasing to respond, wiping out their online contact address, or more directly by telling you it's over.

your service, including your name, address, phone number, and employer. If you don't like what comes up, contact your server.

➤ DO temper your expectations. You really cannot judge your compatibility, nor see a person's true personality, until you get to know him/her face-to-face.

➤ DO understand that cyberdating is subject to the same breakups as real-life dating. You might fall in cyber-love and then get rejected. If you face this experience, check Chapter 23 for tips on handling rejection.

A Warning for Parents!

Mom and Dad, beware! When your kids are at the computer doing their homework, be wary of them logging onto inappropriate sites. There are many stories about perverts who prowl the Web. They take on various poses, lure young people with misleading stories and promises, and can arrange in-person meetings. They may even travel to far-away cities or send tickets to youngsters to meet them elsewhere. While there are some investigators (called syscops) whose job it is to look for these kinds of perpetrators, unfortunately, there are not enough of them to stop this growing crime. Watch out for yourself—and your kids.

In one of the most riveting TV investigative stories, a reporter in Cleveland got a 20-something producer to pose as a 15-year-old girl in a chat room. In just a matter of time, a 40-something guy began to send her lewd sexual invitations over the computer chat rooms. He arranged to meet her in a park, where the reporter ambushed him. Though the man denied everything, they followed him to his car, which he had described to the girl as a white car with a damaged side mirror so she'd know it was him.

Besides the general precautions about using cyberspace to meet people, here are some safety tips to prevent children from inappropriately hooking up over the Internet:

➤ Keep the computer terminal in a family room, not in a private bedroom.

➤ Discuss proper usage with your children.

➤ Monitor usage periodically.

➤ Set specific times when the computer can be used—when someone's home.

➤ Inform kids about potential dangers on the Internet, in the same way you would warn them about abductions. Encourage them to come to you with any questions they may have.

➤ Talk to kids about sex in general so they have a healthy attitude and are not misinformed.

"Why don't you e-mail me sometime?"

When you're face-to-face with a person, you have the opportunity to observe that person's body language and facial expressions. Unfortunately this luxury is missing when you're trying to connect online, where you are instead relying solely on the other person's verbal skills and use of language. This can certainly help you when it comes to in-person meetings, where many singles panic about how to make that approach, what opening lines to use, and what to say.

To add some spice to your messages (and also to translate the sender's notes), it's wise to familiarize yourself with frequently used online idiosyncratic terms. For example, some symbols or shorthand expressions you can use to reflect actions are:

> :) for a smile
>
> ;) for a wink
>
> LOL for "laughing out loud"
>
> BRB for "be right back"

Designs for kissing and physical contact range from the simple to the more elaborate. Get creative in making up your own, just as you would in any "conversation." You can also use different colors or backgrounds to express yourself.

You can learn the ins and outs of these techniques by observing how others use them in chat rooms. Many areas also have guides and help commands, and others in the chat room will give you (sometimes unsolicited) feedback on how you are doing.

Dos and Don'ts for Online Flirting:

Here are some do's and don'ts when it comes to online flirting, besides all the tips above for online cyberdating:

> ➤ DO watch how the conversation is going, and then just jump in. Don't be afraid to be simplistic (just saying "hello") and then wait to see what happens. You can also ask a question of a specific person or the room in general, or say something provocative. These are all the approaches you would use in a real-life encounter, except that here you have that safety to try out anything.

Smooth Talk'n

Connecting online can also be a useful training ground for practicing your flirting skills. You can make mistakes without severe consequences, because you'll never have to "see" that person again. Knowing that no one will ever have to know about strike-outs should give you more courage to try new techniques—and get you closer to your goals.

Smooth Talk'n

A useful book about online dating and sex is *Joy of Cybersex*. It includes extensive lists of services related to cyberdating that you can log onto.

Smooth Talk'n

Remember I've said that attraction happens on several sensory levels, so the more senses you can exchange before you meet a love interest in person for that final sense (talk on the phone, for instance), the better you'll know each other and the stronger foundation you'll have for building that attraction.

➤ DO acknowledge what the other person is saying, using their screen name as you would their real name if you were meeting in person.

➤ DON'T be insensitive to how others react to your flirting. As in real life, note the difference between a response to your advance that takes a step backward and one that shows interest with equal flirtatiousness. Keep in mind that the other person might be shy online. You can apply my old baseball rule to dating: three strikes and you're out. That means if someone seems withdrawn, you can try two more approaches before you decide to move on.

➤ DO understand that flirting online is not as easy as it appears. While you can test out various approaches, developing real skills takes time, energy, and commitment. Use the same creativity as you would in writing a personal note or when making a real-life connection.

➤ DON'T be ambiguous about what you want to say. Instead of beating around the bush or hiding behind confusing or contradictory messages, be clear about your goals and emotions.

Turning Virtual Love into Real-Life Love

Many people ask whether they should meet a cyber-interest for a live date. The story usually goes that they have been chatting with someone for a while and now want to meet.

Of course, the whole point of flirting online is to eventually find a match, meet him/her, and hopefully begin what could be a very promising relationship. However, what if you finally meet your love interest and that person doesn't live up to your expectations?

Obviously, you have to face the fears about doing this. As with talking over a CB radio or maintaining a great phone relationship, the fear is that when you meet in person, the magic will be gone. This is entirely possible. The person's physical characteristics may not be what you like: He may have less hair, she may be more full-figured. However, the advantage of meeting someone in person after you've developed some kind of contact or rapport online is just that. You may be able put aside the fact that he/she doesn't fit what is normally your "type." After all, you may have developed a close, caring relationship before the physical ingredients got in the way. Besides, you could be in for a happy surprise—there's nothing like the eyes of new lovers meeting.

Preventing Online Surprises

Here are some precautions you should take to prevent in-person surprises. Some of these are similar to do's and don'ts about cyberdating that I described earlier.

➤ Be sure that you have been honest in your descriptions of yourself.

➤ Get as much information as possible about each other. You can even ask for a resumé or other information, as if you were interviewing that person for a job. Even "meet" their friends over the Internet, for extra information. Send pictures and talk on the phone beforehand so you can see and hear the way you each come across.

➤ Play private detective. Check out as much as you can about the person before you meet. Look him/her up in the phone book. Don't be afraid to ask for references or friends that can join the chat.

Precautions for Your Live Meeting

Use the same precautions for your first meeting as you would with any other meeting (such as through personal or video dating that I've described in Chapter 4). You may feel like you know the person very well and can trust him/her, but the truth is that you don't really know each other until you meet and ultimately spend time together. For your first meeting, do the following:

1. Meet in a public place (such as a restaurant, a museum, or a movie theater).

2. Meet during daytime.

3. Take a friend along, for safety and also for an independent impression of the person.

Dating Data

Research shows that touch is crucial to our health. Baby monkeys adapted better socially when weaned with real versus wire mothers, and when exposed to play with other baby monkeys. Likewise, human infants deprived of human touch have shown inferior cognitive as well as social skills when compared to infants cuddled by human beings.

A Final Word on Cyberdating

As the Internet becomes more popular as a means to get dates, some singles are finding that cyberdating is a bit too impersonal, that many of the users are not completely above board when it comes to revealing personal information, or that in-person meetings never unfold. It is obvious to me, especially from my radio program, that people really do love to talk and make human contact, a need that will only increase as the mechanization of life, work, and relationships also increases. The more people sit in front of a monitor all day long, the more they will need real human contact.

A similar fear was faced by movie companies, who worried that the advent of videos and easy accessibility at home would drive people away from the cinemas. But, while people do rent videos, they also still go to the movies because, among other things, they want to get out of the house. The same will happen with Internet dating. Though people will sit home and connect, they will still have the desire to reach out and touch someone.

The Least You Need to Know

➤ Used wisely, the Internet can be a valuable tool in meeting new people with whom you would likely never cross paths otherwise.

➤ Always be honest in your communications on the Web, as in person.

➤ Meeting online can lead to real-life love, as long as you're always honest and safe.

Part 2
The Bait

Let me let you in on the biggest secret of all in dating: Sex appeal comes from self-appeal. You are most likely to meet someone when you are feeling your most attractive.

Let's face it. Would you rather date someone who appears insecure and down on life, or someone who is vibrant, energetic, and seems fun to be with? Now, look in the mirror. What kind of image do you see? Would you look forward to having an evening with yourself? Do you consider yourself a catch? If you don't, why should others?

Do you remember the old saying: "Smile and the whole world will smile back at you"? This is absolutely true! Self-confidence can be contagious. If you feel good about yourself, you'll make others feel good about being around you . . . and ultimately about themselves. As you read this section about how you can boost your self esteem, remember this: If you enjoy your own company, others will want to join you.

Would You Date You?

"Girls don't seem to like me."

"I can never get a boyfriend."

"I'm not ugly, but I'm not great-looking either. How will I ever find somebody?"

Do you indulge in negative thinking? Are you constantly dumping on yourself and imagining the bleakest future possible? Right this minute, make a commitment to stop it! Replace self-dumping with self-pumping and images of a bright future—one where you really dig yourself. What happens when you constantly imagine the worst, and put yourself down in front of other people? As my mother always warned, what you say will come true, and everyone around you will believe either the complimentary or derogatory things you say about yourself. So you might as well fill your own, and others' thoughts, with positive images. Practice these affirmations—after awhile, the sentiments will come naturally.

QUESTION: "Who's the best date?"
ANSWER: "Me!"

QUESTION: "Whose company do you enjoy the most?"
ANSWER: "My own."

Why Can't I Get a Date?

"I can't get a date." How many times in your life have you said this? This generalization itself is self-defeating and needs to be wiped out of your vocabulary. *Of course* you can get a date, you just might be paralyzed by fear.

One of the most common reasons for making such sweeping statements is that past rejections and bad dating experiences over the years still haunt you. I refer to these experiences as "ghosts of the past." Once you become aware of these ghosts, do some ghost-busting. That is, separate yourself from past hurts and prevent them from interfering with the present. Remind yourself that you are not a slave to the past. Whatever happened then does not have to repeat now. In fact, you have the power to constantly redesign your life by making new love choices, and carrying out new behaviors that will lead to happier outcomes.

Home Alone

I often hear the following complaint from women: "I know my boyfriend/husband is cheating on me, but still I *love* him." Recognize and believe that you deserve much better and that you're better off on your own than stuck in destructive relationships. Alert friends to your situation so that they can help support you to make healthier choices.

Home Alone

Don't chase after or stay with those who treat you poorly. All you get is bad energy, bad relationships, and no peace!

What May Be Working Against You

In addition to a lack of self-confidence and self esteem, here are other reasons that may cause you to strike out when it comes to the dating game.

➤ You are "too nice." Let's say you're always bringing flowers or paying for extravagant dinners, but girls never seem too interested in you. Recognize that there is a line between being too nice and being a "doormat," which is not an attractive quality.

➤ You're ambiguous about your intentions. Some singles don't get a date simply because they don't ask for one. Be clear about your intentions and don't expect the other person to "read" you.

➤ You're simply barking up the wrong tree. When hunting, you should always chase a prey that you're able to catch. You can determine this through the prey's habits. However, when you set your sights out of range, you'll never catch your prey. Therefore, don't chase someone who is clearly unavailable; you're only setting yourself up for failure. Experienced hunters—or daters—can tell just by looking at someone whether or not they are approachable (e.g. through body language or flirting techniques). You only set yourself up for disappointment when you chase those who don't want to be chased.

You Don't Have to Put Up with Crap

"Use them, abuse them, and they love you."
—Darcy Bonfils, television producer and co-author of The Presley Family Cookbook.

If you are in this kind of relationship my friend Darcy describes—mixing abuse and love—look again! Yes, "crap" is a nasty word but it's a word that is used often by my radio show callers to describe how they feel when they experience bad treatment and downright disrespect. Take the woman who got swept off her feet and then suddenly left out in the cold. Or the guy who spends big bucks on jewelry for his dates but never gets return phone calls. It's easy to end up feeling depressed and discouraged, and decide that dating is, well, not worth it.

Remember, you don't have to put up with disrespect. But also recognize that you are responsible for the kind of treatment you receive. According to my "Mirror Law of Attraction," we bring to ourselves relationships that reflect what our own needs and insecurities are, giving us the opportunity to see exactly who we are in the reflection of the person we are with. This does not mean that you should blame yourself when you are treated poorly. However, if you put up with this kind of treatment, you are sending a message that says that you don't deserve to be treated any better.

Once you realize how and why you bring disappointing dates into your life, make a commitment to not repeat this type of pattern.

Dating Data

Measure how much attention, respect, and love you are receiving from your partner by comparing the treatment to a loaf of bread: Are you getting crumbs, a few slices, or the whole loaf? Trust your instincts; if you feel bad about an interaction, stay away from it. Gravitate toward those who make you feel fulfilled, and away from those who deplete your energies and bring you down like a brick.

Give Yourself Permission to Like Yourself

What will you gain as you gain self-confidence? Sex appeal! People are drawn to self-confidence. I'm not saying you should be an egotistical, selfish narcissist, but neither should you be so humble or self-effacing that you fade into the background or put yourself last. Love yourself enough to be self-confident; this will draw others to you and give you a solid foundation from which to appreciate and love others.

Self-esteem comes from three A's: acceptance, appreciation, and adjustment. Love yourself with the same unconditional love that a mother (ideally) gives a child. That means love yourself regardless of your IQ, your wardrobe, your job, or your looks.

Self-esteem—or the lack of it—is often the result of experience. If your parents and those around you are mindful of the three A's, you stand a better chance of liking yourself. But ultimately, self-esteem has to come from within. It has to be a flame that glows from inside you that says, "I am wonderful. I am lovable. I enjoy me."

You are your own best date and most entertaining companion. Too many people seek dates or mates because they are bored with themselves. If you bore yourself, there is little reason to think that someone else will be thrilled with your company. Consider the following truisms:

➤ You'll never be happy with or truly love anyone until you're happy with and truly love yourself.

➤ People are drawn to those who like themselves. Everybody wants to be around someone who is having a good time. Self-confidence screams sex appeal.

➤ Sometimes, being with someone you feel no connection with can be lonelier than being alone.

➤ Most people don't think highly enough of themselves.

The conclusion? The key to happiness, whether you find a mate or not, is to love yourself.

Your goal is to give yourself permission to like yourself, appreciate yourself, and give yourself the time and attention you would give a lover. Remember the Army's advertising slogan: "Be all that you can be." Do all that you can do, and you'll have all that you can have.

Embrace Your Individuality

A caller to my radio advice show, "LovePhones," once told me: "I've been dating a woman who lately has been treating me like crap. She criticizes me constantly about everything from my clothes to the way I hold my fork. But I can't bear to think of my life without her."

If you find yourself with people who don't appreciate you or who are overly critical, walk away. You deserve more. Learn to train your love antennae to pick up on positive signals, and people who will treat you with the respect and love that you deserve.

One night I stood at a club watching a really cool female punk band, the Lunachicks. The kid to my right told me that he was wild for the guitarist, and that he'd even hung out with her and kissed her once. A few minutes later, the guy to my left said, "I can't stand that short girl playing the guitar," and described how he had met her also and been really turned off by her antics. Same girl, two guys, two opinions. Should she change so that guy number two changes his opinion of her? Should she punish herself because some guy finds her undesirable? Heck, no.

Always remember one person's poison is another's aphrodisiac. The very characteristic or behavior that turns one person off may turn another person on. There's the ultimate proof of this point in the story of Rudolph the Red-Nosed Reindeer, whose nose, you'll remember, made him the butt of the other reindeers' jokes, but was beloved by Santa, who gave him a prime spot at the front of the sleigh. So, if you think your nose is too big, your chest too hairy, or your breasts too small, love yourself anyway. Someone will appreciate you for those qualities!

Exercises to Help You Build Self-Esteem

Building your self-esteem is like having an exercise program to keep your body fit. You have to focus on certain activities and repeat them in order to change your bad habits, improve your outlook, and maintain the benefits. The following exercises will help.

Morning Wake-Up Call

Be your own perfect parent. Think of how you would wake up a child in the morning, with a smile and a cheerful, "Good morning, honey!" If you usually start the morning with a sneer, slamming the alarm, cursing your reflection in the mirror, and dreading the day, use what seer Roberta Herzog calls the "cosmic erasure." Say aloud, "Cancel, clear." Then use your mental TV clicker and change the program in your brain and in your behavior. Look in the mirror and say, "I love you" or "I've got something to make you happy today." Every day, think of one fun or challenging thing you can do, and use that as a motivator as you bounce out of bed. You may feel silly at first, but soon this will come as natural and feel as refreshing as brushing your teeth.

Smile

When you look in the mirror, whether you're shaving, brushing your hair, or checking your reflection in your car's rearview mirror, don't frown and point out your various flaws. Change the program in your brain and smile instead.

Dating Data

As soon as you smile, your facial muscles alter your brain state to a calmer frequency, lifting your mood. Remember throughout the day to turn your lips into a smile even if you don't feel much like smiling. The physical "set" of your muscles will actually create a more buoyant emotion.

Be Your Own Cheering Section

Like sports players need a coach and cheering squad, you need ongoing pep talks to spark up your energy to do your best. When you feel your security waning and your shyness escalating, picture an angel on your shoulder cheering you on: "You can do it!"

Self-Pump (Instead of Self-Dump)

Whenever you feel down or afraid to approach someone for a date, remind yourself of all your wonderful qualities. If you tend to focus on the negative ("I'm too short and chunky," "My nose is too big," "I stutter when I'm nervous"), refocus your energy on the positive.

What happens when you constantly criticize yourself? People will eventually believe you. After all, who knows you better than you? Often we say negative things about ourselves as a kind of protection, to minimize other people's expectations, or to deflect their jealousy. Avoid this trap. Instead, tell others all the terrific things about yourself, what you do, what you know, and what you can do for them.

Try this exercise. Quick, tell me five great things about yourself and list them in the first column of the following table (I'll get to the other two columns later).

	Self-description	Up the Ante 1×	Up the Ante 2×
I am:			

By writing down your assets, you fix them more firmly in your mind. Next, get a tape recorder and record the same information. Before you go to sleep at night, play the tape—the semihypnotic pre-sleep state makes thoughts stick more in your mind.

Try a visualization exercise where you picture your biggest fan making a speech about how great you are. Save complimentary notes from friends and colleagues, and take them out when you need a lift. I have to smile when I reread my mother's birthday cards where, being a master of superlative adjectives, she describes me as "the most wonderful, beautiful, gracious, creative, thoughtful, independent, energetic, stimulating, loving daughter"—I pause on each adjective and drink in how it feels to be that way.

If you have similar cards or letters, put the messages on a small card and keep them in your wallet. Refer to the card while you're on hold, in an elevator, on the subway—whenever you have spare time. Or put these words of praise on tape and carry the tape with you to play in your portable tape player. As you hear the words over and over, they'll become part of your self-concept. Don't feel embarrassed or silly doing this. Take these in as honest truths about yourself.

Another exercise is to toot your own horn. Brag about yourself. Describe your triumphs enthusiastically and extensively. Don't worry about being humble, or acting too full of yourself. People find it sexy and attractive when other people are pleased with themselves.

Now you're ready for the exercise I call "Pump It Up." I love this exercise, and use it at many college lectures and other workshops. Go back to your asset list and get ready to fill in columns two and three. "Up the ante" on each asset—the next highest level of that quality, and then the next level after that. On my "LovePhones" radio show, for example, I sometimes start out the show saying, "Do you feel good? Say you feel good...now better...now GREAT!"

For example, if you wrote "funny" in column 1, write "hysterical" in the second column. Up the ante again in the third column, writing "side-splitting." If you wrote "smart" in the first column, write "most intelligent" in the second column, and then "brilliant" in the third. Now, say "I am" and call yourself aloud the qualities in the third column.

Self-Talk

All of us have a running monologue going on in our heads, as we comment on situations, feelings, and moments in our day. Sometimes the monologue is filled with negative messages ("How could you be so stupid? He really hates you now. You'll never find someone.") Negative thoughts deplete self-esteem and create self-sabotaging actions. We turn people away by the "vibes" we send out.

You can get rid of negative thoughts in two ways. First, picture a street sign in your brain that reads "No dumping allowed." Next, go into the computer program in your brain, print out the negative program (the one that says, "You're a jerk, you blew that, no one loves you"), then use the cosmic erasure. Say aloud, "Cancel, clear," press the delete button and type in a new program, one that says "I'm a neat person," "I am a lot of fun to be around," "I have so many interesting things to do and say in my life," "Lots of people want to be around me because I am stimulating, warm, and fun."

Smooth Talk'n

Be your own public relations agent! Think about what a public relations agent does to promote a product. That person pinpoints all of the attractive features so that others will be interested. Do the same for your best product—you!

Affirmations

Affirmations are a form of positive self-talk. The rule on affirmations is to start your self-affirming statement with "I am" (not "Other people say I am . . ."). Don't start with a negative, such as "I am not fat, sloppy, or boring." When the word "not" is attached to a statement, the mind conjures up the negative images (of fat, sloppy, and boring) anyway. It's like being told, "Don't think about a pink elephant." What's the first thing that comes to mind? A pink elephant, of course. Resist putting thoughts in your head that you don't want your mind to latch on to. Instead, put only those thoughts in your head you want your mind to remember.

Express Yourself

Smooth Talk'n

Avoid saying negative things about yourself in the hope that the other person will say it's not true to bolster your self-esteem. The other person may not bite, leaving you in a lurch.

Do this self-expression exercise. Look into a mirror and think of an encounter with someone. Speak your mind—do this without any fear of judgment, criticism, or disapproval. Watch your face and your expressions, and picture being another person looking into your face. Adjust your face to please you, and practice different looks that make you appear commanding or sexy.

Center Yourself

A lot of self-consciousness, nervousness, and fear comes from a feeling of being "outside" yourself, as you worry about being judged, rejected, or acting foolish. Do the following technique to regain your "center." Take a deep breath and follow your breath into your body, down into your solar plexus (a network of nerves below your rib cage and behind your stomach). Press there with your hand to help guide the breath. Focus on your feet, and feel their connection to the floor. Then press on your "third eye" (the spot on your forehead right between your eyes), concentrating your mind and breath toward that point to focus on your spiritual energy, giving you strength.

Be Your Best

Dress and act your best at all times. Instead of saving your best clothes for special occasions, take them out and wear them! When you look good, you'll feel good, too.

Appreciate what you are, what you have, and what you do. In Japanese Naikan therapy, you say "Thank you" to all the objects and people in your life. Say "Thank you" to your toothbrush every morning for keeping your teeth clean, "Thank you" to the movie seat for supporting you while you are being entertained, and "Thank you" to your mother for all the times she calls to ask how you are. Showing such appreciation makes you realize how many people and things support you in your life.

Forgive Yourself

Emily says, "When I was younger, I constantly went out with guys who cheated on me and treated me badly. Now I try to date men who care about me, but I feel bad and embarrassed about my past, and don't want to share the details with anyone."

Progress and change take time. You may find yourself taking two steps forward and one step back. Appreciate your forward motion. Talk to yourself and accept that you did what you did for a reason. Keep up your affirmations: "I am worthy of love." Acknowledge your progress.

Make Yourself Over

Magazines are full of make-overs. Treat yourself to one. Try new things and take risks. It's fun! Do those things that you always said you'd do if you had the guts, time, or opportunity. This can be as simple as trying a new hairstyle, a new style of clothing, or a new tone of voice. You'll feel empowered by being assertive.

Developing Body Confidence

Most of us have at least one body part we obsess about, a part of us that makes us feel unattractive. The irony is that other people may hardly notice the part that we're so focused on! It can be unnerving to think about someone seeing you in a bathing suit or naked for the first time, with no slimming black dress or dazzling fuchsia sweater to distract their eye. Fears that you won't measure up can put a real damper on dating. Read on for tips on how to conquer your fears.

Posture

How you stand affects the message you send out to the world. There is scientific evidence that posture affects mood—slouching produces a down mood, while standing tall lifts your mood. Try it. This theory seems to validate the old song lyric, "Whenever I feel afraid, I hold my head erect, and whistle a happy tune, so no one will suspect I'm afraid." It also validates the result: "When I fool the people I fear, I fool myself as well."

Here's another exercise to try. Take a deep breath and stand tall. Imagine a root running from your feet into the floor (grounding you, making you feel secure). Now imagine a string running from the top of your head into the ceiling, lifting you up. Picture your spinal column giving you a solid base, where no rejection can blow you over.

Turn Scars into Stars

Everyone has a body part they hate. What's yours? Bobby hates his big nose. Joni gets disgusted with her narrow eyes. Learn to love what you hate. If that part of your body could talk, what would it say? Love me. Ultimately, you can find someone who will love you if not for it, in spite of it. Consider how supermodel Cindy Crawford turned her mole into a million-dollar trademark, or how Barbra Streisand and Meryl Streep have made their unusual noses a part of their distinctive look.

Body Consciousness Exercises

It's hard to relax on a date if you've got the "What-if-she-doesn't-like-my-body" blues. These exercises will help you learn to love yourself—so that other people will!

Home Alone

Most of us have mild dissatisfaction with our bodies ("My nose is too wide" or "My shoulders are too narrow"). But if you experience severe body disgust, what therapists call body dysmorphia, I urge you to seek therapy.

The Look/Touch Exercise

Examine yourself in the mirror. Look at all your body parts with curiosity, without criticism. Ban all negative thoughts, and focus on tactile things: silkiness, softness. As the old song line goes, "Accentuate the positive, eliminate the negative, and don't mess with Mr. In-Between." What are your best features? Play them up. If you have a tiny waist, wear big tight belts to show it off. If you have beautiful eyes, pull your hair away from your face to showcase them.

Now focus on your sexual body parts. I'm always surprised by how many women haven't looked at their genitalia, or how many don't love what they see. After a bath, put a leg over the tub, or lay on the bed and put a mirror between your legs and take a look. It's okay to touch.

The Talking Body Part Exercise

A popular technique in Gestalt therapy involves treating each body part as if it were a separate being communicating to you about how it feels. In this exercise, you "speak" from the body part as if it were a person. In this way, you find out what it has to tell you about its own condition.

For example, say you have frequent backaches. Sit quietly on a chair and close your eyes and put your consciousness into that body part—in this case, your back. Ask, "Back, what are you telling me?" Now imagine being your back and have a conversation with yourself. For example, your back might say, "I am tired of holding you up all day." Press for your back to talk on a deeper, more revealing level, like "I am hurting because I feel like you put a burden on me. I am buckling under the strain of all that anger you are holding in." This exercise can give you clues about what you are really feeling.

This is a great exercise when you have a sexual inhibition or problem. Speak to your penis and vagina and ask it what it feels and needs.

The Moving Body Exercise

Our physical actions both reflect and affect our inner being. For example, a frown reflects the body's inner sense of sadness and also "freezes" the emotional state into that state of sadness. Merely by taking another body position, the physical state can be changed. For example, research in NLP (neuro-linguistic programming) has shown that looking upward lifts the mood. The upward look of the eyes connects, or triggers, the brain to lift the spirits or emotions.

Imagine Your Ideal

Imagine yourself just the way you would like to be. The brain doesn't know the difference between a real image and one you fashion, so it will operate on whatever you picture. Visualize relating to someone in a charming, energetic way. Since your brain doesn't know if the image is true or false, your muscles will behave accordingly—your face will look as if you feel charming and energized.

Athletes have long understood this process of imagery, and will imagine a goal or an action before performing it. You can do the same thing with your love life. Visualize how you want to look, how you want to come across, and how you want your love life to be. Now try to experience how you would feel if all of these things were true.

I also recommend the "repeat performance" technique. Remember a time when you were at your best, your most successful, your most seductive. Picture how you looked, sounded, and acted. Anchor this picture in your muscles and visceral body system by doing something physical (such as pressing two fingers together or snapping your fingers). Eventually, the physical act alone will trigger your nervous system to "remember" the outcome, and fire the appropriate mental and physical state associated with it, making it more likely that you will repeat this similarly successful behavior and positive mental state in the present.

Overcome Your Dependence on Others

In an episode of one of my favorite TV shows, *Silk Stalkings*, Detective Rita Lance, one of the show's main characters, mused, "I had a college professor once who compared the world to a sculpture garden. Men were like statues, striking a pose, rough-edged, hard and cool; and women like ivy, softer, more dependent, forever attempting to embrace the stones . . . (fortunately) I know some women who prefer standing."

This perfectly captures the way in which so many women try to wrap themselves around men, as if their life has no meaning without this attachment. When they do this to unavailable, unattainable men, it's like trying to squeeze blood from a stone. What these women really need to do is focus on themselves—be their own tree, with solid roots, rather than clinging vines.

For example, Josie was going out with a charismatic TV reporter. Every time they were out together, people listened with rapt attention to his stories and opinions. He was constantly being invited places, and Josie loved living in his glow. When he dumped her, she was devastated. She had been living her life through him. Josie wasn't able to achieve true satisfaction, so she sought it through other people. When she lost her boyfriend, she felt as if she'd lost herself.

If you feel that you are overly dependent, follow this bit of advice: "Become the person you're looking to marry." Don't look for a partner to fulfill your dreams. You won't become rich, great-looking, fun, or fulfilled by clinging to someone who is. Rather than seeking a mate to fill your "holes," become whole yourself.

The Dream Scheme Exercise

We all have dreams of how we would like our life to be. Realizing your dream brings you closer to realizing your potential and increasing your self-esteem. Make a list of everything you desire in life, following these rules:

➤ Use the present tense. Say "My body is looking more like the way I like" instead of "I want to lose weight."

➤ Be positive. Concentrate on being cool and collected instead of not wanting to lose your temper. Negatives only reinforce that negative behavior.

➤ Be specific so you can make it real. Think "I will sing more and enjoy free time to take long walks" instead of "I want to be happier."

➤ Make an action plan. Translate "I want a rich guy" into "I want to be rich." Then design a plan of action on how you can make money. Brainstorm possibilities: Ask for more money from your current job, change jobs, or work a second job.

Keep repledging these plans until you start believing you are worthy of happiness and love in life. Obstacles you once thought were impenetrable will melt away—and the love of yourself will draw to you the love you want to share.

Go through all your fantasies and dreams and write them down. Make a plan to realize each dream. Break each dream into seven manageable steps (one for each day of the week). Put the steps in your daily planner or calendar, either written out or in code.

As Nike advertises, "Just do it." Japanese Morita therapy advises the same: Stop obsessing over feelings and just "do what has to be done."

Free Yourself from the Desperate Need for Approval

Almost everyone has mild fears of rejection and a need for approval, whether about dating ("What if he doesn't like me?"), shopping ("If I return this, what will the salesperson think of me?"), or work ("If I speak up at this meeting, will they think I'm foolish?"). The desire to please others can be charming and promise to enhance your self-esteem, but the need for approval becomes a serious problem when you lose your sense of self, your self-respect, and your self-control.

Let's look at a couple of examples. Barbara was so desperate for Kent's approval that she couldn't get dressed for a date without trying on everything in her closet. She would then ask him 10 times if he liked her outfit—turning him off with her insecurity.

Larry was so afraid he'd say the wrong thing to a date that he'd barely speak at all—and women found him either dull or snotty. Ironically, people who desperately need approval sabotage themselves, either suffocating others with demands or driving them away.

How can you break free from seeking approval? Deliberately change your thoughts or beliefs that you need someone else's approval to get by. Realize that the worst that can happen is temporary or tolerable pain. Change your behavior to do what pleases you first. Try to get to the root of your insecurity (perhaps your father constantly told you that you were worthless). Rehearse behaviors that risk disapproval—practice saying no and disagreeing with a date. Decide what you need and either fulfill the need yourself, or ask someone else for help. This can be a simple request ("Please get me a glass of water"), or a more emotional request ("Please give me a hug").

Take Yourself Out on a Date

I am very serious when I say you need to take yourself out on a date. Go out to dinner, a play, or the movies. Treat yourself to the very best. It will raise your self-esteem and give you untold independence. You will never again be devastated if you're alone on a Saturday night, or if someone turns you down (despite the great tickets you got especially for the evening).

Think of something you'd really love to do. Ask yourself out to do it. Make plans, just as if you were trying to impress the most exciting date. Imagine yourself saying yes and getting excited. Mark the date on your calendar. When the day comes, get dressed up as you would for someone special.

I'm not suggesting that you delude yourself into thinking you're going out on an imaginary date with an imaginary friend. What I do mean is that you should imagine another "you" going with you. Have an imaginary conversation about what fun you're having and how great it is to be with you. Say all the things you would to a special date.

This should be a fun, thrilling exercise—one that will help shore up your confidence. Think of it as an inoculation against rejection, a character builder, a self-esteem booster. You'll also gain independence that will serve you through any date.

Discover the Real You

True self-esteem means finding out who you really are. According to a certain psychological theory, the self is made up of different components: the real self (the inner you), the ideal self (what you'd like to be), and the social self (how others perceive you based on the face you show to the world). Think about all those components, and how they operate in the dating world. In the following exercise, describe each of these:

MY REAL SELF (how I really feel): _____

_____

MY IDEAL SELF (the way I'd like to be): _____

_____

MY SOCIAL SELF (how others see me): _____

_____

Getting Feedback

As you must know by now, I am very much in favor of open communication. If you wonder what someone's thinking or what they'll say, ask. If your lover doesn't call, ask why. If you can't figure out what your date meant by that remark, ask. Don't waste time wondering. A date is like a research project—it gives you the opportunity to learn about your own (and others') motivations, fears, and needs. And just like any other research project or experiment, you must collect data to make progress.

Do your dating research. If someone seems interested in you, ask for feedback. If they decide to break up, ask for an explanation (reassure them that you're not trying to control or change them, but just want to learn something for next time). Ask questions like "What did you mean when you said . . . ?" or "How did you feel when I . . . ?"

Be prepared that some people may be unwilling (or incapable) of responding honestly. They may be afraid, inexperienced, or insecure. If you like playing the open talk game, it's best to associate with people who also like open talk, or you may wind up frustrated and unfulfilled.

Beware of Suitors with Unsuited Confidence

The best, longest-lasting relationships are between two people who both have a solid sense of self and who don't try to hide who they really are. But some people may be good at hiding their true self. This section gives you some tips on spotting people with confidence problems.

The Braggarts

Bob loves to wine and dine women, but can't figure out why he never gets a second date. I asked him how he acts on his dates. Bob explained, "I told them they'd never find a guy who would treat them better. I have a fancy car, know all the best wines, and have been places they have only dreamed about." Exuding self-confidence can be positive, but don't overdo it. Bob's excessive self-promotion portrays a desperate need to impress and reveals his deep-seated insecurity that ultimately drives people away.

The Apologizers

Pointing out your weaknesses can be just as off-putting as excessive bragging about your excesses. Sally was willing to admit to me that she's pretty, but if a man compliments her, she quickly tells him how homely she was as a child, or that it is only makeup, or that it's just the outfit she's wearing. Her secret hope is that the man will heap on more compliments to counter her self-criticisms. Instead, men tend to take her at her word and back away. This is self-sabotage at its saddest.

The Manipulators

Peter's girlfriends are always the jealous type, wildly possessive of him. At first, Peter is flattered by their behavior, but he always ends up cheating on them and being mean. Deep down, Peter is projecting his own jealousy and possessiveness onto the girls he dates as a way of denying his own insecurities. Their behavior acts as a mirror of his own, and when he senses this (unconsciously), he gets angry and punishes them for it by pushing them away.

The Abusers

The statistics of the number of women and men who feel mistreated in relationships is shocking. The silver lining in this dark cloud is that the nature of abusive relationships in dating has come more to light in recent years. While this seems like bad news, awareness itself makes singles more determined not to put up with these negative experiences.

Check out Chapter 14, which covers how to know if you're in an abusive relationship, why you might stay, and how to get out.

The horror of date rape has increasingly come to light in recent years, and will continue to affect dating in the new millennium. In the '50s dates were simple: a hamburger and coke at the local diner, a movie, and home by 10. Today those simple days are gone. Dates are costly—not just in money, but in safety! When messages are unclear, approaches can lead to traumatic sexual attacks. Recent infamous cases, like those involving William Kennedy Smith, who was acquitted, and boxer Mike Tyson, who was convicted, have brought date rape to public attention. Preventing these problems requires education about the unacceptability of such assaults, avoiding situations that could lead to danger (like drinking at wild parties), dispelling harmful sex-role stereotypes (that girls owe boys sex or that sexually active girls ask for or deserve rape), awareness of healthy relationships and love, and the importance of communicating clear sexual intentions. Some colleges have even mandated asking and giving permission for various acts ("Can I kiss you?") at the risk of suspension.

The issues of sexual harassment have also more recently come to light. The Michael Douglas/Demi Moore movie about a male worker seduced by his female employer helped heighten public awareness. Avoid dating where one person has power over the other to extract sexual favors. This is a hotbed for harassment. Vivien's attraction to her boss is tainted by the fact that he can offer her a promotion over others more qualified. Georgia is considering dating her high school soccer coach who has offered to put her on the starting team. These types of relationships are a set-up for disappointment, and not "true love" that is based on equality and mutual respect.

Examine how you keep yourself in an abusive relationship. Often I hear complaints from women, "He cheats on me and treats me so poorly, but I *love* him." One guy described to me, "When I get into fights with my girlfriend Kelly she hits me hard and once came at me with a knife. Friends say I should dump her but I love her." To get out of an abusive relationship, trust you can make it on your own, believe you deserve better, and take action to get out. Tell friends so they can support you to stay away from such abusive dating and make healthier choices.

Home Alone

Many stories I hear about unwanted sex take place when the parties are drunk, emphasizing the role alcohol or drugs plays in unleashing inhibitions and bad judgment, and the value of tee-totaling in maintaining clear judgment in dating and party situations.

Smooth Talk'n

Be educated about what constitutes sexual assault and the unacceptability of such "acquaintance" or "date" rapes under any circumstances. Dispel harmful sex-role stereotypes (that girls owe boys sex or that sexually active girls ask for or deserve rape) and discuss healthy relationships and love.

Alcohol and Drugs: False Self-Esteem Boosters

These two stories have a common theme:

➤ "I went to an office party where I had too much to drink. My co-worker told me that I really came on to my boss. I don't remember a thing."

➤ "My boyfriend wanted me to have sex with one of my girlfriends. I was shy about it, but after a couple of drinks I did it anyway. Now I can't even look at the girl when I see her, and I'm afraid that she's after my boyfriend."

Research has shown that alcohol does lower inhibitions. One drink over dinner, in a responsible dating situation, can give you the necessary boost to feel more relaxed and comfortable.

But beware, because excess alcohol leads to impaired judgment, which can get you into trouble. Everyone has a different tolerance level, but the danger level appears to be roughly three drinks. Overindulging leaves you prey to anyone else's desires, and you are apt to do things you wouldn't consider if you weren't drunk. I hear too many sad stories about unwanted pregnancies, betrayals, and contracted diseases because someone drank too much and then claimed that "it just happened."

The Loser Magnet

Janice complained, "I constantly fall for losers, guys who can't hold a job, or who are always down on their luck. Why do I do this?" She does it because it boosts her own shaky self-esteem and gives her a false sense of power. Janice was finally able to see what she was doing: "If I can help them, I feel better about myself, but maybe the only real way to feel better about myself is to do it for me, not for them." Right on, Janice.

The Least You Need to Know

➤ A healthy self-esteem is the ultimate sex appeal.

➤ What you visualize is what most likely will happen, so visualize dating success.

➤ Consider yourself your own best date.

➤ Remember, you don't have to put up with any crap—you deserve the best life has to offer you.

➤ Replace self-dumping with self-pumping.

➤ Enjoy your own company and you'll attract the company of others.

89

Chapter 7

Break Out of Your Shell!

In This Chapter

➤ What makes people shy?

➤ 12 steps to overcoming shyness

➤ 10 steps to overcoming love panic

➤ Symptoms of social phobia

"I just can't go up to talk to any girl. I get so tongue-tied and end up going home alone."
—Mike, sound engineer at a rock music club

Nearly everyone has suffered from it at some point in their lives. Even politicians, seemingly extroverted comics, and celebrities (from Michael Jackson to Barbara Walters) admit to it. Men suffer from it as much as women do. But to win in the dating world, you have to get over it. That is, get over being shy.

What is shyness? At best, it's being reserved; at worst, it's feeling so insecure or fearful of being judged that you don't act like yourself or you withdraw completely. Shyness can be caused by a history of rejection, by rules and behavioral patterns instilled in us as children, and even by chemical imbalances in our brains. No matter what the source, shyness is not something you have to suffer with.

Why Am I Shy?

Shyness may be a result of past experiences of not being accepted or loved. Sufferers may have been bullied or criticized by their peers or by adults when they were children. They may also be copying their parents' own shyness. Or they may have been taught not to be assertive, being told "Don't try that" or "Don't speak until you're spoken to."

Shyness can also be inherited. For instance, 10 percent of the population is born with "stranger anxiety," which is partly caused by the balance of certain chemicals (monomaine oxidase, serotonin, and cortisol) in the brain. Researchers at Harvard University also found that shyness may be governed by the amygdala, an almond-shaped "switching center" in the brain responsible for stimulating reactions like fear and withdrawal. But even if the genes fit, you don't have to wear them. You can change by increasing your confidence.

Disinterest or Shyness?

I've often been asked the question: "Why do some men and women act like they're not interested, when you're almost 100 percent sure that they are?"

Many people are too shy, inexperienced, or socially scared to be up front about their interest. They don't know what to say or what to do if you respond. Or they're afraid their friends will tease them! I'm reminded of the classic scenario of the boy who pulls the girl's pigtails in class, making her think he hates her, when really he likes her. His actions are his awkward way of showing her attention. The lesson: Be more direct if you like someone. Don't play games or act indifferent to cover up your feelings.

Shyness can be charming, disarming (making others less fearful or threatened), and engaging (inspiring others to make you more relaxed and comfortable). But it can also give the wrong impression, and intimidate or frighten others away.

Dating Data

When approaching dating like the stock market, consider if you are a bull (who takes risks and is not afraid to put himself "out there"), or a bear (who is cautious about what's going on).

Shyness may also bore others because of the lack of assertiveness it implies. For example, Kelly complained, "Men always break up with me because they say I'm too nice," when she is really just too laid-back. Whenever someone asks, "Where do you want to go?" or "What do you want to do?" she says, "Whatever." Her ambiguity leaves others with the burden of being in control, and also leaves them feeling confused about who she really is and how they should behave. Kelly should instead speak up and be clear about her preferences: "I'd like to eat Italian food" or "I'm in the mood for a funny movie."

12 Steps to Overcoming Shyness

Overcoming shyness may seem overwhelming or impossible. Not so! It takes effort, just like changing any behavior, but it is very possible—and well worth the effort. Remember, your fears are inevitably much worse than the reality of a situation. Here are some helpful steps to overcome your shyness.

Dating Data

Studies have shown that men often suffer more from shyness than women because they are expected to be more assertive in dating, careers, and life in general.

Step 1. Work on improving your self-confidence (refer to Chapter 6).

Step 2. Understand why you are shy. What are you afraid of? Judd was afraid girls would think he's a loser. "I'm losing my hair and I'm shaped like a pear," he bemoaned. Judd is his own worst critic. People don't see our flaws as we do.

Step 3. Play-act. In the privacy of your home, act out the way you would like to be—taken to the extreme. For instance, walk around the room puffing out your chest and raising your voice. By going to the extreme, you slough off hidden anxieties, embarrassment, and shame, and come back to your center refreshed and reenergized.

Step 4. Mimic someone you admire who is not shy. Imitation is a key to learning. Other people's actions can be a guide on how to act the way you would like to be.

Step 5. Do something in life that makes you feel good about yourself. Start a project, clean out clutter, master a musical instrument. Becoming a success is a potent aphrodisiac to turning you—and others—on.

Step 6. Curtains up! Many people don't bother to look their best some days, either out of laziness or thinking that it won't matter. I'll always remember one hairdresser who chastised me for letting my hair get uneven and unruly. When I offered

Smooth Talk'n

A saying from a "LovePhones" listener, Marianna, that helped her get over her shyness: "Everything in life has an end, so take risks, because you have nothing to lose."

excuses—that I was too busy and had other priorities—he threw his hands up dramatically, proclaiming, "Oh my dear, but every day is show time!" Mothers used to say it in another way: "Always wear clean underwear because you never know when you might get in an accident." So, always be prepared to be seen or discovered whenever, wherever.

Step 7. Forget the "I'm not worthy" routine. Keep your mind on a power track with affirmations. Repeat to yourself, "I am a worthwhile person." No matter what happens, you are. You deserve to have and be what you want.

Step 8. Redefine shyness (not as fear, but as enjoying observing situations).

Step 9. Combat your fear of rejection. Expect and accept that everyone at one time or another gets rejected. Rather than taking rejection personally, decide that you and that person just don't "fit" or the timing is off, and move on to something or someone else to distract and engage you. Read Chapter 20 for more on this.

Step 10. Take risks. Nothing ventured, nothing gained. Or, as my friend Rick McCarty says, "If you don't *take* a chance, you don't *have* a chance."

Step 11. Use self-disclosure. Confess to people that you're shy, so they won't misread you. The confession in itself can be endearing and an ice-breaker to a conversation. If it scares someone away, that person isn't right for you anyway.

Step 12. "Practice" dating. Nothing feeds success like success. As you gain more pleasurable dating experiences, you can feel more confident and your anxieties ease. In one program based on the book *The Shy Man Syndrome*, by Japanese author Nobuko Awaya, shy men are assigned to a woman trainer for 12 two-hour practice dates. These practice dates are combined with group discussions before and after the dates that include role-playing and visualizations (imagining how he will behave and how the date will go). The therapist monitors realistic and unrealistic expectations. Men are taught to accentuate the positive (her smile, the way she leaned on my shoulder) and play down the negative (she didn't squeeze my hand back).

Do Looks Matter?

Feeling good about yourself is a key to overcoming shyness. One way to do this is to look your best. You must believe that you are attractive and worth getting to know better. Don't underestimate the possibility of overcoming any limitations you have in the looks department by making up for it with your energy, excitement, interests, and personality. But do make the most of your looks. Play up your good features with a hairstyle that shows off your pretty eyes, or form-fitting shirts that show off your muscular build, and hide less desirable features. Good grooming always pays off with attention to cleanliness and good style.

Also consider dressing up once in awhile; you don't always have to wait for special occasions. Are you one of those people who buy nice clothes and save them for special days—then rarely end up wearing them? Put away those raggedy old things—unless you can make them stylish, you'd do better to give them up.

Do the "closet-clean-out." A good rule of thumb is to get rid of clothes clutter by clearing out items that you haven't worn in a year—chances are you won't ever wear them. Instead, make room for things you do need and keep your best outfits in good shape. Remember this rule: When in doubt, throw it out.

Let's Talk

How you talk and what you talk about can say a lot about your personality—whether you're timid and shy or outgoing and spontaneous. Learn to speak up and say what's on your mind. Also, listen to your figures of speech. Do you repeat phrases such as "like" (which, by the way, drives me crazy), and "uh"? I once knew a woman who ended every sentence with "that is." Valley girls get made fun of by making every sentence into a question. If your voice inflection goes up at the end of every sentence, concentrate on deliberately dropping your voice at the end of a sentence.

Practice your most inviting, soothing, or comfortable voice. Like a sweet smell, a voice can emanate sex appeal. Speak deliberately, in a low tone, at a medium pace and volume. Then ask the other person, "What's the most interesting thing you did today?"

Also, engage in word-play. My father always emphasized the value of a broad vocabulary. He'd often open the dictionary and test me—now my favorite book is the thesaurus, as I enjoy hours of looking up synonyms for words I'm using even right now for this book, to get the exact right one. If you do this, not only will you be able to understand some people better, you'll also impress others with your knowledge.

To broaden your vocabulary, consider purchasing study guides for GREs (Graduate Record Exams). These review books are available in university bookstores, and contain lists of vocabulary words students need to be familiar with in order to do well on the test. Or, every day, just open up your dictionary and jot down a few words you'd like to learn, and study them while on the train or in your car. My radio producer, Scott Hodges, admitted on the air that he keeps a dictionary in his bathroom, and studies a new page for interesting words every time he is on the toilet.

Practice describing things in interesting ways, with vivid imagery. In radio—called "theater of the mind"—you learn to paint pictures with words. Instead of simply saying she has pretty eyes, say her eyes were "glowing" or "piercing."

Smooth Talk'n

Like everything else, learning to speak up and speak well takes practice. Make it a point to speak to three new people each day, whether at the supermarket, in a movie line, in the elevator, and so on.

Love Panic

Francine stood in front of Rick's door, ready to knock, when suddenly she was flooded with a rush throughout her body. The hallway felt warm, but her hands were cold. Her heart started pounding, and her knees went so weak she feared she would collapse. Adam called "LovePhones" to say, "I want to ask this woman out, but every time I look at her I end up sweating like a pig." And when Jocelyn was out with Tom, a guy she felt was "perfect" for her, she couldn't stop shivering.

Dating Data

Symptoms of love panic are intense terror, trembling, sweating, chest pain, heart palpitations, shortness of breath, choking or smothering sensations, hot flashes or chills, nausea, faintness, numbness, and feelings of unreality.

Francine's flushes, Adam's sweats, and Jocelyn's shivers are symptoms of love panic—frightened feelings you experience when faced with someone you're attracted to. It's like the alarm you'd feel if you were standing on the edge of a 30-story building with no handrail, or if a car was coming at you head-on at 65 miles an hour. People experience these things in situations ranging from giving a speech to having sex.

But what's the difference between love panic and just having a case of the jitters? Jitters can be helpful—to prepare you to deal with a stressful situation or motivate you to solve a problem. Love panic, however, can flood you with so much anxiety that it interferes with your ability to do what you want and to be your charming self.

You're having a serious bout of love panic if your symptoms prevent you from taking your desired action(s), are persistent and frequent, or make you send out the wrong signals. For instance, Francine knew she had a real problem after she vowed never to return to Rick's house again for fear she would pass out at his door.

The 10 Steps to Controlling Love Panic

So how do you handle love panic? Both drug and non-drug therapies have been developed in the past decade to treat panic attacks. What works best depends on the person, but often a combination of therapy and medication is effective. The three types of medications used are benzodiazepine tranquilizers (Xanax, Atavan), antidepressants (Prozac, tricyclics like Tofranil), and monoamine oxidase inhibitors (Nardil). Patients usually take the medication for about six months to a year.

Dating Data

Physical activity burns off nervous energy and increases blood flow to the brain—all of which makes you more relaxed.

Besides medication, try following the 10 steps outlined below, which are designed to help change your behavioral thinking and overall actions:

Step 1. Understand the experience. Examine your symptoms, whether you're experiencing a racing heartbeat or weak knees. Why do you think your body is acting the way it is? For instance, Jocelyn realized that although she thought Tom was perfect, she also knew she wasn't ready to have sex with him like he wanted. As a result, her body was fighting her emotions.

Step 2. Instead of interpreting your racing heartbeat as an impending heart attack, your breathlessness as a sign of suffocation, and your crazy thoughts that you're going mad, label your feelings as signs of fear. Reassure yourself that you feel cold or shaky because you're nervous, and that it's okay to feel nervous.

Try one of my favorite techniques: paradoxical intention. Here you reframe the experience as the opposite of how you would normally see it. For example, instead of identifying nervousness as being a negative, purposefully see it as a good sign—that you are excited for action and that you are turned on.

Step 3. Instead of trying to get rid of your feelings, become mobilized by them; embrace them to propel you into action. My famous rule to follow is: Turn Anxiety into Action. Purposefully slow yourself down by breathing more evenly and letting your energy pour out (energy sparks excitement). The former will make you more sensual and the latter more exciting. Instead of Francine holding back her hand from knocking on the door, she should knock more vigorously.

Step 4. Admit nervousness instead of hiding it. Pretending to be calm and collected often escalates fear and self-consciousness. Instead, confidently announce that you are excited, not scared. When Rick opens the door, Francine should admit: "I'd love to appear calm and collected, but my heart is actually beating a mile a minute, from rushing here and from being excited."

Step 5. Brainwash yourself with positive affirmations. Instead of worrying, "Do I look okay? Does he like me?" fill your mind with self-loving thoughts: "I'm a great person and I'm fun to be with."

Step 6. Rationalize your responses. Instead of worrying about how you responded, reassure yourself that you can always have another chance at another time (to explain your reactions to the person or to behave differently).

Step 7. Distract yourself from your nervousness by focusing on something else. Think about the food you're eating or the music you're listening to, since the brain can only think one thought at a time. These thoughts will replace your anxious thoughts about how you're coming across, how you look, and whether your date likes you.

Step 8. Breathe to calm down. Anxiety causes your throat and chest muscles to tighten, which constricts your breathing—all of which make it difficult to talk. Inhale deeply through the nose and exhale through the mouth. Repeat this three times before you speak.

Step 9. Give yourself an "out"—one that is actual or imaginary—from the anxiety-provoking situation. If you're at a get-together and you see a woman you'd like to speak to but realize that you're becoming noticeably nervous, make a graceful retreat if you have to, and go to the restroom or another spot for an "emotional break."

Step 10. Move and do some activity. Even making gestures can help you to relax and clear your mind.

Dating Data

If you think you're experiencing social phobia, contact the following associations for help:

The Anxiety Disorders Association of America
11900 Parklawn Drive Suite 100
Rockville, MD 20852
(301) 231-9350
Send $3 for postage and handling for a list of therapists in your area.

The New York State Psychiatric Institute
Anxiety Disorders Clinic
722 W. 168th St.
New York, NY 10032
(212) 543-5367

Social Phobia

Shyness and love panic can become so extreme that it is termed "social phobia." You are suffering from social phobia when:

➤ You avoid people altogether. You won't eat, write, or speak in front of people, won't use public bathrooms, and won't answer the phone. You may even refuse to leave your house.

➤ You experience an unprovoked episode of at least four of the above symptoms within a month, or one attack followed by the fear of having another.

Besides medication, the three types of therapy used to treat people with social phobia are behavioral therapy, exposure therapy, and panic control treatment.

Behavioral therapy usually involves breathing and relaxing exercises. These are the prelude to the process of desensitization, which helps people become less sensitive to their situation by reintroducing them in small steps to the sources of their fear while feeling calm.

Exposure therapy involves "in-vivo desensitization," whereby a therapist or guide accompanies a person in the real world to face their fears on the spot, with support.

Under panic control treatment (PCT), the physical sensations of fear that the person usually experiences are aroused in the safety of a therapist's office. For example, if a person feels dizzy when dating, he is spun around in a chair until he is dizzy to make the point that dizziness is survivable—and does not cause heart attacks or death.

Other, more probing therapy includes examining sources of deep emotional conflict that may stem from childhood. During this kind of therapy, some questions I ask my patients are:

➤ What important person in your life have you lost? Losing a parent, close friend, or love—through death, divorce, or other circumstances—can cause you to become afraid of investing emotions in anyone else because the pain of loss is too great.

➤ Were you ever afraid to leave home? Dating fears can sometimes be traced to a time when you were scared to go to school for fear that Mommy would not come back to pick you up, or be there for you when you came home.

➤ What are you afraid of losing if you win the date you want? I know this sounds crazy at first, but some people are really afraid to succeed because deep down there are things they will lose if they win. This is actually called the "secondary gains" of a problem—goodies you get from suffering. For instance, you may complain that you're lonely from having no dates, but you may secretly enjoy the benefits you get from complaining about it: feeling sorry for yourself, getting sympathy from others, or covering up a fear of dating. Some people don't want to give these things up.

➤ Who are you really saving yourself for? Some people hold themselves back from dating because they feel attached to someone already—a past partner (who may have rejected them or died), or even a parent.

It's reassuring to know that even the most extreme forms of shyness can be overcome. You absolutely deserve the joy of feeling confident in expressing the real you.

The Least You Need to Know

➤ Shyness can be caused by past experiences, behavior copied from or taught by parents, inborn traits or predispositions, and certain chemical balances in the brain.

➤ You can overcome shyness by increasing your self-confidence.

➤ An extreme form of shyness is social phobia. If you think you suffer from this, get professional help.

➤ Believe that whatever you do and whoever you are is worthwhile and desirable.

Part 3

The Trap

So, you think you've tracked down the person of your dreams. Now, how on earth do you keep this person from running away? How do you get this new love interest to know you better, to fall for you, so that he/she won't want to be with anyone else? How do you get the date?

From smooth opening lines to seductive flirting techniques, you'll learn how to get your target to notice you. And, when he or she does, you'll learn how to ask for the date in such an irresistible way that the other person will have no choice but to take you up on your offer. And when you do get a "yes," you'll learn how to make that first evening together a date to remember (so that it isn't the last date!). From what to wear to where to go, you'll get all the tools necessary to make a good impression. And when that second date rolls around, you'll get advice on whether or not you're moving too fast or too slow, how to make subsequent dates, how to handle stay-overs and other potentially sticky situations, and more.

Chapter 8

"Is It Hot in Here or Is It Just You?"— Opening Lines

In This Chapter

➤ How to break the ice when you first meet

➤ Pick-up lines that charm or bomb

➤ How to keep the energy between you going

Hot on the heels of "Where do I go to meet people?" is the next, related question: "How do I let him or her know I'm interested?" Many people who've asked me where to go to find that special someone have later admitted not knowing how to approach someone or what to say after they've said hello.

My best advice—that has stood the test of time—is: Be yourself. You can put on an act for the short run, but if you really want something worthwhile to work, you have to be accepted and appreciated for who you are. Remember, everyone is in the same boat as you—looking to be loved. So approach life and love with a positive attitude and expect the best. Realize that others have the same fears and needs as you. So take the risk and say what comes to your mind.

Quiz: Guess Which Lines Work

While being yourself, keep in mind that different people will react differently based on their personalities, tastes, and experiences. For example, many guys approach my attractive assistant, Alissa, using different openers. Just on the basis of their first sentence, how do you think she rated the following three men?

Smooth Talk'n

Remember, anything you say has to "fit" your personality. However, feel free to experiment because meeting people is an opportunity for you to enjoy, express, and expand yourself.

Home Alone

Don't try to play games. If you pretend to be someone other than yourself and the other person ends up liking you, the relationship will be built on lies. If you slip up and reveal the real you (and you will) and your partner finds out that he or she really doesn't like you after all, you've both ended up wasting time.

GUY 1: "Uh, what's your name?"

GUY 2: "Those are great dangling earrings. I wouldn't mind being that close to you."

GUY 3: "Your smile lit up the room here, so I had to come over."

Alissa thought Guy 1's approach was typical, but a little too simple for her. As a result, she feared he could be too shy and not as much fun as she would like. He might be nice to talk to and she might give him a chance, but he didn't get a base hit with her on the first swing.

Although Guy 2's remark was creative, it was a little too close for comfort and forward for her. Alissa was concerned that he could be too much of a fun-loving player. Although she might consider going out with him, she would proceed with caution in case he was too cocky or not serious enough.

Alissa rated Guy 3 as the best possibility. As she said, "He seems like a nice guy with a sense of humor—certainly worth a smile, and probably a date."

Of course, everyone has his or her own comfort level regarding different approaches. Just "hello" or "what's your name?" can be fine. What is too dull for one person may be to the point for another.

Be careful not to jump to conclusions. Everyone deserves more of a chance than just an opening line. Unfortunately, too often we judge people all too quickly, so think about how what you say reflects who you are and affects how others react.

Dating Data

Even the best baseball players strike out more than they get hits; a batting average of .300 is spectacular in the game. For a long time, the great Babe Ruth held the record for the most home runs—and also for the most strikeouts.

You Know What to Say!

Although the idea of approaching someone for the first time may seem terrifying, it's really not as difficult as you might think. You don't have to be a poet or a writer to intrigue and attract someone. Simply say exactly what's on your mind or in your heart.

The basic point that I want you to remember from this book is that it's important to be yourself. There is no perfect pick-up line. The best line is whatever is real for you at the moment. Remember these points:

➤ Charm and sex appeal come from genuineness—being open, honest, and yourself. Whatever is in your mind and heart will come out naturally and sincerely, and that's going to be far more appealing than some contrived set-up.

➤ If you are yourself, the other person is either going to like you or not. If they like you, great; you know they really like you when you're being yourself. If they don't like you, you haven't wasted any time or energy. (Remember, dating is like one of the rules of sales: Don't waste time on rigid "no's" or people who aren't willing to hear your reason or change their minds.)

Smooth Talk'n

Share what you feel (excitement, shyness). If you're self-conscious, admit it; hiding it makes you come across clumsy. For example, Dave is 22 years old, but he looks younger. "Women avoid me because they think I'm too young," he complained. I advised him to say up front, "I know I look young, but you might like that when I'm 80, and anyway, I'm really older than I look and quite mature."

Dating Data

In coaching over 2,000 gay men, Jim Sullivan, founder of the New York–based Dating Strategies, has discovered that single gay men are unprepared for dating because of confusion through teenage years, shame, and a lack of support and role models. They need to know what a date is (a specific time and place with the possibility of future romantic involvement) and how to start a conversation. Sullivan advises admitting shyness (since men, like women, love vulnerable men); say "I'm a shy guy but I find you attractive and want to meet you. My name is Mike."

If you play games successfully and then get dumped anyway, you'll never know what could have happened if you were the real you. Playing games reaps only potential short-term gains, but also long-term heartaches.

➤ Never worry about being rejected. Thinking about the outcome only makes you self-conscious, which can make you clumsy and awkward. Step up to the plate and take your best swing with confidence.

Smooth Talk'n

People become sexier as they talk excitedly about something. You may have had this experience: sitting at a table across from someone you didn't think was very pretty or handsome until that person started talking about something interesting and suddenly you find that person attractive.

Bold or Subtle?

Should you get right to the point and say something like, "I like you. Would you like to go to the movies tomorrow?" Or should you throw out bait and see if the person bites: "I hear you love movies. Did you see . . .? I'd like to see it. Maybe we could go one evening or some weekend, maybe this Saturday afternoon if you're free? What are you up to?"

The key to your approach is to go with your instincts. There are no rules. The direct pitch may be music to one person's ears but static to another. A lot rests on both of your personalities and the mood at the moment. Take Curtis for instance. He approached a woman with the line, "What's up baby. You look sooo good. What's your number?" Curtis claimed this worked for him. I wouldn't recommend this as a general rule, but obviously he was able to pull it off.

Smooth Talk'n

When conversing with someone, use that person's name. Saying her name makes her feel noticed, acknowledged, special, and compelled to pay attention to you. One of the best ways to remember a person's name is to say it several times during the course of a conversation.

Be Creative

One good rule to keep in mind is to be creative. Ambiguity can create intrigue, where the other person tries to "read" an approach sprinkled with some hesitation. Personally, I favor creative approaches that also give the other person "space" to stay or stray away comfortably and without insult or hurt. For example, after a moment of sensuous eye-locking, switch the mood by saying something off the wall like: "If a UFO landed now, what would the aliens say about this party?" or "Wouldn't it be great to rent motorbikes along the beach in Bali? Short of that, I guess we could go roller-blading in the park. Do you feel like it?" or "I missed being at the Superbowl—let's go throw some footballs Saturday afternoon." One "LovePhones" caller reported doing something I love: He goes up to women and gives them a recipe for chicken nachos. Now, there's a sure way to either engage an equally fun-loving mate, or turn away someone who wouldn't be compatible anyway.

Some people's minds make unique and unusual connections that others might not initially "get." If you are like that (astrological air signs often are), and encounter someone who appreciates it, you could be off on a really fun, way out conversation. But beware, if you encounter someone who is more realistic and practical (likely an earth sign), they might look at you like you're crazy.

But go for it. Don't be afraid to come out of left field. Try these approaches:

➤ Quote an interesting phrase. "Some are born great, some achieve greatness, and some have greatness thrust upon them." I saw that on a billboard advertising Shakespeare's *Twelfth Night*.

➤ Ask an unusual opinion about something they would likely know nothing about. For example, ask, "Do you like my hair the color it is or would you dye it red if you were me?"

➤ Pretend you know the person. Say, "I love it when you scrunch up your nose like that. It looks so cute."

➤ Tune in on another wavelength—not to the words, but the feelings behind the words—use you intuition. Say something like, "You sound like your grandmother . . ."

➤ Be timely but controversial. Ask, "How many times have you seen *Titanic*? I didn't get the love scene. I thought she should have given him her life jacket or hoisted him on the wood she was floating on, instead of watching him sink."

➤ Offer help. Say, "I am guessing that you need an electrician to fix your antique lamp and I'm just the person to do it, for free. When can I come over?"

➤ Be goofy. A caller to my radio show recounted how she met her new boyfriend by being goofy. She had never thought of him in a romantic way before, but one evening when they were out with a group of friends, he asked her to get him a beer. When she returned with the bottle, she thought it would also be fun to pour some maple syrup (from a nearby table) down his back. When she did, he responded with the following: "You have two options. Either lick it off or I'll pour the rest of the bottle on your head." She choose the former, and let's just say that have been dating happily for months since.

Smooth Talk'n

Use the "situation" to your advantage. If it's cold outside, remark how she might shiver and offer your jacket. If you're taking a class, remark at how you didn't understand the last problem posed and ask her to explain it to you.

➤ Be far-out. Since the occult is really "in," suggest that you'd love to be abducted by aliens. A female comic I caught on Lifetime's *Ladies Night Out* had a funny routine about how "Everyone I know has been abducted by aliens on a date. I want to be abducted on a date. But I want those aliens with feelers . . ."

➤ Show something outrageous you can do. Paul can roll his stomach. Vera can wiggle her ears. You might stick your tongue out and display your piercing.

➤ Be funny. Humor can be one of the most attractive qualities in a person. You don't have to be Jerry Seinfeld or Conan O'Brien, just be clever. Think of a funny story you heard or talk about something amusing that happened to you.

My Favorite Pick-Up Line Story

Another key to success is to first capture the other person's interest while making sure she feels safe and secure about who you are and how free she is to react or turn away. Women these days are wary about strangers being serial killers, so you have to reassure her that she's safe.

One night, I was eating a sizzling steak alone in a booth in a trendy restaurant when a good-looking guy leaned over my shoulder, ostensibly looking at my plate, and crooned, "It looks good, it smells good, and I bet it tastes good." His provocative glance suggested he meant more than the sirloin. I had to compliment him for how bold and clever he was—even though I wasn't into company and didn't invite him to join me.

Years ago, when times were more innocent and fears (about strangers and sex) less rampant, pick-ups were easier. In these days of caution, people are wisely more wary about strangers, so you have to work harder to win them over, revealing more of yourself to show you can be trusted.

While eating my sirloin, I overheard a pick-up line in the next booth. The guy was telling a woman, "My name is Tom. I live in the neighborhood and come in here often." (Good, I thought, knowing where he lives should make her feel safer.) "I also do my laundry across the street," he offered. (Possible good sense of humor she might appreciate, I registered.) "What's your all-time favorite food?" he asked. (Good next step, I thought, he's engaging her to talk, especially about what she likes.) The guy won; he was soon sitting beside her, and I noticed they left together.

The moral of this story is to be yourself, take a risk, get over your shyness, and let your best self shine through, while knowing that not everyone is going to "take" to exactly where you're coming from at that moment. Be sensitive to what others might need to know or feel to respond to you; and be engaging, but nonthreatening.

Sample Openers

Okay, I know I said you shouldn't worry about using pick-up lines. And you shouldn't. Remember, it's important to just say what's on your mind and not to obsess about the outcome: It either flies or dies. You can always laugh it off. However, I want you to read these sample approaches for the following reasons:

➤ To give you an idea of how many kinds of openers you can use

➤ To help you see that an opening should suit your own personality

➤ To get your own creative juices flowing about how to break the ice

Years ago, I was a regular on a live TV show called *Good Morning New York*, and I did a segment on flirting. ABC-TV weatherman Spencer Christian was the host, and I'll never forget the cute line he offered as an opener:

> "Before I came to talk to you, only God and I knew what I was going to say. But now that I'm standing in front of you, only He knows!"

Since then, I've done many shows about meeting people on the radio, TV, and the Internet. The following are some other suggestions people have shared, used, or just brought up for fun.

Charming Romantic Openers

Being charming and romantic is an alluring, attractive quality. The effort to please and enchant is almost guaranteed to work. Admittedly, some of the following one-liners border on being corny, so say them with a glint in your eye, acknowledging that it's a "line." You're bound to at least amuse someone—remember, a sense of humor is the quality that most attracts men and women today!

> "I'd buy you a drink, but I'd be jealous of the glass."

> "Do you believe in love at first sight, or should I walk by again?"

> Check his jacket label. When he says, "What are you doing?" answer, "Checking to see if you were made in heaven."

> "If I could rework the alphabet, I'd put 'i' next to 'u.'" (A personal favorite of my "LovePhones" co-host Chris Jagger.)

> "Can I have directions?" ("Where?") "To your heart."

> "I had a bad day and it always makes me feel better to see a beautiful girl smile. Will you smile for me?"

> "Why do you want to go out with me?" "Because the alternative is unthinkable." (Said on one of my favorite TV shows, *Highlander*.)

> "If I could be one thing in the world, I would be a tear born in your eyes, living on your cheek, and dying on your lips."

> "Are you okay? That fall from heaven must have hurt."

"Quick, gimme a shot of insulin because you look so sweet, I'm going into sugar shock."

"Ever thank your parents for making you so beautiful?"

"Did heaven open up, because I think I see an angel."

"God may have made all men equal, but He made you without equal."

"Are your feet tired, because you've been running through my mind all night."

"Excuse me, do you have a quarter I could borrow?" ("Why?") "Because I promised my mother I'd call her as soon as I met the girl of my dreams."

"Your father must have been a thief—he stole the stars from the sky and put them in your eyes."

Hand someone a simple but sweet gift like a rose. Then say something like "I wanted to show this rose true beauty." I once read that FDR used this "gift technique" when he was on a political mission. It also worked for Hosea, a "LovePhones" caller from Houston: "When I was stationed in South Carolina, I met a girl who was stationed at the same base. I walked up to her, gave her a rose, and said welcome to Beaufort. That next day, she looked for me on the base to tell me how sweet I was and we ended up dating."

Self-Disclosure One-Liners

It's always a good idea to start off flattering someone you covet (using the openers presented earlier in this chapter). A totally different technique—but also a useful option—is to reveal something about yourself up front to ease the pressure of what you're feeling and to give the other person an insight into who you are. This approach also works best with people who are embarrassed by compliments or uncomfortable with the focus on them.

"This is the first time I've been here. Do you know anything about this place?" (Inviting help engages compassionate souls.)

"I feel funny because I don't know anybody here. Do you?"

"I always feel more comfortable in small groups or one-on-one. I never really liked crowds. Do you?"

"I'm normally uncomfortable going up to someone I don't know, but somehow I felt you'd be friendly." (This disarms the other person and makes him or her less inclined to act rudely.)

Classic One-Liners

There are some questions that have become standard in first encounters. They have the advantage of being simple and nonthreatening, but run the risk of coming across as uninteresting and trite. (For example, asking "What's your sign?" has become a parody.)

"Do you come here often?"

"What's your name?"

"What do you do?"

"Where do you live?"

Sexually Suggestive Lines

What to say to indicate your sexual interest in someone is usually a dilemma. Many people are uncomfortable being direct. It's always best to just let things flow. But the following lines are suggestions people sent or told me. I suggest only considering them once you really know someone, when you are both ready to take your relationship to an intimate level, and when you want to spark some humor into your seduction.

"Is it hot in here, or is it just you?"

"Would you like gin and platonic, or do you prefer scotch and sofa?"

"I miss my teddy bear. Would you sleep with me?"

"I may be no Fred/Wilma Flintstone, but I sure would like to make your 'Bed rock.'"

"I'm interested in having breakfast with you. Should I call you or nudge you?"

"That outfit looks good, but do you know what would look better on you? Me."

"I've been thinking about you all day, so get out of my head and into my bed."

"Do you sleep on your stomach?" ("No.") "Can I?"

Remember, personal style prevails. A young man in a mosh pit at Buzzardfest in Cleveland once asked me, "Will you marry me and have my children?" and handed me a ring. I smile about it to this day, and occasionally wear the ring as a reminder of his sweetness. Wild Pontiax rock singer Mitch Kashmar reportedly tried to romance O.J. prosecutor Marcia Clark after a performance with the line: "Don't sit too close to me darlin', I'm wet as a pack mule and twice as ornery."

Bold and Seductive One-Liners

Keep in mind that these lines are for shoot-straight-from-the-hip types. Some of these lines can be offensive, but they can be funny if you know that the person to whom they're directed can recognize the good humor and won't be insulted.

Jake told me that he used the following line to meet his future wife: "Are those mirrors in your jeans, because I can see myself in them." Although she called him a moron at first, she talked to him anyway. Other lines:

"Levis should pay you royalties."

"My face is leaving in 15 minutes; are you on it?"

"I really like what you're wearing, but I would like it even better on the floor of my apartment."

"Would you be my love buffet so I can lay you out on the table and eat what I want?"

"My name's xxx—that's so you know what to scream."

"What would you do if I kissed you right now?"

Pure Obnoxious One-Liners

When we asked about opening lines on one "LovePhones" show, these were among those called in or faxed to us. As expected, there are always pranksters and jokesters ready with quips. You might be amused by these, but I wouldn't advise using them!

"You cost how much?"

"I got something wrong with my car; want to come take a crack at it?"

"Hey baby, I love every bone in your body—especially mine."

"The word is legs—let's go to my place and spread the word."

"Ashes to ashes, dust to dust, if it weren't for women, my thing would rust."

"How about sitting on my lap and seeing what pops up?"

Many "lines" sound just like that—lines. If so, you can make them sound more appealing and natural by prefacing or ending them with an acknowledgment, such as "Isn't that quite a line?"

Good Stand-Bys

If the previous approaches are simply not your style and don't spark any creativity, here are some other excellent and sophisticated ideas for easy openers:

➤ Talk about current events. Watch TV news or read *USA Today* to get an idea of how stories are told quickly, succinctly, and compellingly.

➤ Cut out interesting or odd stories from newspapers or magazines. My stepfather used to clip all kinds of wacky stories that I could use on my radio shows—like the one about the government being criticized for wasting money on studies about the mating behavior of African fruit flies.

➤ Talk about the weather. This is no longer considered a silly topic due to innumerable earthquakes and other natural disasters, as well as the advent of the Weather Channel.

➤ Talk about common-ground topics. Whether it's a big issue (like whom to vote for) or just an annoyance (like not being able to read the fine print on a menu or being frustrated a train is late), everybody likes to know someone else shares a similar feeling or is having the same experience.

➤ Talk about common interests. Research shows that like often attracts like, at least in initial attraction. Discover something you are both interested in (old movies, animals, music). It gives you something to talk about and makes you feel more at ease and accepted.

➤ Find something in common in your background or lifestyle. Did you go to the same school? Visit the same place for vacation? Read the same book? Be observant. Paula noticed Steve used the word "agreement" and discovered they both attended the same workshop years earlier. While riding the bus, Pat pointed out a vacation poster to Leila and they discovered they both dreamed of going there.

➤ Use the "Opening Story." Keep a journal of the most interesting things you've done, read, or heard about. Talking about something you are passionate about immediately communicates sex appeal because you are at your most attractive when you are involved in what you are saying.

Smooth Talk'n

To sound more natural, adapt your approach to the setting and the person's situation. For example, someone used the following with Michelle, a waitress in Houston:

Customer: "Can I get anything on the menu?"

Michelle: "Sure you can."

Customer: Throws menu on the floor and then asks, "Will you stand on that please?" (Implying that she's on the menu and that he'll have *her*.)

Home Alone

Regardless of how good of a storyteller you are, know when to stop talking; you don't want to bore your potential mate. My friend, ABC-TV reporter John Stossel, told me that you should be able to tell a story within 3 minutes (the length of a typical TV feature), starting out with an attention-grabbing opener.

➤ Talk about a pet passion or pet peeve. Positives are always better than negatives, but passion supersedes all. Remember: She or he who is passionate, attracts. What's your dream: to save the rain forest, travel on the Concorde, write a book?

A Smile Goes a Million Miles

Once when I was in a club, I watched a guy smile broadly at girls until they smiled back. When he approached me, he boldly put his fingers on my mouth to form a smile, and said, "There, that's better." Though I was understandably put off at first by his touching me, after I smiled, I agreed with him—it was better! A safer but similar tactic one guy used: Put a smiley face on a napkin and hand it to her!

Dating Data

Science has proven that smiling improves your immune system by reducing stress, and can make you happy, even if you're not. The muscles used to make a smile trigger mood impulses that are located in the pleasure centers of the brain.

You'd be amazed at how powerful a smile can be in the dating game. Smiling makes you look your most attractive (despite the pouty expressions popular on models). Smiling shows that you're friendly, warm, and open.

Smooth Talk'n

The old saying is true: Smile and the whole world smiles back at you. Research shows that babies smile more in response to their mothers' smiles. The same response is with us all our lives.

In my seminars I usually ask people to turn to the person next to them and smile.

Notice, it's almost impossible not to smile back. Practice finding a smile you like. Look in the mirror and make different mugs until you find one you think looks inviting and feels good. Purposefully make a smirk and turn up the corners of your mouth into a smile. (One of my favorite actresses, Meg Ryan, has this kind of smile.) You'll feel your face, and your mood, lift!

Laughter works even better. My radio show producer uses a gimmick when he meets women. The line he uses is the following: "If I called you Shirley, would you laugh?" Usually, the female laughs, and gives him her real name—and the ice is broken. Saying a spontaneous (or a well-thought-out) joke allows your prey to warm up.

Dating Data

In one survey, women were asked to rate physical characteristics—physique, eyes, smile—in order of importance. They rated smiling first. A smile can even suggest you're richer than you are: In one study, people who made $50,000 a year were found to smile more often than those who made $15,000. Smile, and you're bound to get a smile in return. I'm always surprised when people say to me, "Why aren't you smiling?" As soon as I crack a smile, it changes my mood.

Using Your Voice

Voices are very important to those of us who work on the radio. A voice that is full of energy is likely to get more attention. My "LovePhones" co-host Chris Jagger is infamous for hanging up on people whose first two words sound faint or too hesitant. Brutal as this may sound, people do this all the time in real life. So make the most of your first impression by using a powerful voice.

Say this sentence aloud: "What a pleasure to meet you." Notice where your voice is coming from—probably your throat. Now take a deep breath and repeat the same phrase, but this time make your voice come from your chest. Repeat the phrase again, feeling your voice come from your stomach and then from your groin.

Dating Data

You have only a short time to make that important, and sometimes lasting, first impression. Surveys show people size you up on first glance, which can be as fast as 15 seconds. Then, they make their overall assessment of whether they like you in a minute and a half.

Full-bodied voices are also sexier. A "LovePhones" caller once asked, "My boyfriend says he loves how the sound of my voice is so much deeper and sexier after we make love. Why is that and how can I make it like that more often?"

115

It is common that a huskier and more resonant sound comes into the voice after experiencing pleasurable lovemaking or an orgasm. Called the "postcoital voice," it can be explained by the physiological changes that occur in the body at the culmination of the sexual response cycle, including release of muscle tension leading to general relaxation of various muscle groups all over the body, including those involved in speaking: the vocal cords, throat, and diaphragm. Confidence that comes from a satisfying sexual encounter also leads to more firm and direct communication during sex—and even after—that further enriches the voice quality.

In her seminars and book, *Fine Art of Erotic Talk*, Bonnie Gabriel recommends the following exercises to help develop a sexier voice:

➤ Relax your vocal cords by opening the mouth and back of the throat as if yawning, and speak from that position.

➤ Open the back of the throat and yawn, then keep the lips together, exhale, smile, and push the air out as if silently laughing, and then begin speaking.

➤ Open your mouth wide as if starting to yawn, then count aloud from 81 to 89, punctuating each count with a breath of air.

Breath-enriched sound makes the voice sound more erotic, with the added pay-off that heavy breathing intensifies sexual arousal. Experiment with different sounds on your own, and with your date, but keep in mind that the most appealing voice comes naturally when you are relaxed, confident, and secure in expressing what you want to an accepting, loving partner.

Putting It All Together

So far you've learned about a number of different ways you can approach someone. You also discovered the importance of smiling and speaking in a confident and powerful tone. Now how do you put everything together? For starters, you should smile first and make a comment about your common surroundings. Then you could ask a simple question (not personal, but on a neutral topic) and add something about yourself. This technique accomplishes several goals. It lets the other person get a sense of who you are, makes her feel safe, and helps her decide if she likes you. It also gives her something to respond to—taking the pressure off having to think about what to talk about.

Smooth Talk'n

When you approach someone for the first time, keep in mind that what you say only communicates about a third of your message. The other two-thirds is communicated by your body language—how you stand, move, and react.

For example, imagine you are in a music club. Smile and say something like: "This seems like a fun club" (a neutral statement about a common environment). "I've never been here before" (self-disclosure). "Do you know when the band starts?" (neutral question). "I usually like hard-rock music, but I hear this group has a country sound, and I've been to several clubs in Texas that I like" (leaving a few openings: she can respond to different music styles or to traveling, or turn away!).

Keeping the Gab Going

Now that you've learned everything you need to know about starting a conversation, how do you keep the rapport going and not run out of things to say? Here are a few helpful hints:

➤ **Self-Disclosure.** Recall this technique from opening approaches. Share interesting things about yourself. You emanate sex appeal when you passionately talk about something that interests you. Even if the person is not interested in what you are saying, he can still be captivated by the way you are talking about it.

Dating Data

The 1995 Virginia Slims Opinion Poll found that the biggest complaint women still have about men is that they don't talk enough about their feelings.

➤ **The "Tell."** Everyone has a tell—their Achilles heel or spot of vulnerability. Once you find this spot and discover what your love interest is really touched by or likes talking about, he will, at the very least, enjoy talking to you and, hopefully, become quite attracted to you. In successful sales, it's called "developing the prospect."

To help you find a person's tell, look for clues in his actions or facial and verbal expressions. After working out in the gym, Leigh became accustomed to how guys who body-build stand with their chests puffed out. So when she noticed Tommy's erect posture, she smiled and said, "You look like you work out; can I touch your arm muscle?" Tommy smiled back proudly and offered up his biceps—and his interest.

➤ **Say how you feel.** Communicate how you feel about yourself, the setting, and the circumstances—I feel excited, happy, uncomfortable, and so on.

➤ **Ask provocative questions.** Barbara Walters is famous for this. For example, she once got flack for asking Katherine Hepburn the following question: "If you were a tree, what kind of tree would you be?" Some other questions include:

"If you were a figure in history, who would you be and why?"

"If you were an animal, which one would you be and why?"

Make sure to make sense of the why to reveal some characteristic of the person. For instance, here's a question and two possible answers to the question; each one says something about the speaker:

"If you were a piece of furniture, which one would you be and why?"

"A chair, because people would sit on it and I like to support others. I'm always the person people lean on."

Or

"A rug, because people are always stepping all over me and taking advantage of me."

Now that you have some suggestions about what to say, practice! Overcome any shyness. Nothing beats "just doing it" and then doing it again, to improve your dating skills.

The Least You Need to Know

➤ Like the first few lines of a book or the opening sequence of a movie, the first thing you say will make you stand out or fade away; you may get a second chance, but make the most of your first impression.

➤ Don't play games; be yourself.

➤ Smile and it's more likely that the world will smile back at you. Remember, smiling makes you feel good!

➤ Take note of interesting stories and practice telling them to become a good conversationalist.

➤ Reveal things about yourself, but also ask open-ended questions to learn about the other person.

Chapter 9

Wink, Wink, Nudge, Nudge— The Art of Flirting

In This Chapter

➤ The six rules of flirting

➤ How to show you're interested and read the reaction

➤ Using body talk to your advantage

➤ A 12-step plan to overcome flirter's block

Which approach do you use when you're trying to meet someone? Are you a good talker, engaging others in interesting conversation, or do you sit back and wait to be courted? Do you "come on" strong with sexual signals, or more subtly "flirt"?

Getting someone's attention in whatever way you're comfortable with involves flirting. Flirting was a popular '80s term for trying to get someone's interest in a more subtle way than coming on strong. Unfortunately, flirting has received a bad rap, and these days is usually part of a complaint: "I saw my boyfriend flirting with another girl."

Let the new millennium welcome a resurgence of the positive aspects of flirting. That means, treat flirting as fun and a good way to practice social skills, and to make yourself and your targets feel good.

The Six Rules of Flirting

Besides just being a fun thing to do, flirting can be an effective method for getting to know a person. Remember the following anagram—FLIRTS—to help you get the most out of flirting:

F is for Flattery. The fastest way to a person's heart is to find something you truly appreciate about the way that person looks or acts and then compliment it. However, make sure your compliments are sincere (there's no sense saying "You have beautiful eyes" when they're obviously not).

L is for Listen. Get him to talk about what he really cares about and listen attentively. The most powerful aphrodisiac is your undivided attention.

I is for Interest. Find a common interest. Remember, similar tastes and interests are the best foundations for a good relationship.

R is for being Responsible. Be truthful, careful, and clear about your interests and intentions. Don't hurt or lead anyone on or choose inappropriate flirting partners, such as your friend's boyfriend or girlfriend.

T is for Trusting yourself. Believe that you can do it, survive it, and come out winning friends and feeling good about yourself.

S is for a winning Smile. I discussed the importance of a smile in Chapter 4, so you should be practicing this already!

Benefits of Flirting

Believe it or not, you can derive many benefits from flirting. For example, flirting can:

➤ Help eliminate loneliness by enabling you to meet people.

➤ Heighten your appreciation for what you're doing and where you are (both the specific place and in your life in general).

➤ Boost your ego.

➤ Exercise your technique for meeting people.

➤ Give you feedback about how you come across to others.

➤ Help you make new friends.

➤ Activate your adrenaline and nervous system. When this body system is switched on, it causes your blood flow to increase. This in turn makes you more alert and aroused, more able to concentrate and take action, and more sensitive to touch. It also stimulates the limbic center of the brain, which creates pleasurable feelings.

The Flirting Hall of Shame

Although it has many advantages, flirting has unfortunately earned a bad name. In fact, people who do flirt have been stereotyped as being too forward and too sexually aggressive. For instance, saying "She's a real flirt" sometimes translates into "She's a slut." Although this shouldn't be the case, the following shameful flirts perpetuate this bad reputation:

➤ **Blatant flirts.** They come on too strong, too fast, and overdo it—making the other person feel extremely uncomfortable ("Ooh baby, you're sooo hot . . .").

➤ **Confusing flirts.** They give one message, but mean another: "Yes I might like you, but no, I'm not interested in going out."

➤ **Egotistic flirts.** They are the Don Juans and Don Juanettes who always check themselves out in the mirror and need to make everyone in the room drool over them. They can make you feel like a million bucks, but only to flatter their own ego.

➤ **Controlling flirts.** They flirt just to tease the other person. (They make you think they're interested when they're really not.) These flirts enjoy watching others squirm, and manipulate others into doing things that they wouldn't ordinarily do.

Showing That You're Interested

Remember everyone is sensitive to rejection. So if you are receptive to someone's advances, don't hesitate to show it. One key ingredient to effective flirting is to show interest in your potential mate. Let's face it—everyone loves attention and being noticed. Two ways you can show interest are by giving compliments and by asking thought-provoking questions.

Being Interesting

People usually say to each other "What's up?" I often greet callers with that on my radio show, and they need to have their story ready! Besides being interested in the other person, you also want to come across as interesting yourself! That means be enthusiastic about yourself and things that you have done. Something outrageous or different often works best. A great technique to accomplish this is to keep notes (either mentally or in a notebook) about fun things that you have done.

One of my precious interns at my radio show, Emily, used this technique successfully. As she told me, she grew up in a small town, "so you couldn't make up anything, turn on the charm, or make small talk, because everybody already knew you." But when she moved to the big city, she could meet people "with a clean slate." This made for some exciting (though admittedly also fearful) experiences, where she could dazzle people with things she had done "without them going ho-hum, we already knew that." Talking about her most outrageous experiences, including a thrilling time sky diving, worked great in breaking the ice with strangers.

Delivering the Compliment

Paying someone a compliment is not as easy as you might think. Simply saying, "That's a nice shirt" is not enough to spark an engaging conversation. To deliver a compliment successfully, that is, to open the door for a promising conversation, follow these steps:

1. **Take note of the details.** Do this by:

   ➤ Picking out something she is wearing. This can include a piece of clothing or jewelry, or even a hairstyle.

   ➤ Noticing something about her—her smile, her eyes, or her physique.

   ➤ Paying attention to what he is carrying. ("That's a beautiful leather case.")

2. **Pay attention to what he is doing.** ("You play a great game of pool" or "I notice that you're careful about what you buy.")

3. **Follow up with a question.** ("Where did you find such an interesting piece of jewelry?")

Smooth Talk'n

When asking a question, listen attentively to the answer, instead of worrying about what your next question will be.

Because I have a habit of dressing unusually and wearing funky clothes, many people are always noticing what I wear. When people compliment me on my fluorescent orange boots with the glow-in-the-dark soles by saying "Those are really cool boots, where did you get them?" they can engage me in a conversation about the store I shopped in (which leads to talking about how everyone hangs out in malls these days, how my conservative mother hates them, how they glow in dark clubs, what clubs I go to, and so on).

Asking Intriguing Questions

Smooth Talk'n

Ask open-ended questions rather than ones requiring one-word answers like "yes" or "no." By doing this, you get more revealing insight into the person and more of a chance to assess what he is really like.

What is most people's favorite topic? Themselves. So, ask them to talk about themselves. You've got five W's to consider:

➤ **Who.** Who's your favorite actor/relative/friend?

➤ **What.** What's your favorite thing to do?

➤ **Where.** Where is your favorite place to go?

➤ **When.** When was the last time you treated yourself?

➤ **Why.** Why did you come here?

Avoid answering a question negatively. Let's look at an example. Chester asked Elena if she goes to the movies often. She replied, "No, I don't," and the conversation came to a dead end. Instead, Elena could have answered, "I prefer to hang out at my friends' houses, so we rent videos instead," setting a more positive tone to the interaction, and giving Chester the chance to ask about her friends, which videos they rent, and so on.

Home Alone

Some people don't like being asked questions; they feel put on the spot. You'll sense this if the person only gives you one-word answers, smirks, or simply turns away. If the person does this, quickly turn the tables and talk about yourself.

Dating Data

When the brain hears a negative answer—no matter what it's about—it creates physiological responses in the body and mind of a defensive, protective, and shut-down nature. "Yes" boosts deeper and easier breathing, more even blood pressure, and calmer heartbeats that make for better health and a more positive frame of mind.

The Flirting Flamenco

Dating is like a dance—a matter of synchronizing your rhythms (but not backing someone into a corner). Sometimes you can't tell if a person is totally uninterested or just shy or reserved. Make your approach using what I call the "Flirting Flamenco." It has three steps:

1. **The Approach.** Make your boldest move to gain the other person's attention. This should last a few minutes.

2. **The Retreat.** Back off (sip your soda, dig in your pocketbook) to take the focus off the flirtation and to give the person a chance to assess you.

3. **The Re-approach.** Test the waters. If your target responds, fine. But if not, definitely move on after three tries.

Body Talk

Researchers have estimated that more than half of communication comes from body language—gestures and movements that we make that reveal what we think or feel. So let your posture, facial expressions, and eyes do the talking for you. One cue is often not enough, so to send or interpret a message, combine several cues.

Smooth Talk'n

A playful wink is also a good flirting tool.

Smooth Talk'n

Women have a head start in touch flirting and can be more forward because men are generally less threatened by being touched.

Eye Contact

The eyes are the window to the soul. When you look at someone, you are saying that you are willing to see and connect with them, and you are willing to be seen yourself. You have only to watch new lovers in a restaurant gazing across the table into each other's eyes to know how powerful eye contact can be.

But how much eye contact is too much/too little/the right amount? Research shows that a constant stare makes people uncomfortable. However, a short gaze may mean that the person is shy, insecure, or insincere. The most effective eye contact is where you glance, linger, look away, then reconnect—holding each other's gaze for at least 60 percent of the total time you are together.

Once you've made eye contact, longer looks usually work. Use what I term the "Driver's Eyes." You look straight at the person (like you're watching the road), while occasionally glancing right and left (like you're looking at the side-view mirrors) for relief.

Touch

Touch is comforting and also stimulating. Flirt by touching yourself lightly in a nonsexual, safe way. Primp or preen yourself, smoothing your hair or stroking your own hand, neck, face, or leg. Use an interesting trick based on the psychological principle of modeling—touch yourself wherever you would like to focus attention or where you imagine the other person touching you.

Dating Data

There are many sensitive nerve endings in the skin surface. When they are touched, they set off impulses to the brain that trigger chemical releases and signal pleasurable feelings.

Once you've become comfortable with each other, you can straighten his tie or her necklace, or brush a speck off the shoulder of his jacket. Advance to touching a body part: first covered parts, like the back or shoulder, then hair, and then exposed skin on "safe" areas like on the arm, hand, or cheek. Back off if the person winces or withdraws.

Body Positioning

Research on kinesiology (the study of moving bodies) shows that posture and movement communicate messages. Read and interpret caution or unwelcome signs if the body and head are turned away. Crossed arms could mean he's nervous or closed off. Uncross those arms and see how much more open—and vulnerable—it feels! Better to do that if you want to give the message you're more approachable! Lean in, extend a hand, nod (to signal approval), or puff out your chest or tilt your hips (to show interest). Legs crossed with the top leg nearer the other person signals that you are creating a barrier between you.

Smooth Talk'n

Purposefully copy your prey's posture or movement, to give the subliminal message that you're interested and on the same wavelength. If she rests her chin in her hand, do the same. If he puts his hand on his hip, you do that, too.

Vigorous leg-shaking is a sign of nervousness (a turn-off), while slight movements are stimulating (and a come-on). Mannerisms such as hair-flicking or tie-tugging can be distracting and a sign of discomfort. Also, if someone's hands or mouth are hidden (hands in pocket, or covering mouth), he may be hiding something.

Mirroring or Getting in Sync

When people are in tune with one another, they copy each other's body movements, so one's posture or movements seem like a mirror reflection of the other. Watch how this works—you'll be amused! Observe a couple who seems "into" each other, and notice that if he leans on one elbow, she'll likely do the same thing. If she rubs her lips, he'll reach for his, too. Without even realizing it, people in the seduction mode copy each other.

Body Boundaries

How far away do you stand? Respect each person's "SPD"—safe personal distance—measured by an arm's length, usually about two to three feet. Then test the waters: Wait to see if she gives you clues to come closer (body touches, smiles, open body position). Also give clues yourself. Then do the "distance duet": Move in closer to show you're interested and then withdraw to give her "space" to advance and to show return interest.

Make sure your touches are welcome by "reading" the person's receptivity. Make a gesture first and see if the person resists (moves away) or moves closer or smiles invitingly.

Nonverbal Ways to Tell Him You're Interested

You can also show that you're interested in someone and sense if a person is interested in you without using any words at all. Nonverbal cues of interest consist of what I call "the four P's":

➤ **Presenting.** Present yourself in a sexy and alluring manner. For example, lick your lips, trace the outline of a scoop-neck top, or run your hand down your leg.

➤ **Preening.** Show that you know you're appealing. Straighten a tie, smooth or toss your hair.

➤ **Parading.** Stay close to your prey. Show that you're checking her out (think of an animal circling around its prey). For example, Barry had his eye on Jessica at a party. She, however, was being pursued by so many men that she was unlikely to notice him. But while others courted her and drifted away, Barry always reappeared in her line of vision, until the end of the night when he offered her a ride home—which she took!

➤ **Posturing.** Nibble at food or play with the rim or stem of a glass suggestively. How you stand, sit, and even walk says a lot about you. For example, tilting the head implies vulnerability, extending an arm is inviting, cocking a hip is seductive.

Reading Mixed Signals

Lots of people are confused about whether someone's really interested. As Tara said: "I go to bars a lot and I've had lots of guys come on to me, but when push comes to shove, they walk away. What's wrong with me and what am I doing wrong?"

The odds of hitting a home run in dating (especially in bars) are as high as hitting one in baseball; you are more likely to strike out. Don't wipe yourself out over it. But think about whether you're showing enough interest in return. Sometimes people act a little aloof, especially when they've been repeatedly rejected.

As you flirt and as others flirt with you, I suggest that you test the waters, so to speak. Use the "Flirting Flamenco" and rule of three advances: Put your foot in the water three times while giving the other person breathing space in between to decide how to react to your advances.

To read someone's reaction and to be really good at seduction, you have to become good at tuning in to what a person is doing, thinking, and feeling. Some people are good at it intuitively, and others need more practice. You'll be better at it the more you are not consumed with your own fears, such as worrying about how you're coming across ("Do I look good?" "Is what I'm saying okay?" "Does he like me?"). When you focus on yourself too much, you can't possibly read the other person.

Home Alone

Self-consciousness comes across as insecurity, making the other person more likely to be turned off.

Flirter's Block

Many singles tell me that they often see someone they'd love to meet but are too afraid to approach. Why? They're afraid of being rejected and feeling like a loser or a fool. You must overcome these feelings. Remember the phrase: "Nothing ventured, nothing gained." Risk being the first to say hello; the other person is probably just as nervous as you.

Check off the risks you fear:

➤ **Embarrassment.** Are you afraid to say what's on your mind for fear of being perceived as silly or foolish?

➤ **Shame.** Are you afraid that you'll be disgraced or humiliated and that others will judge you poorly?

➤ **Guilt.** Do you feel you're doing something bad or wrong and that you will be punished for it?

➤ **Rejection.** Are you afraid of being turned down?

My 12-Step Plan for Dealing with Flirter's Block

If you have trouble flirting with someone, don't despair! You can overcome your shyness and inhibitions. Just follow these steps:

Step 1. Identify and express your resistance. Realizing that you have flirter's block has won you half the battle.

Step 2. Review your past patterns with flirting and rejection and reframe your experience. See what you can do differently this time. For example, think, "The last time I tried talking to a girl, she sneered and walked away. If this happens again with another girl, I'll assume that she's in a bad mood rather than that I'm a dud."

Step 3. Forget your past. Don't relive each rejection you ever had. Come to each new experience with a fresh attitude.

Step 4. Stop making overgeneralizations. For example, don't say, "Every time I try to meet someone, it doesn't work out," or "All pretty girls/good-looking guys don't like me."

Step 5. Identify your faulty or self-defeating negative conclusions. Don't say things like "I can't meet someone I like," or "The way I look, I'll never find someone." Expecting negative outcomes predisposes them to really happen.

Step 6. Think positive thoughts. Make more enjoyable predictions. Tell yourself, "I will enjoy this encounter," or, if you are rejected, "It's his loss, not mine."

Step 7. Eliminate expectations. Change your intention about flirting from "scoring" (a date, job, or marriage) to simply being an innocent social interaction to establish a friendship. This reduces anxiety (about failure) and disappointment over an outcome.

Step 8. See things from the other person's point of view. The reason for someone's non-response may have nothing to do with you. The person may have low self-esteem, or be distracted about losing a job, or be involved with someone else. I remember the time I met a top executive and felt hurt that he didn't talk to me. Imagine my relief when my friend told me that he told her, "I can't talk to Dr. Judy now, I just ate garlic and my breath smells terrible!" Here I had wasted my time feeling slighted, and he was worried about being slighted himself!

Step 9. Reassure yourself. "I am a (good/interesting/fun) person." Positive self-talk and affirmations boost your self-esteem and chances for success.

Step 10. Identify the emotional charge on your resistance. "I feel like a failure," "I am a loser." Simply state what happened without the emotion: "I approached her, and she wasn't responsive." Don't add how horrible you felt about it or the negative conclusions you came to about yourself.

Step 11. Identify the true meaning of the fear—that will often reveal its insubstantiality. For example, shame is a feeling that you have done something wrong or foolish and that others will think less of you. Decide instead that there is nothing foolish about your actions, and that others either aren't that focused on what you've done, or that their opinion doesn't matter.

Step 12. Mentally practice flirting so that when the opportunity arises, your actions will flow. Imagine how you would like the encounter to go. Rehearse it over and over, as if you're watching a movie in your head. The more you practice, the more likely you'll behave that way in real life. For example, imagine you're crossing the street and you see a terrific guy. You step up to the curb next to him and make a comment about how much traffic there is today. Or, you're at a card store and you spot a beautiful woman, so you pick out two birthday cards and ask her which one she would prefer getting.

Smooth Talk'n

Expect rejection; everyone goes through it. If you expect the worst, there's nowhere to go but up.

The Least You Need to Know

➤ Besides being fun, flirting can be an effective way of getting to know a person.

➤ One key ingredient to effective flirting is to show interest in that person.

➤ More than half of communication comes from body language.

➤ To become successful at reading people, practice tuning into others' actions, thoughts, and feelings.

➤ To overcome flirter's block, forget past failures, reassure yourself, and anticipate having a good time. Remember, the other person is probably just as nervous as you.

Chapter 10

The Proposition

In This Chapter

➤ How to increase your chances of getting a "yes"

➤ New ways to make your move

➤ How to say "yes" or "no"

➤ What to do when you get no response

So you've spotted someone who strikes your fancy. Now it's time to take the next step: Make the connection. If you're stymied about what to do, you're certainly not alone. "How do I ask her out?" is a question I get asked all the time on my radio show. It seems so simple at first—just ask, right? Yet, why do you feel so nervous and anxious? In this chapter, you learn about what's cool and what's not when it comes to popping the question (not that question—we're working on the first date here).

Welcome to the new millenium of dating. Throw out the old rules you thought you had to follow. We'll tackle new ones in the upcoming sections.

What's New About Asking for the Date

Give up the old way of asking for the date—thinking of it as a "date!" Remember my basic principle: Think of a date as an exciting invitation to spend time together. It's not about dating, it's about spending and enjoying time together and getting to know each other. Think of it as an *invitation*, rather than a *date*. So, what's the best way to do this?

Passé: There is a right way.

In the New Millennium: There is no right way. Do what is natural for you, and remember to be yourself. You'll find more specific suggestions later in this chapter.

Passé: Make the invite "formal" (as in, "I'd like to ask you out" or "Do you want to go out on a date?").

In the New Millennium: Keep it casual. Think of a date as a time to hang out and get to know each other's likes and dislikes. This will help you feel less anxious.

Passé: Ask for a date far in advance in case she's busy or purposefully say "no" so you don't look desperate.

In the New Millennium: Ask when something comes up or the time feels right—it may be last minute, but asking spontaneously could be just what's appropriate. You can always apologize for asking at the last minute.

Passé: Ask if she is "free."

In the New Millennium: Assume she wants to go and then find out if the time is good for the both of you. This concept allows you to approach the situation with self-confidence. If she is busy, you'll find out soon enough.

Passé: Not calling when you said you would.

In the New Millennium: *Always* call when you say you will; if you haven't said when, call (or e-mail) shortly after taking the phone number (even just to say hello).

Smooth Talk'n

Track your progress. Keep a journal of your goals, plans, reminders, and successes. Review these to boost your morale. You can even leave sticky notes on mirrors or doors to remind you to be assertive.

Smooth Talk'n

My friend Donovan, lead singer of the band Nancy Boy (and ex-Calvin Klein jeans model), heartily endorses telling your target's best friend about your interest. She'll then tell her friend, who'll be more prepared for—and hopefully more receptive to—your invitation. That's how he won over his current love.

Preliminaries...

Before asking someone out, brief yourself on the following dating tips to increase your chance of getting a "yes:"

➤ Your invitation should not build anxiety for either of you. Wait for a moment when you feel relaxed.

➤ When asking someone on a date, consider what you enjoy doing. Participating in something you are good at or comfortable with will increase your overall confidence. If you like basketball, take her to a game.

➤ Ask, "What's in it for my date?" Just as President John F. Kennedy said, "Ask not what your country can do for you; ask what you can do for your country." The same basic rule can be applied to dating: Always offer something to others before expecting or asking that something be done for you.

Think of a date not as getting, but giving. When inviting someone to a party, say, "There'll be some people there I know you'll enjoy." Or combat resistance by pointing out advantages, as in, "Come play golf with me. Even if you don't love the sport, you'll be outdoors getting sunshine and exercise, and seeing beautiful sights."

If a prospective date sees what he can get out of the evening, he will be more receptive. What does she like to do? How will the date benefit him? For example, if he is thinking of buying a new car, offer to spend a day visiting car showrooms.

➤ Remember the basic point: Be yourself, instead of feeling the pressure of what you're supposed to do, or even what the outcome will be.

➤ Face your fears about the ghosts of the past. Sammy told me that he saw his kindergarten heartthrob at a reunion but was too scared to ask her out. Sammy remembered the days when he felt fat and awkward as a youngster. With my encouragement, he called her—and was successful!

What Works?

Follow the general principle: Be yourself. That means you should follow your instincts about what feels right for you. If you're going to be liked, you'll get a positive response no matter what you do. Therefore, you have some choices.

Whenever I pose the question on my radio show about the best ways to ask for a date, many male callers respond that they use the direct approach. As Mario said, "I just come right out and ask, 'How'd you like to go out?'" Sean agreed: "I'd be

Smooth Talk'n

Sometimes you can use a friend as an ice-breaker. Abby had her eyes on Charlie, but she was too shy to approach him directly. Instead, she waited until he was with a friend she knew. After some small talk with the both of them, she directed her attention towards Charlie. Shortly thereafter, she had a breakfast date set up with him.

Smooth Talk'n

Plant a seed and watch it grow. Drop the hint and come back to your proposal (returning to the subject three times is a decent rule of thumb, with each time building to a more definitive invitation). When you are asking for the date, be interesting and engaging, and keep the conversation moving while giving him a chance to digest your invitation.

myself. I say, 'How'd you like to go out?'" Sammy, whom I described earlier, ended up using a very simple approach to ask out his kindergarten heartthrob: When he called her on the phone, he said, "Hey, how ya doin'?" Fortunately, she immediately recognized his voice and was enthusiastic, giving him courage to ask, "What are you doing this weekend?", to which she replied, "My weekend's open . . ." He then said, "How about going out? We can get something to eat and go to a movie." She said she'd love to.

Smooth Talk'n

Test the waters, and make yourself attractive in the conversation by being creative. Let's say you want to ask her to go to an Italian restaurant. Talk about how you'd love to visit Italy, and then say you'd fly her to Italy if you had an extra day off, but you'd settle for going to the local Italian restaurant.

Smooth Talk'n

After you ask, don't make that the last thing you talk about. Swing into another topic, so you can complete the conversation on a neutral note. Have a topic up your sleeve that you can talk about, like about what you heard in the news. Don't worry if it seems to be an abrupt change in the topic. That alone can create interest, by switching—and capturing—the other person's attention.

Personally, I favor the subtle approach. That means you go with the flow when asking, making it a natural outgrowth of the interaction—almost so that it doesn't seem like a formal invitation. Popping the question shouldn't come out of nowhere. Ideally, you have both just finished discussing something in which you're both interested and you would like to do together.

I am also in favor of starting the conversation with something that you offer first. That means you should think of entertaining the other person, offering them some tidbit of information that is interesting or a story that is funny rather than you expecting them to carry the ball of the conversation and entertain you. If the other person is the type who likes to entertain, you'll find that out soon enough. But if they aren't, then you've risked turning them off by putting them on the spot. Personally, I am more receptive to strangers when they approach me with a tidbit about why the sky is blue or why hurricanes take on a certain pattern than if they say, "Tell me what you do," right off the bat.

Use a technique similar to what's called "free association," where topics lead into one another. Here's how the flow might go:

You might be talking about what you enjoy (maybe playing baseball) and the last game you did well in. Then remind her about the amazing baseball players who broke the world's record of home runs (Mark McGwire and Sammy Sosa, who beat Roger Maris's 1961 record of 61 home runs) and ask what record she would like to break.

Dating Data

Men who are threatened by a woman's assertiveness may prove troublesome in relationships, as they tend to resist her requests and insist on proving their own superiority or control.

Suppose she answers that she doesn't know. Suggest breaking records, like the number of hours dancing without stopping, and then segue into the suggestion that the two of you ought to go dancing sometime. Then swing into talking about how you heard the tango is a new craze, and that someday you'd like to visit Argentina. Then you can come back to the date—because now she's had a chance to let it sink in—saying how you love to dance and asking if she does. Move into another subject, picking up on the travel theme by talking about your last trip, and then come back to the invitation again. This time you're a little more definitive about whether you will get together (say something like, "What do you think about going out dancing next Friday?").

When and How?

Once you've decided to make your move, when's the right time? Again, follow your instincts. Tune into your own comfort level, as well as hers. Then strike when your iron is hot (when you feel motivated and empowered) and when your intuition tells you he/she would be receptive.

Asking in person has great advantages. Obviously, you can see the person's response (more about this later). However, you (and your prospective date) may feel put on the spot.

Short of that, the telephone has advantages. You can get feedback from what you hear and listen for cues in the other person's voice. In addition, you won't be put on the spot—and if you get a "no," you can easily end the conversation. Choose asking on the phone over other means (e-mail or voice mail).

Smooth Talk'n

This intuition ("psychic dating") may take some trial and error, and some time to develop, but it will come. No matter what happens, your enthusiasm will carry you through the moment.

Smooth Talk'n

The telephone is a tremendous aid in dating. Unfortunately, it is one that men have traditionally been shy about. Get over your phone fears by taking a deep breath, identifying yourself to the person you're calling, and providing some information that connects the two of you ("Remember when we met at Bob's party?"). Talk a short time, and always end with warmth and a compliment: "It was great talking to you" or "Looking forward to seeing you." Women hate abrupt endings.

And of course, let's not forget about the latest craze: e-mail. It's a great tool for shy people, but there really isn't any way for you to gauge the person's response. Even if you have a solid e-mail relationship, pick up the phone and make your invitation. It's better to either hear the person's voice on the phone or see their face in person.

Another new millenium mode: beeper and voice messages. The beeper has become like an answering machine, so you can consider beeping your prospective date. This has an element of surprise, but it's best to keep this method in reserve, to use in case you can't get in touch another way. If you leave a voice message, make it a vague "hello," and not the specific invitation. An exception to this: If you have last-minute tickets to some fabulous event and need an immediate answer. The element of excitement overrides any other caution about using this technique.

Who Makes the First Move?

Forget about leaving it all up to the man. This puts enormous pressure on men to carry the ball and face rejection. Men don't want this pressure anymore!

She can make the move, too. As the role of women in the workplace continues to expand, so does their role in the dating world. People often ask me, "Is it okay for a woman to ask a man out?" and "Do men like women who make the first move?" The answer to both questions is a resounding "Yes!" More men have grown tired of always being the ones to make the first step. In fact, they appreciate women who take the initiative and are relieved to know when a woman is interested in them. In addition, many men (as long as they're not intimidated) find women attractive when they are assertive, confident, and in control of their lives.

Hillary Clinton made the first move on Bill. She spied him in the Yale Law library, went up to him, and said, "If you're going to keep looking at me and I'm going to

Home Alone

Avoid leaving your invitation on an answering machine or sending it in writing. This gives you no chance for testing a response. And you never know whether she really got the message (the cat could have stepped on the "erase messages" button, or if she's anything like me she doesn't get to her pile of mail for weeks). It's better to get a more immediate response.

Smooth Talk'n

When asking someone on a date, offer alternate times. If they can't make it one night, they may be able to make it another. But if that person declines all suggestions, you're better off letting the whole thing drop.

keep looking at you, we at least ought to know each other. I'm Hillary Rodham, and what's your name?" (Bill was stunned and couldn't remember his name.)

Closing the Deal

Asking someone on a date is like trying to make a sale—that is, you are trying to sell yourself. When making the proposition, follow the "Rule of Three Yes's": Ask three questions that will all lead to favorable responses. You never want to ask a question that will lead to a "no." That stops the conversation and injects negativity.

You also want to ease the person into agreement, without making him feel like he's risking too much, and by giving him an out at each stage so as not to embarrass either of you. Of course, you have to do some research first and learn something about the person so that you can figure out how to set up your questions. Then you close the deal by asking three "yes" questions.

Consider this scenario: Bill wants to ask Kate out. He does a little research first and discovers that she likes Kung Fu movies. His conversation opener, therefore, can be something like this: "I heard you like Kung Fu movies."

He then does more fact-finding by asking open-ended questions like, "What's the latest Kung Fu movie you've seen?" or "What's your favorite Kung Fu movie?"

Or, after a conversation about something else, Bill then can close the deal on his date by asking the following three "yes" questions:

1. "So, you really like going to the movies?"

2. "I heard you love horror movies. Is that true?"

3. "Wouldn't it be neat to see the latest horror movie that's playing at . . .?"

Smooth Talk'n

What's even newer: giving both people a chance to call each other. Exchange numbers rather than leaving it up to one person or the other.

Smooth Talk'n

When selling a car, two of the biggest tricks used in closing the deal are to say something like, "So which color do you want?" and then, "How do you want to pay for it? In a three-year or four-year plan?" The first question makes the assumption that you are interested, which encourages your interest further because the dealer is acting as if the hypothetical were a reality. The second question is a clincher because it continues to promote the hypothetical as reality. The question makes you focus on the choices that surround the "yes" rather than on saying "no."

Now apply this method to dating. Ask which day both of you should meet rather than *if* you should meet at all. Or, you could ask, "Would you prefer going to the movies, or out to eat, or both?"

Then Bill can add something along the lines of catching a movie the next weekend: "I'm thinking about going to see (that movie) sometime this weekend. Maybe you could go with me—what do you think?" (Of course, this won't always get you a definite yes, but you gave it a good shot.)

Notice these characteristics of Bill's invitation:

Smooth Talk'n

In case of a lukewarm reception, use another rule of selling: Always leave the door open. You can say, "Okay, I'll call you in a week and maybe we can go then," or "I'm sure we can find something that would be great to do together another time." This keeps your ego from being totally deflated.

Smooth Talk'n

When finalizing the date, consider giving out your business card. I learned the advantages of trading business cards from spending a lot of time in Japan, where it's *de rigeur* to exchange name cards when you first meet someone. By having someone's business card, you won't have to worry about forgetting the person's name, what she does for a living, or how to contact her.

➤ Pose the question as if you're already going and she can join you. This takes the pressure off you to take her out formally and also off her if she says no. You also avoid sounding desperate. (No one wants to board a sinking ship in full sail.)

➤ Be casual and light (this is my favorite suggestion). Don't jump into water that's too deep before you've tested it.

➤ Point out all the benefits of the deal. Folgers sells coffee not by quoting the price but by showing how warm and cozy consumers will feel sharing coffee with their mate early in the morning.

How Persistent Should You Be?

A lot of people ask me how to tell whether someone is interested. Of course, you'd love an enthusiastic "Yes," but my general rule is similar to baseball: three strikes and you're out. That means make three attempts to show your interest, and if you strike out those three times, back off and give up. Someone can turn you down two times for a legitimate reason. Maybe she's really busy. Or maybe he was a little ambivalent. Cut them a little slack. But after three approaches, it's time for you to take your time and energy elsewhere!

Scott asked a girl he liked out and she said "no." Then he bumped into her again, and she lit up, making him think she was interested. Scott took the bait, and called her up again. This time, she was warm, and even though she said she couldn't go, she said she'd love to another time. She could have just been being nice, but it was worth Scott waiting a few weeks and then calling again. This time, she said yes. If she had been busy again, Scott could get ready to cross her off his list.

The only exception to the three-strikes rule would be if the person really gives you encouragement and the excuses ring true. Her mother could be sick. He could be buried in studying for the bar exam and can't spare the distraction. She could be breaking up with her boyfriend. But don't sit around and wait breathlessly. Move onto other things—or other people—and when the time is right and the excuses are sincere, you'll go out eventually.

Getting the Number

So how do you get the phone number? You may be comfortable not beating around the bush. Many of the male callers to my radio show have said they just come right out and ask, "Can I have your phone number?" Take Josh, for instance, who simply goes up to a lady, says "I'd like to have coffee with you sometime. What's your phone number?" He claims this has about a 60 percent success rate for him.

Personally, I favor a more subtle approach. Slide asking for the number into the conversation. While discussing something interesting, say something like, "Well, we should talk more about that." Then add, "How do we get in touch? I should give you my card/ my number. And you should give me yours."

Keeping Your Emotions in Check

When dating, it's important not to have any expectations. Enjoy the process and not the outcome, the journey and not the destination, or you'll be headed for disappointment. The best actions are the ones that come from the heart, that have good intentions and are not caught up with the actual "response." Have fun flirting without worrying whether it'll lead to a ride home, a date, a roll in the hay, or a marriage proposal. Your expectations may also make your date feel obligated, guilty, and resistant. People need to feel free to say yes or no instead of giving in out of guilt, fear of hurting you, fear of retaliation, or fear of anything else that can doom any relationship.

Smooth Talk'n

Having business cards drawn up isn't a big deal. Visit your local print or card shop, or even use your own computer to print out business cards. You can also order personalized business cards through some catalogs.

Smooth Talk'n

For an interesting test of his interest, see his reaction if you disappear for a while (into the ladies' room, or over to talk to a friend). He's interested if he says, "I felt abandoned; where did you go?" and holds on to you tighter, goes looking for you, or seems happy on your return. It's not a good sign if he acts disinterested (to punish you for disappearing, or to prove he didn't care to protect himself), or he is actively talking to someone else and doesn't notice you even after you make yourself obvious.

Accepting the Date

Consistent with my disagreement with *The Rules*, I do not condone refusing dates to prove that you are desirable or not desperate. That includes these:

Smooth Talk'n

Think of a date as a TBC (To be continued) television movie. Be positive and complimentary at the end of the date. Tell the person, "I enjoyed talking with you. Let's do it again."

Home Alone

If dates are constantly made last-minute, are disorganized, or even canceled, reconsider whether this is the right person for you.

➤ The rules say that if he calls at the last minute, you should be insulted and play games, such as pretending that you are too busy and that he should have called you earlier. I say if you really want to see him and you are free, accept the date and have a good time. Be as casual about going as he was about calling you at the last minute. Instead of being insulted, feel good that he was inspired to want to see you now.

➤ The rules say to refuse if he does not suggest taking you to a fancy restaurant or on some special date, but just suggests that you "get together" or "hang out." I say do not immediately conclude that he is disrespectful or not willing to put in any effort. He may be strapped for money or he just wants to spend unstructured time with you. Give it a chance.

➤ In addition, I say that if she breaks dates with her friends in order to be with a guy, be wary about her priorities and reliability. A mature woman keeps her agreements and appointments, regardless of what may come up that can seem more exciting or romantic. There will always be another chance for the exciting date, if he is worth his salt, and she will have proven her trustworthiness and loyalty, qualities you *want* in a date anyway.

Just Say No Gently

Some men and women feel guilty about saying no to a proposition. Take Heather for instance, who said, "Sometimes I get stuck talking to some creep at a party, and I just can't get away. My evening ends up ruined."

I'm really impressed when people ask me how to let a casual encounter down easy. It shows that they care about other people's feelings. When letting someone down, one rule to remember is to always be kind. It could happen to you, and what goes around comes around. So I was pleased when Billy called "LovePhones" and said, "I'm a pretty good-looking guy, and lots of girls do ask me out. I don't want to blow them off because I've been hurt myself and I know what it feels like. What can I do?"

Kudos to Billy for being considerate. People who have been rejected know what it feels like and are more sensitive to not hurting someone else. Similar rules apply to exiting casual encounters as to ending a relationship (as described in Chapter 20). Let someone down easy by reassuring them that they're nice, and by giving a neutral but firm excuse. Here's a suggestion: "You're interesting/that's fascinating/nice talking to you, and it'd be nice to talk to you more, but I need to make a phone call/talk to my friend/get something to drink. It was a real pleasure to meet you."

If the person persists, talk kindly, but drop something into the conversation about another relationship, or say something like, "Please don't take this personally, but I don't feel like talking right now."

Dating Data

It's one thing to be nice; it's another to sacrifice yourself. If you're wasting your time, you're wasting the pursuer's time, too, and you are only being misleading. Disengage yourself nicely, and consider that you're doing both of you a favor.

Psychologically, people who can't break away are usually oversensitive to rejection themselves. Deep down they may have merged with the other person, so that the rejection is also a blow to themselves. These people have to learn to set boundaries and stop fearing that they will be punished for rejecting someone else. For instance, Jackie's mother always warned her, "What goes around, comes around." As a result, she feared that if she turned a guy down, some guy would turn her down, too.

Getting No Response

Remember, dating, like selling, is a numbers game: Learn to welcome the "no's," because they just mean you're getting closer to a "yes." Even the best hitters in baseball get on base only about once every three times at bat—and they also strike out occasionally!

If you get a "no" from a person, don't obsess about it. Instead, pick up your marbles and go to another playground where you might be welcome. Immediately turn your attention to others who might be interested.

A common question I'm asked is: "Why is it that a girl seems interested, but when you ask her out on a date or begin to show you are interested, she doesn't want to speak to you again?"

Unfortunately, when people feel awkward or embarrassed, they may avoid talking to you. You may have jumped the gun interpreting friendliness as an interest in dating. If you approach someone and she does not respond the way you want her to, accept that she was just being nice and did not mean anything more or to lead you on.

If you want to be big about it, you can be the one to use the "Let's just be friends" line, so you don't feel totally rejected. Come right out and say, "It's okay that it's not going to work out between us. I don't expect anything from you, so we can just be friends. That'll work much better for both of us."

Don't Blow Up if You're Blown Off

John couldn't accept women who turned him down. If he approached them and they turned away or said something rude, his temper flared out of control. He was like Jekyll and Hyde: one minute an innocent flirt, the next a raging bull. John and other rejected suitors need to:

➤ Realize that everyone has a right to say no. Don't take rejection personally.

➤ Realize that your hair-trigger temper over rejection is related to your need for instant gratification (getting what you want when you want it). Instead, consider patience a virtue.

➤ Trace your reactions to childhood experiences. Were you spoiled? Did you always get what you wanted? Remember, the world will not indulge you like your mother did.

➤ Identify past events that are currently fueling your present anger. Separate the past from the present so that you can react effectively now. When one woman rejected John, he was flooded with memories of all the other women who had slighted him. Resist this urge, and stay focused on the present.

Smooth Talk'n

If you are easily upset by rejection, interrupt the eruption by stopping and taking a deep breath. Then smile and turn your attention to something else that captures your attention and makes you feel good.

Smooth Talk'n

One of the big upsets about being rejected when you ask someone out is that you wonder, "What did I do wrong?" Maybe nothing—but maybe something. Consider asking someone who has turned you down what they really thought of you. This requires guts. Go for it, though, and learn about yourself. Say, "I know it's not working out between us, but I was wondering if you could help me by giving me some honest feedback." Whatever she says could help you for the next approach.

Dating Data

Research has shown that getting past hurts off your chest is helpful to your physical as well as mental health. A group of people who wrote about their past traumatic experiences for 20 minutes a day for four days had fewer visits to the doctor than those who wrote about trivial topics. In addition, those who wrote about their feelings were happier, less anxious, and seemingly healthier than those who described events non-emotionally.

One Last Pay-Off if You're Blown Off

Treat every experience in dating as a learning opportunity rather than as a success or a failure. You can learn from your own—and the other person's—reflections about you.

I want you to feel good about yourself, and to act naturally, so I don't want you to be too self-conscious about your style. Performance anxiety classically refers to the self-consciousness that destroys your enjoyment of sex, but this can apply to anything you do. As with every experience, assess how you did, take stock (not too harshly or judgmentally), and make adjustments when necessary.

Home Alone

Don't sink away into oblivion if you are dumped or rejected. Instead, use each approach as a learning experience. If you've been blown off, you can make another approach. Just learn what you might have done wrong.

The Least You Need to Know

➤ Don't think of a date as a formal outing. Think of it as a casual time to get to know each other.

➤ Consider dating like selling: Always ask questions that lead to a "yes," and even consider a "no" as leading you closer to an eventual "yes" from someone else.

➤ Don't take rejection personally. Consider that one road not taken leads you down another (better) one.

➤ Keep your spirits up. Never give up hope. Keep trying, and you're bound to find someone special!

The First Date— and How Not to Make It the Last

"Cup your hand over your mouth and check your breath."
—first-date rule (John, guitarist from the Dopes)

So you leapt over the first dating hurdle by asking to get together. Now get ready to jump again, because it's time to put your money where your mouth is and follow through with the real date. As you get ready, there's a lot to think about. You may have anxieties to overcome and preparations to make, and you want to ensure that all goes as smoothly as possible and that you have a good time. In this chapter we'll make sure you do!

Psyching Yourself Up

If your mind instantly fills with images of tripping over your own feet, getting spaghetti sauce on your shirt, or, worse, feeling stupid about not knowing what to say, relax. A first date is bound to be fraught with some anxieties. Here are some ways to calm yourself down while psyching yourself up:

➤ Remember my basic principle: Treat the date as simply a way to get to know each other better, having a good time together, sharing an experience, and learning about yourself and each other.

➤ Remind yourself that your date already likes something about you, or he wouldn't have agreed to go out in the first place.

➤ You don't want to drive yourself crazy thinking about your upcoming date too much, but as with everything in life, a little pre-planning goes a long way. Think through where you will go and what you will wear, and make some mental notes about what interesting things you might want to talk about. Then put it out of your mind. Don't keep changing your mind or trying to make things perfect.

➤ If you are excited about the particular person, indulge fleeting thoughts or fantasies about how you want things to go, or how terrific it would be if it all worked out. Then remind yourself to stay grounded in reality, and curb your expectations.

➤ Resist worrying about what would happen if things don't work out.

➤ You can allow yourself a fleeting sad thought about the frustrations of dating, but avoid over-generalizing that nothing ever works out anyway.

➤ Re-read Chapter 6 to build up your confidence. Remember that you are a valuable person and that it is fun to be with you. If you enjoy being with you, others will, too.

What to Wear

As the saying goes, "Clothes make the man." It's not as materialistic as it sounds though; put simply, this means, how you dress can say a lot about you. Think about what your clothes reveal about your personality as you decide what to wear on your first date. Keep these considerations in mind when choosing your outfit:

➤ What impression do you want to make? Do you want to look professional and conservative, casual yet savvy, or cool and hip?

➤ Dress appropriately for the occasion. You would not want to wear high heels if you are going for a long walk in the park. And you might not want to dress in too-revealing clothes if you're going to a cocktail party with business associates.

➤ Of course, you want to express yourself in your clothing style, but you also want to please and impress your date, and make him feel comfortable. For example, when Paula planned her first date with Rich, she remembered how much he likes motorcycles, so she wore her black leather jacket and high buckle boots—and she was a hit. When Sarah met Stephen, he was wearing gray slacks and a blue blazer, so for their first date she dressed in an equally conservative outfit: white shirt, black skirt, blue jacket, and black pumps.

➤ You can never go wrong in dressing for your date with the KISS rule: Keep it simple. For guys, black jeans and a simple black T-shirt are an easy choice. Take a jacket that can double as a dress jacket. If you're more into fashion, wear a plain or simple-patterned shirt (button-down collars are back in).

➤ Be comfortable. There's nothing worse than having to keep sucking in your stomach because your waistband is too tight, or not being able to sit down because your pants creep into your crotch.

You can always check magazines to see what is fashionable, but do it to expand your ideas and choices, not just to copy-cat. I'm a fan of individuality in how you dress to project your personality, so be free in choosing items that show off who you are, even if they don't follow the latest fashions.

Smooth Talk'n

Never be afraid to ask, "What should I wear?" Though guys will usually not have an idea what to answer, it could yield some interesting suggestion about their taste.

Footwear is often the most overlooked, though I have had callers tell me that they really can tell a lot about what dates put on their feet. For example, if he shows up in Birkenstocks, you can surmise he'll know who Santana and the Grateful Dead are, and that he's a hippie at heart; butter-soft Italian loafers suggest some sense of the Eurotrash scene. Dirty shoes or sneakers are definitely a no-no. A simple pair of boots (Doc Martens, for instance) always works these days. While chunky platform shoes are also fashionable—depending on where you go—you might want to purposefully try different shoes to see what fits your look and feels comfortable on your feet (in case you end up taking some romantic walk . . . or have to walk home!).

Also, don't forget choices about underwear. Even though you (probably!) won't be showing them, they will make a difference in how you feel about yourself. Something new that makes you feel sexy is the best choice: Imagine what you'd want to be wearing *if* they were going to be seen. Sammy wore Tommy Hilfiger gray boxers for his first date with Jenine. Beth chose her favorite satin bikini underwear: white with red hearts. How you feel intimately inside will affect how you project confidence and intimacy.

Another thing: Don't forget your smell. As we discovered in Chapter 2, smell is important in attraction. You can go au natural, or you can pick a fragrance that is your favorite. For instance, "Tommy" is in for men as well as women. Other favorites include Calvin Klein's many varieties, and my personal favorite is "Georgio." Choose the one that works for your body, as each fragrance interacts with body chemistry individually.

Smooth Talk'n

More men are getting formal manicures and pedicures now, without considering this unmasculine. Factor such beauty treatments into your budget. Many shops in cities all around the country offer such services exclusively, and at reasonable prices. Beauticians sometimes even make home or office visits for last-minute services.

Home Alone

While you might be motivated to get a haircut or fresh hair coloring before your big date, be careful. Usually it takes a few days before you get adjusted to the new 'do and for the style to settle in—and that's not to mention the possibility of getting a bad haircut. If possible, make your changes a few days beforehand, to prevent any shocks or disappointment.

Jewelry is also an expression of you. Moreover, it draws attention to parts of you and makes for easy conversation pieces (where you got it, what it means to you, how much you like it). Fashion experts advise that you should never wear more than three pieces of jewelry, and fashion magazines may dictate more rules (such as, no earrings if you wear a necklace), but I believe you should let yourself go and adorn yourself in any way that makes you feel comfortable.

Grooming

Looking your best is not just a matter of the clothes you wear, but also how you take care of your entire body and appearance. Looking your best is important not only for the impression you make, but for feeling good about yourself as well.

Cleanliness

It might seem insulting to even mention, but it deserves a respectful reminder: Get clean. Most people are into the good habit of taking a shower, shaving, and washing their hair before they go out. Many have become conditioned to use deodorant or anti-perspirant. But how about paying attention to some of the finer points of grooming? Pick clothes that are clean and pressed. Make sure your nails are clean—dirty nails have turned up among the top 10 turn-offs in some surveys. And don't forget your toenails—in summer, of course, they're exposed if you wear sandals. And you may never know when you could take your shoes off for that spontaneous walk along the beach or through the grass.

Brush your teeth before you go, and use a mouth rinse or breath-freshener. Also take along some mouth mints or sprays. Commercials are right: A fresh-smelling and tasting breath (to yourself) will add zest to your confidence.

Hairdo

Everybody knows what it feels like to have a bad hair day—it can ruin your mood! Liking your hair can be even more primary than feeling right about what you are wearing, because hair frames the face so prominently. Give yourself time to wash and style your hair before your date, in case you are dissatisfied and want to make changes.

Be judicious about trying out a new hairstyle. Certainly be daring if you like, and if it makes you feel exciting, but also be prepared for the effects of sudden changes. Slicking back your hair if you have always worn bangs or tried to make it fuller can be fun, or it can make you uncomfortable or self-conscious.

Makeup

Of course, you want to put on your best face. Consider how much makeup you will feel comfortable wearing on your date. Be careful about overdoing it. Use less than you normally do for a more natural look, or if you know your date likes a more casual look.

As with other preparations, the first date is not always the best time for experimenting. While it can be fun to try something different, usually it is best to be already comfortable with how you look. This is not the night you want to use that new color foundation or eye shadow—unless you have tried it out before and know whether it looks good on you.

Smooth Talk'n

For something special, consider getting made up at a beauty salon or makeup counter of a department store. But even so, make it your second trip, so you already have some idea how you would look afterward!

Where to Go

So what do you do and where do you go on a first date? The key is to go to a place you'll both enjoy and where you will both feel comfortable. The most confident and comfortable you both feel, the better time you will have—and the better you will come across.

Typical Places to Go on the First Date

Let me first say that any place you choose to go, or anything that you do, can be perfect for you if it suits the two of you and makes you feel comfortable. Go with your instincts about this. But consider the pros and cons of certain situations, and decide whether you can come up with something a little more creative in this new age.

The most common answer anybody gives when asked about where to go on a first date is "the movies." That suggestion certainly serves several purposes. It's a common suggestion, so you don't risk coming up with something the other person is not into.

Smooth Talk'n

It's a good idea to do an activity before going out to eat, so that you have something you can talk about over the food and aren't put on the spot without knowing what to say.

Smooth Talk'n

If you go to a bar, make sure it has some seating and setting for intimacy and that it's not overly noisy, preventing you from being able to hear each other.

Smooth Talk'n

If you're driving yourself crazy drumming up first-date ideas, consider asking your date, "Where would you like to go?" or "What do you enjoy doing most?" Better yet, brainstorm together something you would both enjoy doing.

Going to the movies is safe because you don't have to talk to each other, providing you with some safe distance and less pressure about what to say during those several hours, and still providing you with something neutral (the movie) to talk about afterward. But the downside of the movies is that you really don't get to know each other. You're spending two hours paying attention to the film instead of showing off who you are. It's time to come up with something a little more creative—especially in the beginning, when you don't know each other well.

The other most popular date is "getting something to eat." By going out for dinner, you have the opportunity to talk and get to know each other a little better, while you can still have the safety of the distraction of selecting and eating the food, and talking to the waiter. I certainly can't knock this as a suggestion. But the downside of going out to dinner on a first date is that you are put on the spot: You're facing each other and being forced to talk. If you are anxious about making small talk, this may not be the best place for you to start. As with the movies, you might do well to consider something a little more creative for your first date. Get the best of both possible worlds by doing some activity besides eating.

Another popular first date is "going out for drinks." Many people use alcohol to ease their inhibitions, so drinking becomes a way to ease those first-date anxieties about relating to a relative stranger. Consider, however, that it would be better for you to face the situation of your date without any crutch, following the principle that if you are liked for truly who you are, then the relationship has a much better chance of progressing. Also consider whether being in a bar with singles trying to meet each other would stimulate any memories that would subliminally make you uncomfortable or distract your attention.

New Ideas for the First Date

Keep in mind the purposes of a first date. You want to learn about each other, but you may also want to minimize too much intensity, to ease your anxieties. So while you might want to be alone to some extent, you might not want too much aloneness. That means you might not want to go to a party where there are lots of singles. You also might not want to put your date in too-personal a setting too soon, like meeting your parents or going to a family function.

If you already know that you really want to be together, then anywhere you go is fine. Whatever you share, you will have a good time. But in case you're at a loss for what to do, here are some suggestions:

➤ A picnic in the park

➤ A visit to a museum for a special exhibit

➤ A matinee or evening performance of a play

➤ A live concert in the park on a Sunday afternoon, or a nighttime music club or concert by your favorite band

➤ A ballet

➤ An afternoon trip to an amusement park or a zoo

➤ A walk along the beach, a pier, or any waterfront promenade

➤ Any sport you can do together, such as shooting pool, bowling, or playing golf or tennis. Other sports (such as skiing) involve more time and more complicated preparations, so save these for future dates)

➤ A barbecue in your backyard

➤ An afternoon parade

➤ A street fair

➤ A walk along a boardwalk or through a local marketplace with food stands and shopping stalls (like the Pikes Market in Seattle or the pier in New Orleans)

➤ An arts and crafts festival

➤ A walk with your dog

➤ A flower show or arboretum

➤ A visit to a pier or promenade (The well-known Santa Monica Pier in Los Angeles has booths as well as constant open-air events, like dance festivals.)

Smooth Talk'n

A friend of mine, Matt Feinberg, New York musician and advertising executive, recommends cooking for a woman on a date. He loves to do it because, being "not a guy who's used to dating," it gives him a chance to feel at ease, be creative, be comfortable in his own surroundings, and make her feel good by showing that he cares about doing something to please her. Not only that, it's economical since eating out is so expensive! Women also get impressed by a man who can cook and do the dishes.

Smooth Talk'n

Some men and women are afraid to invite someone to an event (such as a friend's birthday party) for fear the other person won't enjoy it. If you get such an invitation, a great reassuring response would be, "It doesn't matter what we do, as long as we're together."

➤ A walk with a purpose—like to observe local architecture

➤ A toy-shopping excursion to shop for a child

➤ A shopping excursion to help you pick out something you need that might be an interesting experience for them, too (a tennis racket, backyard furniture, a new stereo set or computer)

➤ A buggy ride through a local park

➤ A city-wide festival at the local fairgrounds, such as Renaissance Fairs held in many cities around the country

➤ A comedy club (Remember that laughter not only physiologically turns you on, but it psychologically brings out the best in you. After all, you're having fun, and having fun together is intoxicating.)

Smooth Talk'n

One of my favorite suggestions for where to go (thanks to Jenn Shreve who wrote about her 20 blind dates for *Egg* magazine) is to decide what you have always wanted to see or do—be it bowling or that cool new cyberbar.

➤ A karoake bar (Though a "thing" of the '90s, karoake bars are still fun. The experience of singing together, even if you're out of tune, can bring you close together.)

➤ A coffee shop (These are becoming more "in" and provide a comfortable atmosphere to relax and get to know each other.) Since coffee can activate your body physically (setting off adrenaline and other body sensations), it can also stimulate your love interest.

➤ A night on the town (Get dressed up formally in a tux or gown, and rent a limo to take you to various nightspots. The experience of getting all decked out will put you in a fun, sexy mood.)

Dating Data

Health club consultants, like Kevin Miri of the New York Health and Racquet Club, attest that singles are more serious these days about their workouts than "picking anyone up." But making a date to work out together not only activates you physically and mentally, but gives you a chance to do something healthy together without being dolled up—and it's a good test of confidence and trust.

Being Creative

Coming up with something interesting to do has a lot of benefits. It can add excitement to your first date, simply because it's new for either or both of you. It can also show how much fun you can be, and it can set the stage for a good time, no matter what your feelings about each other turn out to be.

Be as creative as you can in coming up with new ideas. Think about what would be different for you. What have you always wanted to do but didn't want to do on your own? Ask friends for inspiration, or look at newspapers and magazines for ideas about what's going on around town.

Consider these unusual ideas for the first date:

➤ An experimental theater troupe's performance

➤ A yoga class

➤ An afternoon at a health club, working out together, playing racquetball, or taking an exercise class

➤ Sky-diving, hang-gliding, ballooning, or bungee-jumping (for the more daring)

➤ A helicopter ride

➤ A hike

➤ Horseback-riding or bike-riding

➤ Skating or roller-blading

➤ A ferry ride or boat cruise (either in the afternoon or evening) that goes around the city

➤ A trip to a more unusual museum, such as a geological or science museum

➤ A rodeo

➤ A dog, cat, or horse show

➤ An exhibition (gift show, car show) at a civic or convention center

Smooth Talk'n

To make the first date as casual, non-threatening, and non-anxiety provoking as possible, think of going somewhere public. You can always look at the other people instead of just at each other—or talk about them!

Smooth Talk'n

If you can't come up with a suggestion that's at least interesting and engaging, admit confusion ("I'm not sure now what we should do, but I'd love to hear your suggestions") or be provocative ("What's the most interesting thing you've ever heard of?").

153

Know Where You're Going and How You're Getting There

Some dates can be fun when they are totally spontaneous and full of surprise. But the first date is better when the basics are planned—the surprises can come from your interaction and relationship rather than the arrangements. Be prepared about the particulars:

➤ How you are getting to your destination (taxi, bus, train, your own car, car service)

➤ How much time it will take (you want to arrive on time)

➤ What passes, tickets, or identification are necessary (Nothing was more annoying on his first date with Courtney than when Paul forgot to tell her that they were going across the border from Detroit into Windsor, Canada to a club. As it turns out, Courtney needed at least her driver's license to show the border guards. Not knowing this, she didn't bring proper ID, and they had to turn around and change their plans.)

Bringing Gifts

Tokens on the first date are a nice touch, as long as you don't go overboard (too big, too expensive) and look like you're over-anxious to please. Flowers, some small token you know a person would like (a favorite CD), or something associated to what you're about to do on your date (a can of tennis balls) are appropriate.

Dating Dos

Finally! It's time for your date. Here are some tips to help things run smoothly:

➤ DO feel confident.

➤ DO look your best.

➤ DO smile.

➤ DO address your date by name frequently.

➤ DO compliment your date.

➤ DO listen attentively and repeat things your date says.

➤ DO be honest about whether you're interested in seeing the person again. If you're not, the aftermath will be more painful; if you are honest, the positive feedback will be more pleasurable.

Dating Don'ts

Keep in mind these tips to help avoid disastrous dates:

➤ DON'T put yourself in uncomfortable situations (such as ordering messy food—unless you're into an erotic feeding scene, like from the movie *9¹/₂ Weeks*).

➤ DON'T suggest overly expensive places or events for a first date unless you clarify who's paying.

➤ DON'T look at other women/men.

➤ DON'T monopolize the conversation.

➤ DON'T lie about anything (for example, your marital status or your financial situation).

➤ DON'T talk about your ex-relationships.

➤ DON'T become too intoxicated (unless it's with each other).

➤ DON'T make sexual approaches too quickly or insistently—send out vibes and wait for a welcome response.

Being a Good Conversationalist

The art of conversation involves having the confidence to speak freely about whatever comes to your mind (without self-consciousness or second-guessing yourself), but also in a manner that engages the other person to be interested in what you are saying and feel like you are interested in them as well.

Check out Chapter 15 to determine what type of talkers you and your date are (so you do not have unrealistic expectations), and so you can look over some guidelines on good communication. These include: getting to the point (instead of rambling), being open to answering questions, and listening without interrupting.

Your conversation can cover many types of topics, such as these:

➤ Talk about current events or news. For example, if you or the other person likes movies, have a story ready about a new release or the latest on a film star (Pam clinched Charles's interest when she talked about Japanese producer Kurasawa's death). Sports lovers can talk excitedly about the latest baseball records (if anyone's close to McGwire or Sosa's homers). Conspiracy theories about Princess Diana's death can stimulate analytic minds.

➤ Use compliments. Notice—and make a positive comment about—your date's looks (such as eyes or hair), actions (a gesture), expressions, or experiences. Jody was swept away when she slid into the booth at the restaurant and Geoffrey immediately noticed her unusual nail polish!

Smooth Talk'n

Keep notes in your daybook or computer about story clippings and interesting topics you can discuss. Practice by saying them in a mirror or tape recorder, speaking aloud in the shower, or telling a friend.

➤ Ask a question. You might ask, "Where do you work out?" or, "Where's your favorite restaurant?"

➤ Tell an interesting story about what you have done recently. You might have visited the White House or learned a new sport.

➤ Talk about the moment. Tell how you feel about where you are and what you are doing. For example, you might say, "I'm excited to meet you," "I love industrial decor of bistros like this," or "This is my first calm moment after such a crazy day."

Some people seem to be born conversationalists or good talkers. But most people have to learn the skill by practice, getting a sense of what makes other people respond positively. Here are some tips to help you be engaging on your date:

➤ Talk about subjects that are meaningful to you (from cooking to volunteering at a soup kitchen) so the other person can sense your passion.

➤ Choose a subject that can lead to an engaging conversation (like your favorite movies, foods, travel destinations).

➤ Talk about things initially that are positive rather than what makes you mad, so your date will not think you are a complainer.

➤ Use words that are descriptive and rich in imagery (say "sparkling emerald" rather than just "green").

➤ Avoid slang and worn-out clichés ("you know," "like," "uh") that may be a habit but that are boring to hear and don't flatter you.

➤ Be provocative. Ask, "What's your dream for what you would most like to happen?" or "What do you think about the current controversy in the news about…" Or, talk about "My scariest experience growing up…"

➤ Make connections from one subject to another. Use the psychological technique of free association: What does one subject make you think of? For example, if you start with the conspiracy theory of Princess Diana's death, then you can connect this to the movie *Conspiracy Theory*—with Mel Gibson and Julia Roberts, and from there talk about other Mel Gibson movies you enjoyed, such as *Mad Max* and how many sequels you've seen.

➤ Keep yourself as informed and diverse as possible. Keep track of the news so you can talk intelligently about major developments in politics (wars in other parts of the world), economics (drops or rises in the stock market), sports (what season it is for which sport, major players (such as Tiger Woods and Michael Jordan), and entertainment (current movie releases, plays, concerts).

➤ Be surprising. Out of the blue you can interject into the conversation, "Oh, the Czechoslovakian President said in a news conference this afternoon that a poor Russia is better than a rich Soviet Union."

➤ Develop the conversation. For example, if you start out with this statement about Russia (the fact), build on it by saying something like, "I thought that was fascinating" (your feeling). Then expand on that with an explanation, such as, "It was, of course, a statement about preferring democracy to communism," and then follow-up with an engaging question, such as, "Would you ever like to go to Russia?"

➤ Make statements and ask open-ended questions to get beyond just "yes" or "no." For example, ask "What is your favorite food?" instead of asking, "Do you like Italian food?"

PASSÉ: Being afraid to say anything out of fear you'll sound silly, stupid, or foolish.

IN THE NEW MILLENNIUM: Saying anything that comes to your mind, however it comes out of your mouth, without intentionally hurting the other person's feelings, of course. That shows confidence about who you are. Get in touch with your intuition. If it sounds strange to you, say so.

PASSÉ: Being too humble. Holding back saying nice things about yourself.

IN THE NEW MILLENNIUM: Don't be afraid to toot your own horn. Hopefully you'll be appreciated and your date will see your fine points without you having to point them out. But you might as well do just that—point them out. I don't mean that you should be a braggart or give yourself false compliments, but do say nice things about yourself. Talk about your successes and what you've done that you're proud of. Not only might your date be impressed, but he'll see your self-esteem, which will only cycle toward making you feel even better about yourself.

PASSÉ: Being afraid to tell a joke because you're not good at it.

IN THE NEW MILLENNIUM: Remember, I said humor is a most attractive quality. Punctuate your conversation with a joke. Even if you're not good at joke-telling, you can likely remember and practice telling at least one. Or say, "I'm not great at joke telling, so roll with me on this . . ."

Smooth Talk'n

Pose brain-teasers. Example: A baby fell out of a 20-story building and didn't get hurt. Why not? (Because it only fell out of the first-floor window. I didn't say it had to fall out of the 20th floor, only that the building was that high.)

The Pitfalls of Conversation

You might be good at small talk, but still face certain pitfalls. To refine your technique and really be good at capturing—and keeping—someone's attention, keep in mind the following.

Rambling

Have you ever been in a conversation with someone and you feel like you can put down the phone, or even walk away, and they would still be talking and wouldn't know the difference? That happens when you feel you are being talked "at" instead of being talked "with." Talking "at" people comes from chattering on about yourself without being connected to the person who is listening. They key is to engage the other person in what you are saying so she feels involved. You can prevent doing this with certain techniques:

➤ Hesitate while you are talking to give your date space to jump in and react.

➤ Stop after talking awhile and ask a question that involves your date. You can ask for his opinion ("What do you think about that?") or her understanding ("Do you know what I mean?") or empathy ("Can you imagine how that feels?"). If you are ready to turn the attention to your date, you can ask about a related experience ("Has anything like that ever happened to you?").

➤ Use your date's name every now and then to let her know you know to whom you are talking.

➤ Tune in to yourself. If you ever get the sense that you are rambling on and on and that your voice is droning, stop talking and give the other person a chance to speak.

➤ Ask for feedback. Ask directly if he is interested in whatever you are talking about, or if he wants to change the subject.

➤ Avoid talking endlessly and hogging the conversation. Instead, toss the ball to your date, eliciting a response and listening attentively. If you have a tendency to go on and on, develop a sense of timing, or purposefully set a limit for yourself. Sound bites (a quote from a person) on a network news show can be as short as eight seconds. A talk show host usually will let a person have his say for no more than two minutes before making some other comment—no matter how interesting the information. A late-night comic's routine may go for three minutes, but it is punctuated with audience responses. As a radio professional, I know it is best to make a point in only up to a minute. Even President Clinton's radio address in the Oval Office was under five minutes because he noticed that stations carried his report only when it ran that short length of time. Especially in the age of MTV-quick images, the average attention span has shortened, so make your point quickly and clearly.

Getting Over the "I Don't Know" Block

Avoid falling into the "I don't know" syndrome. This is one of my big rules about dating. Not only does it sound boring to say you don't know, but it is never true. Whenever someone is telling me about a date and answers a question of mine with "I don't know," I refuse to accept that as an answer and encourage them to come up with any suggestion or response. And guess what, they always can! So, you *do* know something, and that makes you a much more interesting person.

Try it. Imagine your new love interest asking, "Where do you want to go for dinner?" or "What movie would you like to see?" Imagine first answering "I don't know," then cancel that answer, think a minute, and come up with a suggestion. Any suggestion is better than none. Now imagine the most common question asked on the phone or in a greeting, "How's it going?" or "What's going on?" A common answer is "Nothing." But of course, that is never true! There is always something going on. Saying "nothing" is counterproductive; you risk being judged as a bore, and it stops the flow of conversation. What can someone say after that? Instead, you have so many choices of things to say. You just need the confidence to be able to say anything that comes to you. Then you can talk about something you are doing at that moment, something interesting you did that week, or a feeling that you have.

Touchy and Taboo Topics

Be as natural as you can in saying what you want to say. Second-guessing what the other person wants to hear, and being self-conscious about what you say only makes you come across stilted and unnatural. But a few topics are best to avoid on your first date:

➤ Obviously, noticing other attractive people and pointing them out. This only makes the other person feel insecure.

➤ Talking about your opposite-sex friends too much. This stimulates insecurity and jealousy.

➤ Talking about previous dating successes or horrors. This also stimulates jealousy and puts attention on the relationship with other people instead of what is happening between the two of you.

➤ Subjects about which people are very opinionated. This can be provocative but risky, in case your date is easy to judge and not easily accepting of opposing points of view. Topics that are known to touch off such fervor include capital punishment, gun control, abortion, and homosexuality.

➤ Sex. Launching into talk about sex too early can raise all kinds of anxieties and confusion ("Is he coming on to me?" "Does she always get sexy with guys on the first date?"). If you cannot resist talking about a sexual topic, stick to current events and generalizations about opinions without being too personal ("What do you think about the new morning-after pill—will it make men refuse to use condoms?" or "Do you think they should have rejected that sex-education bill?").

159

➤ Morbid topics are a risk but can be engaging, depending on the other person's interests. For example, I have cared deeply about the Jon Benet murder case (the six-year-old beauty queen found strangled in the basement of her home). I can bring up this subject with others but need to be sensitive about whether they are disinterested or find the subject too depressing to talk about.

Show and Tell

A picture is worth a thousand words. So, besides just talking, think of taking along things to show your date, to illustrate what you're up to, or something interesting that you're into. For example: a newspaper article about you or whatever you're interested in, an award you won, a gift you got from your mother, a photo of your latest vacation.

Who Pays

In this day and age, decisions about who pays for what have become more complicated than in previous dating ages, when the rules were clearer. Up until the '70s, the man usually paid for everything. As more women went to work and the women's liberation movement demanded equality, it became more common for couples to "go Dutch," where the man and woman would share paying. In more modern times, the woman can now pay for the whole date! With these changes, it is even more important than ever to be clear about who will pay for what.

Smooth Talk'n

Even if he earns more than she, she should offer to pay sometimes—he may decline, but will appreciate her offer. Then she can surprise him with something she has pre-paid for.

Here are some guidelines to follow about who pays:

➤ Whoever invites the other person out will pay for the date. If he asks her to go out for dinner, he pays. If she invites him to go to a concert, she gets the tickets.

➤ Whoever has more money might pull more weight paying.

➤ Whoever doesn't pay can offer to contribute— and should be prepared to follow through with the offer if accepted, without being angry or resentful.

Whoever pays should be prepared for whatever the costs of the evening will be—and then some. Bring cash and credit cards (if you have them) to cover whatever you expect to pay, with some added "emergency" money in case something else comes up or some vendors accept some form of compensation other than what you expected. Even if you are being "treated," be prepared to take care of emergencies (as in, he loses his money, you have a fight, and you have to get home on your own steam).

Dating Data

Old attitudes can die hard: Be aware of how they affect your dating. Even though women are expected to contribute more to the financial aspects of dating, some may still resent it, thinking they should "be taken care of" and "treated." And men may still operate with the belief that "I pay, she plays," expecting that sex is payback for paying for the date.

What Works and What Doesn't for Women: E! TV

I recently did a number of really successful TV specials for E! Entertainment TV on "What Women Want." All the experts and real women interviewed agreed with all the advice in this book! One of the shows covered the stories of women who used a dating service for dates. It was fun to follow them through the first contact and see what happened on the first date. After the date, I conducted a group session with the men and women together, to tell what they liked or didn't like about each other—a rare opportunity for feedback, because it rarely happens that you really say what's on your mind after the date!

In the show, we addressed all the issues throughout all the chapters in this book—and particularly those in this chapter.

All three women profiled on the show put a lot of effort into preparing for the date (deciding what to wear, processing past experiences about disappointments). They all formed initial impressions of the men based on the first contact on the telephone about whether the man would be a good conversationalist. One woman was quite predisposed to her date because his voice sounded so resonant and sexy (even though she wasn't crazy about him when they met), which shows how you can score initially but still strike out when you meet face to face when chemistry and other factors play a role.

The women were very clear beforehand about what turned them on or off. Nice hands were a turn-on to one; dirty fingernails were a sure turn-off to another.

The women reviewed their worst dates. For all, too-soon sexual approaches were a real turn-off. Kelly remembered one date where, "When I said no sex, he wanted me to pay." On another traumatic date, she recalled, "I was in his bathroom and it was dirty and there was no toilet paper, and I came out and he was spread on the bed on black silk sheets, in just red underpants. No way. Ugh." Kristen recounted her dating horror, "He grabbed me, was in my face, stuck his tongue down my throat, and said, 'Come on, you can do better than this.'"

What Works and What Doesn't for Men: E! TV

No matter how much you may not like to hear that it's still the case, what a woman looks like still captures a guy's attention! But the good news is that guys these days don't *say* that looks matter most to them. I've certainly found that true in my surveys—and it was true when I worked with E! Entertainment on the special "What Men Want" (a follow-up to the shows we did on "What Women Want"). Three guys were selected (for their charm, good looks, and age) to go on a vacation to Cancun, while the cameras followed them on their escapades meeting women. Dan is a 34-year-old musician and audio engineer with bleached-blond, funky hair who has been divorced for five years; Francisco is a 27-year old-snowboard instructor; and the youngest, at 23, is Matt, a tall, dark-haired writer.

What attracts them? They all echoed honesty, passion, and good communication. Francisco explained further, "I look for some sort of brain first, some kind of pulse, somebody who can hold a conversation and have some interests that I have. And then from there, hopefully she's good looking and funny." Dan added, "I like a woman who can dance, so I see she can move physically." (I agree—watch how a date moves and you can tell how confident and free they will be as a lover.) And Matt wants "a good heart and good morals, money and having a career and all those things in line, who is strong and takes care of herself."

What turns them on? Eye contact and a smile won hand over foot—as you might expect and as I always find in surveys. Turn-offs: being drunk, smoking, rudeness, embarrassing him, too many tattoos, and not laughing at his jokes.

Casual sex is not politically correct these days, but you all know some people still do it. Some guys say they will still judge a girl "easy" if she does it, or worry she'll do it with another guy. Others will go with it "when the feeling's right." But the biggest surprise with the three guys for this show was that they all *said* that sex on the first date was not a good idea ("except maybe on a vacation when everything is accelerated!").

Matt's "date" one night didn't show, prompting the guys to share that rejection hurts, but you gotta get over it quickly by throwing yourself into doing something that occupies you, and hopefully that's fun. I found Dan's rule most intriguing: You can't be friends until six months after you've broken up—to give her time to cool her emotional attachment.

The whole show corroborated the basic point of this book: Guys don't want to play games! They want to be liked for themselves, and they want a woman to be

Home Alone

Getting drunk always led to dating disasters for the men in the E! Entertainment TV show. One New Year's Eve Dan remembers looking forward to his big chance with a girl, with everything going well until he passed out, finding out from her the next morning that his tongue (and other things?) went limp in the middle of the kiss. Francisco remembers one date when the girl had so many shots, she went in the bathroom and passed out on the floor.

herself! They want a woman they can be comfortable with, and who has her own life (not clinging on to his).

To Kiss or Not to Kiss

Blatant sexual advances too early in the game—especially if they are unwanted—are real turn-offs to most men as well as women. You must be really sensitive about reading a person's openness to being intimate at all when it comes to dating: Even a kiss can be a major step.

Before you get to the kiss, you must establish whether the person wants to be touched. This is easy to tell, by reading body language. Crossed arms, standing away from you, or retreating whenever you make an advance (to hold his hand or put your arm around her) is a sure sign to back off. A green light about welcoming any physical contact would include responding if you make a physical contact of any kind (holding your hand tightly, touching your shoulder, putting an arm around you, too).

Of course, if the sparks are really flying between you, planting a surprise kiss or melting into a kiss after looking into each other's eyes will be the most natural thing, and you will not need to think about it. But if that does not happen, test responsiveness to physical contact by making a small gesture (kissing her hand) and seeing whether she smiles (a "yes") or pulls her hand away, frowns, or looks uncomfortable (a "no"). Try a hug and test the same responsiveness. Then, build up to a kiss on the lips by first kissing her neck, and then moving closer to her lips.

The kind of kiss will also depend on your instant attraction and passion. You will dive more into it wantonly if the intensity has already been built before you even touch. Otherwise, you might want to be more romantic and seductive, by kissing very lightly on the side of the mouth and building toward more direct lip contact and more openness. You will be able to tell if there is electricity between you to go further.

Dating Data

Always be aware that singles are sensitive to where a kiss is leading, as well as how far to go, and what the other person expects. Both of you might be more cautious about making advances—not because you aren't interested in each other, but because you are being responsible in this day and age to avoid casual sex and sexually transmitted diseases from even casual sexual contact like kissing. Never kiss if either of you has a cold sore; oral herpes is very contagious.

How To Tell If S/he's Interested

Besides gauging your own interest in another meeting, you of course want to know whether the other person is receptive. The best way to know is to ask for the next date and see if the response is positive, but signs on your first encounter can give you an idea of how much your date enjoyed being with you and whether she or he would like another encounter. Here are some of the signs:

➤ Smiling at you often

➤ Inviting body language—making the same motions as you do (called "mirroring," such as putting hand to chin when you do) and assuming "open" positions (such as facing toward you, with arms not crossed)

➤ Making some contact (holding hands, touching your cheek, or putting an arm around you)

➤ Making reference to a future time together, or responding positively to references you make to future encounters (such as "It would be nice to do that together")

➤ Maintaining lots of eye contact

➤ Being interested in the conversation and keeping it going

➤ Trying to find common topics for conversation

➤ Seeming energetic and enthusiastic about you, about what you say, and about what you are doing together

➤ Complimenting you

➤ Moving close to you (for example, sitting on the same side as you in the restaurant)

➤ Hugging with comfortable body contact; drawing you close

Smooth Talk'n

Figure out what your date needs, and show that you "get" them. For example, instead of just laughing at his joke, you say, "You're so funny," thereby acknowledging what he really wanted to project about himself—that he's funny.

Of course, the opposite of these would indicate more of a yellow light about further contact. These warning signals indicate that things did not go well:

➤ Wanting to end the date earlier than planned

➤ Making no references to the future

➤ Returning non-enthusiastic responses to any mentions you make of future contacts

➤ Showing little eye or body contact

➤ Displaying restrained body language that closes off contact (such as crossed arms and legs, turning away, or hands over mouth or eyes)

➤ Showing little interest in what you are saying, and engaging in restricted conversation beyond shyness

➤ Mentioning other relationships, indicating a desire to set up an excuse about having another boyfriend or girlfriend

➤ Making references to being busy, having many commitments, or not being interested in having a relationship (as a preparation for turning down further dates)

➤ Being preoccupied with other things, such as fumbling with keys, primping, looking away when it comes time to get into the car, or parting at the door (times when some intimate contact could take place)

Home Alone

People just getting to know each other can repeat themselves, but they do not like to be reminded about that faux pas. If he tells you something you heard before, react or respond to another aspect of it.

Six Signs You Might Not Want to Go to Date Number Two

1. He tells you he hates germs and sleeps in a hyperbaric chamber like Michael Jackson.

2. Sucking peas in your nostrils didn't go over too well, especially after they fell out with boogers on them.

3. When you twisted your spaghetti on your fork, it spritzed all over her white see-through blouse.

4. He told you he's worth millions of dollars, but he doesn't have cash for the coat check or valet because his mother handles all his money.

5. He tells you he's dated models and actresses all his life—and you work for a bank.

6. He goes to kiss you and saliva drools down his chin.

How to End the Date

Define the amount of time of the date beforehand because you don't know how the first date will turn out or how much you will like each other. That means you should say ahead of time what time you want to be home, so it doesn't cause any anxiety during the date. Doing so gives you an easy out if you are not having a good time, without either of you having to come up with some lame excuse or feeling hurt or rejected. And if you are really having a good time, you can always extend the time.

If you haven't had such a good time and you really don't want to see the other person again, be sensitive and cautious—and be honest (but not brutally so). Everyone wants to be appreciated—and everyone is sensitive to rejection—so in ending the date, follow these suggestions:

➤ Always say something nice about what you have enjoyed about the person's company and what you have done together.

➤ Add something about it being time to get home because it's late, or because you have a long drive or something to do in the morning.

Smooth Talk'n

Ending the date early always runs the risk of hurting the other person's feelings. Avoid this, if you can, by always looking for some way that you can enjoy whatever is happening and make it interesting for you, whether or not you plan to ever see each other again. If, of course, being together is insufferable, give yourself permission to end it. Do this in a way that minimizes hurting the other person. Without being dishonest, say something like, "I'm having a good time, but I did have a more trying day than I expected, and I have to get up early tomorrow morning, so I hope you don't mind if we turn in a little earlier than we planned."

➤ Point out the differences between you, your lifestyles, or your interests that will make the other person equally see that you are not a great match.

➤ Mention how you are really going to be busy—for the next few months. Emphasizing the long-term will be a dead give-away that you are not anxious for another rendezvous.

If you have both had a good time, the end of the date can be much easier than if you are not sure about each other. But you still might be a little awkward about what to say. My best advice is to be honest. Remember my basic principle about dating: Be yourself and don't play games. That means if you really had a good time, don't be afraid to say so, for fear that you will expose yourself or not be "cool." Be as warm and enthusiastic as you feel. Say openly:

➤ "I had a great time."

➤ "I'd love to see you again."

➤ "Let's do it again soon."

If you have to hold back, or if she doesn't respond positively to your natural reaction, this does not bode well for her accepting you throughout the future of your relationship.

If you had a decent time but are not massively enthusiastic about getting together again, then find something nice to say anyway about your time together, without making any references to getting together again. Let some time pass after the date for the experience to percolate in your unconscious, and for you to either think about the person and feel you would like to call again, or for the impulse and the thought to not cross your mind, giving you a sign that you are really not that interested after all.

Smooth Talk'n

Leave an interesting message on your own answering machine. Ask a question or report a news fact. Change it often, to keep it fresh.

"I'll Call You/E-Mail You/Beep You"

When you're saying good-bye, there is always that awkward moment about whether you will say something about seeing each other again. Because I am a fan of honesty and don't believe in misleading someone by setting up false expectations, I'll suggest that you avoid saying, "I'll call you" if you know you are not going to do that. Nothing is more miserable than leading someone on and having them wait by the phone for your call that will never come. Convince yourself that it is better to leave someone disappointed about not hearing that promise than making a false promise.

After the Big Date

Okay, you cleared the first big hurdle. The first date is over. You can breathe easier now. So how did it go? Do you think you've met the person of your dreams, or someone you'd rather just keep as a friend, or, worse, a dud or a jerk you never want to see again? No matter how a date goes, I'm a big believer in grace after dates. That is, after the date, always call and thank the person for going, whether it worked out or not. Emily received a call from her blind date who said, "I had a nice time with you, but I don't think it's going to work out between us." As much as it hurt her to hear this, Emily knew herself that it wasn't going anywhere, and she appreciated the acknowledgment and the closure his phone call gave her.

Smooth Talk'n

Write down key phrases that he says (you can use the introduction cards at the front of this book) so that you can repeat them back to him when you next talk—everyone loves to be "known" and remembered. For example, Jeff greatly impressed Annie the next time they talked by asking "How's your grandmother?" showing he had heard her mention, in their last conversation, visiting the hospital to see her.

Dating Data

A woman usually expects to hear from a man the day after a date. Men, on the other hand, usually make contact days—or even a few weeks—later. I recommend calling the day after the date—or at least within three days—whether it's to just say thank you or to indicate further interest. If she cares, she'll be happy to hear from him soon (knowing she's on his mind), and if she doesn't care, there's nothing lost.

Ways to Stay in Touch

There are more ways to keep in contact these days than years ago, when the telephone was the only method. Now, you can e-mail, call people via cell phone, or beep people or leave both numeric or voice messages on their pager. Consider how available you want to be by hooking yourself up to all these potential modes of contact. Become aware of all the ways your new date can be contacted so you can decide on the best way to do so.

Even if you are enthusiastic about your date, keep cool. Too much contact (as in flooding her with e-mails, expensive cell phone calls, and pages five times a day) can be annoying and reveal your desperation (a big turn-off). After the post-date thank-you via one of the methods of electronic communication, wait a few days before another contact. Even then, avoid a barrage of approaches. Slow and steady more likely wins the race. There is plenty of time for those luscious, romantic five talks a day, once you both find you want to speak to each other that often.

Get to know the person's daily habits (when he has free time at work, what time she goes to sleep) so you can make contact at available—and not inappropriate or inopportune—times.

Smooth Talk'n

If you are really excited about your date, or if you're troubled, review what happened in your mind. Write it down so you can go over it another time. Or call a good friend you trust for some feedback or advice.

Next-Day Thoughts

After the date, you will invariably have thoughts about how it went. Hopefully you will feel peaceful and satisfied. That's the best sign that things went well and you felt good about yourself and your date. But often, the next day you may find yourself "Monday morning quarter-backing" in a critical review about what you did or said, wishing you had done something differently. Stop these obsessive thoughts by realizing that whatever happened was right to happen, and that if you want to do something differently and the relationship has a chance, you will get another shot at it on the next date(s).

Whether It's Going Anywhere

Now that you got over the hurdle of the first date, it's time to think about whether you are going to go another round and ask for the second date. Again, don't think about it as a formal date. Think about making more time to spend together.

To decide about the next meeting, ask yourself the following questions:

➤ Did we enjoy each other's company?

➤ Did the energy seem to flow? Remember, I talked about energetics in the introduction to this book. By just focusing on your gut, did things seem to go naturally between you, without much effort or "work"?

➤ Consider your time and attention a precious gift. I know this sounds dramatic, but what if you considered that this was the last date you were going to have in a long time (I don't even mean that you would die tomorrow, but that you would be so tied up with work or school that you'd have no time for fun). If so, would you really want to spend that time with this person?

Another Chance

While first impressions do determine how we feel about someone—and even though I've said you should consider your time, energy, and attention precious and not to waste them—there is a point to giving someone another chance. The first date may have been really good, but he may have been on his best behavior. More dates are necessary before you really know someone and can truly judge how he responds to you and other situations. Or, the first encounter may have been a disaster because she was nervous or the situation was unfavorable (such as rain, missed timing, a canceled event) so they deserve another chance.

Playing Games

People play games to protect themselves from being hurt. Some self-help books and articles suggest that people play games to create mystery and keep a partner guessing. You're beginning to know by now why I don't subscribe to this theory. If you play games, then a game-player is what you'll attract, and neither person will be open about their intentions. Eventually the game will break down, and your true self will emerge.

Accept whatever happened on the date, good or bad, by not making it into such a big deal. Resist over-dramatizing that it was either great or terrible and, therefore, that dating is a lost cause. Instead, think about it as a learning experience.

Smooth Talk'n

Start your relationship on an honest foot by playing it straight—act and say exactly what you feel. Remember, honesty is a key ingredient to long-lasting relationships.

The Least You Need to Know

➤ Do something that would be fun and comfortable for both of you, taking into account interests, degree of intimacy, and available time.

➤ Be creative about where to go.

➤ When getting ready, do whatever you can to make yourself feel as good about yourself as possible, to build your own confidence.

➤ Be honest about your feelings about how the date went and your interest in each other, making sure not to lead the person on.

➤ Women as well as men should take the initiative in dating.

➤ Always thank the other person for the date.

➤ The initial phases of dating take time and effort and cause anxiety, but hang in there. Your efforts will eventually pay off!

Chapter 12

The Second Date and Beyond

In This Chapter

➤ Where to go on date number two

➤ Deciding whether this is going anywhere

➤ When you become "boyfriend" and "girlfriend"

➤ Bearing gifts

➤ Open house and stay-overs

➤ What to do after the date

Hopefully the first date worked and you both think you would like to see each other again. Be prepared that the same anxieties will arise about the second date as you faced on your first go-round, including making decisions about where to go and what to say. In fact, these anxieties may escalate because the stakes have increased—after all, now you feel more interested in the person and have more fears about whether it will work.

To prevent these anxieties from building, continue to remind yourselves that you are not "dating" as a formal declaration of a relationship, or permanent interest, or commitment to a future together—you're merely expressing an interest in sharing another experience together. This is the time to really condition yourself into thinking of dating as "hanging out" so you will feel more at ease about making the advance to the next stage.

As each date progresses, you have more of an opportunity to learn about each other and make those decisions about whether you can spend lots more time—and maybe the rest of your life—together. But take it step-by-step. In other words, let things flow. Instead of worrying, trust your gut. See if your mind naturally flows to thinking about the person, wondering how he or she is, and wanting to share what you're doing with him or her.

Asking for the Date

Follow all the same tips as with the first date when it comes to asking for the next get-together—only up the ante a little. On the first encounter you might want to be a little short and sweet. Later you can be a little more detailed and friendly, with longer messages on the answering machine ("I have a great joke to tell you," or "The most amazing thing happened today, and I can't wait to tell you about it"). You can also be more personal ("I hope you're having a great day," or "How was your meeting?").

If you have to leave a message, be clear about when you will call again. It is better for you to say *you* will call again later rather than saying "Call me back"—you might not want to risk wondering why she didn't call back. One of the worst parts of dating is the uncertainty of not knowing if you did something wrong, so you want to do whatever you can to minimize those fears and confusions.

Smooth Talk'n

Remember that practically nothing captures a person's heart more than knowing that they were "heard." So, if she told you about her mother being ill, ask how she is. If he told you he has a major report due at work, ask him how it went.

Always start out the conversation with a comment about your last encounter. A compliment always sets people in a good mood and makes them more receptive to you. You could refer to the new wine you tried, or the funny joke she told you that you then told a friend, or how you saw a painting with that beautiful cobalt blue color of the sweater she was wearing.

Preface your invitation with the fun you will have ("It'll be really fun to . . ." or "I know you'll enjoy . . .").

Keep some topics in the back of your mind for when you want to change the subject and keep the conversation moving, and remember to use the three-step approach outlined in Chapter 11.

Second Date and Beyond: Where to Go and What to Do

Where you go on subsequent dates, and what you do, should all be a natural evolution of the basic principle of dating: getting a sense of each other and how you both approach life. After all, if this relationship really develops into a long-term one—or even marriage—you will be spending a lot of time, doing many things, and taking care of many responsibilities together. Therefore, think of various situations that would reveal how you are. For example, consider the following:

➤ Vary who you're with. You will want to spend time alone, one-on-one, to see how well you can relate to just each other, but also with other types of people (friends, co-workers, family), to see how you each relate and get along with others.

➤ Vary what you do. You will want to plan some activities, but you will also want to spend unstructured time together, to see how you can entertain yourselves without any specific activities to occupy or distract you, and also to see how you make decisions together.

➤ Vary the places you go together. Spend time together at home, to see how you can adapt to a homey situation together, but also plan some outside social activities, such as at a bowling alley or putting green.

➤ Vary the times you are together. Meet in the morning, afternoon, and evening to get a sense of which is the best time for each of you. All of us have preferences for the time we are most awake or alert.

➤ Be indoors (at a museum or concert) as well as outdoors (a picnic or beach).

➤ Include social activities, but also some activities that are mundane. As a relationship develops, people have to take care of simple daily tasks, such as shopping and chores. See how well you adapt to doing these together. Drop off a deposit in the bank machine, or stop into an all-night drug store for that shampoo you ran out of. Ask her to help you buy new sheets. Ask him to help you fix a leaky faucet.

➤ Come up with ideas on your own, but ask for the other person's suggestions. In addition, welcome some disagreements (for example, he wants to go for Italian food but you prefer Japanese that night) so that you can see how you negotiate and resolve differences.

Remember the two cardinal principles of where to go: a setting you feel comfortable in, and something that plays to both of your interests. Now that you've been through your first date, you have an even better idea of what you both feel interested in and comfortable with, so it should be easier to come up with something to do together. She may have already told you how much she enjoys art, so it would be easy for you to check the newspaper and find out about exhibits or openings that are coming up. He may have already told you his favorite sport, so you can check the newspapers and call up to see if you can get tickets.

Review the idea list of first dates in Chapter 11 for your second dates and beyond. Here are some additional suggestions that may not have been appropriate for the first date:

➤ Cook dinner. If either of you enjoys cooking, make a meal for the other.

Smooth Talk'n

It is easy to play it safe and do the same thing in the initial stages of a relationship. If you know what worked last time, the tendency would be to play it safe and do it again. But variety truly is the spice of life, and it gives you the opportunity to learn about each other in different situations. So resist doing the same thing (such as dinner and movies) each date, but force yourself to find something new and different each time—at least for the first six dates.

➤ Take a drive together (to view the fall foliage, to explore a new country road, or even to cruise the strip one evening).

➤ Take a walk together (in a new part of town, on your own streets, or in a park).

Smooth Talk'n

If you're planning to cook for your date at home, make dinner a sensuous experience. For example, choose suggestive textures, smells, colors, and tastes: crunchy string beans, tangy sauces, red tomatoes. Find out if your date is health-conscious, vegetarian, or has special dietary constrictions so you don't turn him off with greasy hamburgers, too-salty appetizers, heavy cream sauces, or too-sugary cakes. Tidy up more rooms than just the kitchen.

➤ Take a tourist tour of your own city. Few people really do the fun things that out-of-towners would do if they visited you. Call your city visitors' bureau, or get the folders and flyers from a local hotel lobby. Take a walking, bus, or boat tour of the city, visit the tallest buildings and historic parts of town, and take a peek at other tourist attractions. Consider the afternoon as well as the evening trips (to nightspots and evening attractions). This will give you a fun sense of being explorers together; you might even get the thrill that comes with traveling to new places together, where you feel it is the two of you in the world.

➤ Take your nieces to a park or zoo. Children often make people feel relaxed and friendly.

➤ Spend the day at a street fair or expo (at your city's exhibition hall).

➤ Go to a fund-raiser.

Ideas for Subsequent Dates

Think of subsequent dates building on the experience of the second date. They should also fulfill certain purposes. As a review:

1. You will want to get a truer and fuller sense of togetherness and see how you work together as a team.

2. You will want to learn even more about how you both deal with different situations.

3. You will want to test how you make decisions together.

4. You will want to know even more about how you handle real-life situations that come up when people are together over a long period of time. That includes how you deal with work situations, other people, health crises, and particularly family obligations and relationships.

With those purposes in mind, consider these suggestions:

➤ Instead of cooking for the other person, consider cooking together. It can be a wonderful experience of togetherness to share the preparations.

➤ Include food shopping together for making the meal at home. It can be great fun to select what's on the menu.

➤ Host a dinner party. Share the above responsibilities and prepare for their guests. The sense of togetherness will be heightened as you work as a team for others.

➤ Do laundry or errands together on a Sunday afternoon.

➤ Make a social visit to family. Go together on a family picnic, take your parents out to dinner, or simply visit your grandmother on a Sunday.

➤ Go to a wedding together.

➤ Visit an aunt or grandparent in a nursing home or retirement village, to get a sense of how you each deal with aging.

➤ Visit a friend who has just had a baby.

➤ Visit a sick family member.

➤ Ask him to drive you to your doctor's appointment or to wait in the waiting room (or even to go in with you if you are anxious about your visit, and already trust him).

➤ Attend religious services.

➤ Attend a funeral.

➤ Spend a Saturday afternoon volunteering together (taking a homeless child to a park or working at a soup kitchen).

➤ Go shopping together. Men traditionally don't like shopping, but they do have to do it some time or another. Choose something that he needs or enjoys, such as even shopping for a new computer. Consider window-shopping, even if you are not prepared to buy right now.

Smooth Talk'n

Choose a video to watch together that has positive outcomes about relationships. *Crossing Delancey* shows how nice guys can finish first. *Selena* is about how love can survive any obstacles, including initial parental disapproval. Research even proves that scary movies or horror flicks stimulate chemicals in the body that encourage intimacy.

Smooth Talk'n

In choosing music to play at home together or to see at a concert, keep in mind how different types of music affect different moods and emotions, by stimulating certain brain chemicals and muscular reactions. If you have different musical tastes (she likes country, he likes classical), learn to appreciate each other's choice. Listen to your collection with the intention of selecting ones that would be conducive to a date. Go through racks at a music store, including compilations with titles about music for love and romance.

➤ Watch a video at home together. While I know this can be a popular suggestion for initial dates, I suggest saving that for later dates, because just coming over can imply some pressure about intimacy and trigger feelings (however unfounded) about not being "taken out and treated."

➤ Enroll in a class together. Learn drumming, dancing the tango, wine tasting, or computer skills. This will extend the contact you have together and imply to each other that you really want to make this an ongoing relationship.

➤ Get a massage together.

➤ Plan a short overnight trip. This can involve some activity (antiquing) or a sport (such as skiing, which involves preparation and time).

➤ Take a self-improvement course.

➤ Take him/her along on a convention trip.

Smooth Talk'n

If you meet somewhere, make sure to both be on time, to prevent either one feeling awkward while waiting. If you're going to a restaurant or a club, make sure you know whose name is on the reservation so she can be seated if she arrives first. Be clear about where you'll meet (at the table, bar, or corner of the club).

Smooth Talk'n

If you really don't want him in your place, be ready at the door a few minutes before the appointed time so you can slip right out. If you live in an apartment building, you can always come right down to the lobby, but making him wait there is a little rude and may be uncomfortable for him.

Bringing Gifts

Small tokens are a great way to show your interest and make the other person feel good. Avoid large items and expensive things in the beginning. Choose something that the other person likes. Jackie gave Jeff a package of golf balls that he had mentioned were his favorite, impressing him with not only the gift, but how she had paid attention to what he said (a sure winner in seduction). Jared brought Kristen a snow globe from each of his out-of-town trips after finding out she collects them.

Some examples of thoughtful but non-expensive gifts include a CD from your favorite artist, a souvenir from a city you have visited, a T-shirt from some event you have attended together, or a book that has meaning to both of you. Think of something that he would use or see often (a pen with some inscription, a paperweight for the desk) that would make him think of you.

Where to Meet

PASSÉ: In the old days, it was only proper for a gentleman to pick a lady up at her place before a date. Suggesting any other rendezvous would be insulting. She would never dream of getting herself anywhere on her own.

IN THE NEW MILLENNIUM: You can meet anywhere for your date, if it seems comfortable and appropriate. Of course, the traditional scenario can seem right: He can come to her house to pick her up, and they can go from there. But he might meet her at work if she has to stay late. Or they can both meet at some convenient place, if time is short and distance is a problem. She can even come to his place in these more modern times.

She no longer needs to be insulted if he doesn't pick her up at home, but if she insists or is more comfortable with that (and also for safety concerns), he might want to accommodate her.

Primping Your Home

Whether you're going to be picked up at home, or plan to go back to your place for a nightcap, review your place with an eye for having company. Do it yourself, or if you have a few days to prepare, get a cleaning service to do a really thorough going-over (save your nickels, though—these services cost about $50 for three hours). If you're rushed for a last-minute visit, go over the essentials.

Think about what he will see when he walks in. Likely he'll come in the doorway and sit for a few minutes in the living room. Put away any unnecessary mess (papers, clothes, boots, dishes). Fluff up the pillows. Collect any balls of dust on the floor (swipe a wet paper towel over exposed areas). Adjust the shades (either closed or open, as you like). Turn on lights to whatever level you want.

> **In the bathroom:** He may ask to use the toilet, so swish cleaner with a scrub brush in the toilet bowl, to get rid of those stains and ugly rings. Don't forget the underside of the toilet seat (especially because he will raise it). Swish through the sink, too. Fold the towels over the rack neatly. Wipe any unsightly blotches or spritz from your toothpaste off the mirror.

> **In the kitchen:** He may want a drink of water, so scrub the sink. Put away any dishes. Have a glass handy so he doesn't have to go through your cabinets.

> **In the bedroom:** Close the door so your bedroom is not visible. But make the bed and throw any scattered clothes into the closet.

Smooth Talk'n

If you have piles of things (magazines, videos, CDs, and mail) that look unsightly, get a nice piece of material (silk or fur) or a pareo (rectangular material wrapped as clothing popular in the islands) and drape it over the pile so it is not visible and also looks somewhat attractive.

Home Alone

As much as possible, put away too-obvious photos, memorabilia, and evidence of other lovers when you expect a date at your house. This causes unnecessary jealousy, insecurity, and questions.

Who Pays?

When you start going on several dates, the issues about who pays can shift from the routine you have set up on your first dates. As you go out more often and spend more money, you might want to share more equally in some of the expenses. And you might want to be more sensitive to who is earning more money. Talk about this without fear, because not doing so has some unpleasant consequences. For example, he might not ask her out to a nice place—or to go out at all—if he doesn't have the money, leaving her thinking that he doesn't care about her when really he is ashamed or simply cannot afford it.

To avoid the problem of too-expensive dates, plan a few activities that do not cost much. For example, go to free concerts in the park, go for a drive, visit museums, or hang out with friends.

Is This Going Anywhere?

So you've been out with this person a few times, but you're still not sure if she is really interested in you or if this is "it." You will likely ask yourself, "Is this going anywhere?" or "Am I wasting my time?" Chances are, if you have to ask, be cautious. It means that things are not flowing so smoothly. If you are really enjoying each other, you will feel right about continuing to be together. As soon as you start wondering about whether you are wasting your time, you might be.

Home Alone

The more dates you have, the more you will also be deciding whether this person is "the one." While this is a natural reaction, it is best in the beginning to take each date one at a time, without making sweeping decisions. Let things evolve at their own rate, without imposing some definitions or expectations on whether this can last forever. You will have plenty of time to make that decision after months of seeing each other.

Timing is everything. Be aware that some people need time to let a relationship grow, while others jump right in and go for broke. If your styles clash, you won't be on the same wavelength. Keep alert to each other's pace for developing a relationship.

Give it time. You could be surprised. Sometimes the fire is a flash in the pan, and when you really get to know the person, you realize you are not right for each other. Or, over time, you could see things that you didn't notice at first. He may not seem to be your type, but you fall for him anyway over time. That happened for Jody. As she said, "I don't usually like men with round cheeks, a beard, or a hairy chest, but I met a man who looks like that and I think I'm falling in love with him. How can that be and won't I fall out of love with him eventually?"

Like Jody, nearly all women and men have a distinct concept of what constitutes a desirable mate. Check back to Chapter 2 to read more about this. These eligibility criteria extend from background and personality traits to specific physical characteristics. Many surveys have proven that 8 out of 10 men put physical characteristics on the top of their list, while women rate personality as most important, with looks ranking fourth or lower. Therefore, it is not unsurprising that Jody is more interested in what this man is like as a person than what he looks like.

While women can still specify details about men they find physically appealing or unappealing (hair, height, build), they can more easily than men suspend such judgments when confronted with a suitor who does not fit that type yet who still captures their heart. Remember the truth of the idiom that looks fade. Identify those qualities of his that you appreciate, and keep concentrating on those.

Instead of affection diminishing, as Jody fears, her more substantive appreciation of this man can grow. In fact, some women have found men who are initially physically unattractive but personally endearing to actually appear more handsome over time, as the man treats them well and their intimacy together grows. Some men these days are getting the hang of this, too.

Red or Green Lights

Along the way, there will be signs about whether the two of you are interested, and whether you are suited for one another. **These are some good signs:**

- ○ He asks what you would like and then does it.
- ○ The amount of time you talk together increases.
- ○ The things you share become more intimate.
- ○ He says "sweet" things (such as, you are gone only a few hours and he misses you).
- ○ You think about each other when you're apart.
- ○ You both put other people on hold when either of you calls.
- ○ You leave some free time (from work or other appointments) to see each other.
- ○ You start to wonder what each of you is doing when you're not together.
- ○ You get a twinge of possessiveness or jealousy.
- ○ You are amused by other things about him that might have annoyed you in others in the past.
- ○ You think about having a picture of her.
- ○ Both of you think about doing things to please the other person.
- ○ You develop experiences that you call your own ("your song," "your place to eat").
- ○ You both feel comfortable sharing feelings.
- ○ You both listen attentively to each other.

○ You do thoughtful things for each other (scraping the ice off her car, leaving him his favorite breakfast at his door).

○ You enjoy each other's company, even if you're "doing nothing."

○ He asks what you did that day, and is interested in hearing your experiences.

○ Neither of you has a desire to date anyone else.

○ Fantasies about meeting anyone else fade.

○ Flirtations from others don't make you flirt back.

○ He buys you your own toothbrush and puts it in his bathroom.

○ You aren't afraid to do and say what comes naturally to you.

○ You express affection freely to each other.

○ You're willing to spend time with her friends or family.

Warning signs it's not working out well:

○ One of you makes all the approaches or invitations.

○ One of you is always hesitant to make definite plans and leaves things until the last minute.

○ You get together only if there is nothing better to do.

○ Some things your date says don't ring true.

○ You find yourself being unnatural, playing games, or being dishonest.

○ Dates are refused.

○ He lies.

○ She plays games.

○ Dates are often broken.

○ You get excited about meeting that new girl your friend wants to fix you up with.

○ You find yourself not feeling special or thinking, "He says that to all the girls" or "She's the same way to every man."

○ She seems unresponsive when you are together, or his attention to you is inconsistent.

○ He doesn't show any affection toward you in front of other people (beyond being shy or not liking public displays of affection).

○ She doesn't tell any friends or family about you.

○ He rarely compliments you or returns any compliments you give.

○ He doesn't ask what you're doing (on an evening or weekends).

○ He doesn't call when he says he will.

○ She won't make any sacrifices or change any plans to see you (especially if a certain date is important to you).

○ She always seems too busy.

○ He doesn't offer any affection (holding hands, hugging).

○ She is critical.

○ Everything is on his terms (where you go, when you go out) and never at your request.

○ You don't "feel" any emotion from him—or for him.

○ He makes too many references to sex too soon.

Home Alone

If you find yourself still looking at other women, don't immediately think it means your date is not the one for you. Some healthy guys (or gals) will keep on looking until the day they die.

The more of these warning signs that apply, the less likely that you are truly interested in each other. Of course, it is possible that other things are getting in the way, but generally, if many of these signs are present, it is best to turn your attention elsewhere.

When You're Really Not Sure

You can usually gauge someone's interest by how he acts. But if you're unsure about someone's intentions, ask and get feedback. It's a good idea to see things straight early in a relationship. Say something casual, like "I had a great time. We should do it again sometime, don't you think?"

Things are probably not going well if you have to ask more pointed questions, like "Is this going anywhere?" or "Are we both wasting our time?" Unless you're really insecure and need such reassurance, you're likely sensing accurately that it is not going well. Trust your instincts—your doubts are likely valid.

What do you do when you get double messages? Ben called about liking a girl he's seen on a few dates, but she's now giving him double messages. Sometimes she's nice when she sees him on campus, and other times she ignores him. She told his best friend that he calls her too much. This may "feel" like double messages, but really the message is quite clear: Back off. Rushing into something too fast makes the other person feel suffocated and crowded. Give her space—get involved in other interests so you don't become overly attached.

Clicking or Clunk?

Everyone has his own pace. "You can't hurry love" went the line of a popular song from the '70s. Remember my theory that each person in dating has his or her own comfort level for intimacy and independence. These days, the phrase used is commonly "I need more space." If someone asks for that space, give it to them.

181

Remember styles in dating (review Chapters 17 and 19). Remember, too, there are those who rush into love and sweep you off your feet, but then cut out suddenly, as if having "love panic." Once they get close, they see flaws and back off. Then there are those who drag their feet incessantly. Fence-sitters (or who I call "Mr. Maybe") suck you in with promises of the future (but never deliver) and try your patience, when you could be treating yourself to attention and love elsewhere.

To truly hit it off, your love scripts must intertwine. But something can throw it off drastically. Be aware of what a date might say that could crush your idea that you are meant for each other. And if your date withdraws, reflect on or ask about what may have upset or disappointed her. For example, Annie was totally taken with her new wealthy and handsome boyfriend, Jayson. She dreamt of long romantic weekends in the Islands at five-star hotels, so when he suggested, "Let's go to some cheesy motel for the night and be naughty," her fantasy was crushed, she felt insulted, and she stopped returning his beeps.

Cutting It Off

"My definition of dating in the Year 2000 is call block," quips my friend, TV producer and reporter Susan Cingari. She said it in humor, but caller ID is not a bad idea so you know who's calling and whether you want to pick up.

Rejecting someone is not a nice task for anyone, but please be kind. Remember karma: Whatever you do to others eventually comes back to you. Acknowledge how you enjoyed meeting the person, appreciate specific things about them (humor or intelligence), and then say something that is honest but non-blaming about why you can't continue the relationship. You can always say that you are already interested in someone else. Never say you don't like them (that can hurt forever), but point out how both of you would be better suited for different partners.

Hit and Run

Julie's problem is not uncommon in dating. She recounted, "I had started a relationship with a man I grew to like. Though we went out only on a few dates, we talked on the phone three times a day and had really intimate conversations. He called me pet names, and his voice had a sexy tone like a boyfriend's would. Then all of a sudden, he disappeared. I am in terrible pain. Should I call him?"

An intense connection that is suddenly, abruptly, and inexplicably broken is extremely painful. Once you have opened your heart in good faith, only to be shut out, you can suffer grave emotional trauma (self-doubt, fear, and insecurity) as well as physical symptoms (tightness in your chest, constriction around your heart, shortness of breath, disinterest in your work, fatigue, and sleeplessness).

Many women and men in Julie's situation question whether they are desirable or lovable. Reassure yourself, and trust that you had reason to believe that this person cared for you. It may not, however, have been as primary in importance for him/her as it was for you.

Friends may advise that you never call this man until he calls you, or that you dismiss him entirely to protect your pride and prevent desperation. But if you are suffering, consider calling him not a disgrace or defeat, but an effort on your part to achieve resolution to this troubling break. Ask for his feedback on what was really going on and what he felt about you, to help you in your future relationships. You might be surprised that his withdrawal could have nothing to do with you, but rather other preoccupying stress in his life that he was fearful to share with you.

When Is Someone Your Boyfriend or Girlfriend?

How you refer to the person you're dating both reflects and affects your level of intimacy. I don't recommend using the terms "boyfriend" and "girlfriend" too casually. All too often people will call my radio show and say, "I saw my girlfriend talking to another man" or "My boyfriend didn't call me." When I ask, "How long have you been going out?" they say, "two weeks" or even "three days." It seems a bit premature to use the term "boyfriend" or "girlfriend" so early in a relationship. By not exaggerating the importance of the person you are dating, you won't feel as bad if the relationship does not work out. And when it does work, the word will have more meaning.

What Did You Call Me?

What does your date call you? How do you define your dating status? Consider some terms and phrases you can use:

➤ "This man/woman I'm going out with." Use for first dates and casual acquaintances.

➤ "This man/woman I'm dating." Use to suggest you may have been out on a few dates but may not be exclusive or committed.

➤ "This man/woman I'm seeing." Reference to show you have been dating for at least a few weeks and plan to move on to a more serious level.

➤ "My girlfriend/boyfriend." Reserved for when you have been dating for a few months and have some level of commitment to spend time together, share experiences, and see each other regularly (but perhaps not exclusively).

➤ "My lover." Reveals an open admission of sexual intimacy that usually implies exclusivity.

➤ "My significant other." This term was created by the Census Bureau to imply that a couple was sharing living quarters and, therefore, aspects of their daily lives. Usually, this term implies a stable or longer-term arrangement. It is also often used in same-sex relationships when someone doesn't want to be specific about the sexual nature of his relationship.

Dating Data

How many people should you date at the same time? You can date as many people as you like, as long as you don't deceive anyone. There's absolutely nothing wrong with playing the field—you get to meet many interesting people while learning a lot about yourself. However, you might prefer to concentrate on one person at a time. Remember, the more people you see at the same time, the less time you have to devote to one person and the less opportunity you have to see whether you can satisfy each other's needs.

Making Subsequent Dates

Now that you've established that you're into each other, you have to set the pace for how often you make contact and how often you get together. This is the tricky part: keeping track of how and where you both stand on whether you are free to date others, or if you are seeing each other exclusively. What number of dates (three dates, or consistent dates for three weeks), events (family functions, meeting close friends, staying over), or sexual activity defines commitment for you both? Make sure you both have the same criteria for this. Nothing is more painful than one of you thinking the other owes you exclusivity. And nothing is more common in dating than getting hurt if you think you're "seeing each other exclusively" but the other person still wants to play the field.

The best course is to take it slowly and not to expect exclusivity until it really becomes clear. You can always test the waters by mentioning that you're going out with a "friend." If he asks more questions or seems disturbed, then you can sense if he cares about your seeing others. If not, he either doesn't mind, isn't ready to take on the responsibility of being yours alone, or is too anxious to ask. If you're truly hassled about it, though, you can always have a discussion about it. Wait until a time when both of you feel relaxed and have time to talk. Start out talking about what exclusivity means in general, and then you can talk about the situation between the two of you (asking, "Are we agreeing to see each other only, or are we still dating other people?"). Listen to the answer and respect the

Home Alone

You are being obsessive or becoming co-dependent if you beep or call several times a day and the other person gets increasingly busy or short in response. Control your urges. If you get a clear message to back off, respect that. Stalking reflects a serious psychological disorder. And if you're the one being stalked, don't hesitate to tell the other person to back off.

other person's needs. The one who wants to have more "space," or isn't "ready" to get more serious, should set the pace, whether you like it or not. You can never force anyone to like you or want to see you.

The more you see each other, the more contact you may have over the phone, Internet, or in person. Trust your instincts about when to call or beep. If you get the sense that you are being over-demanding, trust that and do something else to get the attention you need at that moment. Get busy (with your own work or responsibilities, or a pleasurable activity) to keep your attention focused elsewhere.

Keeping It Going Over the Phone

In a wonderful article written up in the *New York Post*, writers Ron Mitchell and Sacha Mornell write about using the telephone for "reaching out and touching her." They list Law No. 1 as using the telephone for accumulating what they call "date equivalents"— making up for personal interactions to rack up the necessary number of contacts necessary for a woman to feel comfortable before she gets intimate with a guy. A telephone contact, they say, is equal to 0.5 dates, making two long phone conversations equal to one date. (Personally, I'd require three times that amount.)

In another law, the writers suggest using strategically placed phone calls to keep it going, even when you know she is not there. That way, you get the perks from calling without having to have an extensive conversation. Phone calls include:

➤ Leave a voice mail message at her job late at night so she starts work with a nice message from you.

➤ Call after the date before she gets home, saying you had a wonderful time.

➤ Call when you know she's away on vacation or on a weekend, and say you're thinking of her (or even that you miss her).

Stay-Overs

For guidelines about when and where to get intimate, read Chapter 21. Inviting someone back to your lair is a set-up for a stay-over, so your date is bound to wonder whether this is an invitation—or an expectation—for sex. A decline may be colored with a fear of such an expectation, so if you don't intend sex, be sure to be clear about that.

If you've both followed the guidelines in Chapter 21, and if you've both decided you're ready for a stay-over, be prepared. If it's your place, take these actions:

➤ Tidy up.

➤ Stock up on refreshments (drinks, snacks, perhaps breakfast).

➤ Have condoms or other birth control and safe-sex precautions handy.

➤ Keep love aids handy (lubricants, toys).

➤ Buy a guest toothbrush.

Dating Data

In the new millennium, going to her place is equally as likely as going to his.

To be prepared for a stay-over at your date's place, you'll want to take a few things along. A few of the things listed here can fit in your pocket or evening bag, but you might need a larger briefcase or carry-all bag.

➤ Toothbrush

➤ Money, credit cards, driver's license

➤ Contacts case, glasses, or other eyewear

➤ Any pills you take

➤ Key telephone numbers

➤ Appointment book or pocket computer

➤ Change of clothes (so you don't have to go into the subway or show up at work in an obvious evening dress or suit from the day before, letting everybody know you've been out all night)

➤ Anything you'll need for the next day (for errands in his neighborhood or books for class) so you don't have to go home first

Men, Women, and Dating

Men and women definitely approach the dating scene differently (as you'll see in Chapter 16). The following are a few guidelines for both men and women to consider at this stage of the game.

What Men Need to Know: The Woman's Point of View

➤ DO be romantic and sensitive in your words and actions. Send cards. Bring small gifts (flowers or thoughtful trinkets).

➤ DO listen attentively. (Eye contact is critical here; if on the phone, ignore your call waiting.)

➤ DO agree to do things with her family and friends.

➤ DO build her trust by being faithful and truthful, and always "being there."

➤ DO spend time cuddling.

➤ DO learn about her body and erogenous zones. Enjoy afterplay. Take time.

➤ DON'T expect her to date you exclusively and then play around yourself.

➤ DON'T expect or demand sex.

What Women Need to Know: The Man's Point of View

➤ DO take the initiative instead of expecting him to always be the aggressor.

➤ DO loosen up your inhibitions.

➤ DO think of dating as fun without weighing it down with overly heavy emotional complications.

➤ DO let him withdraw once in awhile; understand his need to be alone, to take things slowly, or to have a night out with the guys.

➤ DO accept him without judgment.

➤ DON'T expect him to profess his love for you so soon. (See "When to Say 'I Love You'" in Chapter 15.)

➤ DON'T push him into a commitment or an exclusive relationship.

➤ DON'T snoop.

➤ DON'T nag him into talking about his feelings.

➤ DON'T take everything personally.

➤ DON'T compare him to other lovers (unless it's to tell him he's the best).

➤ DON'T badmouth him to your girlfriends.

After the Night Is Over

As with after the first date, always say something nice about the time you spent together. Don't make false promises about what comes next if you're not interested. But, if you are interested, then go ahead and let him know. He'll welcome the encouragement!

Follow up the parting with a casual phone call, e-mail, fax, cell phone call, or message on her machine saying something like, "I had a great time." Comment on something you shared. Even tell a joke. Keep the contact going. Send a fun card (stationary stores are filled with all kinds of greeting cards for all occasions, or make one yourself) or write a personal note with something poetic or funny. This is the time to start revealing your unique personality even more.

Time In-Between

Now that you've gotten to know each other a little better, you're either getting along or still not so sure. In these early stages, be aware of the following:

➤ Don't jump to conclusions too fast. Follow my six-date rule if you're at all interested. Give someone six dates to really reveal themselves so you get to see them on bad hair days and good hair days and in different situations. Over time, you'll be able to better judge their character and your compatibility.

➤ Stay grounded in reality instead of sliding into fantasy. If he seems like your dream lover, be careful not to be planning your vacation with him already and shopping for your wedding dress. Resist thinking you're already set for New Year's Eve together. A passing fantasy can be okay, but locking into it can be dangerous because you still aren't sure about whether it's going to work out.

➤ Keep yourself busy with your own life so you still have interesting things to share with one another.

➤ If you don't feel interested in accepting other dates, don't—but also don't expect that he has to do the same thing.

The Stages of Your Hooking Up

You're likely familiar with the phrases "We're just casually dating" and "This is getting serious." There's more about making commitments in Chapters 18 and 19. For now, it's worthwhile to know that to get from the casual stage of dating to the serious stage, you actually go through these 10 steps.

Stage 1. The first look. At that first glance, you sense your initial attraction. You're lucky if you feel the draw right away: Research shows it takes those 15 seconds to make your initial decision about whether you are interested.

Stage 2. The first flush. When you're face-to-face, you get a fuller sense of how you interact and whether you feel good being around each other and can talk to each other.

Stage 3. Feeling "in like." You sense you enjoy being around the person and are curious to find out more about him.

Stage 4. Feeling lust. This is the flush of adrenaline that may make your heart pound. Your skin tingles, and you can't wait to feel their arms around you or their lips on yours.

Stage 5. Falling in love. You've spent time together, and you notice he has that savoir fare that makes you melt. He orders wine and you're impressed he knows the vineyards. She talks to your friends and you feel the thrill of pride over your catch.

Stage 6.   Getting over humps. You first imagine you could wake up every morning looking at her without makeup, or you decide you can fall asleep every night even though he snores.

Stage 7.   Speaking words of commitment. Telling each other you could be "the one."

Stage 8.   Practicing coupledom. You spend a weekend playing house, making his bed, cooking her breakfast, and taking your nephew to the zoo. So now you think you might be able to do the marriage-and-kids thing together.

Stage 9.   You move in together and see how you really get along.

Stage 10.   You can get through the rough spots, where you might feel tinges of being bored with him or you're worried that she doesn't look as hot to you that day. Still, you hang in there and it gets better again.

The Least You Need to Know

➤ Choose things to do that you know you both enjoy.

➤ Keep thinking about enjoying what you do instead of becoming involved too quickly.

➤ Be prepared to take things slowly; be aware of each other's pace and comfort with intimacy.

➤ Be sensitive to cues about whether you are getting along.

➤ Always be gracious and gentlemanly about appreciating each other's company, even if it's not going anywhere.

Part 4
Keep It or Throw It Back

The search for love should be fun and bring you happiness. If the prey you've found doesn't bring you joy, but instead, gloom, fear, and insecurity, then the person isn't for you . . . and you're better off on your own.

In this section, you'll figure out if you indeed have found your match. You'll learn about the importance of communication and the differences between the ways men and women approach love. You'll learn how to handle different personality types and how to put a stop to unhealthy behaviors. And when you just can't figure the person out or you're just not happy, you'll learn when and why to end the relationship.

Chapter 13

Are You on the Same Wavelength?

In This Chapter

➤ Getting to know yourself and your date

➤ A quiz to test your dating personality style

➤ Understanding the four basic personality types

➤ Dating game questions

➤ The Noah's Ark test

➤ Matching that makes "sense"

➤ Matching by the stars

This chapter is about making a love connection. It's about finding a mate whose lifestyle, personality, and dating expectations are compatible with your own. While no mate will ever be perfect, there are certain types of people who make better matches. When two people are running on the same track, the connection can be blissful. But when love trains collide head-on, or when their tracks diverge, the pain and disappointment can be overwhelming.

From psychology to astrology, theories abound as to why certain people get along and others clash. While no theory tells the whole story, many offer useful clues about human behavior and compatibility. I've adapted certain personality theories to come up with the quizzes in this chapter. Keep in mind that these are simplifications of some very complex theories and assessments. Use them as fun guides in your search for a lifelong love, or at least a pleasant dinner date!

Basic Dating Rule: Know Your Love Target!

Janet came to me to help her figure out why all her relationships turned sour. Janet is the spontaneous type. An artist, she loves to wear colorful, sequined dresses, and she tends to move around a room like a jackrabbit. At a business party at the art gallery that represents her work, she met the gallery's accountant, Albert. Stunningly handsome, he was wearing a starched shirt and a dark suit, and he spoke slowly and deliberately— unlike Janet, whose sentences tumbled out a mile a minute. Drawn to Janet's energy, Albert followed her around all evening and then offered to drive her home. He lingered at her door as they said goodnight, and Janet, sensing his passion, grabbed him wildly. Standing in her foyer, they embraced passionately.

Janet thought about Albert all week until she finally saw him again at another business function. Sidling up to him, she whispered in his ear, "I'm mad for you." To her shock, he pushed her away and muttered, "I don't want you to do that," making a leveling motion with his hand as he walked away.

Devastated, Janet tried to make sense of his behavior. How could he be so hot one minute, so cold the next? I explained to her that while Albert was so attracted to her "wildness," it probably frightened him—as did his own loss of control. If there was ever to be anything more between them, Janet would have to tone down her behavior and proceed more slowly. She agreed, but decided that Albert was not worth the effort.

My point is not to suggest that you adapt yourself, chameleon-like, just to get a date. But if you are attracted to someone whose outward style is radically different from your own, you may have to be a bit more calculating in your approach. Sometimes it's easier to win over a person if you approach them in their style—even if it's a little against your nature. Albert, the starched-shirt accountant, was probably mortified that Janet came on to him during a business meeting, thus his rude rebuff. If her come-on had been less aggressive (if she'd been more sensitive to his nature), the results might have been different. They may not have walked off into the sunset, but she probably wouldn't have walked away wounded, either.

The Personality Style Quiz

The following quiz will help you assess your own style and that of your love interest. Take the quiz with a partner or with someone you've been dating. If you aren't sure about asking your current love interest to join you in this quiz, take an educated guess at his or her answers.

Dating Data

Over 30 years of research have shown that most people fall into one of four main personality categories (see "The Four Basic Personality Types" later in this chapter). This reflects the dominance of one of the four quadrants of the brain. Brain dominance determines how we think, relate to others, choose jobs, and fall in love. Once you determine which type you are, you'll have a better chance of determining who you like and don't like—and why. And once you know another person's basic type, you have an advantage in influencing or pleasing that person.

I've adapted this quiz from an extensive computerized questionnaire developed by the Ned Herrmann Group in Lake Lure, North Carolina. I've used it for many, many years and know that it works! Answer the questions as they apply to you, choosing the answer that applies most of the time. Remember, most of us are a mixture of personality types, but the results of the quiz may offer you some useful guidelines on compatibility. Be honest!

1. Dates usually like me because I am
   a. intelligent and rational
   b. reliable and punctual
   c. romantic and a good talker
   d. spontaneous and full of fun

2. Dates who don't like me think I am
   a. controlling, opinionated, and argumentative
   b. stubborn, boring, and unemotional
   c. overemotional, hypersensitive, and needy
   d. too wild, unpredictable, and off-the-wall

3. My feeling about love is
   a. it alters your perceptions, making you overlook limitations, and requires you to suspend more rational assessments you would make in other situations
   b. romantic love is transient, so make practical choices
   c. I'm happiest when I'm in love; I don't like being alone for too long
   d. it's magical and inspires me to explore, create, and take risks

continues

continued

4. When it comes to spending money on a date, I believe in
    a. spending when there may be a payoff
    b. sticking to a strict budget
    c. spending on friends
    d. splurging for something special

5. If I disagree with a date, I like to
    a. figure out the right thing to do before saying anything
    b. try to forget it and move on
    c. immediately say how I feel and insist on talking the situation through
    d. consider possible solutions that make both of us happy

6. It would turn me on to hear a date say
    a. "I've been thinking it over and I think we are right for each other"
    b. "You make me feel secure; it's like I've known you all my life"
    c. "I love the way you talk to me and how you make me feel"
    d. "Let's take off on an adventure next week and do whatever strikes our fancy"

7. My idea of a perfect evening together consists of
    a. stimulating conversation or a debate over a new movie or current events
    b. clear plans of what to do, such as something we enjoyed in the past
    c. a romantic dinner and intimate talk
    d. doing something new or going somewhere different or exotic

8. When it comes to sex, I like
    a. when I feel in control and perform well
    b. to stick to proper times and places
    c. feeling close or like soulmates
    d. fantasies and being playful

9. When it comes to sexual fantasies
    a. I have some fantasies, but I don't think it's wise to share all of them
    b. I don't believe in fantasizing when I have the real thing
    c. I like fantasizing, especially about romance, being adored, or giving in
    d. the wilder the story, the better

10. When I consider a future together, I need to

    a. know I have made the right decision

    b. feel secure that things will go as planned

    c. feel warm and wonderful

    d. picture lots of exciting things, some of which I can't yet imagine

To find out your score, total the number of a's, b's, c's, and d's you selected. Multiply each total by 10, and record them in the table below.

Your Score	Your Date's Score
a's _____	a's _____
b's _____	b's _____
c's _____	c's _____
d's _____	d's _____

Now plot your numbers on the matrix below. Use one pen color for your score, and a different color for your date's score. Match the number of your score for each of the four dimensions (a, b, c, d) along the line in each corresponding quadrant of the circle. Start from the center of the circle, "0," and move out to the outer line marked "100." Connect the dots (to make a figure) so you can more clearly see your preferences.

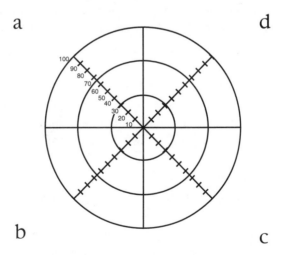

The further your plots are from the inner circles, the more you prefer a particular style; the closer they are to the center and inner circle, the less you prefer that style.

Notice where your plot and that of your date overlap, and where they diverge. The plots intersect in areas where you have the greatest mutual preferences or concerns. For example, if you both land on the same spot on the relaters dimension, it means you probably have a fairly equal desire to express emotions. If your score is high on the creative scale while your partner's is higher on the conservative scale, the two of you may be out of synch much of the time. If you are aware of your differences, you will be in a better position to understand your partner and work through the difficulties that are apt to arise.

The Four Basic Personality Types

No one personality type is inherently good or bad, desirable or undesirable. The challenge is to understand your own tendencies and those of your partner. If you are not in a relationship, you can use this information in your search. For instance, if you are basically conservative but would love a more spontaneous mate, you may have to adapt your style to attract this type of person.

Dating Data

Personality type is just one factor in the great mate equation. Compatibility is another. The key to compatibility lies with the three A's: acceptance, appreciation, and adjustment.

Use your quiz answers to assess where you and your date fit into these four broad personality types:

➤ **Creatives** (mostly "d" answers): Imaginative, free-spirited, impulsive people who thrive on experimentation and taking risks. They are often artists, CEOs, or entrepreneurs.

➤ **Relaters** (mostly "c" answers): Emotional, expressive, sensitive people who value personal relationships and communication of feelings over facts. Psychologists and teachers frequently fall into this category.

➤ **Conservatives** (mostly "b" answers): Practical, organized, detail-oriented people who go by the book and value predictability. They are often administrators, planners, or computer operators.

➤ **Thinkers** (mostly "a" answers): Analytical, rational, logical people who love to win arguments and solve problems. They often choose professions such as banking, law, or engineering.

Creatives often seem a bit off-the-wall, but they are great innovators and often have terrific ideas. If you are attracted to this type, encourage the person to let his or her imagination run free. Don't expect them to focus on details or take "It can't be done" for an answer. Enjoy their fantasies and have fun!

Relaters cherish feelings and relationships. If you are interested in a person of this type, talk a lot and emphasize your feelings and willingness to get along. Ask, "What are you feeling?" instead of "What are you thinking?" Give lots of hugs and attention.

Conservatives often seem picky and unimaginative, which may be frustrating for Creatives, who like taking risks. But appreciate their caution, discipline, and punctuality. If you are looking for security, a Conservative is a safe bet. Be cautious in your approach; don't surprise a Conservative by being overly emotional. Initially, at least, be predictable and punctual to make them feel safe.

Thinkers like to be right and need to know the facts. So, with these people, you wouldn't be wise to come on with a barrage of emotions. Instead of saying, "This will be fun" (a typical Creative response), or "I feel good about this" (a Relater's response), you might ask, "What do you think?" Thinkers can be controlling, which is something to watch out for.

While the cliché is that opposites attract, in fact it is common that "like" initially attracts "like." For instance, creative types who are into fantasy and adventure are more likely to pick partners who share their interests. But what happens in the long run when neither is willing to buckle down and balance the checkbook or attend to household details? All this similarity in temperament may create friction; a creative man may wish he'd ended up with a conservative woman, or vice versa!

Home Alone

Opposites may at first attract, and then repel. For instance, a thinker may be attracted to a relater for her warmth and outgoingness. But as the relationship progresses, he may accuse her of being overly emotional. The thing to keep in mind is that the very traits that are endearing in the beginning of a relationship may be the same ones that drive you apart (if you let them).

Lindsay provides a poignant example of how understanding differences in style can help you avoid devastation in dating. This sweet, shy guy in his late 30s came to one of my seminars where I explained these brain styles. Weeks later I saw him again and he told me how he had been fixed up with a friend and for their date she suggested they go to an amusement park. Frightened of such places (particularly the crowds and rides there) since he was a child, he politely said he would prefer a quiet movie. Suddenly she got furious, he told me, with a flash of anger he would have never understood and would have taken personally, had he not been familiar with the brain style quiz and understood that there was nothing "wrong" with him, and that their types simply did not mix. She was obviously the imaginative, risk-taking "creative" or "d" type, while he was the more organized, cautious "conservative" or "b" type.

The Quick Assessment: An On-the-Spot Quiz

The quiz you just took is most useful when you know someone well or have the time to ponder the various facets of his personality. But what if you've just met someone? Are there clues to help you figure out where he fits into the four basic categories? The answer is yes, and the following questions should help.

1. The Sheet Test. The sheets on her bed are
   a. striped
   b. plain white
   c. flowered
   d. wildly patterned

2. The TV Clicker Test. On TV, he would rather watch
   a. *L.A. Law* reruns
   b. The Learning Channel
   c. *Oprah*
   d. *Beyond 2000*

3. The Restaurant Test. She would rather eat in a
   a. highly recommended restaurant
   b. quaint, old-fashioned place
   c. romantic spot
   d. gazebo or hot-air balloon

4. The Video Rental Test. If we rent a movie, he would most likely pick
   a. *Presumed Innocent*
   b. *Of Mice and Men*
   c. *Sleepless in Seattle*
   d. *The Rocky Horror Picture Show*

5. His Bedclothes Test. Which of the following would he be more likely to wear to bed (other than "nothing")?
   a. blue cotton pajamas
   b. plain pajamas
   c. silk boxers/robe
   d. "Betty Boop" boxers

6. Her Bedclothes Test. Which of the following would she be more likely to wear to bed (other than "nothing")?

   a. cotton pajamas

   b. long flannel nightgown

   c. silk nightie from Victoria's Secret

   d. satin teddy with fur trim

7. His Date Attire Test. Which of the following would he be more likely to wear on a date to go out to dinner?

   a. navy blazer and khaki slacks

   b. gray wool suit

   c. black shirt and slacks

   d. leather jacket with black jeans

8. Her Date Attire Test. Which of the following would she be more likely to wear on a date to go out to dinner?

   a. navy blazer and beige slacks

   b. blue suit and black pumps

   c. flowered dress

   d. sequined jacket and satin pants

To interpret the answers, match the a, b, c, and d answers to the personality types described earlier.

Coming to Your Senses

Our senses play a large part in why we choose dates and partners. Just as some of us are more creative and some of us more emotive, some of us are more focused on scent and others on touch. This section helps you determine which sense dominates your daily experience, and how you can figure out which sense is dominant in another person. Once you know which sense is dominant in your love interest, you can use that knowledge in your seduction.

Think back over your recent relationships. What is it that you first recall about your partners: the touch of their skin, their particular scent, the sound of their voice, their eyes, the feeling of closeness?

Dating Data

Neuro-linguistic programming is the scientific term used to describe the various ways in which we process information.

If your dominant sense is visual, you'll probably create a picture of a person in your mind. If your dominant sense is aural, you are more likely to recall a voice or the songs you listened to when you were together. Kinesthetic types focus on how things feel—his strong arm muscles, her soft, silky hair. Some of us are most sensitive to aroma, with a particular scent producing an instant flood of memories.

How can you tell which sense dominates in people you know well or barely know at all? Pay close attention to the words they use. Visual-type personalities use words to create pictures: "I see . . ." "Let's look at . . ." "I imagine . . ." and so forth. In a restaurant, they may reach for a pen to sketch on the tablecloth.

Smooth Talk'n

By all means be yourself, but also be sensitive to your date's reactions. For example, you may be the spontaneous type, likely to exclaim enthusiastically on a date, "Wow, I have a great idea about what we can do." But if your date is a more formal, conservative type, who could be unsettled (even if attracted to such forthrightness), you might temper yourself a little and present an idea more calmly, to let him get used to it.

Aural-type personalities might use phrases like "I hear that . . ." "I say . . ." "That sounds like a good idea . . ." "Something tells me . . ." and so forth. They may touch their ears when you're talking, or close their eyes so they can hear you better.

Kinesthetic types are touch-oriented; they literally take a hands-on approach and concentrate on how things feel. They frequently use words that describe touching ("I can't put my finger on . . .," "I'm touched that . . .") or textures ("This feels like . . ."). They shake hands readily and hold on longer, and find opportunities to touch you whenever they can. They may rub their chin or stroke their hair as they talk to you. They may also have a difficult time sitting still and move around a lot.

Scent-focused types pay attention to how things smell. They'll sniff the food, your perfume—and probably you!

Putting Your Knowledge to Work

If your love interest is visually oriented, choose eye-catching clothes and try gazing lovingly into her eyes.

If your lover is more attuned to sound, try seducing the person over the phone. Before you make the call, rehearse detailed descriptions of what you're doing and feeling. Have music playing when he comes over.

If the person is a touchy-feely type, wear clothes that beg to be touched, such as silk or fur. Occasionally offer a gentle touch on the hand or shoulder.

Perfume, flowers, incense, and scented candles are obvious devices for attracting someone whose dominant sense is the sense of smell. But since the wrong choice can be a turn-off, ask about favorites.

The Noah's Ark Test

There are countless tests for determining compatibility. Some are scientifically based, such as the Personality Style Quiz, based on personality styles, earlier in this chapter. Others are more playful, based more on common sense than on scientific research. These fun tests are a useful way to encourage openness between you and a date. For example, consider the following hypothetical situation:

Imagine the world has come to an end. There is one boat: Noah's Ark. You can take just one animal as your companion. Which of these animals would you choose: a horse, tiger, sheep, or peacock?

The horse symbolizes a career, the tiger symbolizes power, the sheep symbolizes love, and the peacock symbolizes pride. Following this, a person who chooses the horse might be most focused on their work, and might tend to put relationships on a back burner. Someone who chooses the tiger might need to exert a lot of control over your relationship. Be prepared to give the person who chooses the peacock a lot of attention, compliments, and flattery, and the one who chooses the sheep a lot of affection.

The Dating Game Quiz

TV shows such as *Love Connection*, *The Dating Game*, and MTV's *Singled Out* use simple questions and hypothetical situations to help couples find out whether they are well matched. Here are some questions like the ones from these shows to help you assess your styles and preferences, as well as your date's. If you're not sure about asking your current love interest to answer these questions, take an educated guess at his or her answers.

For each of these aspects, underline the one that you prefer and put a check mark over the one your current love interest prefers:

Characteristics:

Q: Brains: Einstein or beer stein?

Q: Body: slim and trim or muscle-bound?

continues

---

continued

Q: Height: delicate mouse or giant elephant?

Q: Facial hair: baby face or scratchy face?

Q: Sleep style: wrap-around or "Move over, baby"?

Q: Lifestyle: fireside chats or disco inferno?

Q: Dating style: one and only one or play the field?

Q: Hair color: dark fantasy or light and bright?

Q: Underwear: silk boxers or cotton briefs?

Q: Eating: raw veggies or raw meat?

Q: Experience: *Presumed Innocent* or *Basic Instinct*?

Q: Career goals: Wall Street or Easy Street?

Q: Commitment: stay free or landing pad?

Questions:

Q: Which is more important to you: looks or attitude?

Q: Vampires: romantic or blood-sucking freaks?

Q: Do you like Snoop Doggy Dogg or Snoopy the dog?

Q: Where would you prefer to go: Venice or Vegas?

Q: In the morning, sleep in or "rise and shine"?

Q: Do you consider the Internet a superhighway or superdrag?

Q: Do you find strip clubs sleazy or sexy?

Q: Magazines: save 'em or toss 'em out?

Q: Dress up every day or only on special occasions?

Q: Bungee-jumpers: daring or deranged?

Q: Wonder Bra: boon or bust?

Q: Socks with holes: wear 'em or throw 'em out?

Q: Lie to break a date or go out anyway?

Q: On a guy, ponytail or earring?

For these situations, write in what you or your date would say.

Situation	You	Your Date
I caught you with another guy, and now your head is in a guillotine. What would you say to get out of it?		

Situation	You	Your Date
If you were a dessert, what would you be? (The guy who won the date on this one said "chocolate mousse.")		
You're on the *Oprah* show. What's the topic?		
I keep a secret diary. What would the entry read on the night I met you?		
What was your high school nickname and why?		
If you could be a famous cartoon character, who would you be and why?		
If you met me at a crowded club, what would you do to get my attention?		
It's Valentine's Day and you wrote me a love poem. Recite it.		
If you were an ad campaign, what would the slogan be?		

Feel free to come up with your own questions to help stimulate conversation and display your creativity, as well as cue for specifics you want to know about your date.

What's Your Sign?

It's become humorous to ask someone the old 1970s line, "What's your sign?" But humor aside, there may be something to be learned from the 12 astrological types. Your star sign can give you specific tips on what appeals to you and your mate. Learning that there may be reasons why you and your date act in certain ways should enlighten you and in turn make you feel more in control. That sense of control heightens self-esteem. Keep in mind, however, that this method, like the Personality Style Quiz and the Dating Game Quiz, should be used only as a general guide to understanding each other and as a way to spark communication between you and your date, and not as the last word. The following descriptions were developed with the expert help of New York-based parapsychologist Gerri Leigh.

➤ **Aries** (March 21–April 20). These people are strong and always like to get their way. They have few sexual inhibitions, and like to dream up and play out their wildest fantasies. Because they love to be worshipped, tell them that they're great and show excitement during intimate encounters. They love self-expression, so talk things out to your heart's delight (good news for women who want a talking man). But be careful if you need attention, too, because Aries men and women can be selfish.

➤ **Taurus** (April 21–May 21). These people are similar to what Freud called "oral" characters—they like to be fed (either with real food or with love). Superficial dating doesn't cut it; they like the deep stuff. However, bulls tend to be possessive and want to "own" their mate, which can lead to jealousy and smothering. If they're controlling, intrusive, or jealous, try not to get angry; it's just their style. Sensualists at heart, win them with languorous kisses and by wining and dining. Nature lovers, they can be seduced with a walk in the woods or a fur bedspread.

➤ **Gemini** (May 22–June 21). These childlike, changeable folks may make you feel like you're in bed with two or even four people at the same time. So be fresh and youthful and play along with their fun. Try to role-play and plan lots of surprises. However, beware of love turning into a brother-sister relationship. Since they also tend to change their minds often, be sure to pick the right time to approach the subject of commitment.

➤ **Cancer** (June 22–July 22). These homebody romantics will eat out of your hand if you serve them homemade apple pie, and cuddle by the fire looking at old photographs. But beware—you'll have to be the one to light a fire under them if you want to party. Reminisce with them about how you loved them at first sight. Mother them and they'll never leave you for another partner. But since they tend to parent you one minute and want to be babied the next, be sure to set aside time to be lovers. Make those times cozy, with candlelit dinners and bubble baths.

➤ **Leo** (July 23–August 23). Like the lion in the *Wizard of Oz*, Leos search for companions with heart and a lot of courage. Once smitten, they'll pursue you with a strong will and, if you allow them, rule over your life. Whimper, and Leos will roar loudly (crybabies turn them off). Pamper them and they'll purr like pussycats. Treat them like kings and you'll preside as the queen in return.

➤ **Virgo** (August 24–September 23). Since these people chronically analyze things, you're likely to accuse your Virgo of being too critical. But they can just as easily put you on a pedestal. Be confident that they'll care enough to please you and bring you to the peak of pleasure. Virgos are wholesome health enthusiasts. They like to be right and are very organized, planning every detail, so emphasize compromise and challenge them with the following question: "Is it really important to you that we do it your way?"

➤ **Libra** (September 24–October 23). The scales of justice symbolize the Librans' balancing act: they'll be inclined to do anything to keep the peace, including giving in. Their challenge is to stop vacillating and take the bull by the horns when it comes to love. They tend to express what they really feel, and are die-hard romanticists who appreciate beauty and dressing up. Make sure to spoil them as they would spoil you. Take them to the opera or serve them juice in a silver goblet, and watch love blossom.

➤ **Scorpio** (October 24–November 22). Wild, even kinky, desire abounds in these passionate partners, who brandish sex as they do power and money. You won't hear "Sorry, no sex, I've got a headache" from them, and encounters could last all night. Try body-painting or washing each other's hair. Make homemade videos of your love. Tell them you have a "hunka hunka burning love" for them and watch them swoon.

➤ **Sagittarius** (November 23–December 21). Adventurers by nature, better take your Sagittarian on a weekend fling to some faraway place before he goes off alone. But you make the bookings (even for a hotel in town), since they're hard to pin down. Once they commit, though, they'll struggle to be loyal and settle down. How do you seduce a snob? With Dom Perignon champagne and eelskin attaches. Sags get turned on by high-priced tickets. Don't expect homestead living; their house can be in disarray, but they don't care because freedom and being on the go matter more.

➤ **Capricorn** (December 22–January 20). Like a goat holding steadfast on a mountain slope, Capricorn lovers stick to routine. They like simple and traditional styles, like a black dress with pearls. As partners they can seem boring, but don't nag or they'll become defensive and depressed. Let them learn on their own to be more spontaneous, and that love and sex do not just serve a practical purpose. Staunch idealists, they covet the "perfect" partner, but will soon settle for Clark Kent rather than endlessly seeking Superman.

➤ **Aquarius** (January 21–February 19). These humanitarian folks are very sensitive to feelings. They can satisfy your desires, but expect you to do the same for them. If you don't call the next morning, or tell them how wonderful they are, they'll be hurt. Verbal intercourse is the way to their hearts. Turn their minds on and their bodies will follow. But as much as they thrive on intimacy, they're essentially gypsies or loners—friends to all, but owned by none. So don't expect a long-lasting commitment except on the deepest spiritual level, since these eccentric and enlightened souls will likely be off pursuing a million interests and saving the world.

➤ **Pisces** (February 20–March 20). These slippery fishes are hard to catch. Blinded by Hollywood love scenes and idealism, they paint illusions over real lovers, and load them down with high expectations. They pursue until their love objects give in or until they find imperfections. You'll hear them say, "There's chemistry between us" or despair over "The mystery is gone," but they'll be drawn to you if you're the life of the party and boost their confidence.

I've met some people who uncannily fit these descriptions. But of course, even astrological profiles require consideration of much more extensive aspects (rising signs, moon signs, and many others). So treat these very simple sketches as fun, and if you're intrigued, explore the subject further with astrology books and consultations.

The Least You Need to Know

➤ Learning about your own (and your date's) love style can increase your chances of finding a compatible match.

➤ No personality type is inherently good or bad, desirable or undesirable. The challenge is to understand your own and your date's inclinations.

➤ Sometimes it's easier to win over a person if you approach them first in their love style.

➤ Tests and quizzes about personality and behavior—no matter how cursory—can be fun, give you valuable clues about you and your dates, and be a good way to get you talking.

Chapter 14

Dating Disasters and Dilemmas

In This Chapter

➤ What to do when he doesn't call

➤ Breaking out of the dating daisy chain

➤ Dangerous liaisons to look out for

➤ The ugly trio of feeling used, abused, and foolish

➤ Hit-and-run lover alert

➤ What to do with cheating

➤ Breaking out of abuse

It would be wonderful if all of dating was a smooth, happy road. Unfortunately, there are bound to be some bumps and possible painful collisions.

Through every dating horror, painful moment, and disappointment, always remember to maintain your self-esteem. Never do anything to compromise it or hurt yourself. Think of your most precious possessions: your car, your childhood teddy bear, your best suit. You wouldn't want these items to be stained, smashed, and least of all dragged through the mud. Now think of your heart. Handle it gently, even if others don't. If your dating disasters seem repetitive, strive towards less pain, quicker exits, and wiser choices.

Unmet Expectations

When dating, people inevitably make assumptions about what the other person feels or needs. These assumptions can lead to misunderstandings, resentment, guilt, and disappointment. You can prevent these feelings by keeping track of your realistic and unrealistic expectations.

When Laura invited Dave to her best friend's wedding weekend activities, she was hoping to be with someone she could feel close to on such an intimate occasion. Overcome by the feeling of love in the air, Laura wanted Dave to hold her hand and look at her admiringly. Instead, Dave was chilly towards her. Dave later admitted that he had fallen for another girl the week before and assumed that Laura just needed an escort.

Laura's experience teaches us a few lessons:

➤ Know the person better before you get into a situation that stimulates your expectations that this could work out.

➤ Have no expectations, since whatever happens between two people is unpredictable, and since some people react poorly to demands. You get more if you're in "non-demand" mode.

➤ Be clear about the "deal"—what you both want out of the time together. Does he just want to have a good time? Is she looking for romance?

➤ Be honest about other relationships you each have. Ask "Have you met someone else?" If his or her mind, heart, and sexual energy are elsewhere, the relationship becomes confusing and possibly emotionally devastating.

➤ Be aware of your "love script"—the role you want the other person to play. Sometimes the person is either not aware or not interested in your plans, making the outcome upsetting for both of you.

The "Why Doesn't He Call?" Dilemma

It's a common and painful experience: "We had a great time, but she blew me off every time I called," or "We had great sex and then I didn't hear from him." You end up feeling used and foolish. You also begin questioning yourself ("What's wrong with me?"), blaming yourself ("I should have been more attentive or less demanding"), or resolving never to love again.

Home Alone

It's dangerous to hook up with someone to try to change him. People can change, but only if they want to.

Instead of focusing on yourself as the problem, you should consider many other possible explanations. For example, she may be preoccupied with matters that have nothing to do with you. He could be relationship-dysfunctional: a user (who uses people for sex or otherwise and then discards them easily), a loner (who really doesn't relate to others or fails to follow through on plans), immature (who doesn't know common courtesy), or a non-committer (who can't keep up a relationship beyond a one-night stand).

If you've gone ahead and had sex, the upset over being rejected can be escalated. It's even more confusing if you enjoyed the encounter but still get no follow-up response. You search desperately for an explanation but before you rush to blame yourself consider the above possible explanations. In addition, he may not view sex the same way you do (for you it might be connected to love, for him it's just sex). The pain of such realizations may lead you to resolve (wisely) not to jump into bed so fast, until you know the person better, and can better predict their post-sex responses.

Whatever the reason, you shouldn't obsess about it. Learn from the experience. If you feel used, then you gave much more than you received, and you need to make sure next time that you get your needs met, too.

Dating Data

Treat dating as a learning experience—you can learn as much from "failures" as from "successes."

Michael dated a woman a few times. On one date he thought they were having a ball "car dancing" (dancing in the car at a stoplight). When he dropped her off, he started telling her how great he thought she was and what a great time he had, but he could see her eyes glazing over. Being an amateur cartoonist, he sent her a cartoon to ask her out for Valentine's Day, but she never called. "How can she blow me off like that?" he wondered.

People can have a good time, but that doesn't necessarily mean they're really into you. It seems outrageous, but even though you can laugh and talk and even be physically close, it doesn't imply a next time. Obviously, that person was enjoying him- or herself but was just not into you. It's sad, but something you have to realize and accept.

The Dating Daisy Chain

Groucho Marx once joked, "I wouldn't want to belong to any club that wants me as a member." It's a common scenario: Every girl James wants doesn't want him. But every girl who does want him, he doesn't want. I call this the "dating daisy chain." This scenario involves low self-esteem: thinking if someone wants you, he can't really have good taste, because deep down you know you're not worthy. It may also involve self-sabotage: You ensure that you never get what you say you want. Or a twisted love antennae: You're attracted to the wrong ones, the ones who don't want you. Face the

211

truth—no matter what you say, you really don't want to find someone, because no one ever works out!

It's not uncommon to go through many relationships, repeating a pattern, until you finally realize what you're doing. Think of love as a tabula rasa—an empty canvas—where we choose the colors and make the shapes. Or love as your own drama, where you're the producer, director, and all the actors. What leading lady/man are you going to cast? What is the script? Are you in the dangerous *Fatal Attraction* or the more tender *An Affair to Remember*?

Always Going for the Unavailable and Unattainable

Kimberly's dilemma is not an uncommon one: "I'm only attracted to men who have girlfriends or who are married. If they're single, I think there's something wrong with them."

Being stuck in a no-win situation reveals a need for a challenge to prove you are desirable and attractive. Both men and women get caught in this trap, going for someone who is clearly unavailable and unattainable.

To get out of this trap, examine your fears of getting involved, your need to compete (perhaps traced back to childhood sibling rivalry or Freudian dynamics to win one parent from another), and your need to test your attractiveness by stealing someone else's partner. Take up more constructive challenges, like race car driving or rock-climbing.

Also, remember that people are on different wavelengths and have different needs. Peter, for example, thought his last girlfriend was "the one." But she told him she wanted to work on her career and didn't have time for him. If you find yourself in this same situation, it doesn't mean that you're wrong for that person—only that you're wrong for that person at that time. Remember, love (as unromantic as it sounds) has a lot to do with convergent needs—the two of you being in the same place at the same time.

Attracts Only When Already Taken

Heinz wants to know why women always seem to like him when he has a girlfriend, and avoid him when he's free. The answer is simple—some men and women act more confident and carefree when they're involved, so naturally they become more attractive. In contrast, when they're not dating someone, they feel insecure and desperate, exuding unpleasant vibes that repel others.

Living with Ghosts of the Past

We carry with us ghosts of past loves that infringe on current relationships. If you've been hurt before, you might anticipate being hurt again, or protect yourself against it by hurting someone else. April, for example, has stayed away from dating because three past relationships have failed and she doesn't want to get hurt again. Tom got hurt in the past, so now he acts badly toward women first, before they get a chance to hurt him. Healthy love requires entering each relationship fresh, without acting out past love scripts.

Nothing Ever Works Out

Ishmael sat next to me in the booth at a Florida restaurant, talking about the sadness of his divorce and how he had dated women but none had worked out, leaving him depressed, disgusted and discouraged. I had to remind him not to lose heart. Of course, love is not easy to find, and patience is necessary. It's essential not to generalize "Nothing ever works out."

So many women and men feel they are losers in the dating game. They blame themselves for the fact that nothing works out. Even though I don't want you to be too hard on yourself, it can be helpful to take some responsibility.

Leslie asked me: "I'm really bad at relationships. Guys always break up with me after one month. I'm tall and attractive and I have a strong personality, so maybe they get intimidated. What could be wrong?"

Home Alone

Be cautious if an old lover calls to relive the past. Directly ask what her intentions are. She may be feeling nostalgic, have grown and wants another chance, or may simply be using you to fill an empty need.

Home Alone

Men and women can pack on the pounds easily when they're frustrated about dating. Food becomes a substitute for love. Instead of eating, do something else to make yourself feel better. Call up friends, start a hobby, get active.

Remember, one of my favorite rules: What you resist persists, and what you embrace evaporates. It's entirely possible that an attractive, strong person like Leslie intimidates others. If so, play with changing your behavior to see how it affects people drawn to you. Or stay the way you are and enjoy the dating scenarios you create.

Les Liaisons Dangereuses

Although the thought of having a dangerous liaison may seem adventurous and exciting, it may also be exactly that—dangerous. You and others may end up devastated and hurt. Watch out for these potential disasters:

➤ Flirts who try to catch you in their web and use and manipulate you for their own ego.

As John said: "I work with a woman who says she dreams about me kissing her. But she has a boyfriend. What should I do?"

Teases like this woman can be dangerous. She's playing a deadly game and John is the bait. Don't get caught up in this spider web. If you're drawn in, take note of your own vulnerability to getting attention.

➤ Flirtations with associates, friends' partners, and boyfriends' or girlfriends' parents can be deadly.

As Trish said: "My friend's husband followed me into the bathroom at a party and we had a quick one. I have a hard time facing her now."

Examine your own apparent need to mix into a relationship or family (what went on in your childhood?). Learn to control your urges and to think of others and the consequences of your actions before seeking immediate gratification.

➤ Messy relationships in circles of friends should be avoided, like Tom, who is attracted to his ex-girlfriend's sister, who is dating a friend of his. But Tom's ex wants to get back together with him. It's best to step out of the whole mess, since it's loaded with land mines of jealousies and competition.

Home Alone

Some people put their lovers through unreasonable tests and traps that end up backfiring on them. For example, Rosa put a note on her boyfriend's car as though it was from another woman (it said, "I look forward to seeing you"). When her boyfriend didn't mention it, Rosa decided he was untrustworthy—when in fact he assumed it was a mistake and didn't want to upset her. Rosa's test led to an unnecessary and unfair test of his devotion.

➤ Dating several friends is playing with fire.

As Theresa said: "I'm dating three guys who are all friends. Is there anything wrong with this?"

Dating friends gives you a sense of power—that you can control others so much they'll sacrifice friendships for your attentions. Recognize your need for "ego food," and don't be surprised if one day you're the one left out in the cold.

➤ Dating several people at the same time can be stressful. Like for Rosanda: "I'm seeing two guys at the same time, but it's really complicated. How do I choose between the two?" Sometimes it's best not to choose. Enjoy your popularity. Give yourself permission! Say, "Look how desirable I am!" Appreciate the opportunity to see many suitors, to be able to sample many types of people and ultimately to decide who you really like being with more exclusively. Just don't lie or break agreements.

➤ An obsessive attachment to bad boys/bad girls can be deadly. Bridget can't get no-good guys out of her mind, even though she feels used by guys who have girlfriends and call her for late-night sex, or expect her to have sex with their friends. Dawn's ex-boyfriend had been verbally abusive, calling her names. He cheated on her and she cheated in return. Eventually she had to get a restraining order against him, and he was put in jail. "But I still love him," she cried, "and I want him back." Like moths attracted to a flame, Bridget and Dawn are in danger. If you fall into this category, you must examine how allowing yourself to be mistreated reflects your low self-esteem.

➤ The moth attracted to the flame is a dangerous scenario. When you see you're "doing it again," take heed and decide to do it differently this time. As Roger said: "My ex-wife made me feel worshipped, like I was the best, and then dumped me—several times. Then, this new woman did the same thing. I met her last weekend and I had that chemistry for her and fell in love. But she's a real party girl, always drunk and high on cocaine. I left her several messages to meet me somewhere, but she never called." Roger saw a pattern, but wasn't willing to stop it.

➤ Rejected lovers seeking revenge. Many people may feel the urge to become rude and mean when hurt, and try to hurt others back. Mark was on that verge. "I was seeing this woman and brought her flowers and perfume, and then heard rumors that she's been cheating on me. What can I do to get her back?" Don't spread bad energy, punish others for the ill will of one person, or defend yourself by becoming belligerent and rude to all partners. Tune your love antennae better to draw nicer people to you.

Home Alone

Demands for loads of affection can become overbearing for your partner. Back off and give him or her a chance to willingly initiate love and tenderness.

The Ugly Trio: Feeling Used, Abused, and Foolish

When you give your heart innocently and unselfishly, but then feel used, abused, or foolish, it's devastating—but a learning experience.

Brad was dating Nanette for nine months, and had just asked her to move in with him. When his phone bill came, he noticed calls to another state. Since the phone company claimed they were legitimately made from his phone, Brad called the number. A man answered, but when Brad asked for his girlfriend, she was there—with another live-in boyfriend.

Maria had been seeing Peter for six months. Since he was a struggling photographer and she was making good money as a TV producer, Maria paid for everything, including fancy restaurants, Broadway shows, and movie tickets. One night, at a party, Peter seemed to spend a great amount of time with a magazine publisher who came from a wealthy family. Maria dismissed it until months later, when Peter claimed that he was spending weekends with his sister (whom Maria didn't know he had), who was stricken with cancer. Later, a friend told her that she had run into him several weekends on the publisher's yacht, and that they were "an item."

Brad, Maria, and hundreds of others want to know, "How could this happen to me?" "How could I have been so blind?" Double-crossers do their dirty deeds to be in control, to have their cake and eat it too, and to have the security and freedom to find the best "deal." The double-crossed are lulled into false security; they deny the evidence and are temporarily blinded. It happens to the smartest of men and women when they have their guard down. Learn to interview your partners more carefully and to be sensitive to troublesome clues early on. Trust your instincts (Maria had been puzzled to suddenly learn that Peter had a sister, but had unfortunately dismissed her doubts), and tune your love antennae for someone with more honesty and integrity.

Dumped for No Reason: The Hit-and-Run Lover

It's another common woe: "I was dating a guy for eight months. Things were going well, I thought, when all of a sudden he dumped me for no reason. Why did he do this?"

It is very painful to be pursued wildly but then summarily discarded, leaving you confused and frustrated. If this happens to you, you have a right to ask why. Your former love's answer may help you learn more about dating, people, and yourself. Something may have been missing for the other person. An imbalance in feelings while dating is all too common—and painful. It feels great when you are both in the same place, at the same level of interest. But it feels awful when one person cares more than the other. Learn a lesson from a date's quick exits. Obviously, he wasn't playing straight with you, or he would have given you more clues about wanting out. Be more alert to subtle cues that someone isn't committed.

Home Alone

Singles often find holidays such as New Year's Eve and Valentine's Day stressful and depressing. To prevent any unhappiness, make plans with friends—it's better to be with those who care about you than to be alone or to take a risk on someone you're unsure about.

Smooth Talk'n

Conscious Singles Connection has prepared a 40-minute audiotape to help singles lower their stress level and find positive ways to enjoy the holidays. They can be reached at (914) 339-2732.

Play fair and kind in the dating game by not being a hit-and-run lover, who, like a hit-and-run driver, leaves blood behind. Why have someone else's bleeding heart on your conscience? And remember, what goes around comes around. Keep your dating karma (your energy in life) clean.

Skeletons in the Closet

Keeping secrets can be destructive for a relationship, but sharing them at the wrong time or when trust is not established can be even more devastating.

Some people "freak out" when they discover a partner's keepsakes. Keep in mind that everyone is entitled to their personal belongings. If your partner's keepsakes upset you, examine your own insecurities: Are you jealous that you don't have similar memories or important past relationships? Is your current relationship fragile?

Home Alone

Most people keep memories of past loves: gifts, letters, cards, photos. People who save them have a need to remember their history or to be reassured of their past attractiveness. This is fine as long as these keepsakes aren't excuses or escapes from moving on. Monica Lewinsky's now-infamous semen-stained dress has heightened lovers' paranoia that keepsakes can be used against them, as hers was used against President Clinton.

Secrets You Should Tell

Most of us have secrets we'd be afraid to tell others. Yet intimate sharing can be one of the strongest bonds between two people. For this reason, you must think carefully about sharing very private matters, to decide what impact it will have on your relationship.

Example 1:

Sandy: "I'm 28 and still a virgin. I don't want this man I'm dating to know. I'm embarrassed and I don't want him to think he's conquering me."

Some men love to know that they're someone's "first." Face your feelings (embarrassment, fear, worries about how you'll perform), and get over them. Instead of being embarrassed, you should be proud. Keep in mind that sex is not about power, or about a guy owning you. Sex is about two people sharing their bodies and souls with each other, but maintaining their own integrity of self.

Example 2:

Heather: "My boyfriend thinks I'm a hairstylist, but he doesn't know I'm also an escort. I've been saving money for a new car. Should I tell him the truth?"

Yes. If he finds out on his own he'll be furious that you kept such a big secret from him and will likely not trust you again. He may be titillated or threatened by your secret job, but he has a right to know in the interests of safe sex and overall honesty.

Secrets You Should Not Tell

Here are some secrets that men and women have been unsure whether they should tell.

Chrissie: "I live with a guy, but we haven't had sex in ages. So two or three times a week I sneak out of bed in the middle of the night while he's sleeping and go to his best friend's house. Should I tell him what's going on?"

Chad: "I got drunk at a party and ended up spending a lot of time with two girls. I love my girlfriend, but should I tell her?"

Brian: "My girlfriend gets me right to the edge of sex but then stops. She admitted to me that she's gone all the way with other guys, so why doesn't she with me?"

Before you would ever reveal a potentially harmful secret, consider the following:

➤ Examine your intentions. What do you want the other person to give you? If you want absolution from your guilt, work that out in church. If you want to hurt your date, examine why you are so bitter. Sometimes you want to be found out. Often when a mate is unaware, or denies, that you cheat, you end up resenting him for living in denial or not caring enough. For example, it's unlikely that Chrissie's boyfriend doesn't suspect that something's going on.

➤ Consider other ways to get what you want. If you need more love, attention, or sex, ask for it directly. For example, Brian might get his girlfriend to have sex with him if he stops pestering and criticizing her, and if he helps her discuss her fears about love, sex, and any past bad experiences.

➤ Anticipate the impact such a confession will have on the other person. Be considerate. Sharing some sensitive past sexual experiences may make your present partner obsess endlessly about it. When Jake told Alice about his exciting past with an uninhibited woman, Alice couldn't stop counting her orgasms with him and feeling she came up short.

Confronted with Cheaters—Changing Them or Changing Yourself

I get heartsick from hearing so many stories like "My boyfriend cheats on me and lies, but I still love him." How can you love someone who treats you so poorly? That is a sure sign of low self-esteem and a lack of understanding of what love is. And when you do discover that a lover has cheated, anger, depression, and distrust will run rampant.

Accept these feelings as normal, clarify your relationship, and decide whether you can come to a new agreement about fidelity or whether you should break up. Avoid cheating and guilt by not making agreements about fidelity that you can't keep. Allow yourself to rebuild trust without wallowing in disappointment or generalizing that all men or women are rotten and deceitful.

One way to get over the desire for continually new partners when you're in a committed relationship is to always treat each other like new lovers. Often, couples start out dating by putting their best foot forward, trying to impress one another, and then fall into a rut, taking each other for granted. Keep asking each other questions that you would on a new date: What did you do today? Have you seen any good movies lately? What's your favorite food?

Home Alone

Look at every relationship as a mirror. If you're trying to change someone, you're really trying to change yourself through that person.

Eve and the Apple of Temptation

Think before you act. Consider the consequences of any sexual encounter. Angela had been seeing Frank for two years when he proposed. They had become best friends, but the sex was not there anymore. Meanwhile, Angela's old boyfriend has come back on the scene. With him, the sex was hot and Angela wants to taste it one more time before she marries. But it would be far wiser for her to use that passion and to re-ignite what she has with Frank.

Some men and women who are very sensual and open may never stop being interested in others even when they love one person. This doesn't mean they are bad or unsuited for their love—what matters is that they control themselves from acting on their attraction.

Early Promises

Greg's story is typical. "I'm going away to college and I told my girlfriend I would be true to her, but I know I'm going to get there and there will be lots of other women. What should I do?"

Some people pledge fidelity even when they know it will be difficult because they don't want to lose their "steady," even if they want to be free to date others. In other words, they want to have their cake and eat it too.

Rather than break an agreement, it is wiser to be honest. Your partner may be relieved and might also want some freedom. If not, it's better to deal with disappointment up front, and clarify your relationship, rather than cheat and face betrayal and hurt. If your relationship is genuine, you won't need to act faithful, whether you're two states or two streets apart. Forcing someone to promise faithfulness doesn't make them genuinely feel it. And making an "exclusivity contract" before you're ready can make you feel resentful, frustrated, and suffocated. Agree to see others without telling about your other liaisons, unless one becomes significant enough to change your relationship. You could be so upset by the thought of your lover seeing other people that you genuinely want to make more of a commitment to each other.

Snooping

It's understandable to want to confirm your suspicions of a partner's infidelity. Snooping can be irresistible. Amanda dug around in her boyfriend's closet and found a book of letters, including one from a girl that said, "I don't care about Amanda's feelings, what happened between us was great and we can't fight it." Steve read his girlfriend's diary and found entries about her fantasies about other guys he knows. MaryBeth's boyfriend said he was going away on a business trip, but when she listened to his answering machine she heard his ex's voice saying, "All is okay. I'll see you at the appointed place."

Short of hiring a private detective, you can use your own ingenuity to get at the truth, from checking phone bills to credit card receipts. When Lauren spied on her boyfriend, Jack, she found him kissing one of her friends. She then started carrying around a camera, and the next time she saw them together, she snapped a picture of them and had it enlarged. She confronted Jack, and after he lied about the incident, she whipped out the telling photo.

Indeed, Lauren expended an awful lot of energy being sneaky rather than just confronting Jack with what she saw. In general, when you suspect or discover infidelity, don't be afraid to confront your partner directly—however you choose to. But be ready for denials and even lies. In that case, you may have to be a little more creative, as Lauren was. Gathering evidence and direct confrontations can help restore the badly damaged self-esteem that results from feeling fooled.

Long–Distance Love

"Out of sight, out of mind"—is it true? Or does absence make the heart grow fonder and distance lend enchantment? Many men and women ask me if long-distance romances can work. They can, if you keep sharing (by phone, fax, letters, cards, e-mail), plan reunions in enough time to satisfy both your needs for closeness, and keep clarifying your commitment status. But "out of sight" can lead to "out of mind" if the time intervals are longer than your tolerance and need for closeness; if you neglect reassuring each other; and if you develop too-separate lives, interests, and relationships. When Ricky had to move to another state for work and asked his girlfriend to come with him, she refused—not wanting to leave her job and family—and the relationship was doomed. Clearly, being with him was not as important to her as the other anchors in her life. Ricky needed to give her an ultimatum to join him, or to let her go.

Dating Data

If your long-distance love doesn't want to give you the freedom you want, you may have to give it to yourself. If you lose your long-distance love in the process, the relationship wasn't solid enough to last.

Abuse—Stop It Before It Begins

When dating someone, it's important to pay close attention to how you're being treated. If you're being treated poorly in the dating stage, it won't get better—and will likely get worse if you continue the relationship. Don't stand for any abuse, whether it's physical, sexual, or psychological. Also, note how past abusive experiences (date rape, harassment, incest) affect your current relationship in terms of being hesitant to trust and to commit.

Dating Data

Here are some general guidelines to bear in mind to keep you from being trapped in an abusive relationship:

➤ No one deserves to be abused.

➤ No one has the right to touch you or demand sex from you.

➤ You're not to blame for being abused.

➤ Men as well as women can be abused.

➤ Protect yourself from abuse by being assertive, avoiding dangerous situations, and avoiding alcohol and drug use.

➤ If you have been abused in the past, share that experience with a mate who has proven to be trustworthy.

➤ Report any abuse to authorities.

How Do You Know if You're in an Abusive Relationship?

If you are being abused in a relationship, it still is very possible that you really do care for the person, especially when they act kindly or lovingly in spells. You might even tend to deny that you are in an abusive relationship. The following can help you recognize the signs of a destructive union:

➤ If you are being put down/criticized/controlled

➤ If you are ever shoved, pushed, or slapped

➤ If you are ever forced to do anything despite saying "no"

➤ If your partner apologizes for treating you poorly but does it again

➤ If you wish you could get out of the relationship but feel trapped

➤ If you have a history of similar relationships

Dating Data

Most rapes are committed by people who are known to the victim rather than by strangers. A 1991 study prepared by the National Victims Center reports that more than 12 million women have been raped, with 57 percent of the younger women victimized on a date. Prevent date rape by avoiding situations that could lead to danger (like drinking too much at wild parties), dispelling harmful sex-role stereotypes (that girls owe boys sex, or that sexually active girls ask for or deserve date rape), and communicating clear sexual intentions.

Why People Stay in Abusive Relationships

Despite the pain of abuse, some women and men choose to stay in abusive relationships, clinging to excuses such as the following:

Dating Data

Surveys show that one in four women, and up to one in seven men, has been abused at some point in her/his past. A research study on my radio show "LovePhones" revealed that over a third of my callers admitted to some kind of abuse while dating.

➤ "He was my first." People often get addicted to their first love or to the first person they had sex with. They want desperately to believe in the fantasy of a beautiful first love, and are unwilling to face the reality that it has turned ugly.

➤ "We've been together so many years already." Granted, it's hard to turn your back on years with someone, but think of it as an investment. When you've sunk money into a stock that keeps going down, there comes a time when you have to cut your losses and sell, instead of hoping and praying that some miracle will happen.

➤ "I know it can change." People addicted to bad relationships (called "co-dependents") have a problem themselves if they are willing to sacrifice their own happiness and life in order to save an abusive or addicted partner. If you suffer from this sad syndrome, you need to concentrate on saving yourself.

➤ "I'm afraid to lose him." Think about losing your self-esteem instead and convince yourself there will be someone else who will love you in a healthier way.

➤ "If I leave, he'll kill me." When your safety is threatened, you had better get out. True love does not mean being controlled by another person or living in a prison of fear.

Home Alone

More people are aware of abuse when it involves physical blows or forced sexual acts, but not when it erodes self-confidence and self-esteem. But psychological abuse can be just as damaging and even more difficult to recognize, because it can be subtle at first. For instance, Pam was dating Patrick for seven months. In the beginning he would just butt in whenever she spoke, and criticize and contradict her. But over time, his behavior became nastier—telling her to shut up in front of people and calling her stupid when she voiced an opinion. Eventually he began calling her derogatory names. As Pam learned, even though psychological abuse evolves slowly and subtly, it does evolve and is just as damaging as physical abuse.

Getting Out of an Abusive Relationship

Ending abuse is a sign of self-esteem. It requires self-esteem to say "I will not put up with this" and "I deserve better." But it can be very difficult to get out of an abusive relationship when you have limited financial, social, or emotional resources, or really care about the person. You can help yourself break free of an abusive relationship by doing the following:

➤ Recognize that the abuser has a serious problem, requiring professional help.

➤ Realize that you have a choice.

➤ Do not believe threats that you are undesirable or unworthy.

➤ Face the ghosts from your past when you may have been treated poorly and separate these from your present—when you deserve to be treated well.

➤ Repair your self-esteem. Practice affirmations: "I will only be spoken to in loving terms," "I deserve to be treated well."

➤ Take responsibility for your choices. Ask yourself "Why do I allow this person in my life script?" "What do I need to teach myself?" Remember, the people we are attracted to reflect something about ourselves.

➤ Tune your love antennae only for those who will treat you well. Take inspiration from Grammy-winning singer/songwriter Alanis Morrisette, who told me that after years of being treated poorly by a man, she can now tell within 15 seconds of meeting someone whether that person will treat her well or not. While it is not always possible to spot an abuser right away, since most people are on their best behavior at the start of a relationship and others become abusive when they drink, you do have to learn to develop the skill of observing people as much as possible to determine their potential for abuse.

➤ Stop making excuses for the person who is treating you badly and for yourself for staying in the relationship. Sympathy is sweet, but self-destruction is stupid.

➤ Realize you help the other person by refusing to be abused. Only when you stop putting up with the abuse does the abuser have a chance to get help.

➤ Get support from family and friends and professional help to turn powerlessness into empowerment, and to turn being a victim into being a survivor.

➤ Consider legal action to bring the abuser to justice and to further restore a sense of personal power.

➤ Each time you choose to treat yourself well, you are building stronger self-esteem and will ensure that the next suitor treats you well—as you deserve to be treated!

The Least You Need to Know

➤ Resist making assumptions about other people's feelings or needs.

➤ Always maintain your self-esteem, no matter how bad the date was, or how badly you feel.

➤ Examine your dating patterns carefully—they may reveal a great deal about your own personality.

➤ Think twice before having a dangerous liaison. It may be disastrous to both you and others.

➤ Before you tell a secret, evaluate your intentions.

➤ If you were cheated on, allow yourself to rebuild trust in someone else.

➤ Stop any kind of abuse—remember, it won't get better, and you deserve better.

Chapter 15

"Can We Talk?"

In This Chapter

➤ A quiz to determine your communication type

➤ Is your mate a good communicator?

➤ What to do if he won't talk

➤ What to share and what not to share

➤ Communication do's and don'ts

➤ How to read his mind

In a roomful of potential mates, who's the one you'd feel most comfortable with? Likely it's the one who seems "on your wavelength"—someone you can talk to. Good communication is the key to a good relationship. Whether you're the silent type or a talker, you have to feel that you can relate to and are understood by your partner—that you "speak the same language."

However, people do have different styles of communication. If you date someone whose style is different from yours, it is possible to adapt—as long as you know your own style, and what you're adapting to!

Communication Quiz

What kind of communicator are you? Find out your communication type by taking the following short quiz:

1. You've just had a big fight with your friend when your date calls. He tells you that he has just lost his job. You:

   a. Tell him all the details about the argument you had with your friend first.

   b. Warn him that you're upset, but then drop it to listen to him.

   c. Listen and pretend nothing happened to you.

2. You've been dating for a while and have a minor disagreement that you feel could erupt into your first big fight. You:

   a. Need to blow your stack and say everything that's on your mind.

   b. Don't want to talk about it until you both cool down.

   c. Want to forget about the disagreement completely because you feel there's no point in talking about it.

Smooth Talk'n

Paying attention and noticing details are also qualities of good communication skills. It's a tremendous high to feel "heard" by someone. For example, while Andy and Melissa were riding in the car, she got excited when her favorite song came on the radio. The next day, he surprised her with the CD containing that song.

If you selected answer a) to both situations, you have the need to spill out your feelings. I label these kinds of people as Niagara Falls communicators—people who need to pour out their emotions to relieve their tension.

Niagara Fallers clash with Boulder Dam communicators—those who answered both situations with choice c). These people don't like facing and revealing their emotions, either because they're too frightened of their feelings or because they feel it's a waste of time. They usually have problems being intimate because they don't want anyone or any feelings to get the better of them.

Though they are opposites, Niagara Falls and Boulder Dam communicators may be drawn to each other. Boulder Dammers look to Niagara Fallers to unleash or vicariously express their feelings, and Niagara Fallers look to Boulder Dammers to help them control their troublesome outbursts. But ultimately, a match can lead to unhappiness, as the Dammers get too uncomfortable and the Niagara Fallers get too frustrated.

Steamship communicators, those who answered b), are sturdy communicators who aim to be reasonable. They hold a steady course so that they are never running the rapids of uncontrolled Niagara Fallers, but are also never stagnated like the Boulder Dammers. Because they have a little of the two extremes, they can get along with either type of communicator.

Two Boulder Dammers and two Steamships usually get along easier with each other than two Niagara Fallers. This is because Niagara Fallers often blow up easily, leading to fights with no one there to referee.

Talkers Versus Silent Types—Which Is Better?

"When my boyfriend and I fight, is it better to talk it out right away, or talk about it later when we both cool down?"

The answer to this question depends on your communication styles, that is affected by how you both deal with your feelings and anxiety. Some people need to get their feelings out and have an argument resolved right away, or their tension grows. As soon as these types of people have let off some steam, they feel relieved and more connected, and their anxiety is reduced. For others, talking about something right away is what makes their tension grow, so they need a cooling-off period before they can communicate. Neither style is right or wrong, it's just a matter of understanding what works for you and your partner. Then you can adjust and accept each other's way.

When He Doesn't Talk

It's the biggest complaint women have about men: they don't talk about their feelings. The good news is that men are making progress in this category. The bad news is that men still have a long way to go. Women tend to interpret a man's silence as deadly. Often they ask, "What are you thinking?" when they really want reassurance: "I'm thinking of you." Rather than saying, "You never talk to me," it's better to say to your male partner, "I'd really like to talk about (something specific)" because men respond better to specifics and clear requests about what they can *do*.

What's new in this new millennium is that these communication issues don't apply just to men. Interestingly enough, I hear some men these days making the same complaints about women in their relationships.

For example, Brad called me on the radio saying, "My girlfriend gets off the phone too quick. I want to talk to her but she hangs up so fast, and I get really frustrated." One reason for this is that as women become more independent in their financial, social, and sexual roles, some have taken on more of the traditionally male ways of communicating. Also, there are some women who—like the male stereotype—just don't like to talk.

Dating Data

Women and men are conditioned at a very young age on how they should communicate. From childhood, tradition still reigns, where girls are taught to openly express their feelings while boys are taught to hold in their emotions. Girls tend to spend hours on the phone talking to their girlfriends about their problems while boys are taught to solve their problems on their own. Unfortunately, too, some people today still perceive emotional men as being "weak."

The advice in the situations below apply equally for him if *she* won't talk, as for her when *he* won't talk.

"My boyfriend is afraid to express his feelings and has a hard time admitting them. What should I do?"

Be gentle, kind, patient, and reassuring. Some people are scared to reveal their feelings. It makes them feel vulnerable, exposed, and out of control. Reward your mate when he does make an effort to express himself by saying "Thank you. I love when you say how you feel." Or, "I know that was difficult for you to say, but thank you for doing it." Or ask him about his experience in a reassuring way: "Now that you've said that, how do you feel about it? You may have expected some disaster or that you would be hurt. But, see, nothing like that happened."

"My boyfriend has a hard time expressing his feelings. But he did admit that he's scared to because he was hurt once before. What can I do to make him less frightened?"

First of all, appreciate the effort it took for him to tell you that he's scared, and that he was hurt before. Those are two big confessions, and reveal a tremendous effort to open up.

Reassure him that everyone has been hurt sometime, and that being with you will not mean a repeat of the past. Tell him that he can recover slowly by building up his trust again. You can even agree on a label for his feeling—for example, call it the "fear factor." Make it humorous. Every time he feels it, have him alert you. Then both of you can turn it into something funny, like, "Oh, the fear factor is rearing its ugly head again."

"My boyfriend sends out mixed signals about whether he really wants to be with me. When I've confronted him, he's withdrawn. I'm afraid if I confront him again, he'll get tired of me and really break it off."

It's one thing to be a different kind of communicator from your mate, it's another if you feel threatened by trying to communicate. Don't suffer from anxiety. If you need an answer to a question—get the answer! If you push and he ends your relationship, what kind of future would you really have with that type of communicator anyway?

Is Your Mate a Good Communicator?

Take the following quiz to discover how well your mate communicates with you.

Picture the following scenarios:

1. You tell the man you're dating that you're scared to get involved because you once had a bad experience where you got really hurt. He:

    a. Changes the subject, figuring it's too hurtful for you to talk about and he's really not interested anyway.

    b. Turns the table around and talks about his dating experiences.

    c. Asks you what happened.

If he changes the subject, (answer a), you should find out why. Is it because such openness makes him uncomfortable or because he isn't interested (both are bad signs)?

Is he afraid you'll be too hurt to discuss the subject (a better reason but still an avoidance of your feelings)? If he always turns the conversation to his experiences, (answer b), he's too self-centered to care about you. The best answer is c), because your mate shows that he has empathy. The mates who ask questions and say, "Tell me more," care about finding out about the real you and are able to show it.

2. You tell the man you're dating that a friend of yours is miserable because she was dumped by her boyfriend a few weeks ago and you're still upset for her. You then mention her name a few times in the next conversation you have with him. He:

   a. Says he doesn't remember what you said about her before.

   b. Asks you who she is.

   c. Asks you whether you want to ask her to join you the next time you go out.

Remembering what someone told you and doing something about it is a sign of a good communicator and shows the person really cares about you, as in choice c). However, choices a) and b) may show that the person either doesn't concentrate on what you say, or isn't interested enough.

3. You call your girlfriend on the phone and she's chatting on the other line with another friend. You say it's an emergency. She:

   a. Asks you to call her back later.

   b. Puts you on hold and comes back eons later to your line.

   c. Gets off the other line to talk to you.

Placing priority on the relationship and making the other person feel important is a sure sign of good communication and caring. There's nothing more exciting than thinking that you come first, no matter what. Answers a) and b) are not unacceptable, but a c) answer reveals her good character, raises your self-esteem and strengthens your bond together.

4. You tell the woman you're dating that you were hurt by something she did. She:

   a. Tells you that you're too sensitive.

   b. Denies that she did anything wrong.

   c. Apologizes and asks what she did to hurt you.

continues

continued

Defensiveness, as in answer a), and denial, as in answer b), shut down communication and sabotage closeness and openness. Someone who can accept your feelings and examine their own behavior, as in answer c), is the best choice.

5. You tell the guy you're dating that you would like to spend more time with him. He says:

   a. "We already spend a lot of time together."

   b. "Just like all women—it's never enough."

   c. "Okay, but why? Do you feel like we're not close enough?"

Pointing out whether someone is right or wrong, as in answer a), doesn't get to the heart of the matter. Generalizing, as in b), further negates the person's feelings. Choice c) shows that the person is not being defensive, but rather is truly open to what is really troubling you.

6. You're trying to tell the guy you're dating how you feel about something he said. He:

   a. Gets impatient because you're not spitting it out fast enough.

   b. Asks you what you mean.

   c. Finishes your thought for you.

Intuition, as in c), is another high state of communication. People really in synch with each other can anticipate each other's thoughts and can finish each other's statements. It's an exciting and affirming experience—but not one you should expect. Nor should you think that if someone cannot do that with you, he doesn't love you. Answer b) shows that the person is patient and is trying to understand you—a good sign, and certainly better than answer a), which shuts you up and shuts you out.

Mind-Reading

As I just mentioned above, when two people are in sync, they can often tell what the other is thinking and feeling. The feeling is exhilarating when she finishes your sentences, or he says he knows exactly what you mean. But let me reiterate that reading each other's mind is not always possible, nor does it mean you're not right for each other.

"What are you supposed to do when a woman wants you to automatically know everything she's thinking, and then gets angry when you don't?"

You tell her that if she cares about you, she should share her feelings with you and not play mind games. She needs to be more open and assertive when expressing her thoughts and feelings, without expecting you to automatically know her needs.

If you are the silent one, why are you afraid to say what's on your mind? Are you afraid that you'll be judged, sound silly, or be misunderstood? Are there feelings or memories you don't want to face? Or are you afraid of getting hurt if you open up?

To increase your communication, try this exercise. On a piece of paper, write down some thoughts or experiences you'd love to—but fear to—share. Writing them down is an important step to clarifying the experience, feeling the fear, and possibly sharing the feeling.

Some people were indulged by their parents when they were children—anticipating their every need and making sure to meet each of them. As adults, these men and women expect their lover to do the same, and are quick to lose patience with mates who are not intuitive to their every feeling. They need to learn to be patient, accept that their lovers are not their parents, and learn how to communicate their needs without resentment.

Although you may think you're terrible at "reading" people, you're probably better at it than you think. I use an exercise in my classes to prove that everyone is capable of being intuitive.

Find two other people to do this exercise with you. Person A thinks of a situation and assumes a body position consistent with the experience. Person B mimics the body position of Person A and concentrates on what that feels like, and reports on what Person A must be thinking. Person C monitors and adjusts Person B's position to match Person A's position as closely as possible. It's uncanny how often Person B is right in reporting what Person A is thinking.

The exercise proves that concentrating on the other person's emotions and getting into his or her mental as well as physical "space" can help you tune in to others (since a large proportion of the messages of what someone means is communicated through body language).

How Much Should You Share?

Some books about dating tell readers to "hold back" on some of their feelings and not to give away anything. As in playing poker, they want you to keep your cards close to your vest. But, you've probably noted from my advice throughout this book, I don't agree with this type of game-playing. If you feel that you have to resist being yourself, the relationship is not right for you. A good relationship is one where you feel you can ask your partner anything, speak your mind, and do what comes naturally.

But hold on. There are certain limits to what you should share:

➤ Don't talk about past loves unless you are perfectly sure that your date won't feel jealous or threatened. Evaluate why you are discussing the past (are you trying to foster jealousy or boost your own ego?).

➤ Similarly, don't talk about others you may be dating at the same time. This only stimulates competitiveness, disinterest, or judgments that may backfire on you, making the person drop out of a crowded playing field.

➤ Don't confess to something in order to selfishly get over your own guilt. For instance, suppose you told your date that you were busy at work, but really you had a date with someone else. Always assess what the impact of such confessions would be on the person you're seeing. Of course, you should think about—and resist—betrayal beforehand, but once the damage is done, why throw salt on an open wound? Learn to forgive yourself. If you want to have a clear conscience, go to church. Don't expect a hurt person to absolve you and make you feel better.

Handling Some Touchy Situations

Even the touchiest situations can be dealt with if you know how to communicate effectively. Here are two examples:

"How do I tell the guy I'm dating that he's cheap?"

Have a general discussion about money and what it means to both of you. Consider using an ice-breaker so that he's not put on the defensive. Ask him to explain his fears about money. What did he learn in childhood about handling money (he could be copying his father)? Money can also be symbolic of a person's security, so discuss those deeper feelings.

Smooth Talk'n

One way to show a person that you've been listening carefully is to repeat what the other person said. For example, if your date says "I'd like us to be closer," you say, "So you want to be closer." Then follow it up with a question like "Tell me more about what you mean by that."

"How do I tell my girlfriend, who has been under a lot of stress lately, that she's put on weight as a result of using food as a stress-reliever?"

Losing weight involves changing your lifestyle, exploring your emotional needs, and adopting an eating and exercise plan. You may suggest to your girlfriend that she's using food as a way to relax or to comfort herself, and that you'd like to help her find other solutions. Offer support and reassure her that you love her for who she is, not for what she looks like. Suggest that you exercise and eat more healthily together. Never drop hints about how heavy she looks; it will only damage her self-esteem.

Guidelines for Good Communication

There is no one right or wrong way to talk and express yourself. Learn to trust yourself and your style first. Any attempt at communicating will be appreciated and is a step in the right direction. Here are a few points to keep in mind:

➤ Talking is an ongoing process. You can't always cover a topic all in one conversation. If that's the case, end the conversation with: "We can continue this at another time."

➤ When expressing yourself, be as honest and straightforward as you can without beating around the bush. Get to the point and be clear about what you want to say or ask.

➤ Be open to questions. Give permission to your date to ask you anything.

➤ Be a good listener. Learn to listen without interrupting—hold back responding until the other person has finished a thought.

➤ It's okay to be embarrassed. Some topics are scary to discuss. Admit that you feel this way.

➤ Say up front what you think your boyfriend or girlfriend might fear when trying to discuss a topic. Preface the discussion by saying something like, "I don't want you to be hurt" or "I don't want this to scare you."

➤ Practice talking about difficult things: "I'm hurt by what you did."

➤ Not knowing what to say is okay, but you can always come up with some explanation or answer. Nothing is more frustrating in a conversation than to hear a person say "I don't know," or worse, say nothing at all. You can say "I'm not sure why this happened, but it could be because . . ." Or you can ask what the other person thinks or feels.

➤ Don't run away from a conversation. Talking is not always easy. Don't let your anxiety get the best of you. If you have something to say, say it.

➤ Know what's motivating and affecting you. Getting to the bottom of an issue is like peeling the layers of an onion. Talk is often a smokescreen for something else. What is your real need (to be loved, listened to, reassured)?

Smooth Talk'n

When pointing out something you don't like about a date, it's important to say what you *do* like first. Be careful not to criticize your date; criticisms only make people defensive and deflated. When the brain creates a positive image, positive behavior can follow.

Smooth Talk'n

When asking a question or putting in a request, your best chance of getting what you want is to ask without expectations or demands (called "nondemand" requests). Simply state what you'd like without implying punishment or guilt-inducing feelings. This way the other person is free to give willingly or refuse without being defensive.

Communicating Dos and Don'ts

Words can be reassuring by easing your mate's fears, and can be alluring by promising pleasures to come. In order to get to these benefits, keep in mind the following helpful guidelines:

235

➤ DO relax. Anxiety ruins your concentration and confidence. Take deep breaths every time you feel like ending a conversation out of fear.

➤ DO listen to your date.

➤ DO be prepared for repetition. If the issue comes up again and again, it hasn't been resolved. Instead of complaining that your date is nagging, ask "What is really going on here? Why is the subject still bothering you?"

➤ DO be patient. Give the person time to express himself.

➤ DO admit that both of you have differences, which are okay.

➤ DO expect to feel uncomfortable. It's not always easy to confront issues.

➤ DON'T think you have to solve everything at one time.

➤ DON'T put your date down with vulgar terms and expressions. It's disrespectful and cheapens not only your date but yourself as well.

➤ DON'T criticize, judge, or make fun of what your date has to say. You both have to feel comfortable sharing.

The key to having good and open communication with someone is to make him or her feel secure, loved, and respected. Speaking your mind and sharing feelings creates a bond that's sure to deepen your relationship. Doing this in a mutually respectful way also raises your self-esteem—and your partner's.

The Least You Need to Know

➤ Good communication is the key to a good relationship. It requires attention, acceptance, and appreciation.

➤ Understand and accept other people's communication styles, especially if they are different from your own.

➤ You can get non–talkers to communicate more by offering a lot of encouragement and compliments for when they do open up.

➤ Always be respectful, open, and honest.

➤ Give sharing your best effort.

Chapter 16

Men and Women: What's the Difference?

In This Chapter

➤ Sex role stereotypes

➤ Why men and women talk and love differently

➤ Left-brain versus right-brain approaches to life

➤ The new gender war

➤ Exercises for breaking sex stereotypes

Best-selling author and counselor John Gray has summed up the differences between the sexes with this catchy metaphor: Men are from Mars and women from Venus.

Eastern philosophy has always acknowledged those differences between the sexes. The Chinese "yin-yang" symbol shown below depicts the masculine (active, positive) and feminine (passive, negative) aspects of nature as two contrasting, but complementary, parts of a circle. Their interaction is essential to maintaining harmony and balance in the universe.

So if interaction is essential to harmony, why do men and women seem to clash and miscommunicate so frequently? In this chapter, you'll see why men and women express themselves so differently, and what you can do to help prevent or ease the friction that sometimes arises in your own relationship.

Left-Brain Versus Right-Brain Approaches to Life

It's easy to make gender generalizations: Men are stubborn, women clingy. Men love violent movies; women prefer romantic comedies. But are there any facts to back up these contentions, or do most of us simply fall back on cultural clichés? In fact, there is a lot of scientific information to help us understand what most of us sense already—that men and women communicate differently!

Dating Data

The Virginia Slims Opinion Polls taken over the past quarter century indicate that certain sex role stereotypes persist. Women comment that men would rather get lost than stop and ask for directions, are bad cooks, monopolize the remote control, and can't find things around the house without a woman's help. Marlo Thomas once joked that hubby Phil Donahue always asks her where his shoes are, "as if my womb had sonar for his shoes and socks."

Research at the Ned Herrmann Group, with whom I've been associated for many years, suggests that most men are more predominantly left-brained, with their cognitive style being more logical (they tend to focus on problems and solutions). Women, on the other hand, tend to be more right-brained, with more of an emphasis on communication and emotion. This left- or right-brain dominance affects all kinds of everyday interactions and exchanges. The following table describes many of the ways in which right- or left-brain characteristics can show up in everyday life.

How Differences in Brain Dominance Affect Behavior

Left Brain	Right Brain
Values power, being in control	Values love and communication
Is motivated by being right	Is motivated by togetherness and harmony
Needs approval and acceptance	Needs appreciation and attention
Fulfilled by achieving goals	Fulfilled by expression and relating
Hates being told what to do	Accepts direction
More interested in news and sports	More interested in romance novels and self-help
Relates well to objects and things	Relates well to people
Likes to prove things	Likes to improve things
Comfortable with gadgets and hi-tech	Comfortable with gab groups

Brain differences help explain why many men won't ask for directions (he needs to be right), and why many women get upset when men want them to get off the phone too quickly (she needs to gab). Women like to improve things, and will offer to help their mates without being asked (as a sign of love). But men need to prove themselves, so they may interpret a woman's offer of help as an implied criticism (he's just not good enough). It's easy to see how differences in brain dominance can lead to breakdowns in communication!

Communication Styles

Men and women also have different styles of communicating. I've summarized the differences in the following table, based on my own experience as well as on the research of counselor John Gray and linguist Deborah Tannen, author of the best-selling book *You Just Don't Understand*. Keep in mind that these are generalizations. In the past several decades, many men and women have come to see that it is important to "own" both "masculine" and "feminine" parts of themselves. Many men have tried to become more sensitive, while women have made strides in becoming more assertive and independent. Yet certain differences persist, and it's helpful to see how these differences play a part in the dating and mating world. Use these observations as guidelines to expand your possibilities: If one column describes you, consider the usefulness of the other.

Dating Data

What do most women list as their top complaint about men? According to my own and numerous other surveys, one of women's biggest complaints about men is that they are unable to talk about their feelings!

How Men and Women Communicate Differently

What He Does . . .	What She Does . . .
Speaks to make a point	Speaks to share feelings
Says "I"	Says "we"
Interrupts	Invites others to speak
Takes credit when things go right and blames others when things go wrong	Gives others credit and takes blame on self
Talks about facts	Talks about feelings

Differences in communication styles between the sexes are perhaps most apparent when it comes to problem-solving. When a problem comes up, there are three basic factors or steps in discussing it: the problem, the feelings about it, and the solution. Men tend to skip step two, while women tend to dwell on step two.

For instance, let's say a couple is having a conflict with punctuality—he's kept his date waiting enough times that the subject has become an "issue." She says, "It really hurts me when you keep me waiting. It makes me feel that my time doesn't mean anything to you. And when you don't call, I feel even worse." He responds with, "You've got to understand that my boss is forever dumping last-minute projects on my desk that I can't ignore." To which she responds, "How hard is it to pick up the phone? You never even bother to call." And his response, "Look at my cellular phone bill. You'll see otherwise!"

In this instance, the man is using the fact of his workload as a legitimate excuse for his tardiness. The woman, on the other hand, may accept the fact that he is overworked, but still puts an emotional spin on it. In her view, if he cared enough about her, he'd get there on time. The fact that he doesn't means that he doesn't care.

Dating Data

Survey results show that men are just as interested in romance as women, with their top three romantic fantasies being candlelight dinners, sunset walks on the beach, and bubble baths.

It would be easy for the discussion to stalemate right here. His next response might go something like this: "You're being ridiculous. I was swamped, and the time got away from me. Don't cast me as the bad one just because I want to get ahead." You can imagine the downward spiral from here.

Both parties need to step back and follow my three A's: acceptance, appreciation, and adjustment. He needs to acknowledge her hurt and disappointment, and get to the bottom of what she really means, emotionally. In return, she needs to understand and speak his language by sticking to the facts, being specific, and avoiding being overly emotional—at least at first, so they don't turn off and stop talking.

Assertiveness and Power

Assertiveness and power are no longer considered exclusively male traits, with more and more men choosing to express their "feminine" sides, and more and more women realizing that aggressiveness is not necessarily a negative attribute.

Assertiveness

In many cultures, men have traditionally been more assertive than women, and have set out to grab what they want. Women, on the other hand, have tended to be more passive, waiting for things to be given to them. The women's movement has helped change this dynamic somewhat. In the past, an assertive woman was labeled aggressive, or even a nastier term. While times have changed, I still find that women need encouragement to be assertive, and need to take more initiative to ask for what they want.

Power

Traditionally, it is believed that men hold the power in life and in relationships. But feminist and male movement leader Warren Farrell, the first male President of the National Organization for Women, takes a controversial stance. In his book, *The Myth of Male Power*, Farrell points out that men have only the illusion of power. He goes on to say that men are historically the ones who sacrifice their lives in war, suffer more physical illness from work, feel more pressure to perform sexually, get trapped in frustrations that make them abusive, and die younger.

ACE-ing It

How do assertiveness and power factor into the dating game? Well, it's useful to recognize the different ways in which men and women approach life. This recognition can help both men and women achieve the three A's (acceptance, appreciation, and adjustment); the three C's (confidence, compliments, and compromise); and the three E's (encouragement, energy, and empowerment). All these put together—ACE—is your key to self-fulfillment and satisfying relationships.

Coping with Problems and Stress

Traditionally, men and women react differently to problems and handle stress differently, as described in the table on the following page, according to the "six F's" of possible problem-solving behaviors (that elaborate on John Gray's "four F's").

Men	Women
"Fight": Take the offense, blame, judge, justify themselves to feel they've won	**"Fold":** Give in and assume blame
"Flight": Withdraw (going into their cave)	**"Fake":** Put on a happy face
"Focus": Focus on what to do	**"Flood":** Overwhelmed by emotion

Women like talking about problems; it makes them feel better to express their feelings about things even if they don't reach a solution. Men, on the other hand, feel frustrated until they do something to solve the problem.

For example, Paul was stressed out at work, but couldn't figure out how to relieve the pressure. As a result, he neglected his girlfriend, Patty. Hurt that she hadn't heard from him in a few days, she finally called him but he brushed her off, saying he couldn't talk because he was too stressed out. Patty said, "Please, talk to me about it, I'd like to help make you feel better," to which he responded, "I'll call you next week when this project is finished." Patty was hurt, and suspected he was seeing someone else, because if the situation were reversed, her first impulse would be to call Paul so that he could help make her feel better.

Suppose Patty complained, "I'm furious at you." Paul might say, "Leave me alone," or "You're always so demanding. Let's break up." His response only makes the problem worse, because what she really wants is for him to talk to her more, reassure her, and let her help him.

If your discussions tend to reach this kind of stalemate, what can you do? The healthiest approach is for both of you to face the problem and your feelings. Then work through the situation without blame and with each taking equal responsibility for what you do and how you make the other person feel.

On Commitment

Both men and women can certainly be possessive, jealous, or obsessive in love. But traditionally, it has been men who are more skittish about commitment. However, lately I have heard more and more stories from men complaining about the women they love. Either they complain that their love interest is cheating, or that she's ambivalent about commitment. A typical complaint: "I met this perfect woman last week and fell madly in love. Now all I do is think of her and I can't stand thinking of her with anyone else, but she says she wants us to keep seeing other people." This is a trend (explored further in Chapter 15) that certainly shows the tables are turning.

Both sexes can certainly be tortured by the desperate need for attachment, but more often men are possessive in the service of their ego ("owning their property"), while women are trying to satisfy their needs for merging (feeling together).

It has been said that men love like yo-yos: They want to run to the end of the rope to express their independence, with the confidence that the rope will snap back to the secure base of the woman's love, which is more like a favorite blanket or teddy bear—always there to offer warmth and comfort.

Women's love, on the other hand, is usually more stable. Women are usually more ready for commitment at a younger age, partly because they have been prepared for commitment by their upbringing, conditioned through life to share, sacrifice, and compromise.

As society's traditional caregivers, women are expansive and tend to subjugate their own needs to the needs of others. In contrast, men are more inward and focus on their own needs (thus appearing inconsiderate without even realizing it).

Thus, when a woman is despondent about a guy breaking up with her, I encourage her to assess the situation. Does she still think she has to have a man to be happy? Was he really ready to love? Does he have the emotional and intellectual capacity to give, devote, share, listen, care?

Dating Data

National surveys conducted by the Virginia Slims Opinion Poll over a quarter century revealed that 4 out of 10 women find men selfish and self-centered. The most recent survey further reported that almost half of the women polled think men are still more interested in their own sexual satisfaction than that of their partner, only slightly improved from five years ago.

Sex Stereotypes Debunked for the Year 2000

Melissa called my "LovePhones" radio show to ask whether it was okay to have phone sex. She described how she talked to her boyfriends on the phone, repeating hot graphic fantasies, such as, "You grab me and put your hard throbbing member in my mouth."

I asked her, "That's getting right to the heart of the matter fast. Is that what you really want to say?" "No," she answered, "I'd really like to say something more romantic, like 'Lower me gently onto the bed and we'll embrace longingly, our lips lingering lovingly over flesh afire with desire,' but I know guys wouldn't go for that. They prefer the raw stuff!"

Melissa's experience was certainly helping to reinforce sexual stereotypes. But many of these ideas about men's and women's sexuality today are myths, based on outdated ways of thinking. Here are some typical examples:

STEREOTYPE: Men's sexuality is rated "NC-17," while women's is rated "R."

IN THE NEW MILLENNIUM: Many women enjoy raunchy sex, and many men enjoy romanticism.

STEREOTYPE: Men get more satisfaction from sex than women.

IN THE NEW MILLENNIUM: There is no question that men have traditionally had an easier time having orgasms. They tend to climax more quickly than women, and are comfortable with more types of partners, and under more varied circumstances (in a car, a stairwell, or just while making out). Most women need longer, more direct stimulation (from both a physiological and emotional point of view). Part of the reason is that a man's genitals are more exposed, allowing easier access.

In addition, women tend to be less comfortable with their bodies—less than 50 percent of all women admit to masturbation, compared to 96 percent of men. Only a third of all women surveyed experience regular orgasm during intercourse; most report that they can only achieve orgasm in certain ways. But once a woman learns to be more comfortable with her body, she can have as much satisfaction as a man—and this can be escalated by her emotional investment.

Smooth Talk'n

WOMEN: To help him be more romantic, reassure and appreciate him every time he says or does something sensuous. Alternate telling him "hot" things with sensitive things. Read novels or watch videos together with romantic story lines to give him ideas. Trade off by enjoying a hot fantasy of his.

MEN: Encourage your woman to be more comfortable talking about hot sex scenes. Recite them for her as you'd like to hear her say them. Accept her embarrassment. Trade off by enjoying a more romantic fantasy of hers.

STEREOTYPE: Men always want sex—no matter what, who, or where.

IN THE NEW MILLENNIUM: Survey results indicate that it is a myth that men are always clamoring for sex. I've talked to some men who don't want it as much as their female partners. Or they feel that their lack of constant desire means that something is wrong with them. Men are brought up thinking that an unquenchable desire is manly—(making them mourn the passing of their teenagehood, when raging hormones seemed to create incessant desire), when in reality that expectation only creates pressure.

Additionally, it's traditionally easier for men to get sex than it is for women—there are more outlets, legitimate and illegitimate. Thus, for many men, sex and emotion were often separate entities (since they could fulfill the need for sex with very little emotional investment, and be less choosy about who, where, and when).

You might be surprised to hear that many men these days tell me they don't want to have sex right away on a date—particularly if they really like her. Holding back is a sign of their respect, and need for time to be sure about their mutual interest. Nor do they want sex without any involvement. More men are valuing sex *with* intimacy and meaning.

STEREOTYPE: A man who sleeps around is a stud; a woman who sleeps around is a slut.

IN THE NEW MILLENNIUM: Social mores are responsible for cheering the man who sleeps around, but jeering the woman. Fortunately, this stereotype is dying out, as society, and women themselves, accept the notion of sexual freedom and experimentation.

STEREOTYPE: Women are monogamous, but men can't be.

IN THE NEW MILLENNIUM: Surveys have suggested that women can have the same problems with monogamy as men! By the end of the last decade, despite the fear of AIDS, some surveys estimated that up to 8 out of 10 married men, and half of all married women, have had some kind of affair.

Dating Data

In some animal species, the females are the infidels—they like to upgrade their mates to find the most fertile males and those that are most capable of caring for her young.

STEREOTYPE: Women can easily have multiple orgasms, but men can have only one per sex session.

IN THE NEW MILLENNIUM: Research has shown that while the stages of the male and female sexual response are the same (excitement, plateau, orgasm, resolution), the timing has been a little different. Women can traditionally linger longer in the excitement and orgasm phases, leading to multiple orgasms. Fortunately, men can train themselves to control their timing instead of always ending in a quick release. And by learning so-called tantric love techniques, they can not only last, but have as many sexual highs as women.

STEREOTYPE: After sex, men like to just roll over and fall asleep.

IN THE NEW MILLENNIUM: The physical exertion and orgasmic release during sex can certainly produce relaxation conducive to rolling over and falling asleep, but there is no reflex that makes a man do that. Better explanations include fatigue, force of habit (guys learn as adolescents to have a quick release at bedtime), stress relief, and even escape from post-orgasmic intimacy.

Chemicals released in the brain during sex may have a sedative effect (for women too)—but consider that increased blood flow and heart rate have stimulating effects. Women often want more sex even though their partner is finished, often because they did not have orgasm (which can cause discomfort, restlessness, or unquenched desire), but also to enjoy more closeness or the afterglow.

STEREOTYPE: Men are more capable than women of having sex without love.

IN THE NEW MILLENNIUM: Here is one that still has some residue of truth, since I still hear from and treat women who want intimacy but give in to having just sex just to get or keep a man. Men, on the other hand, are much more capable of having pure sexual relationships, saying: "It was nothing, it was just sex." This attitude produces a kind of sexual bribery, with women feeling that they have to give in if they want anything back. But in this new millenium, more women are allowing themselves the freedom of sex without commitment, even though, deep down, they expect and desire more emotional involvement than men do. And as I said a few paragraphs earlier, more men are refusing to have sex just for sex's sake, and are admitting that they find such behavior to be "empty." They want to make love when they truly feel love.

STEREOTYPE: Between the ages of 20 and 30, men just want sex, while women are looking for love. By age 40 or so, the opposite is true.

IN THE NEW MILLENNIUM: There is reason to believe this stereotype. As men age, they are not as ruled by their hormones, and their lifestyle is not as conducive to casual sex, so they do become more interested in relationships. Studies at Florida State University and the University of Kansas suggest that men's sexual motives vary with age. For men under 25, physical release is the key; for men over 30, love takes precedence over pure pleasure. Physical changes account for some of this shift (it takes an older man longer to get an erection and more time to "rebuild" between erections).

But in recent years, men have started reevaluating traditional sexual attitudes and have become more attuned to sensuality and romance at all ages.

It is true that as women age, they become more confident, more willing to express themselves sexually, and more open to sexual experimentation—including sex for sex's sake, without deep emotional attachment. But women of all ages would certainly prefer sex and the context of love.

STEREOTYPE: Guys rush through foreplay, and head right into intercourse.

IN THE NEW MILLENNIUM: Too often, men do what comes naturally—the quick build-up and release. And too often, they don't understand how women in general, and their partner in particular, like sex. But modern men welcome lingering in love—and need some guidance. So, if a man is insensitive to your needs and desires, educate him! Show him what you like, and express your appreciation when he gets it right.

STEREOTYPE: Men love watching two women go at it, while women are turned off by the idea of watching two people together sexually.

IN THE NEW MILLENNIUM: Men have traditionally been more open to unusual sexual practices. Also, society has revered the beauty and sensuality of two women together. In addition, men get turned on thinking that the two women are really putting on a show and warming up for them. However, surveys indicate that an increasing number of women do entertain fantasies about watching a couple (men, women, or a man and a woman) have sex. This is probably the result of women in general becoming more experimental and open about their sexual desires. (But keep in mind that thinking it does not mean you have to do it, and remember that scenes in your mind are not the same as in real life, when people's feelings become complicated.)

While differences exist, there are still some trends and efforts toward bringing the male and female sex drives more in synch. This is possible. Women do take longer than men to get sexually aroused to the same point (because of differences in the male and female sex response cycle), with the result that women tend to need more time, and respond to slower, more sensuous touches (remember the popular song line, "I want a man with a slow hand"). Yet women today allow themselves a wider variety of love-making, with more active, vigorous activity. Similarly, though men have shorter response cycle times, making quicker, faster stimulation more common, an increasing number of men are learning the pleasures of more leisurely love-making.

The Gender War and the Movement Toward Peace

The "war" between the sexes has raged in the past few decades as women have vied for equality in all areas of life. While "war" sounds harsh, some aspects of this combative-ness still exist, but fortunately cooperation is becoming more desired and happily I predict will continue into the new millennium.

I still hear so many complaints from women about men, and from men about women. As I've suggested, women frequently complain that they'd like men to listen more attentively; be more communicative and honest; be less selfish, pushy, and obsessed with sex; and help out more around the house. Men want women to be less emotional, and to stick to the facts at hand during an argument.

According to surveys, women's complaints about men have changed very little in the past 25 years! Only half the women in the 1995 Virginia Slims Opinion Poll report being satisfied with the man in their life—a slight improvement from 1990. When women were asked to list the things in life that please them, men rated fourth—after children, friends, and motherhood.

Interestingly, men think they are doing better than women think they are. Three-quarters of the men surveyed in the Virginia Slims Opinion Poll think they are better able to express their feelings and are more understanding of women's needs than they were five years ago, but fewer women think so. Additionally, men think they've questioned the need to act "macho"; yet over half of the women think the "macho man" lives on. Over half of the women surveyed also think that men are self-centered and commitment-shy. Not surprisingly, few men believe this to be true.

The tensions between what women think about men, and what men think about themselves, have created a new male backlash—many men say they will give less if this is all the appreciation they get. But all is not lost (if all the steps that follow are taken).

Sex roles have blurred, and 7 out of 10 men and women surveyed admit to being confused. Some women admit to wanting to be a woman of the 1990s when it comes to their career (with equal job opportunities, pay, and power), but a woman of the 1950s when it comes to love (being taken care of and being provided for). The woman of the Year 2000 will hopefully not find herself in that struggle-but accept all sides of herself.

Reaching Détente in the Gender War

Men and women must learn to understand each other better and come to a compromise as we enter the new millennium. It's time to end any war between the sexes. To that end, it's important to call upon the following three points:

➤ Accept your differences and communicate your needs. Your partner is not a mind-reader. You've got to express your desires, your frustrations, and your pleasures.

➤ Adjust to your partner's needs and requests. Within reason, accommodate to each other's ways.

➤ Appreciate that men have made progress. Despite the many complaints that women have about men, I must note that overall men have changed. My professional experience, as well as many survey results, suggest that there is a new man, more like what women have been demanding. He's more able to express his feelings, even with other men. He's more involved with children. And he agrees that he shouldn't make all the decisions.

As callers to my "LovePhones" radio call-in advice show have indicated, more men with those proverbial cold feet have warmed up. I get many calls from men bemoaning how they want to make a commitment and need help to do so. Or they can't find a woman who wants to settle down. Or they feel used for sex. On some phone calls, if I didn't hear a distinctly male voice, I wouldn't be able to tell if it was a man or woman complaining, "I'm shy. How do I meet someone?" or, "I got dumped and it hurts so bad." Just the other night a husband admitted that he criticizes his wife because "I guess I feel inadequate."

On my show and in my practice, I try to point out the similarities between men and women. Women need to understand that men have the same feelings, but just handle them differently. A little understanding will make both men and women feel less helpless and more empathic.

How can we eliminate sex role stereotypes? Try retraining your brain. As soon as the thought comes into your head, snap your fingers (to interrupt it) and change the thought to, "Men and women can both be sensitive, aggressive, nurturing, logical, etc. . . ."

Role-Reversal Exercises

"I never heard of a couple breaking up because they understood each other." My long-time friend and men's movement leader, Warren Farrell, opened his seminar last summer about "Resolving the '90s Gender War" with that very line. Try to put yourself in your partner's moccasins—that's the surest way of reaching a true understanding.

Farrell's seminar (open to the public, drawing about 20 of us) was held at Esalen, the New Age center high in the mountains of Big Sur (where Indians had walked in real moccasins for centuries). It had been more than 20 years since my last visit (I was a typical "flower child" from the East, curious about the West Coast "enlightenment" hype), but one step onto the property was enough to transport me back into the '70s feelings of innocence, openness, and trust—states I still believe are crucial to resolving misunderstandings between men and women.

At the seminar, we performed role-reversal exercises, which you may wish to try. The exercises were designed to promote understanding of the opposite sex's way of thinking and to help shake us from our traditional ways of behaving.

First, the dance. We picked partners, and each woman led her male partner, controlling his every move. He had to follow and look at her with awe (what Farrell calls "awe training"). One man said, "It feels wonderful to let someone else be in charge for a change." Another was more skeptical: "I didn't like following. I'm used to being the one in control." A few women enjoyed leading, but most preferred looking up to the man.

Then, we were asked to reconstruct dating choices in adolescence. We started by thinking about the person we would have loved to have asked to the prom. Most women thought of guys who were good-looking and successful (the jock or student government leader). The guys also chose good looks. But leadership? Yawn.

Next came the male beauty contest—a lesson about being a "sex object." The five biggest "studs," as judged by the women in the group, were herded into a large room. As they stood before us, the emcee, a woman, called each of their names. The women, clapping and hooting for the ones they liked best, whittled the group down to the top two "pieces of meat," who then competed on talent and brains. One women asked, "How do you feel about birth control?" Another asked, "What would you do if your girlfriend had to move for her job?" For the talent contest, one guy sang and the other stripped. The stripper won the contest, judged by the women's howls—perhaps proving that sexual seductions have more power than tamer talents.

Next came the "success-object" contest. The women lined up in rows according to income, with those earning over $55,000 in the front row and those making $5,000 or less in the back. The idea was for women to feel the sting (or satisfaction) of being judged by their bank account—as men often are. Money, instead of looks, became the criteria for their being chosen, and the exercise gave women a sense of how men struggle in the dating selection process.

Then came the role-reversal date. The women had to ask a guy to lunch. The men were told to say yes or no, depending on the woman's ability to support him and children.

The men in the group realized that the woman who would normally be their first choice based on looks was not necessarily the same one they'd pick as a provider.

We also played opposite roles on the "date." My date, Brian, asked me questions about my work, and listened with apparent rapture while puffing out his chest. Mimicking a guy, I chatted on, and paid the check. Back in the group, we shared our experiences. One woman nearly cried. "I sat in the last row because I make no money and the three guys I asked out all turned me down. Now I know how devastated guys feel." A guy confessed, "It was horrible, worrying if I was pretty enough."

Finally came the tolerance lessons. After we'd walked in the opposite sex's shoes, we were asked to close our eyes and think about what we'd learned. Had we learned tolerance and empathy? Could we put our lessons to work with our co-workers, family, and friends?

In typical Esalen style, we hugged each other and clapped for ourselves. And we were given a task for the future—to truly encourage equality, we must help train boys for caring and girls for financial independence; we must learn to communicate and cooperate rather than compete.

Farrell added his favorite message: "Women cannot hear what men do not say." Just as the women's movement empowered women to speak up and ask for what they want, men need the same encouragement. When both sexes learn to listen to each other, we can have the loving dialogue that will end the gender war.

The Least You Need to Know

➤ Men and women have traditionally communicated differently, but that doesn't have to stay that way.

➤ Brain differences, as well as child-rearing, account for some of the differences in communication.

➤ Men and women are raised with different expectations and communication styles.

➤ A good way to overcome a discussion or relationship stalemate is to accept, accommodate, and appreciate your partner.

➤ The traditional gender war is far from over—but there have been many gains where men and women have understood and incorporated each other's behaviors.

➤ Role-reversal exercises can help you understand the other sex's dilemmas and give you new insights and behaviors that bring men and women closer together.

Chapter 17

What's Up with This Person?

We've all run into them—the over-emotional types, the egomaniacs, the obsessive types. Is there any way to do a "quick read" on a person before plunging into a possibly ill-fated romance? In this chapter, I describe some basic personality types you may date, and provide clues that will help you figure out what you might be in for. The more aware you are of what makes someone tick, the better prepared you'll be to either accommodate their flaws and eccentricities—or run!

As I've stated throughout the book, the key to success in dating lies in using the three A's: acceptance, appreciation, and adjustment. But sometimes, despite our best efforts, a person's problems might be far larger than we want to take on. If the person you are seeing has insight into their own problems and is willing to work toward change, then it might be worthwhile to hang on. But don't get into situations where you fool yourself into thinking that you can change a person—especially one who refuses to acknowledge a problem and has no desire to change.

Narcissistic Types

There's a long-standing joke that describes the typical narcissist: "Enough about me. Now tell me—what do *you* think about me?" Narcissists are so self-involved and self-centered that they see all lovers and friends simply as extensions of themselves. But they are also very seductive, and will use endless charm and flattery in pursuit of their own happiness. "God's Gift" comes in male and female varieties.

For example, Kathleen was mesmerized by Al, with his dashing looks, red Porsche, fancy suits, and impressive talk about his promising future as a famous movie star. An aspiring actress herself, Kathleen fell for his constant flattery and was seduced by his talk about how great she'd look by his side when he won his Oscar. Kathleen felt her Prince Charming had finally come.

But at an industry party, Al met another aspiring actress who fed his grandiosity even more than Kathleen. Taken with this new admirer, Al began to pick on Kathleen, pointing out how her dresses were getting tighter, and how bags were beginning to show under her eyes, until he finally dumped her for his new "arm charm."

Al is a self-centered exhibitionist, obsessed with flattery, demanding adoration and attention. He also exaggerated his own success, and as if to prove it, exaggerated the success and beauty of the people he dated. Narcissists are so taken with themselves that they are only attracted to others who flatter, embellish, or enhance their image in their own or others' eyes.

While they may seem self-confident, narcissists crave attention because their egos are so fragile. They (and their love interests) become victims of their own "hero-zero" mindset—vacillating between feeling like the "head honcho" or the biggest loser of the year.

Ask yourself these questions to help identify a narcissistic type:

➤ Does the conversation always revolve around him?

➤ Does she lose interest when she's not the center of attention?

➤ Is he grandiose, constantly referring to himself in the same breath as superstars?

➤ Does he make you feel like a million bucks with constant flattery?

➤ Does she have a pattern of supposedly "ideal" loves who end up disappointing her with some fatal flaw?

➤ Is he a show-off, courting compliments?

➤ Does she fall apart in the face of criticism—for example, if you mention that she looks tired or has made a mistake?

➤ Does he fly off the handle if he doesn't get special treatment (the best table at the restaurant, the best seat in the theater)?

➤ Does she use people to get what she wants, only to discard them when she doesn't need them anymore?

If your love interest displays five or more of these characteristics, be cautious—you may have a narcissist on your hands. Most psychologists say that true narcissists are among the most difficult patients to treat—so there is little reason for you to take on the challenge. If you are looking for attention, commitment, and devotion, you won't find it here.

Over-Emotional Types

Joanna was the life of the party, always attracting the coolest guys in the room. But inevitably, after a few get-togethers, her dates would begin to feel uncomfortable. Joanna liked to grab her date's arm—a little too tightly. She also liked to gaze longingly into her man's eyes, with a look that indicated she was expecting affection in return. Within a date or two, she would turn the talk to their fabulous future together—despite the fact that they barely knew one another.

Women like Joanna (and some men, too) love high drama. Their emotions spill out quickly, which makes their dates wonder about the genuineness of it all. On the upside, these people can be charming and engaging; but on the downside, because they're so driven by their need to be taken care of and loved, they can try to make others responsible for them, becoming helpless and dependent, clingy and suffocating.

Such histrionic women often seem "wild" in bed, yet ironically, many are unable to achieve orgasm because of their fears of really letting go.

There's no question that these emotional types are trapped by a desperate need for love. In psychological terms, they are looking for a lover to help them recapture the comfort of the early mother-child union.

Ask yourself these questions to help identify this over-emotional personality type:

➤ Does she cry at the drop of a hat?

➤ Does she squeal with enthusiasm when meeting a casual acquaintance?

➤ Does he ask you often "Do you love me?"

➤ Is she a chronic flirt?

➤ Does she fly off the handle (for example, if she caught you flirting with another woman, would she throw her glass at you)?

➤ Does she talk too soon or too often about how perfect you are for each other?

➤ Does she always ask other people's opinions of what she should do?

➤ Does she have a history of abusive relationships?

➤ Does she always seem to be helping or "saving" others?

➤ Does she seem overly sensitive about rejection?

If you are seeing someone who displays five or more of these characteristics, suggest that she seek treatment. Many people who crave love so intensely are suffering from what's called hysteroid depression (a mixture of over-emotionality and depression). With treatment, these people can develop a stronger sense of self and a greater ability to fulfill their own dreams and needs.

Dating Data

The ancient Greeks thought that histrionic females had exaggerated emotions because they were afflicted with a "wandering womb." Freud believed sexual trauma in childhood was a better explanation.

If this description fits you, learn to enjoy yourself and your life instead of looking for a lover's approval and admiration. Resist the temptation to seek approval. "Re-parent" yourself by picturing yourself being both the little child and the parent giving you the attention you need (thereby learning to rely on yourself instead of making others your "replacement" parents). Check your emotions before you let them loose, and purposefully under-react, so you will actually feel something. (When you exaggerate emotions, you are actually pushing away your true feelings.) If you break up, focus on simple facts of the situation ("He met someone else," "We went our separate ways") rather than exaggerating how you feel ("The world has come to an end," "I'll never find anyone else").

Passive–Aggressive Types

Pam had been dating Tim for four months when she complained to me, "I can't figure him out. On one hand, he says he's more relaxed with me than with any other woman, and I can ask him anything, but then when I do, he complains that I'm like every other demanding woman. When I try to talk to him about his mixed message, he says that nothing's wrong and walks away."

Pam's lover is a typical passive-aggressive (PA) type who gives double messages—come closer, move away. Such a person can leave you on an emotional seesaw between hope and frustration. The "aggressive" part of the person is seething with unexpressed anger, while the "passive" part expresses that anger in subtle ways, such as with "innocent" remarks and little digs that are really intended to hurt.

Passive-aggressives are big on using the "silent treatment" to thwart confrontation. They pretend to cooperate but then don't do what you ask, and shift blame to you, making you feel guilty for being demanding or angry. Because they are terribly conflicted about intimacy and aggression, dependency and competition, they can't express love and either sleep around or completely withdraw from relationships.

Ask yourself these questions to help identify a passive-aggressive type:

➤ If you complain that he's late, does he claim you're too demanding or that it's your fault?

➤ Does he refuse to say "I love you" because he says you should know how he feels?

➤ When you get angry, does he give you the silent treatment?

➤ If you walk ahead of him, does he complain you're rude, but if you hold his arm, does he protest you're crowding him?

➤ Does she pout unless she gets her way?

➤ Does he promise to make love to you when he's in the mood, but he never is?

➤ Does he agree to pick up dinner or make a phone call, and then forget?

➤ Does he forget your birthday, anniversary, and dates, but always come up with excuses?

➤ Is she always lagging behind, dawdling, running late?

If your love interest displays five or more of these characteristics, you may be involved with a passive-aggressive type. If you fall for this type, think about whether you also have a tendency to stifle anger. If you stay with this person, resist doubting your perceptions about situations, and resist the pressure to blame yourself. If your mate back stabs or twists the facts of a story, state your feelings and the facts clearly and unemotionally. Call your partner on his unexpressed anger, and insist that you not be subtly abused.

Dating Data

In his book *Living With The Passive-Aggressive Male*, Scott Wetzler describes three types of women who fall for PA men: the Victim, who willingly suffers humiliation for scraps of attention, thereby losing his respect; the maternal Rescuer, whose cleaning up after him earns his resentment instead of the appreciation she seeks; and the Manager, whose need to control attracts his dependence but incites his rebellion against feeling trapped.

Obsessive Types

Whenever she's out on a date, Jackie is totally distracted with worries that she's forgotten to turn off her computer, which, she's convinced, will blow the machine's memory. And then there's Larry, who is so worried about germs that he can't even contemplate a goodnight kiss without going into a panic.

Both Jackie and Larry display degrees of obsessive behavior. Obsessions range from simple self-doubt to more serious distortions (such as about being contaminated). Many of us know what it's like to have rituals—we walk to the bus every day, following precisely the same route, or we put on our shoes and socks in a certain manner, or we're a bit compulsive about filing. But for certain people, rituals become overwhelming and interfere with normal functioning and relationships.

For example, Jack flies off the handle if his girlfriend moves anything on his desk, even something as simple as a memo pad. Kris wants to look so perfect on her dates that she irons her dress five or more times, causing her to be late. Jason can't get out of the house in the morning because he keeps rushing back to the kitchen to make certain that he's turned off the lights (sometimes checking 10 times or more before he feels "safe" enough to leave).

Home Alone

It's a good idea to suggest that a person get a psychiatric consultation if any behavior becomes too extreme.

Ask yourself these questions to help identify an obsessive type:

➤ Does she repeat phrases compulsively (such as "Don't you think . . .")?

➤ Is he a neat-freak (CDs all in line, books alphabetized)?

➤ Does she constantly doubt herself?

➤ Does he have to repeat certain acts in a particular way (such as locking all the doors in sequence)?

➤ Does she check things (her car, keys, schedule) over and over?

➤ Does he count things repeatedly?

➤ Does she repeat herself and goes over details endlessly.?

If your love interest displays five or more of these characteristics, he may be an obsessive type. Obsessive or compulsive people are driven by a need to control—their lives, their emotions, and the lives of others. Some obsessive types can become extremely successful in positions of power (in politics, business, money dealings), that can be very attractive. On the downside, because they are controlling and are threatened by feelings, they can be rigid, stuffy, and detached.

The need, but inability, to control (oneself, one's emotions, one's life, or others) can lead to serious problems, like alcohol and drug abuse or eating disorders.

Mood-Swing Types

When Joe started dating Martha, he was taken with her passion. If she loved a film, she would describe it as "awesome," and would go on and on about how much she loved it. On the other hand, if she disliked a movie, she'd be totally unable to discuss it reasonably, calling it "repulsive," and commenting that anyone who'd like it must be a total idiot. While the strength of Martha's opinions at first intrigued Joe, the attraction began to wear very thin. He began to realize that with Martha, there were no shades of gray. She had a long, checkered career history, with jobs that started out with promise but ended in disappointment. And it was the same with the men in her life.

People like Martha often seem pretty normal at first. They seem to function on an acceptable level (or even at a high level), but on the inside they feel like lonely, terrified children. They cling to a partner one minute, but push him away when they become terrified of being "swallowed up." This dramatic inner battle becomes totally confusing to an unsuspecting partner, who doesn't seem to be able to find a happy medium in the relationship.

Home Alone

Many dates begin with dinner, lunch, or some other event where food takes center stage. But for the thousands of people with eating disorders (either anorexia or bulimia), a simple meal can set the stage for all kinds of interpersonal dilemmas. Eating disorders are serious illnesses that involve the need to control one's feelings and life, and require intensive psycho-therapy. If you're involved with someone with an eating disorder, urge the person to get treatment.

Ask yourself these questions to help identify this mood-swing type:

➤ Does she cling to you as if her life depended on it, or at other times push you away angrily?

➤ Does he either love or hate people in extremes, calling them the best or the worst (or switching from one extreme to the other)?

➤ Does she seem to use people?

➤ Does he fly into a rage or withdraw if the slightest thing doesn't go his way?

➤ Does she have an addictive personality, relying on drugs, shopping, alcohol, food, or gambling?

➤ Is he "accident-prone"?

➤ Is she endlessly confused about "who she is," or does she frequently say she doesn't know what she wants to do in life?

➤ Does he seem unable to spend an evening alone?

➤ Does she experience dramatic mood swings?

If your love interest displays five or more of these characteristics, he may be prone to extremes in his behavior. If you date a person of this type, expect a roller-coaster ride of emotions—you may be on a pedestal one minute and in the doghouse the next. If you have the stomach for it, strap in for a bumpy ride. Sometimes the disorder is a chemical imbalance that requires psychiatric attention and medication.

Attention Deficit Disorder (ADD)

Sarah called my radio show to complain about her recent boyfriend. The relationship was going reasonably well, but she frequently felt hurt by his inattention. She told me that even when they were holding each other while watching TV, he'd suddenly jump up to make notes in his daily planner, or he'd decide it was time to reorganize his CD collection. Am I so boring that he has to escape?" she asked.

I pointed out that it sounded as if her boyfriend was suffering from Attention Deficit Disorder (ADD). More often recognized and treated in children, ADD also afflicts millions of adults, but usually goes undiagnosed. Because they are creative, quick, unconventional, and spontaneous, people with ADD can excel at work, especially in structured jobs. However, they may fall apart in more unstructured situations such as dating, becoming easily distracted or unable to concentrate.

Dating Data

ADD is a neurobiological disability that tends to run in families. Researchers estimate that about 35 percent of siblings, 80 percent of identical twins, and 40 percent of children with an ADD parent have the trait. Symptoms can be triggered by fluctuations in hormone levels, as well as by increased stress levels and frustration. Medication and psychological counseling can help.

If you date someone like this, don't take his distractions personally. Identifying and understanding a problem is half the battle to overcoming it.

Forgive your date and try to improve your communication. Talk about the problem and schedule private, intimate time that won't be interrupted by distracting tasks. Rather than referring to him as hyper or exasperating, tell him you appreciate him for being so energetic and stimulating.

Depression

Who hasn't felt depressed at some point in life? You know the symptoms—you're "down in the dumps," you have trouble sleeping, you're eating too much or have lost interest in food. Such feelings usually pass. But depression that lasts more than a few days, or is accompanied by feelings of doom or despair, is a different matter.

For example, Paul called my "LovePhones" radio show to say, "I've been dating this woman for six months, and she's become increasingly depressed. At first she just seemed a little blue, but lately she's been sleeping for 10 or more hours a day, and she has even said that she occasionally feels that life just isn't worth living. What should I do?"

Depression is a serious illness that requires medical attention. If you are seeing someone who seems depressed (not just "blue"), urge them to talk with a professional.

Don't blame yourself for a partner's depression, but if you find yourself chronically attracted to depressed people, look inward. Use my "Mirror Law of Attraction" and ask yourself if you're the one who is really also depressed. If so, face your own problem instead of picking lovers who protect you from facing your own feelings of desolation or hopelessness.

> **Home Alone**
>
> Many singles today take anti-depressants of various types in order to overcome the upsetting depression and anxiety that stop them from enjoying dating (much less life in general). Unfortunately, recent research shows that at least 20 percent of people taking certain of these drugs can have sexual problems, including decreased sexual desire, impotence in men, and anorgasmia in women. Studies have shown the anti-depressant Remeron does not adversely affect sexual functioning.

Insecure or Paranoid Types

Gordon called my radio show to complain that his girlfriend was always accusing him of seeing other women, which was simply not true. He went on to say that when he came home, she examined his clothing for hairs and other indications that he'd been with someone else. While she'd always been a little insecure, he felt that she was getting completely carried away with her suspicions and accusations. Was it something he was doing?

I told Gordon to face her accusations honestly. If his girlfriend truly has no reason to doubt him, he must insist that she stop accusing him and work on her own self-esteem and inner security, lest she destroy the relationship once and for all.

Many of us throw around the term "paranoid," but chronic distrust can be a serious problem. Here are some clues for recognizing overly suspicious, paranoid types:

➤ False and frequent accusations that you are looking at someone else

➤ False accusations that you are trying to make your partner "feel bad"

➤ Distrust and over-generalization beyond reason ("All women are just after one thing: money.")

➤ Excessive guardedness ("You can't be too careful about people these days.")

➤ Frequent doubts of others' loyalty

➤ Irrational conclusions ("I saw you talking to that man, which is proof that you're cheating on me!")

➤ Over-concern about hidden motives and meanings ("You and your friends seem to have a secret signal to quiet down when I walk into the room.")

➤ Easily blames or takes offense ("You purposefully ruined my night.")

If your date displays more than five of these clues, he or she may have a seriously distorted view of reality. Don't blame yourself, or constantly try to prove or defend yourself. You don't have to settle for a person whose problems are too large to take on.

Too-Smooth Dudes

Beware of fast-talking, smooth operators, with great lines and too-good-to-be-true promises—they just might be taking you for a ride. You read about such sociopaths all the time in the tabloids—from gigolos who con unsuspecting, naive, and lonely women out of their savings, to polygamists, who keep a string of wives and families.

Sociopaths are often delinquents, thieves, liars, and poseurs (one notorious guy performed surgeries, though he had never gone to medical school). But they are also often bright, charming, and exciting. They're good at seducing women, but inhumanely aggressive once their prey submits. A deep resentment and hatred for women, and inner weakness, may unleash a violent rage.

Catching on to these people (most of whom are men) is difficult because they're good cons. And changing them is nearly impossible, since true sociopaths feel no reason to live by the rules that govern the rest of society and, therefore, feel no guilt or pain for hurting other people.

Be suspicious of slick lines and of someone who sounds too good to be true (the handsome "high-roller" with no visible means of support but lots of slick schemes). Remember the adage: "Fool me once, shame on you; fool me twice, shame on me."

Addictive Behavior

If you find yourself falling in love with a drug addict, whether the drug of choice is alcohol or narcotics, keep this simple thought in mind: You cannot "save" an addict. The only addicts who clean themselves up are those who take steps to help themselves. If you are seriously involved with an alcoholic or drug addict, join a support program (like Al-Anon) and start living your life—for yourself.

Dating Data

Research by Dr. Stan Grof shows that addicts can overcome drug-taking by using a technique called holotropic breathing (continuous inhaling and exhaling that is deeper and faster than your normal pace), which helps you reach deep states of consciousness, insight, and awakening. Contact Grof Transpersonal Training, Inc. at (415) 383-0965 or e-mail gtt@dnai.com.

Rehab counselors may recommend that recovering addicts refrain from commitment to new relationships for a year while they reestablish their life. Be prepared that recovery is a "one-day-at-a-time" process and can be an emotional roller-coaster.

Smokers

Many people are adding "smoking" to their dating criteria list, rejecting those who do.

"I hate that ugly thing hanging out of his mouth," Charlene said. She added, "If he needs something to suck on all the time, why doesn't he stick a pacifier in his mouth?"

No doubt smokers are hooked on nicotine, but psychologically you could say they are stuck in the "oral" stage of Freudian development, where the child has to have something in his mouth to feel secure. The smoking habit is one of the hardest to kick, so if you fall for one who smokes, be prepared to lend tons of support while he tries to kick the habit, or accept it if he won't change.

Deciding Whether to Stick It Out

It's wonderful to be understanding and sympathetic when you fall for someone with a problem. But it's important to know when to cut your losses and cut yourself loose.

If you're in extreme pain, danger, or you are being abused, you need to get out. Also bail out if your partner's behavior is getting you in trouble.

Remember my "Mirror Law of Attraction"—we tend to attract people who reflect our own needs. Examine what your partner's behavior means to you or tells you about yourself. Are you living vicariously through your lover? Are you co-dependent, sacrificing your own well-being to save the other person? Are you hiding behind your partner?

The Least You Need to Know

➤ You can't change people; they have to want to change themselves.

➤ If the person you're dating acknowledges problems and is willing to change, it might be worth staying in the relationship.

➤ End the relationship if your partner is mentally, physically, or sexually abusive, or is putting you in danger.

➤ We attract people who reflect our own needs. What does your date's behavior say about you?

Part 5
Start the Fires

What is this thing called "love?" How do you know if you're really in love, or just in love with the idea of being in love? How do you know if the person you're with loves you? You'll find the answers to these questions in this section.

In these pages you'll also feel confident about saying yes or no to sex, and clarify your intentions and expectations. You'll understand that sex doesn't always translate into love. Understanding and good communication are essential components of a strong relationship, but many people have trouble talking about sex and intimacy. The chapters in this section help you over this hurdle, and safer sex guidelines give you the necessary signposts to help you make responsible choices.

Chapter 18

What Is This Thing Called Love?

In This Chapter

➤ Three essential characteristics of love

➤ Some tests to tell whether it's love

➤ Can love at first sight work?

➤ The stages of love

➤ When and how to say "I love you"

➤ When you can't choose between two lovers

In my years of experience hearing people's stories about love, not surprisingly, I have come up with some thoughts on the subject! For starters, I have come to recognize three essential factors for determining whether someone is really in love:

➤ Do you have compatible needs for independence or togetherness? Some people need time alone or time on their own; other people want to be with their lover all the time, or feel a passionate need to "merge" with another in order to feel whole. In my view, the healthiest relationship is when neither party is overly dependent or independent—when two people are interdependent.

➤ Do you both have a strong desire to make your relationship work? Not all love comes naturally. The daily grind, arguments, outside pressures, and various other factors can get in the way of love, and test your commitment to one another. But almost all barriers can be overcome if you both want to make it work.

➤ Do you experience the intermixing of physical love (sex) with emotional sharing and spiritual connection?

What Is Love?

Love—everyone craves it on some level. And we certainly date in an effort to "find" it. Without it, many people feel a gaping hole inside, their inner child crying out to be held, the adult longing to adore and be adored, cherish and be cherished.

But we use the word "love" to describe our feelings for so many things. You can love your friend, parents, pet, movies, even chocolate ice cream. We use it to describe the hormone-raging lust of teenagehood, but it also certainly applies to the comforting togetherness our grandparents experience in old age. In each case, we mean something a little different.

Who hasn't swooned after meeting someone and exclaimed, "I'm madly in love!" But this is a far different feeling from the deep connection we feel after being in a relationship with someone for years.

According to my definition, love entails the five C's: caring, communicating, compromising, commitment, and cheerleading. But true love also includes honesty, sacrifice, and sharing. In an effort to get at your definition of love, start with the following exercises.

Exercise #1. Describe what it feels like for you to be in love with someone.

_____

_____

_____

Exercise #2. List the top three things that come to mind when you think about love, along with any other thoughts you might have on the subject.

1. _____

2. _____

3. _____

Other thoughts:

_____

_____

_____

Dating Data

In a landmark study of 500 passionate lovers, Dr. Dorothy Tennov listed a dozen components of strong romantic love. These included constantly thinking about the person you passionately desire, longing for reciprocation, the inability to act in love with more than one person at a time, and an "aching" in the heart when uncertain about your relationship.

Putting into words (as in Exercise #1) how you feel when you are in love with someone makes it more real to you, and helps you focus on what's important to you. Once you list the qualities of love (as in Exercise #2) you can reflect on different relationships and see if these experiences were present. If they were missing, you can understand more about why the relationship did not work out. Also answer the questions as you think your dates would, to see if your definitions of love are similar.

Dating Data

Loving touches not only feel good but are good for you! Research has proven that touching strengthens your immune system by stimulating certain chemicals in your brain. Furthermore, the feelings of emotional security that are nurtured by loving strokes facilitate relaxation, which helps guard against stress.

Tests of Love

Is there a simple test to determine whether you are really in love? Of course not. But certainly there are questions you can ask yourself (and your mate) about your relationship. Here are some questions that may help you gauge your level of commitment:

➤ **The Mood Test**. Are you flowering in your relationship or dying on the vine (are you worried, threatened, criticized, etc.)?

➤ **The Sacrifice Test**. Remember the classic test: If the two of you were onboard a sinking ship with only one life vest, would you keep it for yourself or give it to your mate? A more true-to-life related question might be: If you had something important to do, but your mate requested you to do something important for him, which would you do?

➤ **The Thoughtfulness Test**. Do you know your date's favorite treats? Do you go out of your way to indulge him in special ways? Does he do the same for you?

➤ **The Unconditional Love Test**. Would you love him no matter what he did for a living, or if she lost her looks? Do you feel your date is capable of loving you for who you are?

➤ **The Security Test**. When the two of you are apart, do you feel a sense of trust and security, or do you fear betrayal or loss?

While even true lovers will occasionally stumble on the above (and be selfish, ill-tempered, thoughtless, demanding, or insecure), if you are basically happy, giving, thoughtful, accepting, and secure most of the time, you're well on your way to a rewarding love.

Love at First Sight

You see each other across a crowded room. Your eyes lock. Your hearts melt. Immediately you "know": You've found the one you've been searching for. It's "love at first sight"—the instant attraction people dream about. Love at first sight is possible (almost everyone has an anecdote to support the premise), but what is called "love at first sight" frequently turns out to be lust at first sight.

Looks undeniably play a part in such immediate attractions and many times matter too much. All too often on my "LovePhones" radio show, I hear young women exclaim that they are in love because "he's so good-looking," and guys say "she's so hot"—and yet they don't really know or care enough about who the person really is.

Dating Data

Surveys show that many people believe in love at first sight, although more want to believe it exists. On one TV show I did on the subject, half the audience at first said they believed in love at first sight, but by the end of the show, hearing horror stories of how some of these "fairy tales" turned out, three-fourths of the audience had changed their vote.

It takes time to determine how right or compatible a partner is for you. Real love develops slowly as you share and support one another through happy and sad times.

My rule: Enjoy the initial thrill, but have at least six dates before you start seriously thinking he or she is really the "one." Even then, be cautious for the next six months as you observe your mate's character. Watch how he deals with family, friends, children, and colleagues. Is she caring and responsive? Does he tell the truth? Observe her in times of stress. Is he there for you in an emergency?

So how do you deal with the butterflies in your stomach? On the other hand, how do you know if something that doesn't give you an instant rush is worth pursuing? Here are some tips:

➤ Enjoy the excitement of being turned on by a stranger, but don't expect too much at first blush.

➤ Don't dismiss a relationship that doesn't provide instant thrills.

➤ Take time to let lust mature into more lasting compatibility.

Home Alone

Women, more often than men, fall too hard and too fast. So many women cry to me over the radio, "Everything seemed so perfect. Why hasn't he called?" I'll ask, "How long have you known each other?" "Just a few weeks" is usually the answer. After so little time, how can you possibly know enough to predict someone's behavior or explain their actions? Remember, love takes time!

Stages of Love

One thing is certain about love: It changes! Love comes in stages. The first stage is not really love but attraction. If the attraction is accompanied by sexual thrills and excitement, we call it lust. In this "honeymoon" phase of blind bliss, you are usually obsessed with mystery and the desire to impress. You enter a fantasy world of idealizing the other person and imagining how perfect you are for one another.

The next phase is the testing period, where expectations are met—or not—and fears arise ("Is she really the one?" "Can this really last?"). You find out if you really enjoy the same things, if you can rely on one another, if you have the same level of commitment, and if you communicate on the same level.

If your relationship survives the testing period, you will enter a brief period of satisfaction where you'll feel that your fantasy of perfect love could indeed be fulfilled—until reality sets in. The more time you spend with your mate, the more opportunity you'll have to disagree with each other and see each other's flaws and imperfections. Inevitably, one of you might feel grumpy and disagreeable, or come down with some illness, providing a true test of your tolerance and ability to compromise.

You may also start to notice that his hair is thinning, her breasts are beginning to sag, she nags, he spaces out in front of the television. In this testing period, you have to learn to compromise, to accept imperfections, to reduce your expectations, to resolve your differences, and to develop a realistic view of your life together—either that, or you'll throw in the towel.

If your relationship weathers the test of time, you'll end up with more intimacy and commitment, and with the resolve to make adjustments to "make it work." During this time, love deepens, but lust may fade. This creates another challenge—that you not take your relationship or each other for granted. Researchers call this "companionate" or "conjugal" love, which is where you'll find the warmth of a long-lasting relationship.

Dating Data

Some people forget or don't realize that the excitement and passion of new love may not go on forever—it either gives way to something more permanent, or the relationship ends. This may come as a real letdown to someone who fears "He must not love me anymore" when the lust stage runs its course. This can be the reason some people hop from relationship to relationship—to try to recapture the initial excitement or challenge of falling in love.

Too Young for Love?

The feeling of being in love can happen at any age. Steve is 16 and wants to know, "I met this girl, and we want to spend the rest of our lives together. Should I dedicate my heart? Are we too young to know?"

Falling so madly in love that you think you want to spend the rest of your life together is a delicious experience. It can work, of course, even if you're young. You may marry your childhood sweetheart, but the chances are probably slender it will last. There's a lot of truth to the notion that you can't love someone else until you know and love yourself—and it is very hard for young people to truly know themselves. My advice to young people is to enjoy feeling love but don't act on it prematurely.

When to Say "I Love You"

I usually say that when you are in love, you should feel free to say almost anything: "If it's on your mind, let it be on your lips." But many of us feel anxious about telling someone that we love him—and there are some legitimate conditions and considerations.

When to say I love you:

➤ When it's true.

➤ When you want to get it off your chest.

➤ When you've been wanting to say it a long time.

> ➤ When you feel overwhelmed with gratitude for all that someone has done for you.
>
> ➤ When it seems appropriate in the heat of passion (and you know you're not just carried away, or saying what you think she wants to hear).
>
> ➤ When you have your partner's full attention.

Three little words—"I love you"—whether whispered or shouted from the rooftop, have such impact and significance. Many of us have fears about uttering these three little words—fears of feeling silly, of being rejected, or of being misunderstood.

But if you truly love someone, saying "I love you" is a risk you have to take. If you are concerned about what to say, start by expressing your appreciation or with a compliment: "I appreciate you for your support, (or strength, attentiveness, or thoughtfulness)." Then talk about your love in hypothetical terms: "If I could say I love you, without being afraid that you'd be scared to hear it, I'd say . . ." It's always a good idea to reassure the other person that you have no demands in return: "I want to say I love you, but it doesn't mean you have to say you love me back."

What if your mate has just told you he loves you? How should you respond? Obviously, with the truth. If you are not sure of your feelings, say, "That's wonderful. Let's take this slowly and see where it goes." If you are sure of your feelings, try, "I love you back" or tease, "I love you more." Express joy and appreciation: "Thank you for the beautiful gift of your love."

If you don't feel the same way, be delicate responding to "I love you." Your answer may have an impact for a very, very long time. Never say: "I wish you wouldn't say that," "I don't love you back," "That's a bad idea," or "It's too late for that." You can kindly and dispassionately say, "That's such a nice thing to say," or "What a nice feeling"—something that clearly doesn't return the feeling but acknowledges it.

When not to say I love you:

➤ To force your mate to say or feel it in return.

➤ When you're afraid your partner doesn't feel the same thing.

➤ To get something from someone in return.

➤ To convince yourself you feel it.

➤ To prove to yourself you can say it.

➤ To get someone to have sex.

➤ Because you've always dreamed of saying it.

➤ When you're not sure.

➤ Because your mate has said he's in love with someone else.

➤ When you don't have her full attention.

➤ When you've barely met the person.

Jumping the Gun

"What do you do when you think you love someone, but it might be too early to tell her?"

If the relationship is right, you won't need to play games—you'll be able to say what you feel. However, there is such a thing as jumping the gun. For instance, Eli had been seeing Rita for only two weeks when he told me, "I want to say 'I love you' to her. Is it too soon?" Of course, there is a chance that she feels the same way, in which case Eli's impulse would be welcome. But generally, two weeks is hardly enough time to get to know someone, much less love him. Early proclamations of love run the risk of making the other person suspicious of your intentions, burdened by your needs, and turned off by thinking of you (however unfairly) as insincere or desperate. It's safer to say, "I really like you a lot," "I feel tremendous affection for you at this moment," or "I'd really like to spend more time with you."

Examine what is behind your need to profess your love so soon (control, loneliness, or insecurity). Eli realized, "I don't have too many women notice me, so if one does, I have to say it to keep her because I'm afraid there won't be another." Eli needs instead to believe that the world is abundant—and that eventually the right person will come along.

Torn Between Two Lovers

I am always hearing from people who ask if it is possible to love two people at the same time. In almost every case, the person is asking for a specific reason—because of feeling torn between two lovers.

For example, Mitch called my "LovePhones" radio show to say that he is dating a woman he really cares for—she has a terrific career, is wonderful with his family, and makes him feel so comfortable. However, he still has feelings for his former girlfriend, and still sleeps with her on occasion—and finds the sex much more satisfying. While he loves his fiancée, he can't stop lusting after his old flame.

Many men and women find themselves split—they are physically attracted to one type of person and emotionally attracted to another. While it is unreasonable to expect that one person will satisfy all of your needs, if you cherish and value monogamy, your happiness depends on finding a mate with whom you want to pledge exclusivity. It's a little tough if you're unable to merge these two competing sides of yourself (referred to as the Madonna-Whore Syndrome" for men or the "Daddy-Don Juan Syndrome" for women). The trick lies in embracing and integrating your competing urges.

I encouraged Mitch to imagine his current girlfriend as being incredibly sexy, more of a "bad girl." She may also be looking for an opportunity or "permission" to express another side of herself. I also suggested to Mitch that if he couldn't work out his conflicts and integrate his competing desires, he might be wise to hold off on making any commitments or to look for someone who's a better mixture of what he wants.

The Changing Face of Love

The beauty about love is that once you give yourself permission to feel it, you can experience it many times over—in different ways, perhaps, but in satisfying variations. You can always feel devotion, intense caring, trust, excitement, and spiritual connection.

Sophia recalled the first time she fell in love, with Rick: "I was the happiest girl on Earth. I felt I was doing exactly what I wanted, with the person I wanted." But they eventually broke up, and for years afterward she didn't feel the same way about anyone.

Sophia found that she kept comparing her new dates with Rick. "At so many other times with so many other guys," she said, "I always wished they were different, more like Rick." Finally, years later, she met Court. While she did not feel, as with Rick, that he was perfect for her, by this time she had changed her priorities. She wasn't looking for perfection, she was looking for someone to connect with on a deeper emotional level. Sophia called it "love" again, but the criteria, definition, and experience of it had changed.

Starved for Affection

Part of love is expressing affection. However, I often get calls from people who complain that their lover is not affectionate enough—or at all. People who think they are in love but feel deprived of affection are either so overly desperate and demanding that no one could possibly fulfill their needs, or, more likely, they sabotage themselves by getting into relationships that do not satisfy their need for affection. It's also possible that their styles are just different—one is more "touchy-feely," one more reserved.

But if you find yourself picking mates who withhold affection, it's time to ask yourself a few questions. Do you feel unworthy of love? Indeed, many women grow up with fathers who never hold them or say they love them. These women go on to choose men like their fathers and then try to change them as a way of repairing the early hurt. Learn to recognize when you are trapped in such dysfunctional attachment, misperceived as "love."

All You Need Is Love

I frequently get calls from people asking, "Is it possible that if you love each other, you can overcome anything—different religions, backgrounds, careers?"

It is possible. You can be so committed that you can withstand all kinds of barriers and pain. Unfortunately, such devotion was more likely in the covered-wagon days, when people were hardier and more loyal. In modern times, both men and women all too often run when the going gets tough.

In addition, our society has not always nurtured and supported loyalty. It's enough to make you cynical. But I say you should not accept that. Do your part to spread love and keep good energy going. You can overcome any odds and find and create the magic called love, any way you define it.

The Least You Need to Know

➤ Our definition of love can change over time and with different experiences.

➤ Ask yourself important questions about honesty, loyalty, and thoughtfulness before determining whether you are really in love.

➤ Love at first sight may be only lust—but lust can sometimes develop into love.

➤ Love progresses through several phases, including attraction, testing, satisfaction, and "companionate" or "conjugal" love.

Who's Afraid of Commitment?

I'm frequently asked, "How can I tell if she's the one? How do I know if this relationship will lead to marriage—or if I'm even ready for that step?" Commitment tends to progress in phases, but there are a number of clues that can tip you off as to where your relationship stands.

In the best case, you've both decided to dedicate yourselves to one another, to pledge your hearts for a lifetime. But what happens if your partner is not feeling exactly the same way? Or what happens if you're being pursued by someone, and you want to take things slower? Unfortunately, not everyone arrives at the commitment stage of a relationship at the same time. In this chapter, I talk about commitment, including how to spot "commitment phobes," and what to do if you're the one with cold feet.

You Know It's Serious When . . .

Single men and women often ask me how to tell if they really care for someone and are ready to settle down. Basically, if you're asking the question, you're still not sure. But here are some signs that can help you tell how serious you're getting, in two stages:

Stage I. You know you're getting closer to making a commitment when:

➤ You don't make many plans with your friends because you'd rather be with him.

➤ You start saying "we" instead of "I" or "you."

➤ You answer on her behalf (for example, the waiter asks what you'd both like to order for dinner, and you know exactly what she'll want).

➤ You start gravitating toward couples instead of singles.

➤ You no longer keep track of all the single people you know or date.

➤ You find yourself more interested in romantic movies and love stories.

➤ You like hearing stories about others who have fallen in love.

➤ You no longer panic about her checking your answering machine or opening your drawers.

➤ You get tickets to some event and instantly think of taking her instead of your best buddy.

➤ You find yourself thinking of ways to please her instead of just yourself.

➤ You wonder about what furniture and belongings you'd both give up when you move in together.

Stage II. You know you're getting close to a proposal when:

➤ You would rather be with her than with anyone or anywhere else.

➤ You say you're tired of the single life and really mean it.

➤ You think more in terms of your future: how and where you will live and work.

➤ You have a newfound interest in weddings.

➤ You consider money differently—with an eye toward buying a house, for instance.

➤ You expose secrets to each other that you wouldn't tell anyone else.

➤ You enjoy fantasizing about what your children will be like.

➤ You really want your families to get along.

➤ You picture yourselves growing old, sitting on some porch in rocking chairs together.

If the majority of these signs seem to apply to you, consider becoming comfortable with the idea that you are one step closer to settling down and making love work. Take the next step and discuss these signs with your mate to see where you each stand in your relationship.

Rules of Commitment

Here are a few simple rules about commitment that, if kept in mind, will help you avoid a lot of heartache and frustration:

1. Believe it if he says he doesn't want to make a commitment.

2. Believe it if she says she doesn't think she'll ever find Mr. Right. She's challenging you to try to fit the bill, but chances are you won't be "it" either. Do you really want to audition for this difficult role?

3. Believe him if he says he doesn't like discussing his feelings. If you love to talk, you will be miserable in this relationship—and you're a fool if you think you can change him.

4. Believe him if he says he doesn't want to change. Don't take pity or feel challenged, although it's very tempting to think that you can show him a happier way.

Men with Cold Feet

"When it comes to commitment, a glacier moves faster than my boyfriend!"

"I have been with my boyfriend for three years and he refuses to discuss our future. I have asked him if we can talk marriage, but he simply won't. Am I wasting my time with him if he won't discuss the subject?"

Dating Data

It was the complaint of the 1980s: men who wouldn't commit, men with cold feet, "Peter Pans" (men who just won't grow up) who loved to date but were terrified of settling down. While complaints about commitment seem to have leveled off, some "commitment phobes" still abound.

If you are trying to catch someone who doesn't want to be caught, you better decide how long you can continue the pursuit. But think about this: If you truly wanted a commitment, you would probably be with someone who was more willing to commit! Keep in mind my "Mirror Law of Attraction": We are attracted to people who reflect a part of ourselves. Women who find themselves with noncommittal men frequently have some unconscious motivation not to commit themselves.

Fence-sitters rarely change until they have to—that is, until they are faced with the loss of something they truly value. If you're running out of patience with a noncommittal mate, an ultimatum will certainly put him to the test. But be careful—once you make an ultimatum, you have to follow through or you lose credibility.

When a pattern continues for many years, it is often difficult to change the relationship. As the partner, you may have to be the one to change—your expectations, that is.

If you put up with a mate's continued ambivalence or distance, that's all you will get. The only way to find out what your mate's intentions are is to ask directly; and if you are reluctant to ask, you might ask yourself whether you really want to know.

Be wary if either of you turns love into a game of control. You'll know that's happening if one of you is pushing for a commitment, and the other resists because of feeling controlled. In that case, back off and give each other some time, until you can approach again out of true caring and not a need to control.

Women with Cold Feet

Men are typically pegged as the ones with commitment problems. But many women have cold feet too. For example, Stephanie told me: "As soon as a guy shows he cares about me, I brush him off."

If you see yourself in Stephanie's shoes, think about why you back off when men advance. Some women with commitment problems have low self-esteem. Remember the cliché, "I don't want to belong to any club that would have me as a member." It's important to value the people who see your worth. By brushing off people who like you, you are devaluing their opinion, and yourself!

Dating Data

As men are becoming more comfortable making commitments these days, they are complaining more about women who don't commit. Women are realizing their own problems in this department, too.

Women with commitment problems may also be looking for a challenge. These women constantly need to test their attractiveness. If you fit this description, you have to start believing that you are desirable, and make the catch as valuable as the chase.

Finally, some women, like some men who have cold feet, are afraid of being suffocated. Certain "commitment phobes" were smothered by parents who made all their decisions and influenced all their choices. Sometimes a fear of commitment is really a fear of repeating the same scenario—having a mate who is too attached and too involved, just like their overbearing parents. If you see yourself in this example, resist repeating the pattern. Feel more secure in your independence. Go out only with people who have their own lives and who will not try to live through, or take over, yours.

Dating Data

Today, more and more women want to be a parent—even if they don't have a man in their lives. According to a survey I analyzed for *New Woman* magazine, a whopping 40 percent of 16,000 single women said they would consider having a child on their own.

Tips for Recognizing Cold Feet in Men and Women

Here are some signs that your love interest has commitment problems:

➤ He says outright he's not ready to settle down.

➤ She frequently complains there are no good men "out there." (Hint: There are, but she attracts those who aren't ready for a commitment because she's not ready herself.)

➤ He looks for—and finds—imperfections and faults in all the women he's gone out with.

➤ She tends to withdraw whenever she's pursued.

➤ He's a workaholic—too busy for a relationship.

➤ He breaks dates at the last minute—even with a convincing excuse.

➤ She says she wants a relationship, but her love history indicates that she doesn't.

➤ You're always doing the calling and pursuing. He never takes the initiative.

➤ When you give an invitation, he says he'd like to go but can't give you an answer yet.

I Need My Space!

Having someone tell you "I need my space" is painful. It usually means that you want that person more than he or she wants you. But if you are the one demanding some space, you may be feeling suffocated by too much intimacy.

Remember I said that for any relationship to work, both people have to have similar needs for separateness or togetherness. If you and your partner are at different stages in your psychological development, you may have very different needs for intimacy—which can cause real problems in your relationship. If your partner is demanding "more space," get to the bottom of what he means. Does he really want to separate, or does he simply need a little breathing room? Sometimes, if you are able to leave him alone, his trapped feeling will subside, and he'll come back willingly.

For example, Diane had been dating Scott for nine months when he asked her for a little "space." She was devastated, because she really loved him with all her heart. But wisely, she stepped back and didn't call him. Within a few weeks, he called and the relationship got back on track.

Keeping Secrets

Some people run from commitment because they have a hidden shame or fear of rejection. Often this is the result of some secret (you never graduated from college; you have herpes; you once broke the law) that makes you feel as if you are just not good enough. What is the solution?

➤ Change your thinking, from "No one will love me if they know my secret" to get over your shame and fear, and decide that you deserve some happiness. If you do have a secret that will affect your partner, such as herpes, discuss it now! Remember, your partner has a right to know.

➤ Examine how you are using your secret or your shame to avoid or escape commitment.

➤ Trust your true love by showing him the real you—but only after you feel he's earned your trust and you know him well (after at least six months).

➤ Carefully select the right time to discuss your secret, and make sure your love understands you're revealing your secret out of concern for the relationship.

➤ Be prepared for possible disappointment or rejection. Not every one will be able to handle your secret.

Sabotaging Relationships

Along the road to commitment, many couples face dilemmas about faithfulness and other crises that sabotage the relationship. For example, Mike admitted, "I seem to have a problem staying faithful. Every time I have the opportunity to cheat with a beautiful woman, I can't stop myself." You will always be confronted by others you find attractive, but that doesn't mean you have to go after all of them (or any of them for that matter). It sounds as if Mike needs to feel that he can attract beautiful women—that his ego needs constant reassurance.

In John's case, his girlfriend is the one with the wandering eye. "My girl is always looking around, staring at attractive men. She compares it to admiring a piece of art. But I hate it, and I've told her that a million times. What should I do?"

Since John's girlfriend has heard and ignored his objections, there is not a lot he can do—except reassure himself that, after all, she is with him. Although looking is not the same as touching, if you've made your feelings known and they are being ignored, take heed. Chances are, she's gazing around for a reason (and it's not just art appreciation). She may not be ready to settle down, and is checking out other guys to see whether she's interested in pursuing someone else. If you're involved with someone who can't or won't stop looking around, despite your objections, take the hint and look for love elsewhere. You'll drive yourself crazy if you stay in the situation.

Constantly comparing a present love to an ex can be another way to sabotage your making a commitment. It's natural to compare your present lover to past loves. But remember, we often idealize old relationships, forgetting the pain, insincerity, and other flaws. While it's fine to indulge your private love history occasionally, don't overdo it. Put your energy and imagination into your current relationship—not into the past.

Overcoming a Fear of Commitment

If, in reading this chapter, you recognize yourself in any of the "commitment phobes," is there anything you can do to overcome your fears? The good news is yes, but as with any other significant change, overcoming your fear of commitment will take hard work—and a commitment to change! Here are some tips:

➤ **Face reality.** Realize that no one person will ever fulfill all of your needs (no one is perfect).

➤ **Re-prioritize.** Decide that focusing primary attention on your mate is something you value (rather than valuing playing around).

➤ **Control yourself.** If you have a wandering eye, stop yourself every time you turn to look at other women.

➤ **Examine your need to pursue others** (for attention or proof of your desirability), and get those needs satisfied in other ways.

➤ **Confront any anger or tension.** In your relationship deal directly with your mate, instead of escaping him by running to other relationships.

➤ **Create a different love script.** Replace the one of you as a swinging single with one of you as a committed partner.

Moving Too Fast

Before closing this chapter, I'd like to point out that not all commitment problems fall on the shoulders of the one resisting the commitment. In certain situations, one person in the relationship may be applying pressure too soon and may be trying to move the relationship along too quickly.

For example, Marie had recently met Joe, and within a few weeks had decided that he was the man of her dreams. At 34, she felt "Why waste time when you know?" But Joe felt no sense of urgency, and in fact was put off by her insistence. Marie seemed so hungry for attachment that it was scaring him away. In this case, Joe sensed that he was being cast in Marie's love script—and he felt that she couldn't possibly know him after only a few weeks. He was beginning to feel that it wasn't him that she loved, but rather the idea of being in love.

Home Alone

Ultimatums are risky. If you say to your partner, "Commit to me or good-bye," be prepared to leave if your terms aren't met. Crying "wolf" only tells your partner that your word means nothing and that you are easily manipulated.

If your love interest is resisting your urge for commitment, examine whether you really are moving too fast. Think about whether you are truly in love, or are casting your mate in your love script without sensitivity to who he is or what he really wants.

Evaluate your pattern of choices. Do you constantly attract people who seem sensitive about commitment, who draw away, or who move too slowly? If you tend to move quickly in relationships, make this clear from the start. Explain, "If I really like someone, I tend to go fast." If your partner balks or seems to pull back, then you should pull back, too. Being sensitive to your own and your partner's needs for intimacy or separateness is the key to fulfilling both of you individually, and to finding a balance between you.

The Least You Need to Know

➤ Always believe it when someone tells you he or she has problems with or is unwilling to make commitments.

➤ Both women and men can have fears and resistance to commitment.

➤ Trying to change a "commitment phobe" is frustrating, if not downright impossible. Examine your need to attract these types of people.

➤ If you move too fast, wanting a commitment, you may not be truly in love but have a desperate need for attachment.

Chapter 20

The Dating Duo: Fighting and Jealousy

In This Chapter

➤ Why lovers fight

➤ The 10 topics lovers fight about most

➤ Assessing your anger style

➤ Eight steps to stopping arguments

➤ Rating your jealousy meter

➤ Slaying the green-eyed monster

At some point in dating, you are bound to disagree—from simple things like which movie to see to more complex issues like handling finances. Believe it or not, disagreeing is part of any healthy relationship. It enables couples to pinpoint their individuality, and to determine what triggers each other's anger, how to handle the anger, and how to resolve differences. However, constant fighting can be a warning sign in dating. As the saying goes, anger is one letter away from "danger." If you can't agree early in your relationship, think of the trouble you'll have ahead, when life together gets more complicated.

Disagreeing disintegrates into chronic arguing or fights—that can sabotage your relationship—when you refuse to respect each other's point of view. Worse yet, you begin to resent each other, and go over the same points ad nauseum, in a stalemate.

Another element that can sabotage any relationship is that "green-eyed monster" we call jealousy. Jealousy can range from the superficial, for example, being envious of another person's body, job, or car, to the not-so-superficial—that your mate may leave you for someone prettier or richer. However, one thing that all types of jealousy have in common is that they breed on your own fears and insecurities. As with any other emotion, you can learn to control it or slay the monster on the spot with lots of self-esteem and confidence.

Top 10 Topics Couples Fight About

Being prepared for the pitfalls in a relationship can help you work through them. As soon as you notice the following common sources of tension in your dating, realize that it's to be expected. Then focus on the following solutions, rather than staying stuck in stalemates.

1. When to see each other
2. How often to see each other
3. Flirting with other people
4. Being late
5. Forgetting important dates (birthdays, anniversaries)
6. Being faithful
7. Who spends how much money and on what
8. How you spend time (watching too much TV, going out with friends)
9. The amount or type of sex you have
10. Family (when and whom to visit, their disapproval)

Anger Styles

Your style of handling anger and arguments can be explained in a manner similar to explaining your communication style (see Chapter 12). The two most common styles are withdrawing into the silent treatment ("He's mad and won't talk to me"), or expressing ("I have to talk it out to feel better"). Obviously, these two styles clash. Work on accepting and compromising, so both of you can have a chance to either cool off quietly or let off steam. Admit your style to each other, so you don't feel the other person is punishing or rejecting you (it's just their way). Then agree to take turns accommodating each other. (You can keep quiet for awhile, and choose a time for a civilized discussion.)

Why You Fight

There's always a deeper issue fueling a fight. For example, all of the top 10 arguments listed earlier are smokescreens for the real complaints: "You don't think about me enough," "You don't love me enough," or "You don't care about me enough." Once you recognize the real feeling and address that real need, you can move toward a deeper intimacy.

Different Values

Joe called my "LovePhones" radio show with this complaint: "Because of an accident that happened at work, I collected $45,000 in worker's compensation. My fiancée wants me to use the money as an investment in a house. But I bought a T-bird and plan to use the rest of the money to purchase other 'fun' things. Now we argue about it all the time and my fiancée even says that she's not sure she wants to be engaged to me anymore."

Joe and his fiancée obviously have different priorities. She wants him to buy a house as a sign that he's ready to settle down. His resistance and his types of expenditures may be a sign that he's just not ready to make that commitment. Instead of arguing about the "smokescreens" (what to spend the money on), Joe and his fiancée need to talk about each other's deeper needs and feelings, and the issue of their commitment.

Battles Over Control

Many fights are really over whether you or your partner needs to be the boss—and make all of the decisions. If you tend to argue over silly things, you are most likely competing over who gets his or her way. It would be a real breakthrough if you could just stop when you notice a fight over these repetitive, meaningless issues and admit, "I just need to feel in control right now."

Misunderstandings That Stem from the Past

Many times people argue because they both just see a situation in a totally different way. We each wear our own special "glasses" through which we see the world. For example, Jim wants to simply go out with his friends and have a good time. Darla, his girlfriend, instead suspects that he's looking for another woman—what her ex-boyfriend did.

Before starting an argument, examine your own personal fears as well as events that happened in your past. Are you really mad at the person, or just scared that the past may be repeating itself?

Fighting as a Turn-On

Some couples endure, or purposefully invite, the pain of fighting in order to enjoy the pleasure of making up. Arguing does stimulate physical arousal that can be channeled into sexual excitement. But beware of this motivation because it can erode your relationship. Find more constructive ways to spice up your passion for one another.

Getting Over Peeves

The best love is unconditional, such as the love mothers feel for their children. But when it comes to dating, you usually find something that eventually bugs you. As

Roseanne's TV sister Jackie admitted to her new beau in one episode of the TV sitcom, "I bite off my nails and spit them across the room!" She may leave her shoes lined up on the floor, he may leave the milk carton spout open, or his dirty underwear lying around. Everybody has something—decide if you can deal with it!

Let others' habits stop annoying you by concentrating on improving yourself. If you need to make your date feel "wrong," examine how you need to justify any self-defeating generalizations you might make about men or women (for example, that men never do anything to help out around the house or that women always nag about what men don't do). Focus on the behavior without blowing it out of proportion. Consider whether the behavior is worth bothering yourself about. Some things are just not worth your time and energy; put the peeves in proper perspective and concentrate on more important priorities.

Constant Complaining

Mike is upset because his girlfriend picks on him about everything. "She yells at me for silly things, like wearing gray socks with blue jeans, or not closing the door behind me. What's going on with her?"

Unrelenting nags and complainers are either copying the way their parents behaved, or are dissatisfied with their own lives and are taking it out on their mates. Keep in mind that naggers only keep nagging because they aren't stopped. Tell such arguers firmly that they'll have to speak to you respectfully or not at all, and to hold their tongues when they're about to start petty attacks. Ask them to examine how they can turn their own life around to fulfill their dreams so that they don't take their frustrations out on you. If naggers and complainers felt better about who they are and what they do, they wouldn't focus on your inadequacies.

How to Stop Fights

Arguments have a certain pattern that leads to an escalating cycle of unexpressed needs, unfulfilled needs, and misunderstandings. Brandon and Sue hadn't made love in three weeks. Brandon lost his sexual desire because he lost his job and felt miserable. This caused Sue to feel rejected and undesirable. At a party one night, when Sue noticed Brandon talking to a pretty woman, she immediately felt threatened, and nastily called him "a pig."

To stop these types of arguments and prevent them from occurring in the future:

➤ **Nip problems in the bud.** Mountains grow out of molehills. Sue was already building up weeks of resentment and hurt since Brandon had been neglecting her sexually. She was ready to blow her stack. Talk about your needs or complaints when they're small and you first notice them.

➤ **Clarify behavior.** Hold off blowing your stack till you get the facts. The truth is, Brandon knew the woman from work and she was married. He had no intention of going out with her. Sue jumped to conclusions, given the colored glasses of hurt she was wearing.

➤ **Explain how each other feels and ask for support when necessary.** Brandon withdrew from sex and Sue without letting her know how he was feeling—leaving her feeling insecure and vulnerable to losing her temper.

➤ **Get to the bottom of what the argument is really about.** Ask the question "What am I really upset about?" On the surface, people seem to be arguing about money, time, household tasks, or sex, but they're really arguing about deep emotional needs that are not being met. If your girlfriend complains that you spend more time with your friends, she's really trying to say, "I need to feel important."

➤ **Say what you want.** Don't be afraid to express the real need you have and ask for what you want. If Brandon had asked Sue for support and Sue had asked Brandon for reassurance, they wouldn't have had the misunderstanding that they did.

➤ **Exercise self-control.** Before exploding, take a deep breath and hesitate one moment. Purposefully do something else—walk away, smile, even say you feel you're about to explode but don't really want to.

➤ **Correct irrational or negative thoughts.** Don't assume the worst before you know the facts. Usually, the other person is not trying to do you in, humiliate, shame, or embarrass you; they're usually just trying to cope with their own problems.

➤ **Look for relationship patterns.** Are you getting revenge for what others in your life have done to you? Look at deeper issues: Do you feel insecure or deprived in life in general and are you taking it out on this person or situation?

Jealousy Barometer

Jealousy consumes your self-esteem, sabotages your confidence, and ultimately scares any potential good catches away. But, as with any other emotion, if you recognize it and turn it around, you can harness it—for your dating success!

The following quiz will help you gauge your potential for jealousy. For each question, score yourself on a scale from 0–10, with 10 being the most true of you, and 0 being the least true of you. When you're done, add up your total score and record it at the end of the list.

Score from 0–10

_____ **1.** I worry that others get better dates or more dates than I do.

_____ **2.** I compare what I have to others.

_____ **3.** I wish I were like some other woman/man who dates a lot.

_____ **4.** I feel better when I think I have something or someone that another person might want.

_____ **5.** I tend to buy clothes or use language to impress other people.

_____ **6.** I date people who I think my friends would admire or envy.

_____ **7.** I'm insecure about how much my love interests like me.

_____ **8.** I pout or scold if I think my date is looking at others.

_____ **9.** If my date flirts with somebody else, I freak out.

_____ **10.** As soon as I walk into a room, I gauge how I compare to others.

My total score: _____

What Your Score Means

If you scored 0–20, you don't have to worry about killing the green-eyed monster—you've already learned to control it. Most of us compare ourselves to others once in a while. This is okay as long as you keep your eye on your own ball, feel good enough about who you are, and use others as examples to motivate you to be your best. Sometimes even a tiny bit of possessiveness can make your mate feel that extra spark of being prized. A score of 20–50 is a warning that comparisons are eroding your confidence and that competitiveness is blinding you from your own potential success. A score over 50 is a danger sign. You are short-changing yourself by thinking you are less than others, comparing, or copying them rather than being yourself. This makes you act irrationally out of fear and insecurity, which further sabotages your dating opportunities and damages your self-esteem.

Smooth Talk'n

In overcoming jealousy or envy, keep in mind the rule of the 12-step program to overcome addictions: God give me the courage to change the things I can change, accept the things I cannot change, and the wisdom to know the difference.

Slaying the Green-Eyed Monster

Most of the quiz questions deal with comparison. Your ultimate goal should be to be yourself—constant comparison will just keep you from achieving this.

Of course, there are traits worth emulating, but they don't include having bigger breasts or a fancier car. Instead of focusing on superficial concerns, think about the following:

➤ **Work on developing confidence.** Often, what we envy in people is their confidence. What we admire in others is often what we want for ourselves. Don't waste your time focusing on things you can't change—your height, for example. Concentrate on things you can change—your assertiveness, attitude, or self-esteem. Even if you don't have his big bank account or her 34C bra size, walk around with the confidence as if you do; you can have the feeling of having what you want.

➤ **Recognize the roots of your jealousy.** Did your parents always compare you to your siblings ("Why don't you get good grades like your brother?" "Your sister never gave us any trouble.")? Resolve that you don't have to live with the ghosts of the past.

➤ **Trace your insecurity.** Tasha's mother went through three divorces—no wonder she doubted her traveling boyfriend's fidelity. Knowing the reason for your feeling gives you more control over it.

➤ **Make a "life philosophy" fix.** You may think the "grass is always greener," but everybody's garden has patches of brown. If you wish you could snare a Prince instead of a frog, consider Princess Diana's reported depression, eating disorders, and dating miseries, shrouded in scandals and subject to palace and public disapproval.

➤ **Refocus your thoughts.** When you feel pangs of jealousy, envy, or insecurity, refocus. Snap your fingers or use another action that interrupts your train of thought. Then let a new thought step in to replace the destructive one. Rather than obsessing that your date is attracted to another woman, turn your attention to what you can do to spark some energy between the two of you.

Developing Confidence

Jealousy stems from insecurity and low self-esteem. Confidence slays the green-eyed monster, so if this is your problem, turn back to Chapter 6, in which I discuss self-esteem. Whenever you become flooded with doubts about your own self-worth, keep these tips in mind:

➤ **Do affirmations.** Immediately turn your mind to all the wonderful things about yourself. Even if you are not convinced about the truth of these good things at that moment, force your mind to think these things. After all, the "bad" or "critical" thoughts you have about yourself are no more true than these positive ones (the brain, like a computer, only knows what you put in it). It's like kicking a bad habit—force yourself to stop thinking destructive thoughts by substituting constructive ones.

➤ **Make "life philosophy" corrections.** Instead of believing that others having more means you have less, believe that other people have special qualities, and so do you. The more abundance around you, the more resources available to you.

➤ **Practice imaging.** Picture yourself on a first date; everything is going beautifully—you're smiling, the two of you are chatting comfortably. Review these scenes as if you were watching a movie in your head. The mental rehearsal makes it more likely that this will happen in real life.

➤ **Become the type of person you are jealous of.** Make the lifestyle for yourself that you envy in others. Tasha always feared that her boyfriend was going to cheat on her, and she imagined him having a fabulous time with any number of irresistible women. Deep down she wanted to be that "irresistible woman," desirable and leading an exciting life. Once she started concentrating on making that true of herself, she was more fulfilled in her relationship and herself.

Controlling the Green-Eyed Monster on the Spot

Quiz questions 7–10 test how well you handle jealousy on a real-life date. You flunked if you are distracted by the idea that your date is about to leave you for someone else. If you are convinced that you are not good enough to hold someone's attention, you will probably convince this person of the same thing. Yolanda, for example, is always comparing herself to other women, telling her boyfriend that so-and-so is much more attractive, outgoing, and so on. Eventually she may convince her boyfriend that another girl is a better match—but more likely, she'll just push him away with her neediness and insecurity, and she'll lose him anyway.

You also flunk if you get so flooded with fury over a date's flirting that you fly off the handle. For example, Danielle told me, "At a party recently, I saw my boyfriend talking to another woman. I stomped over and made a scene, and dragged him away. The problem is, now he's not talking to me. What did I do wrong?"

Losing your cool is the worst thing you can do—you're allowing your jealousy to overwhelm your common sense. You may think you are showing the extent of your passion, but in the final analysis, your theatricality only reveals your insecurity. Do you enjoy losing control? Do you think it is an attractive quality? Will it get you what you want (attention, devotion)? Your answer to these questions should be "No."

If you feel yourself losing control, tap that stronger place inside yourself that communicates "I feel deserving, and I don't like that behavior." Take a deep breath at the moment and calm yourself down. Distract yourself with something that makes you feel good about yourself (do not flirt with someone else in revenge). What is the worst thing that could happen (that your boyfriend or girlfriend will leave you)? Reassure yourself that you can deal with the outcome of this situation, whatever it may be (you are not going to fall apart). Then calmly, when the two of you are alone, tell your mate what you saw and describe your concerns. Ask for an explanation of what was really happening (to see if you misperceived the situation) and describe how you felt when you saw the two of them talking.

For example, you might say, "I was really upset when I saw you talking to that woman. I felt embarrassed, jealous, and was totally afraid of losing you. Can you tell me what was really happening?"

Jenine did it the right way. When she saw Brian flirting with another woman, she felt flushed with anger and fear. But instead of rushing over to interrupt, she waited until the next night when she and Brian were sitting together on the couch watching a video. She brought it up in a positive context first: "I love the way we are together." Starting out being positive about the two of you allays defensiveness, reinforces your self-esteem, and sets the tone for working out any problems. Then in a more casual (non-accusatory) tone, Jenine reported what she'd seen, "The other night I noticed you were talking to Lisa, and it seemed pretty cozy. I was wondering if you could tell me what was going on inside you so I really know and I won't jump to conclusions." If you can, add reassurance, "I really want an honest answer. I don't want you to feel defensive or worry about my reaction."

When Brian admitted he found Lisa attractive, instead of flying off the handle, screaming, or throwing her glass of wine at him, Jenine said calmly, "That upsets me," and asked for more clarification, "What does that mean about our relationship?" That precipitated a conversation about their commitment and about how they both felt about fidelity.

While Jenine and Brian managed to have a balanced conversation and work through the jealousy crisis, not all of your discussions will work out this way. However, keep the following in mind: Communicate and clarify your feelings. Give each other reassurance, to help you grow individually and as a couple. And remember, knowing the truth is always better than being consumed by jealousy and imagining the worst.

Are You Jealous of the One You Love?

The phrase "penis envy"—coined by Freud to refer to the feeling women have of being "less than" a man—has become politically incorrect and the concept has been challenged. Somewhere along the line, psychoanalysts conceded that men suffer from "breast envy" or "vagina envy"—feeling inferior to women because they lack the equipment to nurture and feed, or to receive pleasure through penetration. Critics have eschewed both concepts. But sexual characteristics aside, there's no doubt some men and women get hooked up with certain mates because they really wish they were them!

Rose is a prime example, as she told me: "My former lover was a personal trainer. I broke up with him because he was always flirting with the women he trained and I couldn't take it."

"You're really jealous of him, aren't you?" I asked her. She was surprised to be "found out," and admitted it. He had a gorgeous body, all the girls drooled over him, and he was cocky and confident. Rose wanted all that for herself. It is not uncommon for women (and some men) to date people whom they want to be like—they feel that if they possess the person whom they so admire, then they can vicariously have the lifestyle or qualities they admire.

Do you complain that your lover spends too much time doing things that don't involve you? Are you jealous of his friends? Have you tried to keep her from doing things that don't involve you? Do you try to involve yourself in everything he does? Do you criticize his work, yet think of him as perfect? Do you feel that he is "God's gift" but you are nearly invisible? Are you always imaging that others are trying to steal your lover away?

If you've answered "yes" to any of these questions, read on!

Poisonous Possessiveness

Irrational jealousy over a lover's friendships reveals your own insecurity. It is unreasonable to demand that your lover drop her friends—and it's cruel to ask a lover to choose between her friends and you.

If your lover is the jealous one, threatening to leave you if you don't drop your friends, ask him to examine why he feels threatened. Reassure him to the extent that it is possible, but then insist he back off. Tell him to stop living with ghosts of his past (past betrayals) and build his self-esteem, or he may really lose you.

Home Alone

Many jealous people put their lovers through "tests," which can backfire!

For instance, Sara put a note on her boyfriend's car windshield, in which she pretended to be a secret admirer. When he didn't tell her about the note, she fumed, thinking that he was unfaithful and didn't love her. Or consider Laura, who was constantly telling her boyfriend to go out with other women, to get "experience." When he finally did as she asked, she screamed at him for betraying her. "But you made me do it," he protested. "I was testing you," she cried, "and you failed." Such tests are usually unfair to the other person, who is blind to your motives and whose actions you may be quick to misinterpret. Instead, ask directly for the reassurance you need.

Does Your Date Foster Your Green-Eyed Monster?

Is it possible that your jealousy is not self-perpetuated, but triggered by your lover? Some people provoke others' jealousy out of insensitivity, thoughtlessness, hostility, or self-protection (hurting others before they get hurt themselves). For example, Paula's boyfriend told her, "My other lovers were much more energetic in bed. Why aren't you?" Such comparisons are a sure way of making someone feel insecure, and less likely to respond sexually! Mates should build, not break, your confidence.

Refusing to Let the Green-Eyed Monster Die

Steve's girlfriend, Saundra, gives him the third degree whenever he walks in the house. Recently, an old flame called, and Saundra lost it, insisting that they were seeing each other behind her back. When Steve brought Saundra roses to express his love, she snapped, "What, did your other girlfriend turn them down?" If your jealousy is making you behave irrationally, take a big step back. You are going to alienate your lover by constantly putting him on the defensive.

Focus on your feelings. Why are you so insecure? Has your lover given you any real reasons to doubt him? If so, why are you still involved in the relationship? Work on the problem so that it doesn't exist. Jealousy is unattractive, off-putting, irrational, and a surefire way of sabotaging all of your relationships. Rather than studying your mate for possible infidelity or petty indiscretions, work on your own self-esteem.

The Least You Need to Know

➤ All couples have disagreements (they're usually called arguments or fights); think of them as "differences." It's how you resolve your differences that determines whether your relationship will last.

➤ Most arguments are smokescreens for the real complaints. Remember, deeper issues fuel a fight. Get to the real need and satisfy it; the real problem and solve it.

➤ Jealousy eats you up; celebrate others' successes and grow under their glow.

➤ Turn envy into personal evolution—to become the best you can be.

Chapter 21

When Sex and Love Become Bedfellows

In This Chapter

➤ Deciding when, whether, and with whom to be intimate

➤ Can friends become lovers?

➤ Having sex to get love

➤ What part sexual fantasies play

➤ Keeping the fires burning

➤ The new sexual trend

You have been on a few dates, and the two of you seem to "click." But now comes the tricky part—sex. No doubt about it, sex is complicated. For some people, sex is purely a physical act, sought for the purpose of arousal, release, and pleasure. But for many others, especially women and an increasing number of men in this new millennium, sex means truly making love; they want an emotional connection, an act of giving and receiving affection and sharing feelings.

Whether you are 15 or 50, sex without love poses problems. Before you take your relationship to the next step, think carefully about your own, and your partner's, feelings. While it is tempting to act in the moment of passion, remember that sex changes a relationship for good—often for the better, but not always. In this chapter, I help you sort out the complications so that you can deal with them before you act, so no one gets hurt, and sex ends up being a good experience.

Dating Data

Having sex with people we love and feel loved by is emotionally and spiritually fulfilling. And research indicates that it can also be good for your health. When you engage in sex, your body releases certain hormones and chemicals (including endorphins, the "pleasure chemical") into your system that have immune-enhancing effects. These physical and psychological effects make the act even more rewarding and desirable—and make the choice of having sex and with whom much more important.

Making the Decision: The 10 Commandments

Obviously, the decision to have sex is a personal one. Some people (however unwisely) still choose to have sex without any emotional commitment. There are several criteria I strongly urge you to consider before making the decision to have sex. Hold off until:

1. You really trust one another with your emotional and physical health.
2. You are able to communicate openly about your needs and desires and how you feel about each other.
3. You understand each other's attitudes toward dating and sex.
4. You understand your own physical, emotional, and sexual needs.
5. You have spent time together nonsexually.
6. You have observed how she treats other people.
7. You have observed how he behaves under pressure or in emergencies.
8. You understand the consequences of having sex.
9. You are willing to be responsible about birth control and safe sex.
10. You've had at least six dates.

Dating Data

Dating coach Jim Sullivan says the stereotype of gay men rushing into sex still prevails, seeing a date—or themselves—as sex objects. In teaching the value of intimacy, he imposes a three date moratorium on sex.

The First Time

Sharing yourself sexually for the first time is an important step, and one that should not be taken lightly. You will likely remember this encounter forever, and it may influence your feelings about sex and love, so make sure your first experience is a positive one. Rachel recently called my "LovePhones" radio show to say, "I'm 26 and have never been sexually active. I have a fear of sleeping with the wrong person. I want it to be special." The fear isn't necessary, but her concern that the first time should be special is warranted. Make sure your first lover is considerate, caring, thoughtful, and giving. Be proud, not ashamed, of being a virgin until then.

Men, too, have anxieties about their first time. For example, Barry called to say, "I'm 22 and still a virgin. I've met a girl who wants to have sex, but I'm really nervous. What should I do?" It's natural to feel silly, embarrassed, or ashamed about being inexperienced—especially when you think everyone else is sexually sophisticated. Don't try to pretend that you are experienced; share your nervousness and appreciate your naiveté.

A caring partner will appreciate your honesty and the opportunity to teach you. If not, walk away—this is not a person to trust with your intimate feelings.

You can eliminate some performance pressures by talking together. Agree to take it slow, and that things may not be as great as you both expect. Spend some evenings just exploring one another's bodies through massage. Give each other feedback on where and how you like to be touched, making a more natural flow into lovemaking.

Too many men and women express regrets to me about their first time—that they felt pressured into

Home Alone

I still hear many men these days admit that if a girl submits to sex on the first date, he worries that she'll give in to other men, and even thinks of her in such old, pejorative terms as "slut" or "loose."

having sex, that it wasn't special enough. Don't do it just to "get it (virginity) over with." Think before you act, so you'll have no regrets later.

Saying No to Sex

It's essential in this new millennium to put an end to the fear of saying "no" to sex.

It boils my blood when people feel pressured to have sex. This isn't just a problem for women. Men often feel pressure, too. It takes a lot of security to say no. But I urge you, if that's how you feel, to say no! Don't worry about sounding foolish, being embarrassed, or ruining any spontaneity. It's better to be sure about such an important decision, so there are no misunderstandings or poor choices.

Valerie was so nervous about when to have sex, it even kept her from dating: "I get so nervous when guys ask me out. I keep thinking that somehow, sex will come up. It makes me so nervous that I never go out with anyone." Realize that YOU have control over what happens. Valerie's nervousness is extreme and implies some sort of early trauma or bad experience. In any case, recognize that you can readily set the limits. At the beginning of a date, if you feel any pressure, spell out your intentions. Be direct. You can say something like, "I find you attractive, and I want to go out with you, but I don't want to imply that I will jump into bed. That's a really important step for me that takes time."

Dating Data

Surveys have shown that more and more women are being cautious about sex. Also, more support groups exist to encourage "Love Can Wait."

Don't put yourself in compromising situations. If you have any doubts about a person, don't accept a date. But if you are out with someone who is more forward than you are comfortable with, make your feelings clear. You might even bring up the subject of sex in a very general way. For instance, mention that you heard something about casual sex on the radio or in the newspaper. State your opinions; put the issue right out on the table. For example, you might say, "I believe people should wait to have sex. They should care about each other. I'm simply not into casual sex." If your date becomes angry or loses interest, let him go. A person who doesn't respect your feelings on such an intimate issue is not someone to trust with your heart, body, or soul.

Remember I've pointed out in several places in this book that men in this New Age are increasingly open about their desire to wait for sex. When Jared and Jean were making love and she stopped his hand from going up her dress, he said, "That's ok. I can wait." (And wait he did—three months!) And, the three men featured in the E! Entertainment special "What Men Want"—all in their 20s and 30s—all said they prefer not to jump right into sex.

Ways to Say No

Saying no can be difficult. Here are some additional handy phrases to help make it easier:

> "I really like you, but I'm not ready for sex."

> "We have to get to know each other better."

> "Being intimate is very special to me, and I have to trust the person first."

Using Sex to Get Love and Vice Versa

On my "LovePhones" radio show, I frequently get calls from women who complain that they are only having sex with their boyfriends out of fear of losing them, and they ask me if they should do it. For instance, Jane called in and said, "I keep getting involved with men who sleep with me but then won't call. What am I doing wrong?" Perhaps more surprisingly, I get similar calls from some men.

My advice is to hold off having sex until you really know someone and what he wants out of a relationship. You can't possibly know someone's true intentions early in a relationship. If you find yourself jumping into bed too soon, examine your self-esteem and deeper emotional needs. I'm heartened to realize that as we enter the new millennium, more listeners who call me about this will finish their own question and say to themselves what I have long advised: "If he leaves you over that, he is not worth it." But progress is slow, and though they know the right thing to do, many women are still struggling over this.

Too many people have sex when what they are really looking for is love. If you sleep with someone whose feelings are not the same as yours, you are bound to end up feeling hurt. It's a mistake to have sex with someone you don't really know with the expectation of receiving love, just as it's a mistake to mislead someone into thinking that you care when all you really want is sex.

Some people (admittedly more men than women) love the thrill of conquest and will "work" the relationship until they get what they want. After that, they lose interest. If you've ever been in this situation, you know how easy it is to blame yourself—for not being interesting, sexy, or attractive enough. Instead, recognize you were being used, and be wise to prevent it from happening next time.

For instance, Anita called and told me about a man in her economics class. "This attractive guy in my class flirted with me shamelessly and wrote 'I love you' on my notebook. He called me a few times and once we had phone sex. After that, he stopped talking to me. What's up?" It is very possible that this man either got what he wanted, or realized he wasn't going to get exactly what he wanted, so he pulled away. Anita should be glad this guy came and went so quickly. Also, I urged her to take responsibility for her own actions. After all, she engaged in sexual phone games with a man she barely knew. As the saying goes, if you cast your net too wide, you're bound to snag a few bad fish.

How Can You Tell if Someone Just Wants Sex?

As I mentioned in Chapter 13, the Virginia Slims Opinion Polls, taken over a quarter century, revealed that women still complain that men treat them as sex objects. So now let's consider how you can tell if someone likes you for who you are or is interested in just one thing—sex? Put him to the test: If you hold off on sex, what is his reaction? If he disappears, you know his intentions. If he sticks around, talk about your fears of being wanted only for sex, how having sex changes the relationship for you, and how you need to know you're cared for. Spell out the qualities that you value: listening, giving, and communicating.

Be wary of dates who:

➤ Plant persistent sexual innuendoes in the conversation.

➤ Don't seem to listen.

➤ Have no history of long-term relationships.

➤ Make no or rare references to the future (phone calls or dates).

➤ Feed you challenging lines such as "You're the only girl I ever felt anything for" or "You could be the one to finally make me change my ways."

➤ Only call at the last minute or in the middle of the night.

➤ Agree to meetings only on their terms or at their request.

➤ Leave you feeling used, empty, or frustrated.

Using Sex to Manipulate

Having sex just to please or keep another person is not only damaging to one's self-esteem, it is manipulative and misleading. For instance, Sue's boyfriend lives in another city. She explains, "When he comes to visit, we make love but I don't always feel comfortable about it. But I don't want to do anything to make him think I'm seeing someone else. What should I do?" I suggested to Sue that she be honest, and if he is uncomfortable with her discomfort and decides to leave, perhaps the relationship was not on solid ground to begin with. Unless Sue expresses what she wants and needs, she'll never truly feel loved. Furthermore, by deceiving her boyfriend, she is not giving him a chance to really know her or please her if there ever was a chance for that.

Tara doesn't like certain positions in sex but explains, "I do it because I know my boyfriend likes it and if I don't I'm afraid that he will find another woman who will." Let him. How do you think you "have him" anyway if you're sacrificing your self-esteem and self-respect just to keep him? Ultimately, the relationship is not going to work out because Tara's boyfriend will probably sense that she is desperate and willing to sacrifice her own self-esteem for his affection. As a result, he may start treating her poorly. Good relationships are built on honesty and trust, not dishonesty and manipulation.

Expecting Sex

Be wary of your expectations that a date will lead to sex. No one likes to be taken for granted or pressured. For example, Tom met Lisa while she was on a business trip in Florida. They hit it off, and he invited her back for a weekend and even offered to pay for her trip. When she got there, he took her luggage into his room. Lisa freaked out and was upset that he assumed she would be having sex with him. The moral: Spell out your expectations, even if it seems forward or kills the spontaneity. Or better yet, don't have any expectations!

Just Sex

I'm frequently asked, "Is it possible to have a purely sexual relationship without any feelings being involved?"

Some people are just not looking for love or a long-lasting relationship; sex serves as a momentary thrill or satisfaction of an emotional or physical need. If both people feel the same way (and practice safe sex), no one gets hurt (like in the trend these days for "buddy sex," in which friends have sex but agree not to be committed to each other).

While such arrangements are possible when both people feel the same way, many people think they can pull it off only to discover that they really expect more or end up feeling more than they thought they would. Just as you should spell out your intentions about wanting to wait before becoming intimate, be equally clear if you go out with someone with the hope of having sex (and not much else). Say something like, "I'm not looking for a commitment, so please don't feel hurt if I don't end up calling you or giving you what you want. Sex may not mean as much to me as it does to you." This is a bit cold, but it's certainly a fair alert.

I hope you come to see that the best sex is in the context of a loving, committed relationship. But if not, before you engage in an act that for you is devoid of feeling, consider not only your intentions, but also your partner's feelings. My suggestion is if you don't feel anything for the person you are sleeping with, but you know that person has feelings for you, move on before you cause a lot of heartache.

The best sex merges the physical act with an emotional and spiritual attachment. As one man I know put it, "She's the paint, I'm the brush, and the bed is our canvas, to create our beautiful painting of love."

The Sex/Love Split

After years of counseling patients and fielding calls on my "LovePhones" radio show I've heard from a lot of people who are confused about sex and love. In particular, I commonly hear the following two types of questions that are related to an important issue called "splitting."

Smooth Talk'n

Some men still seem to have difficulty expressing feelings of love during sex, but have less of a problem expressing themselves physically. In these cases, what seems to be insensitivity or obsession with sex is really a fear or inability to communicate verbally about love. These men should own up to their partner to prevent misunderstandings.

The first type of question:

"How come I can have great sex with a woman but, as soon as I start to develop feelings for her, I don't get turned on anymore?"

The second type of question relates to being torn between two opposite-type lovers:

From men: *"I like these two women: One is gentle and sweet and the other is a real tiger in bed. I'm torn. How do I decide between them?"*

From women: *"I'm dating these two men: One would be the perfect husband and father—the kind of guy that my parents would love—and the other is a real exciting 'bad boy.' I wish I could mesh them into one guy, but I can't. What can I do?"*

Separating sex and love can lead to an intriguing but disturbing dilemma referred to as the "Madonna-whore syndrome" in men or the "Daddy-Don Juan syndrome" in women. Here, the "sufferers" split lovers into either sweet, nice people or wild, sexy ones. Sex becomes desirable only with the latter, not the former.

Smooth Talk'n

Sex is not the only way of expressing love. Be creative; there are countless warm, emotionally satisfying ways of communicating and sharing. Keep in mind that lack of self-esteem, loneliness, or boredom won't be cured by sex.

While I frequently encounter this problem with married people, it also occurs with singles who are torn between two "opposite" lovers. For instance, Bill was enamored of Jill, a sweet, gentle woman, who had all the qualities he wanted in a long-term mate. And she adored him and wanted to marry and start a family. The problem was, he found her boring in bed. Bill was also seeing Liza, a woman who had few of the qualities he valued for a wife and mother of his children, but who really turned him on sexually. Liza was fond of Bill but wasn't interested in settling down. But every time Bill decided to totally devote himself to Jill, he ended up calling Liza for a "roll in the hay."

Men like Bill are compelled to seek a challenge, and often devalue the very people who most value them. They think they are looking for the "perfect" person who combines all of the values they supposedly want with the sexual attraction they crave, but in reality, they can't let one person be everything to them.

If you recognize yourself in Bill's scenario, it's time to retrain your brain. Rather than separating sex and love, insist on having one with the other. Take a look at your relationships: Do you stereotype men as either fathers or lovers and women as either mothers or lovers? If so, look at your partners clearly. Are they really so easily pigeon-holed? Allow your mate the opportunity to express both roles. Communicate all your fantasies, desires, wants, and needs (sexual and otherwise) and give your mate a chance to fulfill the many sides of you.

Admit that both sex and love are equally important and possible with one person. Discover that your lover is trusting, honest, steadfast, and a wild lover. These traits are not mutually exclusive!

Turning Friends into Lovers

It's a very common question I'm asked on the radio: "I like this person but how do I make him/her my boyfriend/girlfriend without ruining the friendship?"

Friendship is the best basis for love. So I find it charming when people ask me how they can change a friendship into a romance. It can be tricky—you have to be willing to take a risk that might put your friendship in jeopardy. Most people who admit they want something more would rather stay friends than risk losing what they have. But keep in mind that becoming romantic may not ruin the friendship; if you take the risk and your friend responds positively, it will strengthen it. And if your friend does not reciprocate your feelings, at least you know where you stand and can direct your energies elsewhere. Of course, it's up to you to gauge whether the potential rewards are worth the gamble—but I'd recommend going for it.

It can be tough to broach the subject of attraction with your friend, especially if you fear that your feelings are not going to be reciprocated. Remember the saying, "It is better to have loved and lost than never to have loved at all." Talk your feelings over, sharing your mutual expectations and fears. You could have the happiest experience of your life. One man posed the change this way. He told his friend: "Our friendship is over," and then, after a pregnant pause during which she was confused and nervous, he added, "Now, let's try being more than friends."

One of my adorable interns at my radio show, Lee, has an inspiring story about turning a friend into a lover. She had been hanging out with a guy, shooting pool, watching videos, and hiking, for six months until one day while riding on a bus home from the movies, he leaned over after a stall in the conversation, took her face in his hands, and kissed her softly. Her first reaction was, "Oh my God," as he explained, "I've been wanting to do that for a really long time," to which she teased encouragingly, "Well, are you going to do it again?" His next kiss was deep and months later he proposed. "The friendship was what made me love him," Lee told me, "because I learned I could really trust this guy and could tell him anything."

If it looks like you can't turn the friendship into love, it's up to you to control your longing, to keep the friendship close, but not intimate. As with any unrequited love or impossible situation, don't waste your energy wishing or hoping. Julie said, "I have strong feelings for a friend and I know nothing is going to happen between us but every time I see him with another woman, I get jealous. How can I overcome this feeling?" As soon as the feeling overtakes you, switch your mind to planning or doing something for yourself. Focus on finding someone who can be both friend and lover. Figure out what you like about your friend and be open to someone else who possesses those qualities.

Who Makes the First Move?

Just as described in Chapter 8, more men today are relieved when a woman takes the initiative in sex because it takes the pressure off them to always advance or perform. But men can also be a little intimidated by a sexually aggressive female. Tony was divorced four years ago and now is back in the dating game. "Are women really this fast now?" he asked me. "I like candlelit dinners, and they seem to want to get right to it!" At the end of Tony's date, the girl said outright she'd like to have sex. "I was so bowled over by such a bold female," he admitted, "that I was really worried about whether I could get it up for her."

While it may make you feel uncomfortable to know sex is expected of you on a date, not being approached can leave you feeling undesirable, frustrated, or confused. Cybil dated Howard six times but complained, "He was a perfect gentleman, but I was jumping out of my skin, wanting him to do something. I was wondering if he was gay, strange, or impotent, and what was wrong with me." Courtney also complained, "I've been seeing this guy for three months and he's only kissed me. I can't help feeling he doesn't want me. I also don't want to be the one who does everything first. What's up?" Find out from him whether he is shy, inexperienced, or afraid of getting hurt. Explain that you feel uncomfortable being the initiator (but don't fall into sex-role stereotypes of expecting the man to make all the first moves).

If someone doesn't make a move, don't immediately assume you're not attractive enough. Find out what else is going on with that person (another relationship, inexperience, fear of rejection, embarrassment about themselves, their body, sex). Take a risk and state your own interest.

Cybil did the right thing. On her next date with Howard, she was open with him and said, "I've really enjoyed being with you, and I wonder why we haven't kissed because we've had a great time, and I wanted to kiss you." Thankfully, Howard was willing to be equally honest. He explained that he was afraid of making moves too quickly and that

Cybil might consider him too forward. Howard's openness about his fear, and Cybil's reassurance, were just the right triggers to give them permission for their first kiss.

How Important Is Sex?

Couples often fall "out of love" when the sex that was once good falters. For instance, Darlene called my "LovePhones" radio show and remarked, "Our sex life was great, but it's now so boring. I'm tempted to throw in the towel or at least to have a little fling. My boyfriend doesn't seem to mind that the passion has cooled."

Dating Data

A University of Minnesota study found that more than half of the students surveyed said they would move toward divorce if the passion ever went out of their marriage.

Every couple has to decide how important sexual compatibility is in the relationship. Lust and passion does tend to cool over time, and it often takes considerable effort to "keep the fires burning."

Face your sex problems head-on. Do you have different sex drives, a sexual problem (such as premature ejaculation or inability to orgasm), or different preferences for positions, acts, or fantasies? Are you willing to work on the sexual aspect of your relationship? If not, then you should probably consider letting the relationship go. Sex doesn't have to be a top priority in your relationship but if sex problems are driving you apart or pushing you to infidelity, then there are issues to be addressed.

Finally, examine your dating history. Do you have a pattern of sexual problems with partners? Is there a specific problem that keeps recurring? Are you choosing relationships that bring out this problem? Since sex is so personal, problems in that area can be a smokescreen for other troubles, such as fear of intimacy or commitment.

Many people take a lover's sexual problem personally. For example, when a man is having erection problems, the woman may feel it's her fault, that she's not attractive enough. Or if a woman is having problems with orgasm, the man may feel inadequate as a lover. Self-reproach or blame only makes the situation worse.

Home Alone

If you're just starting a relationship, and the sex isn't satisfying, or you're already thinking about straying, you're setting yourself up for failure.

Dating Data

The Trojan Shared Sensation Survey of 800 young lovers aged 18 to 29 revealed that two-thirds of couples said sexual pleasure should be equally shared. This increased the longer the relationship, but as expected, men rated physical attraction more important than sharing, while women preferred the reverse. Men appeared to be less selfish than you'd think, since 4 out of 10 men said pleasing their partner was more important than their own pleasure. In other arenas, the highest sharing was in sexual fantasies and body rubs (87 percent), the covers (80 percent), and clothing (71 percent), yet only about half said they had foreplay or afterplay. Dating couples are ahead of married couples in some sharing, with 22 percent of daters sharing sexy e-mails compared to 14 percent of married couples, and three times as many unmarried couples as married couples sharing bathing or showering. Women were more likely than men to question their partner's sexual past, but less likely to tell about their own (around 70 percent of women asked their partner if they ever had unprotected sex, a one-night stand, or an HIV test, yet only about half of women spilled their beans on those matters). One-third said they insist on using condoms every time they have intercourse, yet only a quarter said they share in putting it on (though this is definitely advisable to ease resistance, ensure use, and to increase fun).

Different Sex Drives

Karen's boyfriend is ready for sex at any time, but she is not. She wonders, "Is there a chance for us?" Possibly. As with many couples, Karen and her boyfriend have different sex drives; no matter what's going on, he's ready, whereas her feelings are much more affected by her mood, the situation, how much time they have, and many other factors. Just as with other aspects of the relationship, decide how high a priority this part of your life is. Then, to make the relationship work, accept each other's differences and make compromises.

Some people have a naturally higher sex drive than others, but libido levels are related to many factors, both physical and psychological. This should reassure you that ups and downs are normal and do not signal the death knell of a relationship and that changes and adjustments can be made.

Dating Data

Sex drives are affected by hormone levels that themselves can be decreased (by illness or medication) or increased. Research has shown that women who make love weekly have twice as many circulating hormones as those who have sex sporadically or not at all. Also, certain foods are reported to boost hormone production, especially those that are high in vitamin B-12, vitamin K, and zinc.

Fantasies

Many people worry about whether their sexual fantasies are okay. Of particular concern is fantasizing about someone else when you are making love to your partner. For example, Mike told me, "I fantasize about my friend's girlfriend when I'm with my own girlfriend."

Whether or not this is a problem depends on the reason for the fantasy. Sometimes, our fantasies have to do with things we want sexually that our partner isn't willing or able to give us. Other times, fantasies allow us to experience feelings that we don't feel free to express to our mates. For example, Mike was a virgin when he hooked up with his more experienced girlfriend. Thinking about someone else during sex with her was his way of making up for his inexperience and for expressing his upset and jealousy about her other relationships.

If you are able to discover the purpose of your fantasy, you can decide if it is healthy or damaging to your relationship. In Mike's case, he needed to get over his anger toward his girlfriend and his insecurity about his relative inexperience. When he realized what was going on inside him, the fantasies stopped. In other cases, the fantasy can be helpful, to show you what you would like to do or feel with your present partner. Once you realize this, consider expressing, revealing, and sharing your fantasy with your partner.

Self-Pleasure

Engaging in self-pleasure (masturbation) is a natural act even when you're having sex with someone you're dating. Women who feel upset and inadequate after discovering the guy they're dating masturbates need to realize that, while it is possible urges are not being satisfied, it is also possible he just needs normal private time.

Afterburn or Afterglow?

Many people, especially women, have complicated, intense reactions after having sex. Some fall into what I call "after-sex addiction"—becoming intensely attached to someone after having sex, even if you didn't care all that much for the person before. The experience of "giving your body" makes you feel more invested in the relationship.

At the other end of the spectrum, other people retreat after sex, as Carla found out. "After dating Ken for a short while, we had sex. The next day, he didn't even want to talk to me. I still like him, and at least want to be friends. What's his problem?" If you really want to know, ask him. Don't waste one minute wondering, hoping, or torturing yourself. You may not get a satisfactory answer, since a person who retreats after intimacy may not be able to give you the response you need. But at least you've relieved some of your own anxiety by asking the question. Be prepared to let the relationship go if he isn't prepared for or receptive to your devotion.

Just as I mentioned about dating in general earlier in this book, having sex is an opportunity to learn about yourself and people. Always get feedback. Ask your partner, "What did our relationship mean to you? How do you feel now? How do my actions affect how you feel? What did I do to affect how you acted?" Ask without implied criticism or demands. This means a magical combination of what I call "non-demand dating" (not expecting any response) and "informed dating" (learning from your experience). Your mate may be too immature, inarticulate, or inexperienced to answer you honestly, or he may not have insight into his own motives or feelings. But at least you know you've tried.

Spicing Up Your Sex Life

Kevin called my "LovePhones" radio show and said, "My girlfriend likes to role-play. One night she wanted to dress like a reindeer and make me Santa." I asked, "What would YOU like to be?" He answered, "I'd like to be a musician and have her be a groupie." My advice:

Go for it!

Do you have a favorite fantasy "sex script?" Or is there a particular sex scene from a movie or book that turns you on? There is nothing wrong with imagining or acting out fantasies, as long as each partner is into the scene. Be creative. You have nothing to lose but your inhibitions.

Many people have idiosyncratic sexual desires or fetishes. For instance, Larry called "LovePhones" and said, "I really want my girlfriend to take nude pictures of me with her bra on my head." Carla called and said, "I get excited having sex when other people are around, like in the mall or parking lot." Fantasies and desires are very revealing. Think about your own; what do they tell you about yourself? How do your desires make you feel (safe, secure, risqué, rebellious, different)? If you're not hurting anyone, then it's fine to consider acting out your fantasies or indulging your fetishes.

If, however, you are using this behavior to escape a real relationship and intimacy, reconsider and focus on some healthier activities.

Dating Data

Couples only dating for a short time who want to heighten their capacity for loving instead of just having sex for sex's sake should try tantra, the ancient art that transforms sex into an extended loving meditation that includes sexual healing; energy exchanges; and new positions, techniques, and ways of touching. In fact, the practices are a wonderful form of safe sex, as they include meditating together through breathing exercises, preparing baths, and massaging each other without the intention of sexual arousal, and spending defined time (from 2 to 10 minutes) together twice a day breathing, talking, or hugging and just gazing at each other. Read Charles and Caroline Muirs' book, *Tantra, the Art of Conscious Loving* (see references in Chapter 1).

Battles Over Control

Over the years, as the world has become more complex and daily life more stressful, I've noticed that more and more people tell me about their interest in sex acts involving dominance and submission. There is nothing wrong with playing "master and slave"—it can even be constructive, where one person is in control and the other takes orders. But the most extreme form of this behavior—sadomasochism, in which partners derive satisfaction from inflicting and enduring pain—is a serious disorder that reveals an inability to experience love, intimacy, and vulnerability. People who need to experience pain during sex are also usually numb to loving emotions. Furthermore, they may be so afraid to show their true needs for nurturing or love that they mask their needs with aggression. While some people may defend their indulgence in such activities, I feel most need professional help to release themselves to love.

It cannot be denied that even to less extreme degrees, couples get involved in power struggles in and out of bed. As Roman says, "My girlfriend acts like a drill sergeant. She bosses me around and doesn't listen. During sex, she tells me faster, harder. It's all for her. When she's finished, she rolls over and leaves me there." Roman has a female partner who behaves as many men do—selfishly! Roman needs to ask himself if he is looking for someone to control him, because he is afraid of being controlling himself.

I suggested to Roman that he make control a deliberate game with his girlfriend—that he practice being the commander-in-chief for a change and that they then take turns.

311

Playing the extremes can be a helpful technique for couples to reach some kind of middle ground.

An All-Sex Alert

Keep in mind that whether you are straight, gay, or bisexual, the issues dealt with in this book all apply to you. The feelings, conflicts, and solutions are the same no matter who you are and with whom you get involved. But some questions that arise regarding dating are specifically related to sexual orientation, as many people ask me whether their actions or thoughts mean that they are gay or bisexual.

Bi-Curious: The New Sexual Trend

Bi-curious is a word of the new millennium—meaning those men and women who think they're basically attracted to the opposite sex but who also feel intrigued about or have experienced sexual encounters with someone of the same sex. It has been joked that the worst thing about bi-curiosity is that reading the personals takes twice as long—but the best thing is that you have twice as many choices for dates.

As much as our society has come a long way in being more accepting of people with varying sexual orientations, there are still pressures both from outside and from within. I encourage everyone to value, trust, and accept themselves, but sadly I hear so many men and women who doubt themselves and worry about their impulses and feelings.

As Jim said, "I've had a girlfriend for two years and I'm not gay, but I'm attracted to my best friend who is a guy. Why do I feel this way?"

As Pat said, "I love my boyfriend, but my best friend, who also has a boyfriend, kissed me one day. I had some feelings about it going further. What does this mean?"

This could mean that you're beginning to "come out" and realize your homosexuality, or it could also mean that, as in the case of about one in four men, you're at a point in your life where you are experiencing some level of thoughts or attraction to the same sex (that doesn't mean that you do anything about it!). Think about what this person represents to you. Is he a mirror reflection of yourself (so attraction to him is a way to appreciate yourself), an image of the way you'd like to be (and therefore a sign of the qualities you should develop in yourself), a curiosity (that can also be quite normal), or just a natural attraction that you have always felt but suppressed?

Be aware of how acting on your attraction could impact your current relationship—always think of the consequences of your actions before acting on them. Every fantasy does not have to be acted out immediately; thinking it through can have value in its own right.

If you find yourself with a bisexual lover, you may face a dilemma like Craig: "I've been dating a girl for three years and she just told me that although sex is amazing with me, she also has a female lover. I can't share her. What should I do?"

You can't force a person to only be with you, no matter what sex that person's attracted to. If you don't want to share her, you'll have to let her go. However, don't think that your sex with her was inadequate in any way. The need for someone else, of whatever sex, is not about what you lack but about her needs that you alone cannot fulfill, no matter how great the sex between you is.

The Least You Need to Know

➤ Ideal sex is with someone you love, fulfilling both physical and emotional needs.

➤ Clarify your intentions and expectations about sex and love so that neither person is misled or disappointed.

➤ Feel confident about saying yes or no to sex.

➤ Understanding and good communication is essential for good sex.

➤ Accept your sexual urges, feelings, and desires; self-love is important for happiness within yourself and when choosing a partner.

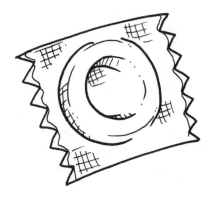

Chapter 22

Approaching Sex Safely and Sanely

In This Chapter

➤ Making sure you don't get pregnant when you don't want to

➤ Safer-sex activities to reduce the risk of disease

➤ Condom-sense

➤ Sexually transmitted diseases (STDs) to watch out for

Birth control and safe sex are topics that must be covered in a book on dating—especially in these times, when there are still so many unplanned pregnancies, and high risks of sexually transmitted diseases. If you avoid these subjects, you certainly are not ready for a sexual relationship.

With so much information available, there is no excuse for not being informed about issues regarding safe sex. Since the goal in love is to find a relationship based on honesty, openness, and trust, I admit that sexuality today is tricky business. You can't always accept someone's word that he or she is disease-free or using birth control. You must protect yourself—both from pregnancy and sexually transmitted disease. This chapter gives you the information you need to make informed choices and to stay safe.

Dating Data

The 1996 Durex Global Survey of Sex and Condom Use of over 10,000 adults from 15 countries showed that of the factors considered most important when making love, protection against having an unwanted child was rated by only 16 percent of the respondents, not catching or spreading the HIV/AIDS virus was rated by 18 percent, and not catching or spreading other STDs was rated by only 5 percent.

The highest rated concern was satisfaction of self or partner, 27 percent and 37 percent, respectively. Women rated avoiding unwanted pregnancy as being more important than men did. Thailand and Germany were the countries most concerned about not catching or spreading HIV/AIDS.

Pregnancy Prevention

"Where do babies come from?" is a question little kids commonly ask. But you'd be shocked, as I am, to know how many adults don't understand the basics of how male and female bodies work, all of the activities and conditions that can lead to pregnancy, and the ways to prevent conception.

I get so many calls on my "LovePhones" radio show from men and women who are confused about the basics of reproduction. Many also have a sketchy understanding of birth control, and the risky behaviors (other than penetration) that can cause pregnancy. It seems that a lot of people need very basic and important information.

There are four basic types of contraception: barrier, hormonal, sterilization, and natural methods. Consult your doctor or a family planning clinic for specific information and for advice on the best method for you. Women as well as men should take responsibility for protecting themselves, and it's not a bad idea to use two methods to be doubly sure.

Barrier Methods

The barrier methods include condoms (for both men and women), diaphragms, and cervical caps. These methods are readily available and have no side effects (although an occasional person is allergic to latex or the spermicide used with diaphragms). These days, condoms can be purchased in almost any pharmacy and in many other stores as well. Buy only latex condoms, as the lambskin variety is not effective in preventing some diseases.

Dating Data

Never reuse a condom. Also, while you can leave a diaphragm in place for several hours (insert more spermicide if you have more sex), don't forget to remove it!

Diaphragms and cervical caps are available by prescription. Women must visit a gynecologist or family planning clinic to be fitted for these devices. When used with spermicidal jelly or cream, diaphragms and cervical caps are highly effective; although their effectiveness drops significantly without the spermicide. The message is obvious—use the spermicide.

Dating Data

Fortunately, women are taking more and more responsibility regarding condom use. A major survey of condom use reported that among individuals practicing safe sex, condoms are carried by 70 percent of men and 56 percent of women.

Care should be exercised to ensure the effectiveness in placement and removal of these methods, and that requires being comfortable with touching your genitalia.

Hormonal Methods

Hormonal methods of birth control include the Pill, Norplant implants, Depo-Provera, and the IUD. All of these methods require a visit to a gynecologist or family planning clinic, and all involve some expense and have some side effects. These may include bleeding, headaches, depression, and changes in appetite or sex drive.

The Pill is highly effective when used properly, but some women forget and miss doses. If you have trouble remembering to take the Pill, consider Depo-Provera, hormonal shots that are effective for 12 weeks. Another option is Norplant, slow-release hormone capsules that are implanted directly under the skin (usually on the upper arm), that last a few years. If you want to get pregnant, the Depo-Provera shots can be discontinued, or the Norplant capsules can be removed at any time by a trained physician or other health care worker.

The IUD, which stands for intrauterine device, is available by prescription. Made of plastic or copper, the device is placed in the uterus where it thwarts pregnancy in one of two ways: either by preventing the egg from being implanted in the uterine wall or by preventing the sperm from fertilizing the egg. IUDs have endured some controversy and suffered in popularity, although many physicians consider them safe and reliable.

Natural Birth Control

Perhaps the least effective birth control methods are so-called natural methods, such as withdrawal, or planning sexual encounters according to the rhythm method, checking the woman's body temperature, or checking the consistency of the woman's vaginal mucus. Withdrawal requires that the man pull out of the woman's vagina before he ejaculates. This is problematic for at least two reasons: One, many men do not have this kind of control, and two, sperm is involuntarily released before ejaculation.

The rhythm method involves timing sex around a woman's cycle, avoiding times of higher fertility during mid-cycle or ovulation. The trouble is, some women have irregular cycles, or get sloppy about keeping track. Even if you're careful, you can get pregnant at any time during your cycle. If you are serious about avoiding pregnancy, think twice before relying on "natural" forms of birth control.

Sterilization

The last resort for most people of child-bearing age is sterilization (tubal ligation for women, vasectomy for men). Sterilization involves surgical procedures that should be considered permanent (although some men do have their vasectomies reversed). Unless you are absolutely certain that you never want children or you have the number of children you want, choose another method.

Smooth Talk'n

Discuss contraceptive options with your partner, and possibly go to a health professional together. Cooperation on both ends is essential for effective birth control and satisfactory sexual relations.

Morning-After Pill

In 1998, the FDA approved the morning-after pill. It is a strong dose of birth control pills composed of female hormones and is used only as an emergency procedure to prevent pregnancy from unprotected sex or failure of a contraceptive method. This method should not be considered a form of birth control. It is effective only 75 percent of the time, compared to the 99 percent effectiveness of other accepted birth control methods (condoms, diaphragms, IUDs, pills). Physical side-effects include headache, stomach upset, nausea, vomiting, and potential harm to the fetus if pregnancy has already taken place. Any over-use can disrupt the menstrual cycle and hormonal balances, which can adversely affect bodily functions and delay fertility when desired.

Male Contraceptives

The possibility of male contraceptives other than the condom has been explored throughout the last decade. Some advances have been made in developing experimental methods, including pills, injections, and implants (similar to those available for women), though progress in this area has been slow. Many drug companies have been hesitant, research funding has been limited, and there is some skepticism about men's cooperation in techniques other than the condom. However, surveys have shown that men have been receptive to considering new ways.

The Scoop on Sexually Transmitted Diseases (STDs)

I am continually amazed by the number of people who call my "LovePhones" radio show to ask about medical problems but who are too terrified or embarrassed to see a doctor. If you have any concerns about your health, put that embarrassment aside and get to the doctor right away. Many young people avoid seeking medical advice out of fear that their parents will find out. Your health is more important than your shame and fear of punishment. Use the opportunity to talk with your parents about sex, or request a private consultation with your doctor and be completely open about your problems.

An STD (sexually transmitted disease) is any disease acquired primarily through sexual contact. Most STDs are caused by bacteria, viruses, and other microorganisms. Some are hard to detect and all can lead to serious health problems (including infertility and death) if left untreated. Medical diagnosis and treatment is essential.

Statistics indicate that 12 million new cases of sexually transmitted diseases are diagnosed each year, many in women and people under the age of 25. In addition, more than 50 million Americans currently suffer from STDs. That's about one in every four men and women. "Old" infections (gonorrhea, syphilis, and venereal warts) are resurfacing, and more than 20 new diseases have been identified in the past decade.

Dating Data

While I outline many STDs in this chapter, this book is not an exhaustive medical reference. For more complete information, see your doctor, go to your local library or bookstore for books about this topic, or call the STD hot line (see Appendix B).

You might think that only people who are promiscuous are the ones accounting for these high numbers—but it's important to realize that it only takes one time having sex to be exposed to some disease.

HIV and AIDS

AIDS (Acquired Immunodeficiency Syndrome), caused by HIV (Human Immunodeficiency Virus), has forever changed the way we think about sex. By far the deadliest STD, AIDS is transmitted through body fluids such as blood and semen. An estimated one million Americans are infected, with the largest risk groups still composed of homosexual men and intravenous drug users. However, more and more heterosexual women and teens are infected every year. They put themselves at risk by thinking "It can't happen to me," and have unprotected sex or excessive sexual activity, and are uneducated about the risks. While treatment options now exist, there is no known cure for this disease.

The fear of catching AIDs has helped some single men and women talk openly about sex, to think seriously about commitment and intimacy, and to put their health above instant sexual gratification.

Getting Tested

People fear getting tested for HIV, yet it is the only responsible thing to do in these times. Worrying is a waste of time. Take action and find out the facts. David was going for his results and panicked, "What if I'm positive?" Instead of just obsessing, suffering from what my friend, television producer Frank Hagan, calls "Afraids," use this anticipatory anxiety to make yourself aware of dangers and to motivate yourself to behave more safely in the future.

Other Viral Infections

Genital herpes is a virus that produces blister-like lesions on the genitalia, buttocks, anus, and certain other areas. It can be present and contagious without symptoms, and is easily spread. Fortunately, the symptoms, especially at first outbreak, can be treated with medication, but the virus stays in the body. About 40 million American men and women have herpes. Condoms reduce the risk but do not necessarily cover all the areas where the virus may be present. Also, oral herpes (cold sores on the mouth) can be transferred in oral sex to genital herpes. The stigma of having herpes must be overcome, and care must be exercised in sexual activity. Outbreaks can be controlled by reducing stress and even taking medications (like Valtrex) as "suppressive therapy." Wash thoroughly. Avoid foods with arginine, like chocolate and nuts, and eat foods with lysine, like chicken eggs. Don't feel guilty and let yourself love!

Dating Data

Remember that when you have sex with someone, you're having sex with all of that person's partners. That means if your partner is promiscuous, you could be having sex with many people!

Genital warts (human papilloma virus), spread by anal, oral, or vaginal sex, produce hard fleshy bumps on the internal and external genitalia. Though usually harmless, they have been linked to certain cancers of the penis, vulva, cervix, and anus. While warts may disappear on their own, they may also be treated by a doctor, who can remove them by freezing, burning, using chemical solutions, laser therapy, or when necessary, surgery. The good news is that, unlike herpes, genital warts don't pop up again on their own.

Infectious mononucleosis (the "kissing disease"), caused by the Epstein Barr (herpes) virus, results in mild to extreme fatigue and fever that often lingers for months and requires a great deal of rest and stress reduction.

Hepatitis C

The hepatitis C virus, equally as debilitating and deadly as HIV but overshadowed by the latter in recent years, has reached epidemic proportions with about four million Americans estimated infected, four times the number of those who are HIV positive. Thirty thousand new infections develop each year, one third of whom die. The virus is exceptionally dangerous, and is called a "phantom" disease, because there are no early warnings (in comparison to Hepatitis B's evident symptoms of fatigue, fever, appetite loss, yellowing skin) and it can be easily misdiagnosed as effects of a bad cold or drinking binge. Undetected, the virus can incubate in the body for 10 years, becoming evident only at advanced stages of liver disease leading to bleeding, delirium, and death. Like HIV, the Hepatitis C virus is transmitted through contact with blood products, by sharing needles, snorting

Home Alone

Carefully screen your sexual partners, asking about their sexual histories and tests, since STD sufferers are often unsure of how and when they became infected. Keep close track of whom you have sexual contact with, since millions of unsuspecting sufferers unwittingly pass diseases along to others (like "Typhoid Mary's"). You are responsible to inform others of infection.

cocaine (damaging nasal passages), infected blood transfusion, sharing toothbrushes, tattooing, and even in childbirth. Up to 20 percent of cases likely result from sexual encounters (vaginal or anal intercourse and possibly exposure to semen and vaginal secretions containing small amounts of blood).

Bacterial Infections

Chlamydia, the most common STD, affects millions of people each year. This infection causes inflammation of the urethra, which can eventually lead to chronic pain and sterility in women and testicular problems in men. Many women experience no symptoms in the early stage of the disease, while in men, the symptoms are painful urination and the discharge of pus from the urethra. The disease is treatable with antibiotics.

Gonorrhea (commonly referred to as the "clap") has resurfaced in recent years with some drug-resistant strains. The bacteria lives in moist, warm cavities—such as your mouth, throat, rectum, and urinary tract (and cervix in women). Symptoms include frequent urge to urinate, painful urination, genital burning and itching, or unusual yellowish discharge from the penis or cervix. Fortunately, it can be treated.

Pelvic Inflammatory Disease (PID) occurs when a bacterial infection from an STD (gonorrhea or chlamydia), IUD, or other source spreads from the lower genital organs to the reproductive organs (tubes, womb, ovaries, abdominal lining), causing scars that prevent passage of fertilized eggs and complications leading to infertility or tubal pregnancy. Symptoms include a yellowish discharge, painful urination, spotting, fever, nausea, vomiting, and pelvic pain caused by swelling or tenderness in the cervix, uterus, or surrounding tissue, which are easily spotted during a routine gynecological exam. PID may be exacerbated by douching or use of intrauterine devices that force the infection further into the reproductive channels.

Epididymitis is a common infection in men, affecting the tubes that carry the sperm from the testicles, and caused by various STDs, other infections, and abnormal structure of the urinary tract. Treatment includes antibiotics and bed rest, elevating the scrotum on a towel between the legs.

Syphilis is one of the more serious STDs, caused by the spirochete (a corkscrew) bacterium that can attack any body part. If untreated, it can progress to disability, dementia, and death. The infamous WWII epidemic was brought under control in the 1950s with the discovery of penicillin, but surprisingly, reported cases have doubled over the past decade (to 130,000 a year). The disease starts with chancre sores (pimple-like lesions) and if untreated, progresses to fevers, aches, and rashes, ultimately invading the eyes, heart, nervous system, bones, joints, brain, and other organs, leading to death in the final stage. A doctor's diagnosis (with blood tests) is necessary, since symptoms "mimic" other diseases such as heat rash and measles.

Fungus

Candidiasis, also know as a yeast infection, is caused by an overgrowth of a fungus that naturally lives in the vagina, mouth, and intestine of healthy people. As many women can attest, during periods of stress or after a course of antibiotics, the fungi can grow out of control, with symptoms including a thick, white, curdy discharge, itchiness, redness, swelling, and odor. While it is important to get an accurate diagnosis, yeast infections are readily treated with an antifungal medication that is now available over-the-counter at the pharmacy.

Parasites

Pubic lice (crabs) is one of the few STDs you can get from clothing, bedding, towels, and possibly toilet seats, as well as from direct sexual contact. It is cured by treatments such as Rid or Kwell, which you can get from a pharmacy. Make sure to wash everything carefully.

Dating Data

STDs can "Ping-Pong"—partners can infect and re-infect one another continually. The reason is that one or both partners may be asymptomatic, so the disease may go unrecognized and untreated. This can happen with everything from yeast infections to herpes.

Safe Sex Steps

The safest sex, of course, is no sex. But short of abstinence, you can protect yourself by making responsible choices. First, avoid risky behavior and always use a condom. While condoms are not foolproof, when used properly they are highly effective in preventing most sexually transmitted diseases and pregnancy. Choose latex condoms, since they are sturdier and less porous than the lambskin varieties. Be wary of gimmicks such as flavored or colored condoms that are often made of inferior materials. Stick to condoms made by well-known and responsible companies (with brand-names like Trojan and Ramses). Avoid oil-based lubricants such as Vaseline, since these products can damage the latex, causing it to tear.

Practice health-promoting behaviors—regular checkups, breast exams, and testicular exams—to detect any problems early.

Communicate thoroughly with your partners and ask specific questions about their sexual history. Finally, never allow yourself to be talked into unprotected sex; "just once" is no excuse. Unprotected sex is like playing a game of Russian roulette.

I've often been asked, "If someone says he was tested for HIV twice and came out negative, should I believe him and have unprotected sex?" Absolutely not! Some people act as if a negative test gives them a license to go wild. That's absurd. Has your partner had sex since his negative tests? With whom? He could have been infected after the test. There are no exceptions—always practice safe sex!

Rating Safe Sex Activities

The challenge is to make these safer sex behaviors VENIS (very erotic non-insertive sex). **Safer sex activities include:**

➤ Dry kissing

➤ Hugging

➤ Frottage (rubbing against each other)

➤ Massage

➤ Mutual masturbation

➤ Solo use of sex toys

➤ Masturbation displays

➤ Watching sexy videos

➤ Telephone sex

➤ Cybersex (love messages on the Internet)

➤ Tantric sex (extended love-making techniques from the Orient that don't involve penetration)

Riskier activities include:

➤ Open mouth or deep tongue kissing

➤ Oral sex (with condoms or dental dams)

➤ Vaginal intercourse with a condom

➤ Anal penetration with a condom

➤ Urinating on unbroken skin

Unsafe sex activities include:

➤ Vaginal intercourse without a condom (even if pulling out before ejaculation)

➤ Oral sex without a condom (even if pulling out before ejaculation)

➤ Oral sex or vaginal penetration without a condom during a woman's period

➤ Rimming (tonguing the anal opening) without protection

➤ Anal sex without a condom

➤ Swallowing semen or urine

➤ Sucking blood or other blood contact from different body parts

➤ Sharing sex toys

Condom-Sense

I mentioned this earlier in this chapter, but it's worth repeating: Condoms are highly effective in preventing the transmission of STDs, but they must be used properly and consistently. Condoms can break, and they don't protect all body areas that might be infected (as with herpes).

Many men and women still have resistance to and questions about condoms that they need to overcome, as in the following examples.

Kristen: "My boyfriend wants to have sex, but he won't wear a condom because he says it doesn't feel good, and he'll lose his erection. He said he'll leave me if he has to wear one, and find a girl who doesn't care."

If he won't be responsible, by all means let him leave! As he goes out the door, remind him of phrases like, "If you really love her, wear a cover," or the more tongue-in-cheek, "Put a helmet on that soldier if he's going into action." Warn him of the dangers to himself too, and reassure him that he can always regain his erection if he loses it.

Peggy: "I had sex with an ex-boyfriend, and he didn't wear a condom. I have never had sex with anyone else, but I know he has. Could there be a problem?"

You bet! One slip-up is enough. You can't be careful yourself and sleep with someone who isn't. One young girl told a heartbreaking story on "LovePhones" of how she had sex for the first time and got infected with HIV. She shared a riveting poem to warn everyone:

"A tisket, a tasket, a condom or a casket."

Home Alone

Avoid novelty condoms, but some reliable companies are now making latex condoms in shapes that contribute to sexy sex. For example, the new Trojan Shared Sensation has alternating rows of bumps and ridges designed to please her and a flared design that's roomy at the tip for him. For more information and a free sample (if your over 18), call 1-800-4 TROJAN.

Dating Data

Statistics, unfortunately, show that not everyone is wise. Some estimates show that while approximately 9 out of 10 college students have sex, less than half use protection.

The Durex Global Survey of Sex and Condom Use showed that while Americans are seen by other countries as being the most willing to use a condom with a casual partner, they are actually only fourth in a list of countries (behind Thailand in first place) in which men always use a condom.

Carrie told me, "I've had sex with seven men and I thought I loved them all. Almost every one refused to use a condom. Why is it that men refuse to use condoms?" Many men claim that condoms reduce sensitivity. This is a terrible excuse. A partner's resistance should not stop your insistence. Be proud to be responsible. Learn to keep the condom handy and to put it on efficiently (make it part of your love play). Learn to compensate for any physical insensitivity by attuning all your senses.

It isn't only men who may object to condoms; some women have similar resistance. They may dislike the thought of a barrier, enjoy feeling a man's ejaculation, or just be afraid of implying a man is not "clean." If you feel this way, examine your feelings to prevent them from interfering with smart behavior.

Dating Data

Besides condoms for men, it's important to consider barrier protection for women for safe-sex purposes. One method is a "dental dam." Imagine stretching a condom-like material in a rectangle shape over the vaginal area. (In a severe pinch, non-microwavable Saran plastic wrap can also be used.) Although this may seem unappealing, it clearly prevents skin-to-skin contact. Dental dams are not readily available in stores, but can be obtained in specialty shops like Condomania, or in women's sex boutiques like Eve's Garden (119 W. 57th Street, New York, N.Y. 10019, (800) 848-3837 or (212) 757-8651).

Rules About Sexual Health

Smart sex in the new millennium requires that you:

➤ Protect yourself (through abstinence or condoms).

➤ Never make a mistake or allow an exception to safe sex practices.

➤ Ease up on using protection only if both partners were virgins when they met, or if both have tested negative for AIDS, and then had sex with each other exclusively.

➤ Talk about your sexual history. Say something like, "Before we have sex, we need to talk about diseases, safe sex, and our sexual pasts."

➤ Discuss what method you are going to use for safe sex.

➤ Find ways to enjoy intimacy other than through sex.

Unconscious Motivations

Our behavior is always influenced by our mind. Sometimes, though, you may not realize what deep motivations drive what you do—and this can get you in trouble. It's my job to help you become aware of these motivations, so that you can make smart and safe choices about sex.

Always consider your deepest needs and conflicts. For example, I was shocked to hear Diane tell me that her boyfriend insisted on having unprotected sex with her, even though she had genital warts, and that she readily agreed. He got the warts, too—and deep down, Diane was glad because she took it as a sign that he would stay with her.

Chris was going into the service and his girlfriend wanted desperately to become pregnant, even though Chris feared—rightfully—that they were not ready to start a family. I insisted he not let this happen just to please his girlfriend, and suggested she explore her deeper need: to prevent herself from being lonely while he's gone, or to ensure that they have a bond. Couples need to establish their bond before making a baby; those couples who become parents know the stresses that a child can put on a relationship.

The Importance of Being Honest

It's a moral and social responsibility to let your sex partners know about your health status. You do not have a right to put another person at risk, nor does anyone have the right to expose you to risk. There are plenty of stories about people flirting with the Russian roulette of disease. For instance, Roseanna told me: "I had unprotected sex with my ex-boyfriend, and he told me later that he is HIV positive. I've been tested, and I'm going crazy waiting for the results."

There will always be people who tempt fate by deliberately practicing unsafe sex. These people are depressed or angry and want to hurt themselves or others. For instance,

Rich called my "LovePhones" radio show to say he had herpes. "I'm furious. I got it from some woman I slept with and I'm going to give it back to as many other women as I can. I don't care. I've been hurt a lot and now others can suffer along with me. I'm lonely and miserable, so why shouldn't they be?"

This vengeful attitude is dangerous and seriously disturbed. But you can't always tell who these people are. That's why it's important to practice safe sex in all situations. If necessary, let Rich's behavior scare you into safe sex practices.

It's a crime to deliberately spread the HIV virus. In some precedent-setting legal cases, such behavior is considered "assault with a deadly weapon."

With better public awareness and more organizations that are dedicated to public health, it's possible to get the information and support you need. To find out where to get more information about STDs, see Appendix B in this book.

The Least You Need to Know

➤ It's essential to be responsible about preventing unwanted pregnancies and sexually transmitted diseases.

➤ Abstinence and virginity are commendable, but if you have sex, practice safe sex every time.

➤ Overcome any shame or embarrassment about speaking to partners or doctors about pregnancy prevention and safe sex.

➤ Get the facts, share your feelings, and stay safe.

Part 6
Going Back into the Jungle

Being rejected is never easy. Nor is dating after a long spell in a monogamous relationship. This section helps ease both experiences—whether you've broken up, gotten divorced, or been widowed. Here's advice for all situations to help you move on and find the love you deserve.

Everyone wants to be himself or herself, and to share with another human being. Honor that connection. Decide right now to do your part to make everyone you come in contact with feel loved. Thank everyone you date for what they bring to your life. Start with simple things, like "I want to thank you for taking me to that movie. I might never have seen it without your invitation." Even if you have had a less-than-perfect evening, say, "We may not be perfect for each other, but I've still enjoyed our time together. You are a nice (special, interesting) person." Treat every date as an opportunity to see that there is value in every encounter. With that attitude, you will never feel empty—even if it's not true love.

Chapter 23

Getting "No" and Letting Go

In This Chapter

➤ Knowing when it's over

➤ The right and wrong ways to end it

➤ The "Frightful Five" blow-offs

➤ The nine phases of dealing with rejection

➤ Letting go

➤ Patching things up

Now that you've learned how to get a relationship going and make it work, it's time to deal with the flipside: getting out without falling apart. Rejection is difficult for the one who feels "dumped," but also for the one who wants it over.

"My boyfriend told me he loved me," Denise wailed, "so how can he turn around the next week and say he needs his space?" Easy. He meant he cared at one moment, but that didn't mean it would last forever. While it's never easy, and always disappointing, you must learn to move on when love ends for your lover but not for you.

The first and most important question you should ask yourself after a rejection is: "Why waste myself on someone who doesn't want me?"

And if you are the one initiating the breakup, why waste time and energy for both of you? If you thought you were wild about someone, but are now having doubts, what do you do? What's the best way of disentangling yourself, while being both firm and kind? Read on for those answers.

Dating Data

For tips on how to deal with a rejection when you want to approach someone, check out Chapter 9.

Deciding to Break Up

In at least one relationship you'll have in your life, inevitably the day will come when you ask yourself, "Is this working?" or "How long should I keep at this before it's really over?" or "When's the right time to break this off?"

Only you can determine your limits of tolerance for working on a relationship. Some people look for instant gratification, and as soon as their needs aren't being met, they're out the door. Others hang on forever, hoping and praying things will get better. Neither approach is ideal, but it helps to know where you and your partner fit along this continuum.

Think of dating as a long road punctuated by traffic lights. Red lights signal danger, yellow lights require caution, and green lights mean keep going (but proceed cautiously since you never know when a car might run a red light!).

You know you are at a green light if your mate:

○ Has positive, close, friendly relationships with family, friends, and co-workers.

○ Is responsible and trustworthy.

○ Is a good communicator (listens and empathizes).

○ Is open to commitment.

○ Can express feelings and be intimate.

○ Displays respect for self and others.

You're at a yellow light when:

○ You've been hurt by him before.

○ Friends are giving you warnings or telling you negative stories about her, though you're not sure they're true.

○ There is a history of bad relationships.

○ You recognize in yourself a pattern of attraction such that you always end up hurt.

○ You fall in love too fast (without testing and observing).

○ Either of you has a cheating past.

○ The two of you are always talking about ex-partners.

○ You spend too much time just "hanging out" without doing anything meaningful.

○ He cancels or forgets dates.

○ She sends "mixed signals"—one minute you're great, the next you're ignored.

○ One of you feels deprived and unfulfilled or complains of not getting enough attention.

○ You wait by the phone or feel you are wasting your time "waiting" for the other to come around.

You know you're at a red light and it's time to put on the brakes when:

○ You're experiencing more pain than pleasure.

○ You're being mentally, physically, or sexually abused.

○ She betrays you or cheats on you.

○ You feel used, abused, or foolish.

○ He keeps secrets (like not revealing a home number or never inviting you over).

○ She constantly blames, criticizes, or denigrates others (parents, friends, co-workers).

○ Either of you has a lot of unresolved anger toward the same or opposite sex.

○ There is a clear reluctance to commit (indicated by statements like "Marriage is a disaster" or "I'll never settle down").

○ He is pushy, controlling, or obsessed with sex.

○ Friends warn you with evidence you don't want to believe (unlike you, they're not wearing "love blinders").

○ His life is dangerous (involves guns, drugs, illegal acts).

Excuses: Holding on When You Know You Should Let Go

Even when trouble is obvious, it can be tough to let go. I hear lots of excuses from people who are unable or unwilling to leave a relationship, including:

➤ "We've been together a long time." For instance, Jennifer told me: "My boyfriend's cheating, and now he says he doesn't want to be with me as much as before, but I don't want to break up. We've been together for five years." It's natural to get attached to people in our lives, but consider "reframing" the way you view the situation. Instead of regretting all of those "lost years" if you gave the relationship up, think of how many more years you'd be investing in being miserable if you stayed, consider that you've learned valuable lessons, and need to move on for a better future.

➤ "He was my first." As Pam told me, "It's not working out with this guy I'm seeing, but I'm having a hard time letting go because he was my first." As I pointed out in Chapter 18, you'll probably always feel a special attachment to your "first," but you can't sacrifice happiness for sentimentality.

➤ "But I still love him." Keisha explained, "I know I should stop going out with him—he cheats and treats me bad—but I still love him." Love yourself more, and treat yourself to someone who treats you well. You can always love the person, but that doesn't mean you have to be together.

➤ "I gave her everything." I recently talked to a guy who told me: "I really liked this girl and bought her lots of things. In fact, I just bought her a $50 sweater, and the next day she broke up with me! What can I do to get her back?" Save your money and your self-esteem and let an ungrateful and unwilling mate go. If someone clearly doesn't want you, regardless of your gifts, you're trying to buy love, a sign that you may be low on self-esteem. The result is disappointing anyway, as the other person usually ends up loving you less.

Sometimes we need a kick in the pants to get out of a really bad relationship. Laura told me, "My boyfriend drinks too much and has been unfaithful. When I tell him I want to leave him, he says he'll never let me go. He tells me that the problem is that I'm unhappy with my life, and I'm blaming him. Is it my problem?"

What is your problem, is that you are putting up with this man's psychological abuse and manipulation. His drinking, cheating, blaming, and threatening are sure signs that he is the one who is desperate, disturbed, and in need of help. Don't allow his threats to intimidate and paralyze you. Life is too precious to waste, so don't spend another minute being miserable and treated poorly. Be firm about your complaints, expectations, and intentions. Take action—get legal counsel or an order of protection if you think you need it. Insist that he get counseling, and get support for yourself (from friends, a therapist, or a 12-step program for people in relationships with alcoholics) to shore up your self-esteem. Then bless the guy and send him on his way.

Reading the Warning Signs

Most of us can tell if a relationship is going sour, but often we want to ignore even the most obvious clues. You've got to trust your instincts. Here are some telltale signs that you are about to get dumped:

➤ She stops returning your phone calls.

➤ He has endless excuses for why you can't get together.

➤ She displays affection less frequently (not holding you, not returning a hand squeeze).

➤ She talks about "me" instead of "we."

➤ He never talks about future plans.

➤ She ignores intimate talk ("I really like you," "We get along so well together") when you raise it.

➤ He's inattentive and distant.

➤ She's slowly removing all of her personal items from your house.

When you're smitten, it's easy to ignore signals that a relationship is going south. And it's natural to want to make the one you love love you—especially if that person considers himself hard to catch. Cathy's is a typical story. "I've been seeing this guy who lately has been rather indifferent and mean. I've also heard he's been seeing another woman. But I don't want to lose him. How can I get him to see that I'm the right one for him?"

Imagine hitting your head against the wall. Does it hurt yet? If it doesn't, would you hit it harder? When will it hurt so much that you'll be forced to stop banging against the wall? Consider emotional pain like that physical pain: When will your heart hurt so bad that you stop running after people who make you unhappy? Imagine that every time your heart is broken, your heart muscle gets chipped and torn. Be as protective with your emotions as you would be with your body.

Finally, I'm frequently asked if bad sex is a good reason to end a relationship. Yes and no. Bad sex is often just a smokescreen for other problems: lack of communication, lack of attention, unresolved hurt or anger, lack of trust, and more. Before condemning a relationship because of bad sex, carefully explore the reasons behind it. Having no sex is a warning sign that something is wrong, since it indicates a withdrawal from closeness, intimacy, and sharing.

Be Prepared

If the handwriting is on the wall—you sense it's over though you're not ready to admit it—how can you prepare yourself? For starters, ask for feedback. Be blunt; ask him if the signals you think you are detecting are the ones that he wants to be sending. If you have to force the conversation, you probably have your answer right there.

Prepare yourself for being alone by rekindling those friendships that you may have neglected during your relationship. Also, make an effort to make new friends that have no connection to the two of you. Protect yourself from constant reminders of your ex. If you and your soon-to-be-former lover have "your" special places, try going there with other friends to establish a new association in your mind. It is too easy to get sentimental about the restaurants, movie houses, and hang-outs where you used to meet. "Detoxify" these places, or after a few relationships you may find yourself without any place to go!

If you are handed one of the five lines below, don't beg or plead. Realize he or she wants the relationship over. You can ask for more explanation, but really what you want is to know it was once real, you once were loved, and still can be lovable. Hopefully you'll get some reassurance, but accept the end and move on.

Disappointing Dating Scripts: Making the Best of It

Bree was really excited about her date with Jason. She had her hair and nails done, bought a new outfit, and even bought some new things for her bedroom. She had been looking forward to the evening for weeks and was sure they would end up in bed.

They started the evening at the movies, where Bree put her hand on Jason's knee. When he didn't respond or return her touch, she began to worry. Outside, after the movie, he told her that his stomach was bothering him and he thought he'd just go home. Bree was disappointed, and felt foolish. Was Jason really feeling bad, or had she misread his flirting with her so heavily when they met? Whatever the case, Bree realized that her expectations had led to disappointment.

Bree had fallen into a common trap: "writing a script" for an evening without really considering the actual role of the other person. We write their part without thinking about their needs, expectations, moods, or plans. Bree wrote a script for romance with Jason. When the evening didn't go as planned, she felt horribly let down.

It's impossible to script every experience in life, because people are so unpredictable. If things don't turn out as you plan, make the new events work for you. Instead of bemoaning Jason's unresponsiveness, Bree decided to welcome that Jason went home; it gave her free time and inspiration to start writing the novel she'd been thinking about for two years. See how you can "reframe" what happens—no matter what someone else does, you can turn it into something personally fulfilling.

Home Alone

Most of us have heard one (or all) of these blow-offs more than once. I call them the "Frightful Five":

"I love you but I'm not 'in love' with you."

"I thought we both knew it wasn't going anywhere/was just sex."

"There's no chemistry."

"Let's just be friends."

"I met someone else."

When You Are the One to End It

Most of us know what it feels like to be dumped: the pain, humiliation, anger, and hurt. But the time may also come when you must do the dumping. Is it possible to minimize the other person's pain? Are there rules that govern breaking up?

Consider this scenario. As Paul described, "I've been dating Jill for a few months, and I really like her—as a friend. I recently met a woman I feel passionately about. Jill is terrific, and I know she loves me. What can I say or do to let her down easy?"

If you have ever been on the other side of the fence, like Paul, you will probably be sensitive to the following "Do's" and "Don'ts" for breaking up with someone:

➤ DON'T break up over the phone (too impersonal).

➤ DON'T break up before a major holiday, anniversary, or any day important to the "dumpee" or the two of you (birthday, anniversary, Valentine's Day, Christmas, death of a parent)—an otherwise happy day will be tinged with pain, or an already painful day will become more unbearable.

➤ DON'T criticize or blame the person for what he may or may not have done.

➤ DON'T use one of the "Frightful Five" blow-offs, like "I love you, but I'm not *in* love with you" or "I never really loved you." These words tend to linger painfully.

➤ DON'T get wrangled by guilt into changing your mind.

➤ DON'T hit below the belt, with phrases like "I just don't find you very stimulating" or "You were awful in bed."

➤ DON'T accept the "bad guy" label (both people lose when it's over).

➤ DO talk about it as a mutual decision ("It's right for both of us") so the rejected party doesn't feel so out of control.

➤ DO be respectful, giving the other person the opportunity to work through feelings.

➤ DO reaffirm that there was something good between you. (The "dumpee" often feels invalidated, as if her feelings never mattered or weren't real. She may need reassurance that the relationship was real, and that she really was cared for).

➤ DO remind the dumpee of wonderful aspects of himself (to boost his self-esteem).

➤ DO point out your own resistance and responsibility ("I'm not ready for a commitment," "I can't be true to someone yet"). The "dumpee" may try to reassure you, but stick to your guns and say "You deserve better." This may help prevent her self-blame and depression.

➤ DO spell out the terms of the separation clearly ("We shouldn't call each other") so that there is no room for misunderstanding.

➤ DO be firm. If you leave the door open even a crack, you are inviting the dumpee to try to change your mind.

Remember the Golden Rule: "Do unto others as you would have others do unto you." This is a good time to put that rule into action.

Dating Data

While women think that men have an easier time after a breakup, research shows that men may actually suffer more. When men get involved in an intimate relationship, they share otherwise repressed emotions. When they break up, they tend to keep their pain hidden, which often leads to physical complaints (fatigue, headaches, and so forth). Women, on the other hand, are more open about suffering, and tend to surround themselves with friends and family to help ease their pain.

Dealing with Rejection: The Nine Phases

If you are the one who is being dumped, be prepared for the "stages" of rejection. While the pain may be awful, each stage is part of the healing process. The stages generally follow the sequence described in the following bulleted list, but the steps can alternate with each other. Dealing with rejection is a lot like dealing with other kinds of loss, and the stages are similar:

➤ THE DENIAL PHASE: "This can't be happening." During this stage you may find yourself waiting for the phone to ring, not believing that the relationship is actually over.

SOLUTION: Acknowledge reality and acknowledge your feelings about it. Accept but do not dwell on shame and embarrassment, and all the "shoulda/woulda/coulda's" ("I should have known better," "I could have been sexier").

➤ THE BARGAINING PHASE: Driving yourself crazy, thinking that "If I get my hair cut," or "If I just let him have sex more often," or "If I don't call her for a week," he will change his mind.

SOLUTION: There's only one solution: Accept that it's over.

➤ THE LONELINESS PHASE: Feeling as if no one understands or cares.

SOLUTION: Surround yourself with people who do care, and who openly say so. Remind yourself often that you are loved.

➤ THE HEARTBREAK PHASE: Feeling like your heart is really breaking. You may even feel pain in your chest, or want to throw up when you think of that person or if you see your ex with someone else.

SOLUTION: You can go on. Rub your hand over your heart to soothe it. If you are feeling really bad, snap your fingers to interrupt the thought, and fixate on something that makes you happy. Do not drive yourself crazy with thoughts that your ex is blissfully happy while you're miserable. Only your experience counts, and only your efforts make you happy.

➤ THE BLAME PHASE: Pointing the finger at yourself or your ex for what each of you did wrong.

SOLUTION: Decide that neither of you is at fault but that both of you are responsible for the breakup.

➤ THE DEPRESSION PHASE: Feeling sad, worthless, and foolish. You may have trouble eating and sleeping, and you may imagine that you'll never find anyone to love again.

SOLUTION: Allow yourself to feel your pain, but do not wallow in self-pity. Keep busy with exercise or projects.

➤ THE ANGER PHASE: Feeling furious for being rejected.

SOLUTION: Allow yourself to experience the anger, but don't exaggerate it, or tack it onto all your past hurts. Don't let yourself become bitter.

➤ THE ACCEPTANCE PHASE: Finally believing it's over. You no longer expect your ex to call, and you begin to feel at peace.

➤ THE HEALING PHASE: Getting your life back. You are now ready to go out with friends and to meet new people, and you are no longer dwelling on your ex.

Letting Go: The 18 Steps

Christina's is a typical story: "I've been dating Chuck for two years, and I really love him. A month ago he broke up with me, saying that he wanted to date other women, but I can't seem to move on. I can't picture myself with anyone else. He says he loves me, but that he'll never treat me the way I deserve. He keeps encouraging me to go out with other guys. What does all this mean? How can I get him back? He wants to be friends, but I only want to see him if I can get him back. How can I stop thinking about him all the time and get my life back?"

As the old song goes, breaking up is hard to do. But it's time for Christina to let go. It's the crucial step in moving on to a healthy life. The following list gives you some tips and exercises that can help with the process:

Step 1. Practice thought-stopping. It's normal to have recurring thoughts about your ex. One way to wean yourself is to decide on a specific time of day where you will give yourself over to the thoughts (such as nine o'clock at night, for 10 minutes). If you find yourself obsessing at other times, force yourself to "change the channel" in your brain, or pick yourself up and do something constructive—take a walk, water the plants, clean out a closet.

Try this exercise: Think about your ex. Now think about being in love with someone else. Now think about your ex. Now think about getting a raise at work. Now think about laughing with a new friend. Now think about a pink elephant. See how you can control your thoughts?

In Japanese Morita therapy, you do not wallow in your feelings; you simply do what you have to do each day to function—and concentrate on those actions. You brush your teeth in the morning, you get dressed for work, and you talk to new potential mates. It's that simple.

Step 2. Recognize the quality that you miss in your ex and find a substitute for it. Focus on the qualities you liked in your ex. Was he funny? Great in bed? A good listener? Realize that these aren't such unusual traits—they do come along in other people, and you will encounter them more than once in a lifetime. Enjoy those qualities in other people or find other ways to enjoy them. Go to funny movies, or take up a sport yourself.

Step 3. Instead of bemoaning the end, celebrate it. In this technique, called "paradoxical intention," you wish the very opposite of what you think you prefer. Put on some music, uncork the champagne, jump up and down, and yell "Good riddance to bad rubbish!" Then honor your time alone.

Step 4. Be your own cheerleader. Remind yourself of all the good things about you. Make a list of those qualities and reread the list.

Step 5. Call all your friends and have them reinflate your ego. Get your pals on the phone and ask them to remind you of all your wonderful traits. Let them take your side. When Georgette was dumped, she called her best friend, who reminded her, "You are beautiful and smart and funny and fun to be with."

Step 6. Understand the situation realistically. Dee was devastated when her boyfriend decided not to leave his wife for her. He said he loved her, but was worried about his kids, his business, and his wife. If she had looked at the situation realistically from the beginning, she may not have been as devastated. While she shouldn't punish herself, she should have been prepared for the possibility.

Step 7. Be realistic about dating in general. While I certainly feel that you should pump yourself up, don't expect that everybody will love you.

Step 8. Accept your responsibility, not as a way of blaming yourself, but to learn. Go over all the sides of the story. Was he mean, cruel, insensitive? Blame him, and then face up to the fact that you pick men like that. For example, Francine realized she wanted Paul to be what he wasn't. She had overrated him and expected more from him than he was able to give, overlooking an obvious problem—he had said he wasn't looking for a commitment.

Step 9. Reaffirm that you deserve to be treated well. Remember how you would treat a child or best friend—you would be loving, protective, and reassuring. Treat yourself that way.

Step 10. Do a "relationship review." Recognize the patterns in your past relationships to prevent the same problems in the future. What type of person do you go for? What happened at every stage—who started the relationship, who made the decisions, what was the tone of the relationship (fun, sharing feelings, fighting), what did you do together (music, art, ideas, books, movies), who ended it? If you see a pattern that displeases you—you're always the caregiver, you try to "buy" love, you're frequently attracted to people who are already involved—make it a point to make changes.

Step 11. Indulge in pleasure. Make a list of things that make you feel good: getting a massage, listening to music, taking a walk. Indulge in these pleasures at least one a day.

Step 12. Keep a sense of humor. Research has shown that laughter strengthens the immune system. On this basis, seeing the lighter side of your situation is a positive step in your healing process. Imagine your ex in a silly situation, or go see a funny movie.

Step 13. Feel empowered. Consider that you chose for the relationship to be over. Even if you think he dumped you, consider that your energy helped create the outcome. Decide "I wanted it over." This is no more real or unreal than any other explanation.

Step 14. Do deeper work. Help the little child inside who is still hurting from past losses. Imagine yourself as this little child, and also imagine yourself as an adult protecting this child from being hurt, holding and comforting her.

Step 15. Purge your anger. Write your ex a letter, pouring out your hurt, disappointment, and anger—but don't send it. That's a good way to purge your feelings.

Home Alone

Some people are so distraught over a breakup that they talk or think about killing themselves or someone else. No one person holds the key to your self-worth. If your hurt and rage are this severe, or if your ex is threatening to hurt himself or you, seek professional help immediately.

Step 16. Rebuild trust. Erica's dilemma is common enough: "My first love stabbed me in the back after I put my complete trust in him. Now I am wary of people and always protecting myself." Resist generalizing; not all men or women are alike. See each person as an individual. In your imagination, line up all those who have hurt you in the past and imagine throwing them in the garbage or picture them incinerating. Now you have a clean slate. Of course, trust gets shattered after you're hurt, but try to put the past aside. If you live in fear, imagining that people are not trustworthy, this is the reality that you will create. Accept the challenge of tuning your love antennae to people who are more trustworthy, and who are worthy of your trust.

Step 17. Welcome your dreams. As Brenda asked, "It's been seven months since my relationship ended, and I have constant dreams about the situation. What can I do to stop them?" Instead of seeing your dreams as obsessions, believe that your mind is trying to work through the pain on a deeper level.

Dating Data

Researchers at a Midwestern university helped women who were depressed over lost loves to use their dreams to heal their pain. All the women were having recurrent dreams of bumping into their ex and feeling devastated by the experience. The researchers trained the women to put a new ending on the dream, one where they walked away from the encounter smiling and feeling happy. Some women imagined they were with another man, others pictured being happy on their own. The women were told to review the script before going to bed, to set the story in their mind.

All the women felt better about coping with their loss using this technique, and the majority reported recovering sooner than they expected.

Step 18. Repair your self-esteem. Amanda's cry is typical: "My boyfriend left after two years. What's wrong with me?" Nothing. Not everyone can appreciate your value, but you need to continue to do so.

Revenge

It's natural to want to anger, humiliate, and hurt the one who has hurt you. "I'd like to make her life hell, and make her suffer like I'm suffering," said Pete after he was dumped by Liz. "I'll get him for hurting me," Kaetlin vowed after Jorge cheated on her.

Don't waste your energy on revenge. As much as your ex might deserve your wrath, you are standing in the way of your own happiness by not letting go. To purge yourself of these feelings, tell your ex how mad and disappointed you are. But then take responsibility for yourself and move on. Be glad that the person is out of your life, and that you endured a bad relationship for three months instead of four.

Moving on can be especially difficult if you've helped a lover through a particularly bad time, only to have him leave you when his life got back on track. Try to be glad that this person's well-being is no longer your concern. But then look for patterns in your own life: Are you always the caretaker? Are you always on hand to "save" a lost soul? If so, be grateful that you've gotten this out of your system.

It is okay to indulge in fantasies of revenge (for a short while, anyway), as long as you don't act on them. Don't dwell on your ex. It is better to bless him, spread white light around you, and get on with your life. Remember, "Living well is the best revenge."

When Your Ex Refuses to Get the Message

You think you've done all the right things. You've leveled with your ex, telling her that your heart isn't in this relationship, and that it's over. But what if she refuses to get the message? Is it possible that you're sending the wrong signal?

Some people become obsessed when rejected. For instance, John's girlfriend continued to call, sometimes five times a day, for months after they broke up. When he didn't return her calls, she would show up at his house. John asked, "How do I get her off my back? I feel like joining the witness protection program."

It is very disturbing, and often frightening, to be pursued obsessively. Clearly, the woman's attachment to John went far deeper than their actual relationship, probably mirroring something in her family. Such an obsessive lover needs to be told she is a good person and cared for, but that your closeness is over, and that pursuing you is not acceptable. Insist that she get counseling. If such behavior persists, go to the police for an order of protection.

Be firm. Don't give in and get back together because of feelings of guilt. Any inconsistency in your behavior will be interpreted as a sign that you don't really want out.

Dating Data

If you truly want to end the relationship, don't be tempted to sleep with the person "one last time." Having sex will only make the breakup harder.

On the other hand, what if the lover who recently left you calls and says she wants to see you? Be cautious. If she was so sure that the relationship was over, what has happened to change her mind? Is it loneliness, boredom, or a true change of heart? Proceed slowly to find out what she wants. When it comes to sex, be especially slow and cautious. Sometimes sex with an ex is good because you're free of commitment or problems, but a roll in the hay won't get you the love you want. Watch out for "yo-yo" lovers—the kind who vacillate between wanting you and wanting freedom.

"Why is sex always better after breaking up?" Sometimes it's easier for couples to have great sex when their commitment and relationship problems (arguments, miscommunications, angers) are put aside, and when they have dropped any expectations. Also, the tension of a breakup can seem to intensify passion. It's like the popular song goes: "The best part of breaking up is making up." But beware of starting arguments just to fuel your love.

Not Fully Cutting the Cord

"Is it okay to keep in touch with an ex-boyfriend of three years if I'm now seeing someone else?"

"Is it normal to still have feelings for an ex?"

Both situations are "normal." Some people can totally sever a relationship and never see an ex again. Usually this happens if the relationship was fraught with pain and anger. But if you truly cared, you will always have a soft spot for that person. Past lovers are a part of your life and your personal history. In fact, at certain times in your life, you may feel an urgent need to get in touch. Often during major transitions (marriage, divorce, death of a parent or spouse, kids leaving the nest), people want to contact ex-lovers to be reminded of good times, or to resolve some issues. This connection can make you feel vital and acknowledged.

But before picking up the phone, think about what you are looking for. Review the relationship and what the person actually means to you. How did that person make you feel? What is he symbolic of? What were you going through in your life at the time (college days, your first job, junior year abroad, the prom)? Then, consider the other person. It might be that your call is the last thing that person needs right now.

Repairing the Hurt

What makes breaking up so traumatic? Often, there are many unresolved emotions and unfinished business. If you see an ex too soon, you risk triggering those unresolved feelings and fantasies, which will prevent you from moving on. But when the time is right, such reunions can also be a valuable opportunity to work through some unfinished business. Sometimes you'll discover that all of the feelings of unworthiness or rejection that you've been harboring are overblown. Such realizations allow you to move on to new relationships.

Don't rush a reunion with your ex—give yourself plenty of time for the wounds to heal. When you are both ready, get together and review what happened. Explain the things that hurt you, what you wanted, what you feared, and what you miss. With distance and a fresh perspective, any lingering pain may ease, and a new love may emerge.

Many of us entertain the fantasy of seeing an ex and having him or her say, "You were right all along. Take me back!" This would restore your feeling that you—and your love—mattered! It is possible for this to happen.

Dating Data

Research has shown that it can take half the time of the relationship to get over losing it, and even then 10 percent of the pain remains. But it's different for everybody, and if you find yourself in turmoil after a year, or if you can't function (eat, sleep, work, etc.), get professional help.

It happened for Didi. Didi had been very much in love with Kirk when he left her. While she'd gotten on with her life, she still had feelings for him and always wondered "What if. . .?" Ten years passed, and after a serendipitous meeting, Kirk called. They got together and talked about their lives. He explained that he and his wife were "just friends." Their sexual relationship had long since died, even though the marriage was intact. Hearing this, Didi realized that the longing she felt for Kirk all those years was suddenly gone.

When Kirk left her years before, he fed Didi the classic line, "I love you but I'm not in love with you." Soon after their breakup, he fell "madly in love" with someone else.

Now he was telling her that this love too had died, and his sex life was barren. It seemed like poetic justice to her. Kirk went on to apologize for hurting her, and to express his feelings of remorse.

Kirk's apology and expressions of regret were what Didi needed to deal with her residual pain. It helped her realize that she hadn't imagined his feelings for her, and that she was probably better off having Kirk as part of her past than part of her present.

Can't We Patch This Thing Up?

More often than not, when things go really sour, it's better not to look back. Getting back together will only work if both of you have worked on the problems that caused the relationship to founder. If you decide to give it another go, you both must also express your commitment to giving it a fresh start. Only under those conditions is it worth trying to patch things up.

Wanting to reconcile is a common dilemma: "When my boyfriend broke up with me I kept begging him to take me back. Why isn't he listening?"

You must already know from previous chapters in this book that I'm no advocate of game-playing. Instead, I encourage you that if you have needs and feelings, express them. But I do think there is one time when you should hold back—when your emotional needs are out of proportion to the reality of the relationship. There's a big difference between saying, "I don't want to break up, I love you" and "I can't go on without you." The latter, acting desperate, pitiful, and "clingy," will only drive your lover away, since such desperation tends to trigger contempt and disgust (often because the person fears that your desperation may trigger his own). Your desperation also sends a clear signal that you are hanging on for your own needs—it is less about your true love for him than about your need to prevent feeling abandoned, and to play out your "love script."

Even if you have strong feelings for your ex, don't go crazy or make a scene. Imagine yourself surrounded by white light, being happy without the person. You can suggest reconciling, saying something like, "It would be nice to get back together." But don't put your life on hold, just leave the door open. Then pull yourself together, look your best, go out, and have fun. Your patience may pay off.

In letting your ex know you still care, don't make demands. People have to choose to be with you freely, not out of guilt, loneliness, or sentimentality. If your ex is asking you to do things as friends, take the bait only if you can control yourself. If you can't, keep your distance. As painful as it may be to say no, it will be less painful in the long run.

The Least You Need to Know

➤ Everyone faces rejection at some point in life.

➤ Someone may not love you, but you must always love you.

➤ There are predictable stages of dealing with loss.

➤ It's better to leave a bad relationship and get on with your life.

➤ You will survive any breakup, no matter how painful.

➤ "Living well is the best revenge."

Chapter 24

Getting Back in the Saddle

In This Chapter

➤ Changing your old views

➤ Rebuilding self-esteem

➤ Dating when you have kids

➤ What will others think?

Each year, 1.2 million marriages end in divorce. That means 2.4 million people reenter the singles life again. Most have been married for about 10 years, and about 70 percent will marry again. But making it work the second (or third) time around depends on how much you've learned from past mistakes and how well you've reassessed yourself and your needs.

The New You!

You deserve a life again! Being alone doesn't have to mean being lonely. Allow yourself to feel passion and give yourself permission to love again. Use the following guide to change your way of thinking.

Old Way of Thinking	New Way of Thinking
Restrictive: Dating is not for me	**Permission:** All possibilities are open to me
Punitive: I have no right to go out	**Supportive:** I have a right to enjoy myself
Fearful: I'm afraid to commit, get hurt	**Confident:** I can risk again, I won't make the same mistakes
Excuses: I have no time to go out	**Freeing:** I can figure out how to make love work

The loss or death of a spouse/lover is traumatic under any conditions, especially if the relationship has in many ways been good. Some divorced and widowed men and women feel so spiritually attached to their partner that they cannot move on to date others. Death is particularly traumatic because it can happen so suddenly.

To move on with your life, try a technique I call "completing unfinished business," in which you have an imaginary conversation with your ex or departed one and say all the things you wish you could have said when he or she was with you. Imagine asking for, and receiving, permission to go on with your life.

Rebuilding Self-Esteem

Being out of the dating game for a long time can make you feel insecure, frightened, and hesitant. "I've been out of that world so long," Jack said, "I have no idea what people do!" Many people struggle with guilt and feelings of being a failure. Take Leila, for example: "I couldn't make it work with Greg, so I'm really frightened to try again with someone else."

Parents negotiating child support and custody may have particular emotional conflicts (confusion, frustration, sadness, anger) at this time. Professionals have become particularly aware of the "father depression" that some men suffer from when they are saddled with child-support bills, but deprived of being with their children.

It is especially important for people who carry a lot of emotional baggage from the past to be aware of those feelings and try to prevent them from spilling into their new relationships. Recognize your fears and remind yourself that the past does not have to repeat itself. Reevaluate all your strong points (your character and your experience). Trust that there will be people whose company you will enjoy and vice versa.

Single-Parent Dating

Alone again, you are entitled—when you're ready—to get back in the dating scene. Inevitably, you will have some practical concerns, and many fears and confused feelings: "When am I going to have time to date when I have children to take care of?" or "How am I supposed to be an example to my teenage kids when I'm playing the field also?" You will probably experience guilty feelings as well: "Will it upset my kids if I start dating again?"

These fears and feelings are all normal, and knowing that you're not the only one to feel this way can ease some of the pressure.

Dating Data

Most problems have practical solutions. If you need someone to baby-sit your kids, consider grandparents, your ex, friends, and neighbors.

Saying Good-Bye to the Old and Hello to the New

One big reason why newly single people resist re-entering the dating world, is that they are stuck in past relationships. My favorite technique to help you get past this is called "completing unfinished business." Because there are many things that have gone unsaid in such a relationship, in this technique you have an imaginary conversation with your ex or departed one, saying all the things you wish you could have said to the person. Simply the experience of getting things off your chest can free you from the weight that you have been carrying. The more mired you are in the past, without clearing those, the more you will simply not "see" something good that will come your way. Freeing yourself up from thoughts, and holding onto the past, allows you to be more open and receptive to the new opportunities that are bound to come your way.

The New Lovers' Dilemmas

If you're about to date a single parent, but have never been married or had kids yourself, be prepared for differences in responsibilities and attitudes. Some couples adjust easily: Garth, a never-married man, was ecstatic that dating Barbara included a "ready-made" family with her two young children. Others face problems: Sue had a problem sharing her boyfriend with his ex-wife and little girl. She was resentful that he saw his ex-wife every other weekend, and felt threatened and left out.

Unfortunately, if Sue wanted to continue dating her boyfriend, there was nothing she could do but accept her boyfriend's package: ex-wife and child. If you're in this same situation, it's important to discuss your feelings and get the reassurance you need. Also, don't waste time worrying about the ex; switch that energy to making your own relationship work. In addition, share time just with the child, so the two of you form a bond.

A Ready-Made Family in the Deal

With divorce rates high, and an escalating number of young women having babies without marrying, there are large numbers of single parents in this new age on the dating market. Despite being more accepting of single life on their own (I've

349

mentioned how one major survey showed more than one third of single woman feel no longer desperate to have a man), most single parents would like to find a loving partner to raise their family. Fortunately, some singles welcome the idea of an instant family by marrying a single parent. Others (especially never-married singles) may resist the idea. Be prepared for such reactions and how you will cope with them.

Greg's ex-wife had serious drug problems, so he got custody of their two small children. "It's rough," he sighed, "because a lot of girls just don't want me when I tell them about the kids. They're not ready to be a mother to some other girl's babies. It's tough because they're girls I want." Greg's discouragement comes from picking the wrong type of women. In fact, there are many who would welcome him with his family. Rather than blaming his status for his new dating problems, Greg has to accept his situation. When you're a parent, the kids come with the dating deal, at the top of the list. You might change other things about you (where you live or work), but you're not going to change the fact that you have children.

Tell a new date about your family situation at the beginning of your relationship. Recognize some initial resistance, that could be based on fears, jealousy, or competition (he's upset you spend more time with your kids than with him, she's worried you spend more money on your kids than on hers). These can be resolved by talking them through and making compromises. But, if a new partner is unwilling to work out these realistic problems, sabotages your parenting, or rejects your responsibilities and their role in parenting, consider passing up the relationship. Even if you love the person, the potential arguments and resentments that will arise over time will erode your relationship and create havoc in your family.

What About the Kids?

Of course you want to be a good parent. But consider yourself, too. Realize that your happiness will spill over into how you treat your kids and what example you set for them. It is important, however, to be prepared for all the feelings that your children may have in reaction to your dating.

Dating Data

Ask about your child's feelings: "What do you think about (the person you're dating)?" or "How do you feel about me dating/having a relationship?" It's important to show that you respect your child's feelings, but do not let those feelings interfere with or rule your dating. Show that you are considerate of, but not controlled by, your child.

Keep in mind that your children will always be upset about the new love in your life no matter how much they like him or her. Deep inside, children want their family back together again. Any newcomer is bound to be perceived, even subconsciously, as a stranger who is sabotaging their fantasy. It is crucial to understand this dynamic and recognize why your children may resent the new person in your life.

One way to deal with this is to introduce your kids only to someone who really matters to you; casual dates may only confuse them. Also, put feelings into words for children who may be afraid or unable to express themselves: "I know how disappointed you are that your father and I are not together, and I understand why you may dislike my new boyfriend." Or, simply affirm the child's feelings: "It is normal to feel angry at me and my new girlfriend."

You should also share some of your own feelings: "This is a difficult adjustment for me, too." And, reassure your child: "No one will replace your mother," or "No matter what, know I love you."

Dating Data

Some parents avoid the difficulties of dating by immersing themselves in their children. While this can be a welcome relief and offer joy and needed attention, such escape and living vicariously through children—or over-absorption in them—can be unhealthy for all concerned.

When a New Lover Meets Your Child

When you decide that it's time to introduce your new mate to your child, refer to your paramour in casual terms at first. For example, you might say, "I'd like you to meet a good friend of mine." Try planning an activity together. This not only makes the child feel included, but it also dilutes the anxiety of a face-to-face meeting.

Most kids become anxious about their parents dating. Their distress can range from worrying about being displaced in their home to being replaced by their parent's new found love. The child might also be very judgmental of whom their dating, and simply not "approve."

When 13-year-old Ben called me, he was distressed that his mother was dating a much younger man (not much older than his older brother.) He also didn't like watching this person order his mother around. He feared that his mother might be sexually and

Smooth Talk'n

In planning an activity together, make it playful. For example, go to a baseball or basketball game, shopping, or to the movies. Do something together in neutral territory first, outside of the child's home. This lessens the chances of the child feeling invaded or imposed upon at home.

financially used, and he was afraid that she would be hurt badly. I encouraged Ben to talk with his mother abut his fears and concerns, while reminding her that he loves her and has her best interests in mind. I also told him he might have to accept her decision whether or not he likes it, but that he should also reflect on how his mother's choice was reflecting his own anxieties about dating, as he was at that age to start thinking about mates, and probably fears repeating his mother's problems.

Sleep-overs should be reserved only for serious relationships and only after your child has had opportunities to get used to your suitor's presence. Your child should also be told first that your relationship has taken a more significant turn. This shows respect for your child's feelings, and portrays sex as a very serious step in a relationship.

What Others Say

Others—friends, family members, co-workers—will always have their own judgments and opinions about you dating again. Some may sound ominous and scary: "You shouldn't be going out so fast, give yourself time to recover" or "No one's going to want someone with the baggage of kids." These opinions are just that—opinions. Remember, what others say is only a reflection of their own fears or experiences and does not have to be true for you. Take such advice with a grain of salt.

Where to Meet People

Review all the suggestions in Chapter 2 on where to find a mate. However, pay special attention to places that would draw other divorced people or divorced people with kids. Remember, meeting people in the same situation as you is just as important as meeting people with the same interests. This is especially true if you and the other person both have children, since each of you will understand the responsibilities and limitations that being a parent places on dating. Keep in mind that you can bring your child to any of the "hunting grounds." Children can serve as both company and ice-breakers for starting up a conversation.

Divorced men and women can find innumerable clubs and organized activities especially for them listed in specialty newsletters and community newspapers. Local religious centers are also a good resource. Playgrounds are particularly good places to meet other single parents. People there are usually free-spirited, which sets the tone for an anxiety-free meeting. Watching others play with their kids also gives you the opportunity to observe their kindness, thoughtfulness, and generosity. Other resources include children's events and activities (many are listed in local newspapers), school groups, and single-parent clubs.

Seniors

Age can affect all the issues concerning re-entering the dating world that are described above in this chapter. But there are some added concerns. These include social stereotypes, and personal attitudes, fears and proscriptions that are often a carry-over from youth.

I invite—and implore—you to keep my overriding rule in mind:

You never have to retire from love!!!

That means you are never too old to date and enjoy the companionship and intimacy that being with a romantic interest can provide.

Now that you have that in mind, here are three additional important principles:

➤ Romantic interests can be a great boost to your self-esteem and joy in life.

➤ You are entitled to love.

➤ There are always opportunities to meet people and find new love.

Smooth Talk'n

While statistics do show that there are more single women than single men in higher age groups, numbers do not have to discourage you. Believe that there is someone for you. Also, look outside the traditional eligibility criteria (younger men, other cultures, different socio-economic backgrounds).

Dating Data

Research shows that people's eligibility criteria changes as they get older. Whereas physical attraction is high on the attraction list for younger people, companionship, shared interests, and compatibility plays a bigger role in relationships as people age. This is reassuring to those who fear waning physical beauty.

Recognize what your resistance is to being open to new love, in order to prevent it from paralyzing you. For example, change your belief system, to eliminate the concept about "dirty old men" or how inappropriate dating is for your age. Boosting your self-esteem is crucial, in this country and decade when youth is so valued. Follow the suggestion in Chapter 6 about boosting your self-confidence. Change your thoughts from "I'm too old" to "I'm full of life and new interests." Take a deep breath and project feeling happy, open, and available. Discard self-defeating lessons learned from your era, like that women should not approach men or that it is shameful to place a personal ad. Instead of focusing on your diminished strength, energy, or physical abilities, appreciate the wisdom about life and people that comes only from age, telling yourself that you can only enjoy this stage of life having been through whatever you have experienced. Reframe your defeatist attitude, from "I'll never find anyone" to "There is always someone who will cross my path who will see how wonderful I am." Every time you think "I can't . . ." rephrase it to "I can" or "I will." Remind yourself that dating enriches your life, keeps you active and alert to explore new avenues of enjoyment and growth.

The old adage "You won't meet anyone sitting home alone" becomes even more pressing for older singles, who can have a tendency to stay at home. Getting out of the house is crucial to increase your chances of meeting someone. If you cannot get self-motivated, ask friends to consistently call to encourage you and insist you come out to join them. Accept invitations to get out and about even if you are not eager to go. Once you get there, you will be surprised at what a good time you can have.

It is often said that older people become "set in their ways," making it more difficult to adapt to new situations and people. You may have developed anxieties about certain situations, or be rigid in your habits (eating, bedtime, TV watching). Yet, in order to adapt to dating, it is crucial to remain flexible and open to change. In reality, the maturity and security of old age can afford you the wisdom to be able to accept the idiosyncrasies of others, and therefore be able to make the compromises that are necessary to any new, or good, relationship. While at 25 years of age you might never have considered a man shorter than you, or a woman who does not look like Claudia Schiffer or Demi Moore, at 55 you may have a different set of values. Change can be just what you need to give you a renewed excitement about life. Being secure about who you are can allow you to consider going off your beaten path, without fear that something drastic will happen.

Dating during the retirement years has certain potential advantages. Newfound freedom from work or family responsibilities can lead to more available time and attention. In addition, you could have more clarity about financial resources. There are also increased opportunities to take advantage of events and places to go meet people when you are not limited by time

Smooth Talk'n

As your financial status becomes more set as you get older, it is that much more important to clarify how dating costs will be handled. It takes courage to discuss who treats, but such clarification is important in order to avoid confusion or upset.

Smooth Talk'n

Replace fear with a renewed challenge to find new interests and excitement, in order to be open to new people and experiences, and to feel good about yourself (that is the ultimate quality of sex appeal at any age).

constraints or fatigue, or have no free time to in the day or evening, or are not able to travel at will. In fact, this can be the time for you to take up those hobbies, or learn those skills, that you never had the time to do before, like going sailing, joining a gym, or taking courses at the local "Y."

Sex in the Older Years

Like I said about love above: "You never have to retire from sex."

Research supports this view, that continued sexual desire and behavior can be a sign of psychological, as well as physical, well-being. Sexual interest and activity results in a self-supporting cycle, between a positive self-image and outlook on life, and physical benefits from increased blood flow, stimulation of body chemicals and heart rate, and muscle exercise.

Since body image greatly affects sexual desire, it is that much more important as you age to keep yourself looking as good as you can. Consider hairdos and clothing styles that flatter you. Treat yourself to a make-over if that would make you feel good. Physical fitness is also important. Follow an exercise program tailored for particular age groups, for safety and appropriate motions targeted at body types and physical ability.

Feeling good about yourself is a precursor to feeling open to another. For those who find sexual sharing an important component of their happiness, self-pleasuring can be extremely useful in the interim when a partner is not available. Research has proven the physical benefits of such activity, including less atrophy of tissues, and fewer genital problems in those who remain active, compared to those who do not engage in such behavior. While often shrouded in silence and shame, solitary pleasure through-out the lifespan is more common than you may think. Surveys show that up to a third of older men and women continue to enjoy some self-pleasuring.

Dating Data

Many older men and women fear for their sexual potency as they age. While changes certainly occur in both sexes (men needing more time to get aroused, and women needing added lubrication after menopause), sex drive can remain high and performance adequate. In some cases, sex drive increases with reduced fears of pregnancy and increased self-acceptance.

When a Spouse Has Died

Losing a spouse/lover is traumatic, and requires much mourning and adjustment. Some widows and widowers find themselves open to another relationship, falling in love again as a way to heal the hurt and loss. Others find themselves unable, or even resolved, never to fall in love again.

If you were blessed to have enjoyed a long and pleasurable union, it is certainly sad to lose that connection. You can of course decide that there will never be anyone else for you and you have no desire to date again. But some loving spouses deep down would like to find love again, especially knowing how wonderful it once was. Appreciate your blessings, but also respect your desire to continue enjoying such an experience.

The death of a spouse creates certain idiosyncratic conditions when compared to separation or divorce. Self-blame and/or guilt may be less (associated with "What did I do wrong?" or "How was I not good enough?"), considering that you were not the cause of the loss. Finality of the loss through death also eliminates the stage of mourning where you try to get the lover back, or feel pained if s/he is with someone else.

Yet some widows and widowers feel so attached to their partner, they cannot move on to date others. Friends may try to fix you up, but you insist there can be no one else in your life. Commonly, the one left behind feels that to fall in love with someone else would mean to betray the departed beloved. This is especially true of older singles, who enjoyed a long and happy marriage. There is certainly no rule that you must date, or get into another relationship, and the choice is entirely personal. The decision should depend on what truly makes you happy. But for those who want to date again, but cannot due to fear or other resistance, there is a way to help get over this hurdle.

Smooth Talk'n

Statistics show that sexually transmitted diseases of all kinds are predominant in older age groups. Protection is therefore warranted at whatever age.

Besides the "completing unfinished business" technique described above, another useful technique for widows is the "set me free" exercise. This helps free you from guilt about dating someone else. Imagine your spouse in the room, pledge your love, and ask permission to move on to love someone else in this life. Really see your ex in your mind's eye smiling at you, acknowledging the love between you, and cutting the cord between you, allowing you to get on with your life on this earth. If it makes you feel better, you can agree to meet in an afterlife. Bless each other and the love between you and then allow yourself to really experience the feeling of detaching, so that you can be open to love someone else, should the opportunity arise.

The Least You Need to Know

➤ You're entitled to date and love again—at any age or under any circumstances.

➤ Having children does not make it impossible to find dates, but make sure that new partners understand your situation.

➤ Kids will always want the family to be whole again—recognize this so you can understand your child's behavior regarding your dating.

➤ Only introduce your child to someone you're dating seriously—casual dates can be confusing.

➤ Friends, family members, and co-workers will have their own judgments about you dating again. Remember, what matters most is what you think and feel.

➤ You never have to retire from love.

A Final Word

Wow! Have we been through the world of finding love! I've tried to think of everything, making this tome an encyclopedia, but if you have something you'd like to add, write to me at the address given at the bottom of the order sheet in the back of this book.

Thanks for being aboard—and keep on reading for fun exercises and more helpful info in the appendixes.

Blessings to you from me.

Fun and Revealing Exercises

In this section of the book, you'll find some fun and simple exercises designed to reveal aspects of your personality and love matches. Some are based on more extensive and even scientific methods that I have simplified here to make them easier to do and interpret. I have used many of these exercises in my therapy practice and workshops over the years, so I know you can learn from and enjoy them. Use them to gain a little knowledge about yourself and your date, and as a stimulus to get you to talk about yourselves, your interests, feelings, and needs.

Exercise 1: You in Your World

The purpose of this exercise is to explore how you see yourself in your world. I have done this exercise with thousands of individuals, couples, and families over the years. It's based on a psychological technique called "projective drawing," a well-researched and practical tool for estimating a person's view of themselves in the world.

Some people have a hard time expressing in words what they think and feel. But the way in which they draw a picture often offers clues about their inner feelings. Emotional nuances emerge from drawings, regardless of artistic skill.

Draw yourself in the drawing space at the end of this appendix. I'm purposefully not giving you any other specifics—don't worry about how you draw, just don't use a stick figure.

Interpreting Your Drawing

Keep in mind that the following interpretations are generalizations, so use them as a guideline only. Intensive professional analysis of drawings can take hours!

The page symbolizes your world. How you place yourself on the page indicates how you see yourself in your world. If you placed yourself in the middle of the page, it shows that you think of yourself as being at the center of your world. This could suggest that you are also centered (secure) inside yourself.

If you placed yourself off in the corner, it could mean that you need to improve your self-esteem and sense of importance. Placement to the left of the page suggests that you may be stuck in your past; to the right implies that you think more of the future. Drawing yourself at the bottom of the page suggests that you are "grounded" and feel more secure thinking about what's real and focusing on factual things and safe feelings; a figure at the top of the page can imply your enjoyment of fantasy and imagination.

How large did you draw yourself? A too-large figure (in relation to the page) can suggest confidence in yourself, a desire to stand out, or a degree of narcissism. If you are too self-centered, you need to think of others more. On the other hand, if you drew yourself too small, it suggests that you may feel insecure or lost in the world.

This exercise should be fun and spontaneous. If you think too much about what you're doing, or try to guess the outcome and influence the interpretation, you ruin the validity.

Exercise 2: Your Real, Ideal, and Social Selves

The purpose of this exercise is to gain insight into what you think of as the "real you," as opposed to how you would like to be or what others think you are. This exercise offers clues about things that you would like to change about yourself. It also offers insight into the image you present to the world—which may or may not be the one you want to project. Finally, the exercise can help you integrate your three selves.

Describe yourself in the table on the following page. Use as many adjectives or phrases that come to you. Write these down spontaneously without editing them.

Me as I See Myself	Me as I'd Like to Be	How Others See Me
I am:	I'd like to be:	Others see me as:

Interpreting Your Descriptions

Look closely at the adjectives you used in each column and compare the ways in which they differ. Connect any adjectives by drawing a line between them with a pen. The more similar the adjectives, the more comfortable and fulfilled you feel—your real and ideal images are in synch.

Review the adjectives in each column and put an "x" through the qualities you do not want to have. Imagine those no longer being a part of you. Now highlight with a highlighter or put a star next to the ones you like. Close your eyes and imagine yourself being this way—this makes it more likely that you will be.

Exercise 3: Body Talk

The purpose of this exercise is to show how body confidence is the key to self-confidence. Look at your drawing from Exercise 1, or look at a picture of a male or female form in a magazine. Rate how positive or negative you feel about your various body parts (with 0 being very negative and 10 being very positive). Write the numbers on the picture.

If any part gets a rating below 5, have a "body conversation." Imagine what that body part would say to you and what you would reply in order to feel more positive about it. For example, describe what your arms/breast/penis/hips are saying to you. If you write, "I'm fat, please love me, I can't take the pressure," you might consider responding, "I love you anyway, don't feel bad, it'll be fine."

Exercise 4: Love Criteria

The purpose of this exercise is to identify your "love criteria"—the picture of who you are looking for and the qualities to which your love antennae are tuned. What qualities are you looking for in a partner—intelligence, attractiveness, or a sense of humor? In the following table, check the qualities you think you have, what you're looking for in a mate, and whether any of your past lovers had the qualities you desire.

Qualities	I Am. . .	My Past Loves Were. . .	I Want a Mate Who Is. . .
sensitive, caring			
thoughtful			
adventurous			
honest			
trustworthy			
easy-going			
fun to be with			
boring			
affectionate			
uncommunicative			
bossy			
shy			
sexy			
outgoing			
smart			
other qualities:			
_____			
_____			
_____			

Exercise 5: Blind Date

The purpose of this exercise is to gain a sense of your perfect image of a mate. Imagine you are waiting for your blind date to arrive. What do you picture the person looking like? What do you imagine talking about? How do you imagine feeling?

Exercise 6: My Perfect Vacation

Vacations are the perfect opportunity to experience your romantic vision and passion to their fullest. The purpose of this exercise is to help you focus on that image. Try getting a date to do this exercise, too; that way, you get a chance to see if your visions and interests are compatible.

Draw yourself and your date on the perfect vacation in the drawing space at the end of this appendix. Where would you be? What would you be doing?

Interpreting Your Drawing

Some people like vacations that are restful, with little activity and lots of opportunity to "chill out." Others prefer adventure and action. If you want to loll on the beach but your date wants to tour museums or ride the rapids, you may not be as compatible as you could be.

Exercise 7: What Dating Feels Like

The purpose of this exercise is to gain an insight into how you feel about dating. Draw anything that you feel inspired by when you think of "dating"—it can be forms, people, shapes, or whatever you like. Use colors if you can. Draw in the drawing space at the end of this appendix.

Interpreting Your Drawing

How do you feel about the drawing? Is the emotional tone dark (signifying sad feelings related to dating) or bright and light (happiness in dating)?

What are the shapes? Are they round (soft, cozy impressions of dating), arrows or bolts of lightning (excitement), zigzags (implying confusion or both negative and positive feelings), or sharp and jagged (suggesting hurt or angry feelings)?

Exercise 8: Writing the Movie of Your Dating Life

The purpose of this exercise is to show how you are in charge of your life by writing a movie of your dating life.

Elsewhere in this book, I share one of my favorite concepts with you—that you are in charge of the movie of your life. When people call my "LovePhones" radio show with questions about a relationship problem, I ask them to imagine a movie of their life. I ask, "What movie do you picture yourself in? What movie would your mate picture himself in? Do the movies have similar themes? Does your mate know the role you have cast him in?" Whether you realize it or not, you are always writing, directing, producing, and acting in all the roles of your life movie. Is yours a comedy or tragedy, an action adventure, or PG- or R-rated fare?

Jot down the following:

Title of the film:

_____

Main characters:

_____

Director:

_____

Producer:

_____

A summary of the plot, including critical scenes in the movie:

_____

_____

Interpreting Your Movie

Decide if your movie is the way things went in reality or the way you really want them to go. What is happening? Does the guy get the girl? Are they fighting? Is there tragedy?

If you like the scenes in your movie, you can rehearse them over and over in your mind to make them more likely to come true.

Have your date do the same and compare your movies. Do the plots overlap? He could be in an action adventure and you could be writing a romance story—if so, your love lives may not be on the same track. Tell him your story and see if he can enjoy playing a role in it.

Exercise 9: Shared Storytelling

The purpose of this exercise is to get you to weave a story together about your date that you both can enjoy.

This is one of my favorite exercises. I use it with couples to get them to focus on sharing a love story and working well together.

Throw out a line to start the story. Then your date adds a line. Take turns until you think the story is complete.

For example, he says, "We're having breakfast on our hotel terrace on the beach on the Greek island of Mykonos." She says, "I'm feeding you a champagne-dipped strawberry. Your fingers lightly glide up and down my thigh." He goes next.

Interpreting Your Story

Examine the story carefully. What actions did you add? What did your date add? Were your details sexual? Romantic? What feelings did you describe? Are your lines more emotive than his or vice versa? How well integrated is the story—did you start the story one way, only to have her shift gears? If so, you may be at odds, and frequently find yourself feeling alone in your relationship or often disagreeing. Or are you on a parallel track? If so, you both may have the excitement of adding new ideas to spark one another. Do you embellish one another's lines? This is good sign that you appreciate and support each other's real-life story.

If you find yourself somewhat at odds, are you both interested in getting in sync? Start another story and see how much better you agree on where the story goes. Doing this can help you learn to resolve differences and accommodate each other.

Exercise 10: Things I'd Like Us to Do Together

The purpose of this exercise is to discover common interests between you and your date.

Make a list of the things you like to do, and have your date do the same. Then go through your own lists and assign priorities ("1" for the thing you most enjoy, and so forth). Compare your list with his to see where you overlap. If none of your interests overlap, you may want to reconsider this relationship.

What I Like to Do	What My Date Likes to Do

Exercise 11: Be a Reporter

The purpose of this exercise is to help you focus on what you really want to know about someone to get better acquainted, and to help you be more assertive about speaking up and asking for what you want.

As a psychologist and former news reporter, I am used to asking lots of questions. This exercise helps you learn how to ask the right questions to help solve your dating dilemmas.

If you have questions about your date, or if you are wondering about a certain behavior, be a reporter. Interview the person, asking questions as if you were an objective third party doing a story about him or her, without any emotional investment or fears. Try not to jump to conclusions, do stay calm, and get the facts as well as the feelings. Ask simple background questions such as:

➤ "Where were you born?"
➤ "Where did you go to school?"
➤ "What have you saved from your childhood?"

Then ask fun questions such as:

➤ "What's your favorite color?"
➤ "If you were an animal, what would you be?"
➤ "Who is your hero? "

Then think of something that happened between the two of you that you wonder about, and ask about that:

➤ "What did you mean when you said . . .?"
➤ "Remember when we . . .?"
➤ "Why did you . . .?"
➤ "I'm really curious . . ."
➤ "What were you thinking when you . . .?"

Exercise 12: Your Own Personal Ad

The purpose of this exercise is to write a personal ad to clarify what you think you're looking for in a date, and to see how you would describe yourself.

In as many words as you like, write about yourself. Then describe the person you are looking for.

Examples of Personal Ads

Personal ads should let your personality shine through, and clearly state what you are looking for. So be honest and creative! Looking at samples of personal ads can help stimulate your own creative juices.

Here are some phrases that people used in their personal ads for a contest I hosted for Details magazine. I picked these samples because they represent some particularly vivid descriptions:

➤ "Jane Fonda look-alike seeks rich, well-heeled TV exec."

➤ "Prince or sheik sought. Into art and beauty."

➤ "Spring fever, into tennis and Sunday brunch, looking for love match."

➤ "Priceless '60s mint condition, presently garaged, looking for experienced driver to step on my accelerator."

➤ "Looking for well-built muscle man—not too kinky, but into body worship."

➤ "Into religion . . . I pray you come."

➤ "Likes to talk after you-know-what—no overweight, sweaty, or hygienically challenged persons, please."

➤ "Fifth Baldwin seeks Barbie with brains."

➤ "I admit I'll soon have to join Hair Club for Men."

➤ "By day I'm a mild-mannered businessman who does origami; by night I'm a winged creature who battles the forces of evil. If you're my damsel in distress, let me be your superhero."

Drawing Space

Drawing Space

Drawing Space

Drawing Space

Resources

Clubs and Organizations

Single Gourmet
133 East 58th Street
New York, NY 10022
(212) 980-8788

Local clubs available in about 18 cities in the U.S. and Canada; contact local directory assistance. Offers dining events with mingling opportunities, often mixed with various outings such as theater, sporting events, or trips. Membership fee (initial, $75, renewal $40; includes newsletter and reciprocal membership in all Single Gourmet clubs), plus cost of dinner or event.

Parents Without Partners
401 North Michigan Avenue
Chicago, IL 60611
(800) 637-7974
e-mail: pwp@sba.com
www.parentswithoutpartners.com

National organization with local chapters around the country. Offers activities for single parents of all ages with children. Membership fees (for example, $30), plus fees for some activities (for example, picnic, $3).

Outdoor Bound
18 Stuyvesant Oval
New York, NY 10009
(212) 505-1020
e-mail: britwalks@aol.com
www.ramblers.com

Outdoors and travel club offering various trips with varied activities from rafting to camping. About ten thousand people on mailing list. Membership fee $30.

12-Step Programs
Nationally available, contact your local directory assistance.

Based on the famed 12-step addiction model, these self-help groups offer frequent group support meetings for people with similar life issues ranging from alcohol or drug abuse (AA or DA) to overeating (OA) and love and sex addictions (LSA).

UJA-Federation
130 East 59th Street
New York, NY 10022

National organization with local affiliates in various cities offering events, trips, courses; for example, Business and Professional Singles, Resource Line.

Christian Singles International
P.O. Box 100
Harrison, OH 45030
(513) 598-2883
e-mail: chrstsngls@aol.com
www.christiansinglesnews.com

Maintains list of 150,000 people and claims 1,400 marriages. Lists personals and articles. Membership $29.95/year.

Book and Music Stores Offering Opportunities for Reading, Listening, and Eating

Check local listings in superstores, such as:

Borders Books and Music Stores
Barnes & Noble Bookstores
Media Play

Restaurant Chains

Check local listings for "theme" restaurants, like:

Planet Hollywood
Hard Rock Cafe
All Star (Sports) Cafe

Dating Services

Together
Corporate Office: 161 Worcester Road
Framingham, MA 01701
(508) 786-0606

Matches made on basis of questionnaire ("Compatibility Evaluation Guide") and in-depth personal interviews. Travel opportunities also available. Offices in 35 U.S. cities, London, and Toronto. Different membership plans (average annual cost about $1,000).

Visual Preference
297-101 Kinderkamack Road
Oradell, NJ 07601
(800) 533-1712
www.visualpreferenceusrc.net
www.firstnationalnetclub.com (Tri-State)

After personal interview, matches made on basis of video or photo exchanges. Glamour makeovers for females included. Cost based on individualized program.

Great Expectations
1640 South Sepulveda Boulevard, Suite 100
Los Angeles, CA 90025
(310) 477-5566

Offices in about 50 cities (not including New York). Choices made by viewing videotapes of clients. Costs about $1,000 to $2,500 per year.

Conscious Singles Connection
243 West End Avenue, Suite 1504
New York, NY 10023
(212) 873-7187
(914) 339-2732

Matches made by member profile through questionnaire and interview. Also has inspirational tapes, as well as guided Meditation for Singles to survive the holidays alone.

SoulMates
P.O. Box 8691
LaJolla, CA 92038
(619) 259-4321

Matches made by working one-on-one with a consultant, or by personal selection from a library of photographs and profiles, and voice mailbox system. Relationship skills seminars also offered. Of thousands of clients, a 70 percent success rate is claimed.

Field's Exclusive Service
317 Madison Avenue
New York, NY 10017
(212) 391-2233

On the basis of your answers on a questionnaire, this "marriage broker" gives you a list of people. Fee starts at $50 for three names and depends on the level of service.

Courses

New Life Expo
218 West 72nd Street
New York, NY 10023
(800) 928-6208

Symposium held in various cities around the country, consisting of 150 lectures, workshops, and exhibits on holistic health, alternative medicine, psychic phenomena, and environment discoveries. Admission $15 plus workshop fees.

The Open Center
83 Spring Street
New York, NY 10012
(212) 219-2527
e-mail: nyoc@micro-net.com
www.opencenter.org

Offers over 600 events, including lectures, workshops, conferences, and retreats, each year, centered around holistic learning and culture, and led by world-renowned experts. For example: classes in Buddhism (drawing large crowds with equal numbers of men and women) and conferences on alchemy in Prague and the Holy Grail in Wales.

The Seminar Center
1776 Broadway, Suite 1001
New York, NY 10019
(212) 655-0077
e-mail: info@seminarcenter.com
www.seminarcenter.com

Extensive listing of seminars on subjects from health to photography and selling, with inspirational best-selling authors and celebrities.

YMCA/YWCA and YMHA/YWHA
Local chapters in various cities around the country. Contact local directory assistance. Offers support groups, courses, and activities on various themes from "How to Flirt" to "Letting Go and Moving On." Cost of events varies from $2 and up.

Magazines/Newsletters

Local city magazines, like *New York Magazine*, can be found at newsstands. Check events listings and personals.

Houston Single File
2476 Bolsover #608
Houston, TX 77005
(281) 496-DATE

Monthly subscription $20, call for similar magazines available in some areas.

Travel Services

Richniks/Perks
362 West 23rd Street
New York, NY 10011
(800) RICHNIK

Offers social, recreational, and travel opportunities for singles.

HEDONISM
Book through travel agent for good prices. All-inclusive vacation package to Jamaica, known for its almost entirely singles patronage and uninhibited atmosphere.

Club Med
40 West 57th Street
New York, NY 10019
(800) CLUB MED
www.clubmed.com

All-inclusive vacation packages at villages around the world offering varied sports and activities. Sixty percent of travelers are single, median age is 35, and two-thirds are professionals. Membership fee, plus cost of trip (week-long, over $1,000).

Information on Health Issues

ASHA (The American Social Health Association)
P.O. Box 13827
Research Triangle Park, NC 27709
(800) 230-6039
www.ashastd.org

Or call the National STD hotline: (800) 227-8922

SIECUS (Sexuality Information and Education Council of the United States)
130 West 42nd Street, Suite 350
New York, NY 10036
(212) 819-9770
Fax: (212) 819-9776
for AOL members: siecusinc@aol.com
for other service members: siecus@ibm.net
e-mail: SIECUS@siecus.org
www.siecus.org

Planned Parenthood Federation of America
810 7th Avenue
New York NY 10019
(212) 261-4300
Fax: (212) 246-1845 or (800) 230-PLAN
e-mail: communications@PPFA.org
www.ppfa.org/PPFA

Alan Guttmacher Institute
120 Wall Street
New York, NY 10005
(212) 248-1111
Fax: (212) 248-1951
e-mail: info@agi-usa.org
www.agi-usa.org

GMHC (The Gay Men's Health Crisis Inc.)
129 West 20th Street
New York, NY 10011
(212) 807-6664
Fax: (212) 337-1220
www.gmhc.org

Dating Quiz

Take this test to see how good you are in the dating game and how to improve your dating skills. The answers to this quiz can be found at the end of this section.

1. List the top three things that men say attract them to a woman:

   _____

   _____

   _____

2. List the top three things that women say attract them to a man:

   _____

   _____

   _____

3. Which of the five senses is the most powerful in attraction?

   Circle one:

   Sight

   Smell

   Hearing

   Taste

   Touch

4. If you were going to whisper sweet nothings in someone's ear, which ear would you whisper in?

   Circle one:

   Right ear   Left ear

5. What are the words that women most want to hear?

   _____

   _____

6. What are the words that men most want to hear?

   _____

   _____

continues

continued

7. What do both men and women (according to surveys) most want to hear?

   _____

   _____

8. What is the best way to "pick up" someone?

   _____

   _____

9. Where is the best place to go to meet someone?

   _____

   _____

10. How many approaches should you make before you give up on a dating prospect?

    _____

    _____

11. What's the best way to show someone you're interested?

    _____

    _____

12. How do you know someone's interested in you?

    _____

    _____

13. What is the best way to deal with rejection?

    _____

    _____

14. Who is the best date?

    _____

    _____

15. How many dates should it take before you know someone is "it"?

    _____

    _____

16. What is the best test of love?

    _____

    _____

17. List three qualities that make for the best-lasting relationship:

_____

_____

_____

18. What is "condom-sense"?

_____

_____

19. Why do men roll over and go to sleep after sex?

_____

_____

Answers to Dating Quiz

1. Top three things that men say attract them to a woman (see Chapter 9).
2. Top three things that women say attract them to a man (see Chapter 9).
3. Smell is the most powerful sense in attraction (the messages go straight, and therefore quickly, from the olfactory bulb to the brain).
4. Whisper sweet nothings in the left ear to connect to the right (romantic) side of the brain.
5. Women most want to hear the words "I love you" and "You're beautiful."
6. Men most want to hear how good they are.
7. Both men and women (according to surveys) most want to hear their name.
8. The best way to "pick up" someone is to be yourself.
9. The best place to go to meet someone is where you feel comfortable, so you will shine. Other good choices: where energy is alive (sporting events, amusement parks, concerts).
10. Make three approaches before you give up on a dating prospect.
11. Show someone you're interested by admitting it, complimenting him or her, and making eye contact.
12. Assess someone's interest from his or her body language.
13. Deal with rejection by switching attention to what makes you feel good, and realizing that one hit in three is a good batting average.
14. You are your own best date.
15. Follow a six-date minimum.

16. The best test of love is going through crises together.

17. Qualities of best-lasting relationships (see Chapter 15).

18. Condom-sense is using one every time.

19. Men don't have to roll over and go to sleep after sex; they're tired, or have trained themselves that way, or they may want to escape intimacy.

Index

S

I have had many requests over the years for copies of articles and tapes of my work. Finally, we are pleased to make some of these available. To receive your free newsletter, be part of the mailing list, request information, offer suggestions, or order items, please fill in the form below, tear it out, and send it to the address indicated. Thank you and I look forward to hearing from you and fulfilling your requests and interests.

Name: _____

Address: _____

City _____ State _____ ZIP _____

Country _____

Telephone (Daytime) _____ (Evening) _____

Fax _____ E-Mail _____

❑ Male   Age_____   ❑ Single   ❑ "LovePhones" listener
❑ Female   ❑ Married   On which station _____
                                   ❑ In relationship City _____
                                   ❑ Divorced
                                   ❑ Widowed

Please:

_____ Put me on the mailing list.

_____ Send information. Specify: _____

_____ Order the items checked below.

_____ Contact me about being a sponsor.

_____ Contact me about Dr. Judy coming to speak to my organization.

_____ Note these suggestions: _____

_____ Other. Specify: _____

Please check the following items that you are interested in.

Videotapes ($24.95 each):

__ V11 Video of lecture on Creativity in Love
__ V12 Video of college lecture on sex I
__ V13 Video of college lecture on sex II
__ V20 Video of Dr. Judy and Jagger at rock festivals

Booklets ($9.95 each)

__ Booklet I of "The Best of 'LovePhones'" (including calls, lists, "LovePhones" facts, jokes, e-mails, and "LovePhones" dictionary)
__ Booklet II of "The Best of 'LovePhones'"

Articles by Dr. Judy (each copy $1.00):

__ P12 "Pillow Talk—What Loving Couples Say in Bed"
__ P14 "Panic Attacks"
__ P15 "Sexual Compatibility"
__ P16 "Too Tired for Sex"
__ P19 "New Year's Resolutions"
__ P20 "Good Judgment: Making Wise Choices"

You can order the popular items below.

Item Description	Number of Copies	Price Each	Total Price
Color photos (5x7 for $5.95, 8x10 for $9.95):			
P10 Autographed photo of Dr. Judy in radio station			
P11 Autographed photo of Dr. Judy and Jagger in radio station			
P12 Autographed photo of Dr.Judy with rock star at music festival			
Audiotapes ($9.95 each):			
A11 Best of "LovePhones" I			
A12 Best of "LovePhones" II			
A13 Advice from Dr. Judy on love			
A14 Advice from Dr. Judy on dating			
A15 Advice from Dr. Judy on sex			
CDs ($16.95 each):			
C11 Best of "LovePhones" I			
C12 Best of "LovePhones" II			
C21 Dr. Judy and Jagger Music for Love I			
C22 Dr. Judy and Jagger Music for Love II			
T-Shirts ($25.00 each):			
T1 Generation Sex t-shirt			
T2 T-shirt with photo of Dr. Judy and Jagger			

SHIPPING & HANDLING CHARGES	**Merchandise Total**
Up to $20 .... $4.75	**Sales Tax** (New York state residents pay 8.25%)
$20.01 to $30 .... $5.75	
$30.01 to $40 .... $6.98	**Shipping & Handling** (use table to left)
$40.01 to $50 .... $7.98	
$50.01 to $75 .... $10.75	**Total**
$75.01 to $100 .... $12.75	
$100.01 to $150 .... $14.98	
Over $150 .... $15.98	

Send this form, along with a check or money order, to:

Planet Love
59 Commerce Street
Staten Island, New York 10514

Please allow 4–6 weeks for delivery. Payment to be made in U.S. funds. Price(s) and availability subject to change without notice.